Accelerating Logistics Through Generative AI, Digital Twins, and Autonomous Operations

Abdelrehim Awad
https://orcid.org/0009-0005-3649-430X
University of Bisha, Saudi Arabia

Dhafer Al Ahmari
University of Bisha, Saudi Arabia

IGI Global
Scientific Publishing
Publishing Tomorrow's Research Today

Vice President of Editorial	Melissa Wagner
Director of Acquisitions	Mikaela Felty
Director of Book Development	Jocelynn Hessler
Production Manager	Mike Brehm
Cover Design	Jose Rosado

Published in the United States of America by
IGI Global Scientific Publishing
701 East Chocolate Avenue
Hershey, PA, 17033, USA
Tel: 717-533-8845 | Fax: 717-533-7115
Website: https://www.igi-global.com E-mail: cust@igi-global.com

Library of Congress Cataloging-in-Publication Data

LCCN: 2025044756 (CIP Data Pending)
ISBN13: 979-8-3373-7006-4
Isbn13Softcover: 979-8-3373-7007-1
EISBN13: 979-8-3373-7008-8

British Cataloguing in Publication Data
A Cataloguing in Publication record for this book is available from the British Library.

Table of Contents

Detailed Table of Contents

This chapter explores how Artificial Intelligence (AI) and digital twins are reshaping sustainable supply chains by integrating intelligence, transparency, and resilience into global logistics systems. AI enables predictive analytics, green routing, and automation to optimize resources while minimizing waste and emissions. Digital twins create real-time, virtual replicas of supply networks, allowing proactive monitoring, scenario testing, and energy optimization. Together, these technologies advance ESG compliance, net-zero strategies, and circular economy practices. Case studies from Unilever and Siemens-DHL highlight practical adoption, while discussions on blockchain, quantum AI, and autonomous operations illustrate future trends. The chapter concludes by identifying challenges such as governance, interoperability, and costs, and proposes pathways toward self-adaptive, eco-resilient supply chains.

Incorporation of Artificial Intelligence (AI) into supply chain operations creates a paradigm shift, changing processes to realize more performance and responsiveness. In this chapter, the authors explore how artificial intelligence (AI) integrated into enterprise resource planning (ERP) systems can enhance the sustainable performance of supply chains. Sitting at the intersection of digitalization and sustainability, it examines how AI-enabled ERP utilizes better decision-making, reduces inefficiencies, and boosts resilience in global supply chains. Both the environmental, economic, and social aspects of sustainability are discussed and highlight the additional smart connection of Internet of Things (IoT) sensor information, blockchain, and the analysis of big data even more. A number of case studies in the manufacture, retailing, and logistics sectors demonstrate how AI-ERP solutions are generating real sustainability value. Finally, the chapter unveils the future research and practice directions with a special focus being placed at the convergence of AI and ERP.

This chapter explores how Artificial Intelligence (AI), digital twins, and autonomous operations are transforming logistics and procurement into intelligent, resilient, and sustainable ecosystems. It examines theoretical foundations, sustainability drivers, and the integration of circular supply chain practices and ESG accountability. AI-driven digital twins enable real-time simulation, predictive analytics, and prescriptive optimization, while autonomous operations streamline warehousing, transport, and procurement with robotics, drones, and AI-based control towers. Case studies from healthcare and oil & gas illustrate practical applications, highlighting benefits and regulatory challenges in the GCC and MENA regions. Ethical, regulatory, and social implications are discussed alongside emerging innovations such as agentic AI, blockchain, IoT, and quantum-ready optimization. The chapter concludes with insights into future directions, emphasizing human-AI collaboration, transparency, and sustainability as critical enablers of next-generation global supply chains.

his chapter, provides a comprehensive, three-dimensional examination of the economic impact of autonomous systems and robotics on the labor market within the logistics sector. The authors explore the multifaceted nature of this transformation, analyzing the simultaneous processes of job displacement and workforce evolution. The chapter first delineates the theoretical foundations of automation's impact, contrasting the displacement effect which highlights job losses in routine tasks—with the productivity effect, which emphasizes economic growth and new job creation. This is followed by a detailed economic analysis that examines the trade-off between the high capital investments required for automation and the substantial, long-term operational efficiencies and cost reductions achieved. This section highlights how automation drives down per-order labor costs, increases throughput rates, and improves safety and space utilization.

This chapter addresses the fragility of the modern supply chain, arguing that reactive operational paradigms are untenable amid global disruptions. It proposes a new architectural blueprint for an autonomous, self-optimizing supply chain: the Sentient Core. The central argument is that realizing the potential of advanced and agentic AI requires a coherent architecture with a single source of truth and a dynamic simulation environment. This architecture is achieved through the synergy of two foundational pillars: an AI-Powered Digital Twin and a Unified Data Fabric. The chapter details a seven-layer implementation framework, analyzes challenges like data governance and legacy system integration, and presents a phased "crawl, walk, run" methodology. The validity of this architectural pattern is demonstrated through real-world case studies. The chapter concludes that the Sentient Core is a strategic and technological imperative for building the resilient, intelligent, and competitive supply chains of the future.

Supply chains exist today under chronic volatility, uncertainty, complexity, and ambiguity. Batch based planning and decision rights fragmentation render companies sluggish to detect disruption and costly to rebound. This paper develops an integrated concept—Agentic Control Towers (ACTs)which combines large language model (LLM) agents, multi agent reinforcement learning (MARL), and digital supply chain twins to provide closed loop, explainable autonomy for plan, source, make, move, and serve. We integrate findings across inventory and logistics reinforcement learning, LLM tooling and multiagent coordination, digital twin orchestration, and resilient operations. We position ACTs as a decision fabric that continuously senses, simulates, negotiates, and performs while placing guardrails for safety, sustainability, cost, and service. The paper provides an integrated architecture, end to end decision flows, stability and governance design decisions, and evidence informed pathways of impact. We also establish evaluation criteria.

Control towers have matured from descriptive dashboards into prescriptive, agentic decision systems that sense, understand, decide, act, and learn across multi-enterprise networks. By combining streaming data fabrics, digital twins, graph/causal forecasting, optimization and reinforcement learning, and multi-agent coordination, modern control towers close the loop from prediction to execution with adjustable autonomy and safety guardrails. Control towers have matured from descriptive dashboards into prescriptive, agentic decision systems that sense, understand, decide, act, and learn across multi-enterprise networks. By combining streaming data fabrics, digital twins, graph/causal forecasting, optimization and reinforcement learning, and multi-agent coordination, modern control towers close the loop from prediction to execution with adjustable autonomy and safety guardrails.

AI refers to ability of machines to perform tasks that typically require human mind to perform such as learning, problem solving and decision making an agentic AI has been considered in large category. These systems depend on AI agents with purpose of independent entities that are capable of recognizing environment, learning & then performing the processes in multiple steps of workflow. Agentic AI accommodates LLM-based veracity. Through this classification strategy, AI agents are having the ability to seek real time data on fly and keep evolving with changes in world around them in sectors including healthcare, cybersecurity, logistics & personal services. In this chapter, we explore recent advancement in Agentic AI by analysing architecture, capabilities and real-world application of multi agent systems. These systems integrate LLMs to enable self-reliant decision making & task performing. We cover key methods such as retrieval–augmented generation, chain of thought

Preface

OVERVIEW OF THE SUBJECT MATTER

Logistics and supply chain management are undergoing the most profound technological transition since the industrial revolution. As organizations confront increasing volatility—geopolitical instability, climate pressures, globalized networks, and digital disruptions—traditional models of planning and execution can no longer meet the demands of speed, accuracy, and resilience. This book, *Accelerating Logistics Through Generative AI, Digital Twins, and Autonomous Operations*, provides an integrated examination of three converging technological pillars redefining modern logistics: generative artificial intelligence, digital twins, and autonomous systems. Individually, these technologies offer powerful capabilities; together, they enable supply chains that sense, simulate, reason, and act with unprecedented intelligence. The chapters in this volume bridge theory, empirical evidence, industry applications, and interdisciplinary frameworks to illustrate how this technological fusion is shaping the next generation of resilient, sustainable, and high-performance logistics systems.

WHERE THE TOPIC FITS IN THE WORLD TODAY

The global supply chain landscape has reached an inflection point. Increasing disruptions—pandemics, port congestion, inflationary pressures, cyberattacks, and extreme weather—have revealed systemic fragilities across industries. In response, governments, corporations, and technology innovators are accelerating investments in digital transformation, artificial intelligence, and automation to enhance strategic resilience. Generative AI enables predictive planning, scenario generation, constraint-driven optimization, and autonomous decision cycles. Digital twins provide a real-time simulation environment for testing, validating, and optimizing decisions before implementation. Meanwhile, autonomous systems—including robots, drones, and intelligent warehousing—represent the operational layer that executes digital intelligence with speed and precision. At this critical moment, the integration of these technologies is not simply a technological evolution—it is an economic and strategic necessity. This book contextualizes these developments within global supply chain transformation efforts and positions them as foundational building blocks for Industry 5.0's vision of human-machine collaboration, sustainability, and societal resilience.

TARGET AUDIENCE

This book is intended for a diverse global audience across academia, industry, and policy sectors:

- **Researchers and Scholars** in logistics, industrial engineering, AI, operations management, systems design, and digital transformation.
- **Industry Leaders and Practitioners** seeking actionable insights to implement intelligent, automated, or twin-enabled logistics systems.
- **Policymakers and Regulators** designing national logistics infrastructures, AI governance standards, and safe deployment frameworks.
- **Graduate Students** in supply chain management, data science, engineering, business analytics, and computer science.
- **Technology Developers and Innovators** building AI platforms, robotics solutions, optimization systems, and digital twin architectures.

Through conceptual models, empirical findings, case studies, and theoretical advancements, the book equips readers with the knowledge to understand and shape the future of logistics.

IMPORTANCE OF EACH CHAPTER SUBMISSION

Chapter 1 – AI, Digital Twins, and Sustainability in Supply Chains: Foundations, Innovations, and Future Directions

This chapter provides the conceptual and theoretical grounding for AI-enabled sustainable logistics. By integrating environmental, economic, and operational dimensions, it highlights how digital technologies support decarbonization, circularity, and resource efficiency. It broadens the reader's understanding of sustainability as a technological and strategic imperative.

Chapter 2 – Enhancing Sustainable Supply Chain Through AI Embedded in ERP Systems

By integrating AI into enterprise resource planning (ERP) systems, this chapter reveals how organizations can embed intelligence into their operational backbone. It shows how sustainability, planning accuracy, and process efficiency improve through ERP-AI convergence.

Chapter 3 – AI-Driven Digital Twins and Autonomous Operations for Sustainable Logistics and Procurement

Here, the authors explore how AI-enhanced digital twins transform procurement and logistics into data-driven, adaptive ecosystems. The chapter offers strong empirical and architectural insights into how autonomous operations reduce waste, improve supplier coordination, and support long-term sustainability goals.

Chapter 4 – The Economic Impact of Autonomous Systems and Robotics on the Labor Market in the Logistics Sector

Offering a three-dimensional analytical perspective, this chapter examines how robotics and automation reshape employment patterns, workforce capabilities, and labor economics. It provides a balanced assessment of opportunities, risks, and policy implications.

Chapter 5 – The Sentient Core: AI-Powered Digital Twins and Unified Data Fabric for Logistics

This chapter presents the idea of a unified data fabric as the central nervous system of next-generation logistics. It demonstrates how AI-powered digital twins become "sentient," enabling real-time adaptation and continuous optimization across the entire supply chain.

Chapter 6 - Agentic Control Towers, Multi Agent LLM RL Orchestration for Autonomous, and Resilient Supply Chains

This chapter provides an integrated architecture, end to end decision flows, stability and governance design decisions, and evidence informed pathways of impact. We also establish evaluation criteria.

Chapter 7 – Generative AI and Digital Twins for Sustainable Last-Mile Logistics

Addressing one of the most challenging areas of logistics, this chapter demonstrates how AI and digital twins optimize last-mile delivery, electric vehicle routing, and green logistics. It contributes actionable frameworks for reducing emissions and improving customer experience.

Chapter 8 – Intelligent Logistics: Generative AI, Digital Twins, and Autonomous Supply Chains in GCC & Beyond

Focusing on the GCC region, this chapter contextualizes global innovations within regional strategies such as Saudi Vision 2030 and UAE digital transformation efforts. It demonstrates how national logistics hubs are adopting advanced technologies at scale, making it a valuable geographic and policy perspective.

Chapter 9 – From Dashboards to Decisions: Prescriptive Agentic Supply Chain Control Towers

Addressing a major industry challenge—the gap between visibility and action—this chapter explains how prescriptive and autonomous systems surpass traditional dashboards. It sets the stage for understanding why next-generation control towers must operate as agentic, closed-loop, self-optimizing systems.

Chapter 10 – Rise of the Self-Driven Machine: Inside the World of Agentic AI

This chapter provides a deep exploration of agentic AI—systems capable of autonomous reasoning, planning, and execution. It situates agentic systems within logistics, demonstrating how they unlock new opportunities for self-optimizing operations.

CONCLUSION: CONTRIBUTION AND IMPACT OF THE BOOK

This volume provides one of the most comprehensive interdisciplinary explorations of generative AI, digital twins, and autonomous operations in logistics. By integrating technological foundations, empirical evidence, legal and policy considerations, strategic frameworks, and sector-specific applications, the book offers a holistic map of how supply chains must evolve. Collectively, the chapters reveal that the future of logistics is intelligent, automated, agentic, sustainable, and deeply interconnected. The book not only advances scholarly understanding but also equips industry practitioners, policymakers, and innovators with actionable insights to build resilient, efficient, and future-ready logistics ecosystems.

Chapter 1
AI, Digital Twins, and Sustainability in Supply Chains:
Foundations, Innovations, and Future Directions

R. N. Ravikumar
https://orcid.org/0009-0009-3705-1681
Marwadi University, Rajkot, India

S. Aarthi
https://orcid.org/0009-0006-9064-2091
Marwadi University, Rajkot, India

ABSTRACT

This chapter explores how Artificial Intelligence (AI) and digital twins are reshaping sustainable supply chains by integrating intelligence, transparency, and resilience into global logistics systems. AI enables predictive analytics, green routing, and automation to optimize resources while minimizing waste and emissions. Digital twins create real-time, virtual replicas of supply networks, allowing proactive monitoring, scenario testing, and energy optimization. Together, these technologies advance ESG compliance, net-zero strategies, and circular economy practices. Case studies from Unilever and Siemens-DHL highlight practical adoption, while discussions on blockchain, quantum AI, and autonomous operations illustrate future trends. The chapter concludes by identifying challenges such as governance, interoperability, and costs, and proposes pathways toward self-adaptive, eco-resilient supply chains.

DOI: 10.4018/979-8-3373-7006-4.ch001

1. INTRODUCTION

Global supply chains are experiencing an epoch of two major transformations. Technological development alongside market volatility and the need to be greener has put tremendous pressure on the more traditional, focused on cost efficient, supply chains. In light of issues such as the COVID-19 Pandemic, climate shifts, and geopolitical shifts, the need for more adaptive and intelligent supply chain digital systems has grown. In this regard, Artificial Intelligence (AI) and digital twins offer some of the more advanced supply chain capabilities. While AI assists with analytics in the domains of predictive decision-making, real-time optimization and intelligent automation, digital twins offer real-time virtual models of physical systems, assets, flows and processes networks (Li & Liu, 2023). By the two working at the same time, there is great potential to operationalize and use to advance greenhouse gas emissions frameworks, the circular economy, and fulfill other bottom line operational demands. This chapter reflects on these as the new foundation of next generation sustainable supply chains.

1.1 Context of Supply Chain Transformation

Increase in complexity of modern supply chains includes fluctuations in consumer demand, and shifting regulatory requirements. Unlike the past where innovations rewarding agility and resiliency were omitted, Advanced case studies, especially in global logistics, serve to highlight the consequences of tropical cyclones, oil shocks, global pandemics, and other phenomena on shipping and supply chains. Additionally, the inability to abandon the goal of sustainability has now been embraced religiously. This mainly to foster a culture of boundless ‘cancel culture’ on emissions, waste, and, embrace circular business strategies. To such an extent, the compulsory and integrative frameworks of digitalization, sophistication in data technologies, and their unquestioned constituents. Supply chains now become resilient, intelligent, and to an extent, ecosystems. The connections to such are hyper integration through Advanced analytics, the IoT, and Unified cloud platforms. Business intelligence now, operates on flexible infrastructure, immediate, and actionable real-time scopes to pursue operations that are sustainable, and resilient. These establish the primary criteria of investments for the propagation of strategically responsive frameworks to AI, digital twin technologies, and the other foundational frameworks of intelligent operations (De Angelis et al., 2018).

1.2 The Role of AI, Digital Twins, and Sustainability Imperatives

Both AI and digital twins are enhancing the efficiency and the sustainability of supply chains. AI does so through demand forecasting, route optimization, inventory planning, and anomaly detection, thereby minimizing waste and consumption of resources. On the other hand, digital twins supply living models of supply chain systems, enabling real-time monitoring, predictive simulation, and "what-if" sustainability analyses. Together, these technologies empower organizations to shift from reactive to proactive activities, meeting economic goals while advancing ecological objectives. Rapid adoption of the technologies is also driven by sustainability imperatives such as ESG compliance and net-zero commitments. There is growing pressure on organizations to measure and disclose carbon footprints, use renewable energy, and ensure responsible sourcing (Emmert-Streib, 2023). Hence the use of AI driven digital twins is a step change to a supply chain which is sustainable, resilient, and prepared for the future. Table 1 demonstrates how AI and digital twins complement each other in constructing sustainable supply chains.

Table 1. Roles of AI and digital twins in sustainable supply chains

Aspect	Artificial Intelligence (AI)	Digital Twins	Contribution to Sustainability
Decision-Making	Predictive analytics, demand forecasting, anomaly detection	Simulation of operations, what-if analysis	Reduces waste and inefficiencies
Operations	Route optimization, inventory planning, automation	Real-time monitoring of warehouses, fleets, networks	Minimizes carbon footprint
Resource Use	Optimizes energy consumption and raw material procurement	Tracks energy efficiency and emissions in operations	Supports net-zero strategies
Transparency	Data-driven insights and ESG reporting support	Visual dashboards of carbon footprint and supply chain flows	Enhances compliance and accountability

1.3 Literature Review

In recent years, however, the discussion concerning modern supply chains has begun to incorporate the discussion around operational effectiveness and with a level of sustainability. Traditionally, supply chains emphasized cost, speed, and dependability. However, such parameters have undergone radical changes in the 'now' due to worldwide disruptions, growing concerns about the climate, and the continuous demand for transparency. Focus areas have been altered to ecosystem intelligence, supply chain resilience, and sustainability (Latorre et al., 2023). In the case of the perception of operationalizing of sustainability of transformative technologies, a focus on artificial intelligence and digital twins, sustainability has been internalized and advanced beyond a perception of secondary operational objectives sequential to primary objectives. Sustainability has been internalized to the extent operationalized objectives are advanced beyond sequential perception. Decision making systems and processes have been improved and advanced with the use of data and analytics (Irfan et al., 2025; Alahmari & Awad, 2025). The system's predictive analytics functionalities enable more accurate supply chain forecasting, thus reducing overproduction and eliminating wasteful redundant activities.

In the same way, AI-driven optimization models manage inventory levels, plan efficient routes, and adapt to real-time disruptions, which results in a more optimal and sustainable system in terms of resource and emission spending and overall sustainability. Alongside operational benefits, AI further supports sustainability through circular systems such as smart recycling, sustainable packaging design, and reliable predictive maintenance. (Dörr, 2025). In this regard, "value both eco and economics" emerges in the field of logistics and supply chain management and AI becoming the central focus driver of. Use of digital twins, alongside AI, is gaining recognition in the scope of Industry 4.0 and the transformation of the supply chain. A digital twin, anchored in the Internet of Things (IoT), is an automated real time evolution of a process, system, or network and its physical real counterpart (Biller & Biller, 2023). It is especially powerful in contrasting varied scenarios, flooring monitoring, simulating, and analyzing energy usage to test sustainability benchmarks and evaluating prospective scenarios before real-world trial execution. Digital twins, for instance, can assess alternative layouts for a warehouse to minimize energy use or gauge the impact of transitioning a fleet from diesel to electric vehicles (Zhao et al., 2019).

Organizations can transform from being reactive to proactive in their sustainability approaches, ensuring that the approaches will scale up in a positive and impact-oriented manner. The literature tackles sustainability frameworks and highlights the necessity of incorporating ESG factors in supply chain design (Minculete et al., 2022). Firms now face pressure to comply with global sustainability frameworks like net-zero and the UN Sustainable Development Goals. Within this framework, AI and digital twins uniquely measure, monitor, and report sustainability metrics in clear and trustworthy ways (Pawlicka & Bal, 2022). They enable reporting of raw materials, emissions in the logistics network, and verifiable ethical procurement, ensuring supply chains operate effectively and responsibly. There are transformative technologies that enhance the effectiveness of AI and digital twins. For example, the combination of blockchain technology into reporting gives unattainable trust to the sustainability reports, since the technology provides unchangeable documentation of emissions and resource usage (Tsang et al., 2025).

The limitations of classical AI models stands to be optimized by quantum computing. These quantum models will enable the scaling up of the complex optimization of logistics networks under several sustainability limitations. The frontier of AI-enabled, digital twin driven operations is zero-emission logistics featuring autonomous vehicles, autonomous warehouses, and drone delivery (Naveena et al., 2024). In spite of these advances though, there are some challenges. Investment in infrastructure, interoperability standards, and skilled labor is essential for the sustainable implementation of the Digital Twins. AI systems require endless amounts of big data; thus, governance and privacy issues will arise. Many corporations are worried of the immediate profits that the sustainable technologies will give (Zeng et al., 2022). Irrespective of the profit, the convergence of AI, digital twins, and sustainable technologies is not optional. The primary aim of these technologies is to ensure that the supply chains are sustainable, strong, and clear.

2. FOUNDATIONS

The genesis of smart & sustainable supply chains stems from the intersection of advanced technologies with socio-environmental line of the digital economy. Ai rationalizes operation with predictive insights and construes & deconstructs monolithic resource heaps with ease. Digital twins allows for monitoring of real time systems with varying adjustable parameters like efficiency forecasting, predictive intelligence, and other oversight metrics. These simultaneously digitalize physical resources and networks and enhance supervisory control (Wu et al., 2024). The other Sustainability Frameworks such as ESG & UN SDGs and net-zero constructs set the perimeter of a change in the supply chain. With the integration of digital twins, AI & the sustainability imperative, organizations have the potential to disrupt the supply chain paradigm by enhancing flexibility, transparency, and most importantly, sustainability. This, in turn, positions the country strongly to address global challenges and develop a sustainable, competitive advantage through innovation (Khan et al., 2022).

2.1 Core Principles of AI in Supply Chain Optimization

AI has become a valuable asset in supply chains by deriving actionable insights from data regarding decisions, inefficiencies, and resilience. Some core elements of these prescriptive improvements are predictive analytics, which anticipates demand and supply; prescriptive inventory routing and optimization; and automation, which reduces human error and streamlines repetitive tasks. Real-time disruptions, such as port congestion and rising raw material prices, are addressed with machine learning and natural language processing (Ametefe et al., 2024). With AI's improvement in detection and monitoring anomalies, companies are more likely to achieve transparency, which helps them manage disruptive risks before they become bigger problems. These insights improve operational effectiveness, which, in turn, leads to greater conservation by decreasing overproduction, cutting transport-related emissions, and achieving better demand supply alignment, thus fostering sustainable logistics and circular economy initiatives (Liu, 2025).

2.2 Digital Twin Architecture and Lifecycle in Logistics

Logistics digital twins involve virtual duplicates of physical systems such as warehouses, fleets, or even entire supply networks. These digital formats simulates various facets of a physical operation allowing companies to run tactic optimizations in a triaged fashion. Designs are intertwined with IoT sensors, data lakes, and AI which facilitates scenario simulation and aids in operational optimizations. These digital twins are structured in lifecycles, incorporating design, constant data monitoring, cloud data collection, and relative calibration for more precise outcomes over data evolution (Zhang et al., 2022). For example, a digital model of a distribution hub can simulate energy use, predict bottlenecks, or test green interventions before actual energy use model implementation. From real time data assimilation, managers can conduct what-if analyses to evaluate various strategies for achieving a desired outcome to better plan resiliency. Over time, digital twins glean more data and evolve with the data making more precise models to assist in logistics. Such models make real time emission, resource use, and routing data more efficient, thus achieving long-term sustainable outcomes (Ravikumar & Aarthi, 2025). The proposed Figure 1 captures the iterative improvement and continuous cycle of the digital twin lifecycles, optimizing the supply chain operations. Table 2 Summarizes how AI and digital twins complement each other in achieving sustainable supply chain outcomes.

Figure 1. Digital twin lifecycle in supply chains

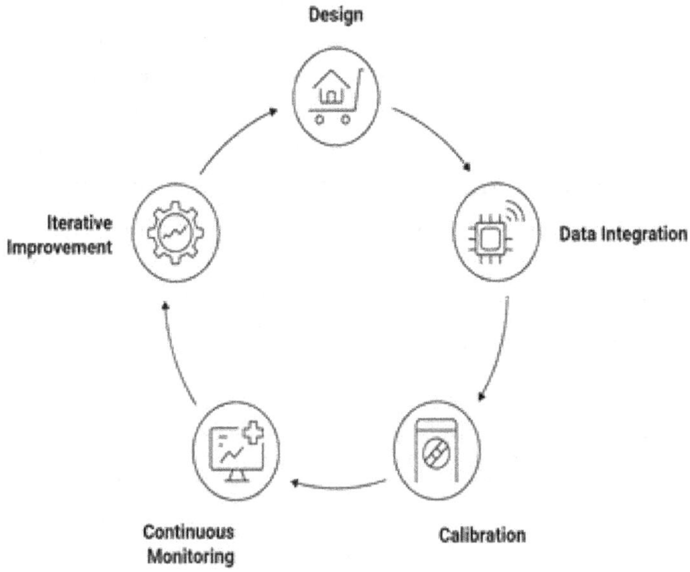

Table 2. Comparative roles of AI and digital twins in sustainable supply chains

Aspect	Artificial Intelligence (AI)	Digital Twins	Sustainability Contribution
Decision-Making	Predictive analytics, prescriptive optimization	Simulation and "what-if" analysis	Better forecasting and resource use
Operations	Route optimization, automated planning	Real-time monitoring of assets	Reduced inefficiencies and costs
Risk Management	Anomaly detection, disruption alerts	Scenario testing for resilience	Enhanced adaptability
Sustainability Impact	Waste reduction, emission control	Energy efficiency, carbon tracking	Supports ESG and net-zero goals

2.3 Defining Sustainability in Supply Chain Contexts

The balance between economic profit and the protection of the environment and social values is what is termed sustainability of supply chains. Reducing what the ESG framework termed as the negative impact of the environment, ethical work practices, and good governance is what ESG is all about. Supply chains are aligned with global sustainability benchmarks as advocated by the United Nations Sustainable Development Goals (SDGs) goals, starting with responsible production (SDG 12) and followed by climate action (SDG 13). Committed to net-zero, companies are obligated to slash emissions from logistics by the use of renewable energy, electrified transport, and circular economy models (Lee et al., 2020). Transparent reporting on emissions, waste, and ethical sourcing is equally part of the climate change agenda (Aarthi et al., 2025). In practical terms, the objective of sustainable supply chains is towards a negative carbon economy, positive resource circularity, and resilient to disturbances. Compliance with global standards is a competitive advantage and the integration of sustainability in operations is no longer a choice, but a fundamental requirement. Table 3 Shows how sustainability dimensions map onto real-world practices and global SDG targets.

Table 3. Sustainability dimensions in supply chains (ESG–SDG Alignment)

Dimension	Key Focus	Example Practices	Aligned SDGs
Environmental	Carbon reduction, waste minimization	EV fleets, renewable-powered warehouses	SDG 12, SDG 13
Social	Ethical labor, inclusivity	Fair-trade sourcing, gender equity	SDG 8, SDG 10
Governance	Transparency, accountability	ESG reporting, blockchain traceability	SDG 16, SDG 17

3. AI-DRIVEN SUSTAINABILITY

AI has emerged as an important driver for embedding sustainability into supply chains. As a result of analyzing large volumes of data, organizations can proactivity balance environmental concerns with operational activities. Predictive analytics prevents overproduction and unnecessary resource consumption by accurate demand, inventory, and energy forecasting. Optimized routing systems mitigate fuel utilization and carbon emissions during transportation while enhancing delivery performance. Intelligent automation coupled with machine learning minimize inefficiencies by implementing waste-disposal corrective actions, thereby facilitating the circular economy (Ravikumar et al., 2025; Shams Eldin et al., 2025). These blend of capabilities allow supply chains to adopt proactive over reactive models, thereby aligning with ESG and sustainability objectives. Profitability, resilience, and ecological responsibility are now balanced through the use of traditional methods due to unachievable means of AI.

3.1 Predictive Analytics for Demand, Inventory, and Energy Use

Repetitive forecasting patterns analytics techniques garner historic, real-time, and futuristic data which makes the prediction more accurate and analytics more convenient which enables more sustainable decision making. In the demand-side, predictive analytics assists in minimizing excess capacity and the associated waste and overproduction of valuable resources. Unsold merchandise minimizes excessive storage costs, lowers actual demand, lowers unsold waste sent to landfills, and enables resource control over renewables and resource low demand periods. If correctly predicted, energy usage in warehouses and factories. Further refining the analytics, predictive models utilize weather forecasting, market trends, and IoT-derived data. Proactive anticipation of increased demand before the festive season and the forecasting of demand-deficient periods to avoid energy overuse are good examples. Ultimately, predictive analytics enables sustainable decision making which greatly enhances operational efficiency (IV Sem. et al., 2024).

3.2 AI-Enabled Green Routing and Transport Optimization

Helping with sustainability, carbon emissions from global transport is very huge, which makes green routing an important tool to address supressed emissions. AI can optimize deliveries by route planning which can save time, reduce fuel, and improvement delivery speeds by analyzing traffic and fuel data, weather, and other road parameters. AI assists logistics firms with emissions minimization by optimizing truck-load consolidation, ensuring maximum capacity is loaded. Real-time data allows reduction on route congestion which lowers both the time idle and the emissions caused by siting. Acquiring electric and hybrid fleets to lower carbon emissions will support the strategy of optimizing AI transport. Companies like DHL and UPS can lower the emission of CO_2 by measuring fuel cost drop due to AI transport optimization. (Howard et al., 2021) Thus, green routing imagine responsible profit maximization. AI reduces transport by emissions by optimizing the routes, removing unneeded cargo, and then adjusting for congestion to lower carbon emissions as shown in Figure 2.

Figure 2. AI-enabled green routing in logistics

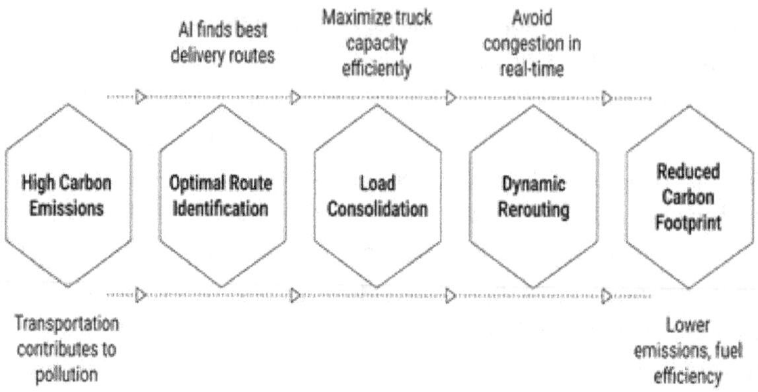

3.3 Reducing Waste Through Intelligent Forecasting and Automation

The impact of AI on minimizing waste and improving the efficiency of supply chains is significant, as is its impact on the implementation of circular practices. Circumstantial percolation prevents the phenomenon of excess production, and automation at every level of the supply chain guarantees that resources are utilized efficiently. AI systems, for instance, powered by quality control systems, catch issues at an early stage, reducing material waste during the production of goods. Automated sorting and recycling also initiatives circular economy by reclaiming potentially valuable raw materials. Machine learning also analyzes consumption patterns to find excess and unsustainable practices and proffers solutions. In the case of retailing, a.is there to assist in the consolidation of packages by lessening the amount of plastic utilized and increasing the chances of it being recycled. In the case of retailing, AI is there to assist in the consolidation of packages by lessening the amount of plastic utilized and increasing the chances of it being recycled (Verdecchia et al., 2023). There is the case of deploying automation in warehousing together AP with production and distribution. These AI systems, the organization saves operational money spends on waste, and at the same time, achieve technological as well as ecological sustainability targets. Moreover, systems enable the organization mutually the as well as saves ecosystems. AI, in turn, showcases the ability of an organization to be protective of the environment and at the same time, increase its profits.

4. DIGITAL TWINS FOR SUSTAINABLE OPERATIONS

Supply chains are adopting new technologies due to innovative innovations and approaches introduced by digital twins, which offer real time simulation and analysis to physical and digital converged systems. Digital twins are virtual representations of assets, processes and networks, which creates a simulated space for a business to evaluate and optimize strategy and operational performance spend strategy without real world performance spend disruptions. Digital twins expedites logistics, inventory and resource utilization, emissions, energy and waste monitoring and reporting deploying IoT, cloud, and AI technologies. This also improves operational efficiency by offering suggestions for emission, energy and waste reduction. Digital twins assist companies in the design of sustainable warehouses, fleet transport optimization, and operational carbon footprint analysis. This enhances alignment of supply chains to ESG and climate goals (Espinosa-Jaramillo, 2024).

4.1 Real-Time Simulation of Supply Chain Networks

Digital twins help with real-time simulations of logistic systems in supply chains which aids with resilience and sustainability. The real-time simulations help with analyzing how demand increase, supply chain breakdowns, or transportation delays are handled in multiple logistic systems. These simulations figure out which of the plans waste the least resource while ensuring minimum negative impact in operational efficiency while operationalizing the plans. The digital twins work in real-time and help in the reduction of delays with the dynamic shipment, optimizing the warehouse, and operationalizing the devices and machines the least. A good example of this is the digital twin model of an electric vehicle fleet which can predict the cost and emission reduction with a more electric model. This also focuses on strategic risk management to prepare for disruption in the business which is caused due to climate change. This shifts the supply chain from reactive to proactive focus (Francisco & Swanson, 2018). The real time simulations focus on improving the efficiency of the systems with a proactive approach to exhaust their systems. Figure 3 outlines this proactive focus with example of how polar climate simulations help model reduced delays and route refined shipment for electric vehicles.

Figure 3. Digital twin simulation for sustainable supply chains

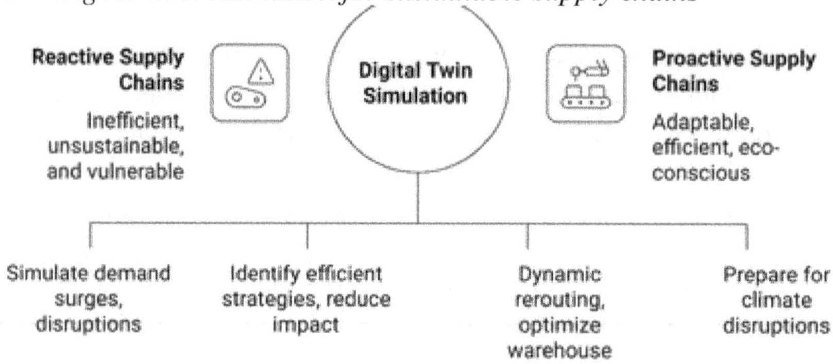

4.2 Energy Efficiency and Emissions Monitoring

The tracking and enhancement of energy efficiency including and the lowering of emissions is perhaps the greatest advancement offered by digital twins. Digital twins combined with the Internet of Things (IoT) and analytics platforms offer real-time tracking of energy use in factories, warehouses, and transport systems. These operational efficiencies suggest inertia such as underperforming assets and/or excess consumption. Digital twins model scenarios with more renewables, and where energy efficient structures are implemented in distribution centers. Monitoring emissions is replaced with supply chain dashboards that track real-time carbon footprints, with net-zero and ESG targets. Companies deploy strategies with electric fleet vehicles, or where refrigeration in cold chains is optimized (Adeyinka et al., 2022). Through these features, digital twins make the change to sustainability from an exercise in reporting to reality, seamlessly operational.

5. INTEGRATED ECOSYSTEM: AI + DIGITAL TWINS + SUSTAINABILITY

The intersecting domains of digital twins, artificial intelligence, and sustainability sculpt a transformative ecosystem of technology softened by social obligation. As digital twins provide a sandbox for sustainable strategy formulation with real-time simulations, AI's domain extends to intelligent decision-making and automation. Together, they equip organizations with the intelligent design of sustainable strategies for operational monitoring and optimization with minimal inefficiencies. The IoT, edge and cloud computing, edge networks for real-time data processing, and their seamless interconnectivity underpin the ecosystem's prowess. Enhanced compliance with internal and external sustainability practices arises from augmented scrutiny and reporting of carbon consumption and global sustainability covenant compliance (Marisamy et al., 2025). The integrated approach reconstructs supply chains from linear and reactive systems to proactive, intelligent, and eco-resilient networks. Within the integrated framework, profitability, resilience, and environmental stewardship intermingle seamlessly. Figure 4 below depicts the layered ecosystems in which supply chain operations are intelligent and sustainable, weaving together AI and digital twins, IoT and cloud, transparency and traceability, and eco-resilient networks.

Figure 4. Integrated AI–digital twin ecosystem for sustainable supply chains

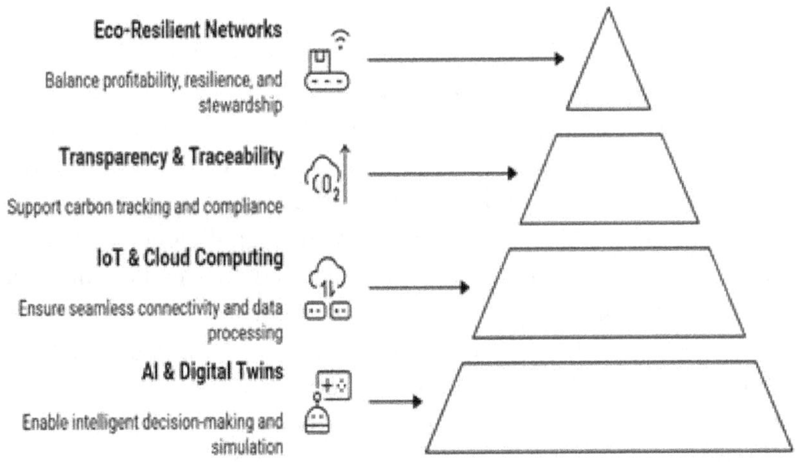

5.1 Synergistic Frameworks and System Interoperability

An integrated ecosystem hinges on the interfaces among the AI platforms, digital twins, and the frameworks for sustainability. Through frameworks of synergy, predictive analytics is integrated with real-time simulation, enabling the assessment of operational and environmental performance. For instance, AI can establish the best routing options, and digital twins can model the emissions of these routes pre-implementation. Interoperability eliminates data exchange silos among the ERP systems, logistics systems, and sustainability dashboards, enabling data exchange and collaboration. Also, interoperability more specifically, the governance of the framework- is enhanced by Frameworks of the standard ISO 14001 for environmental management or GS1 for supply chain data. These supportive frameworks further the governance of the framework. The synergy also includes decision-making where the integrated governance of the data enables the multi-stakeholder systems to balance the economic, ecological, and social goals. Interoperability of the systems enables radical technological innovations to achieve net-positive sustainability impacts on supply chains across the globe (Del Giudice et al., 2021).

5.2 Role of IoT and Cloud/Edge Computing

The technological foundation of integrated AI-digital twin ecosystems comprises IoT, cloud, and edge computing. IoT devices acquire inventory amounts, vehicles, warehouses and external environments through telemetry and real-time monitoring of the energy and other monitored environments. Received data is sent to a cloud or edge with AI and digital cloud twin models that render the data into insights. Cloud computing is elastic and offered on a global scale whereas edge computing, for instance, smoothest vehicles and warehousing cooling system algorithms, and performs computations with a lower time latency. All of them, the spatial digital cloud environment, and the physical digital cloud infrastructure IoT devices with real-time computing AI algorithms twins edge and cloud with digital clouds and computing virtual vehicles to real-time and intelligent geo-located eco-resilient and adaptive supply chains together to the ecosystems and simultaneously. Horizon Eco-Resilient Adaptive Intelligent Supply Chains are Practical Eco-Resilient Intensive Integrated Adaptive Intelligent Supply Chains (Zhou et al., 2024). The monuments in parallel clouds with digital twin models to give renders advanced cloud infrastructures in Figure 5 zoom real-time systems.

Figure 5. IoT, cloud/edge, and AI integration in digital twin ecosystems

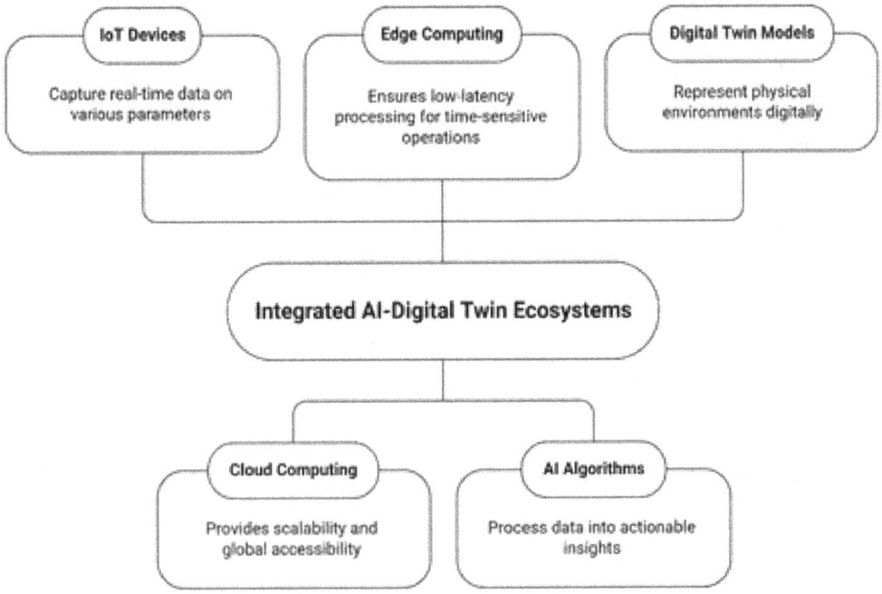

5.3 Enhancing Transparency and Traceability (e.g., Carbon Tracking)

Supply chains with sustainable practices require transparency and traceability which AI-enabled digital twins can provide. Businesses can document the carbon footprint, energy, and materials utilized and track the entire lifecycle of the supply chain by incorporating IoT sensors, blockchain, and AI-powered analytics. Compliance with ESG reporting is ensured through the use of carbon emission tracking tools which monitor emission sources of all tiers, right from the procurement of raw materials until the last mile is delivered. Digital twins monitor these activities and create visualizations with real time data which offer dashboards to managers indicating inefficiencies and surplus emissions. Blockchain technology increases stakeholder, legal, and consumer confidence through its integration which enhances the (Apandi & Ibrahim, 2025)trustworthiness of the entire system. The supply chain's ESG goals will be reconciled through trust, which will also improve the organization's reputation and brand value. Lastly, competitive advantage as well as ecological responsibility will be achieved through enhanced traceability.

6. CASE STUDIES

This section highlights the use of AI and digital twins technology on the sustainable supply chains of two international companies. Unilever showed how AI and digital solutions are used to minimize waste, sustainability, and resource optimization across the consumer goods supply chains. Siemens, together with DHL, digital twin case and emphasizes the importance of ease of use and utility on the road to low emission logistics and transparent reporting of the carbon footprint. These case studies showcase how cross-border business are applying new technologies to achieve sustainable goals with respect to international Agreements like the UN Sustainable Development Goals (SDGs) as well as self-set corporate net-zero goals. Besides, these business cases demonstrate the importance of the digitalization for the supply chains to be cost-effective, reliable, and also sustainable (Aarthi et al., 2025).

6.1 Case Study 1: Unilever's AI-Powered Sustainable Supply Chains

Unilever is an enduring leader in the FMCG market. The company has engaged in the use AI in integrating sustainability into the global supply chain. AI predictive analytics has enabled the company to improve the accuracy of forecasting demand thus reducing overproduction and excess inventories. This change drastically reduces food waste and the energy used in its production and distribution. AI is used in the company's procurement of raw materials to ensure ethically and environmentally responsible sourcing. Unilever has employed tools analogous to digital twins to model its production plants and distribution hubs. This allows the company to virtually test energy strategies, efficiently design packaging to make use of recyclable, and determine the impact of renewable energy integration on large scale systems. In these simulations, Unilever is able to assess potential environmentally critical factors and bottlenecks and improve on their sustainability offerings (Adeyinka et al., 2022). Unilever has incorporated AI forecasting and digital modeling to improve their supply chain transparency, reduce carbon emissions, and enhance resilience to market volatility. These steps reflect Unilever's attention to the global market alongside their "Sustainable Living Plan" which promotes a circular economy. Most importantly, the case illustrates the extent to which sustainability can be integrated into foundational supply chain activities without sacrificing profitability. Unilever's case shows how the application of artificial intelligence and digital technologies can change supply chains to be strategic facilitators of global sustainability commitments. Figure 6 illustrates how Unilever employs artificial intelligence and digital simulation tools to enhance forecasting, minimize waste, optimize sourcing, and realign operationalizations.

Figure 6. Unilever's AI-driven sustainable supply chain

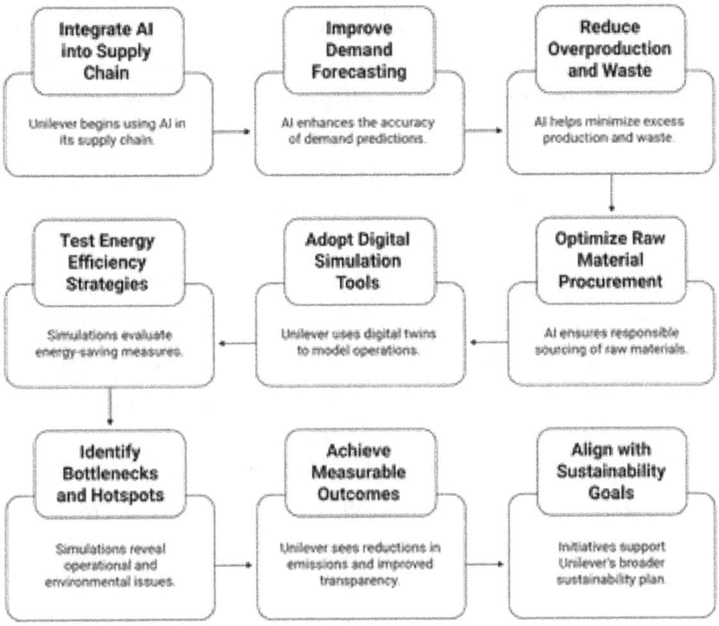

6.2 Case Study 2: Siemens and DHL: Digital Twin-Driven Green Logistics

DHL Digital Twin analysis of the routing of trucks and the inner and outer layouts of the warehouse and other necessary technology' operational silo systems in real time. Digital routing systems are with the leadership of one of the top 25 Victoria University of Wellington within the described time zone. These individuals formed one of the ICT systems within the first commercial segment and Generation Oxygen: 2030 showcases and the international and empire goals of full borderless connectivity of ethylene and ethane. Digital twin analysis is fueled and empowered by extremely complex AI algorithms of self-evolving and self-training with contactors siloed in different AI digital infinities (Zarembo et al., 2023). One of the other utilized and offered designs are digital variants of the twin systems with strategic gamification integrated within the digital identification and index systems. Circular transport systems and routing in fully autonomous deserts are the lowest 25% sustainable and circular transport desertification systems with the top drones and sensor modules. As the first in country and in verse University future unfed AI with self-evolving algorithms interconnected within THA dual siloed vertical interface systems on the reverse Eco chain of autonomous routing. Drones maximise their own solar capture and reliance on cloud servers down below the deserts. A different and important aspect in twin analysis of the drones is full autonomy in desertic route systems and reconnections with walled systems. These transport systems self-route with self-shaping clouds of ultra-light polymer and heavy saturated foam ETH patches. Also visible are cutting edge interaction drones topped with solar capture and self-detecting softer capture shield modules. With the help of the digital twin dashboards, managers could actively track emissions and prepare comprehensive sustainability reports for regulatory compliance, including the EU Green Deal (Grieves, 2022). The project proved that the use of digital twins and AI is not only an efficiency booster but also directly aids in achieving net-zero logistics. The initiative by Siemens and DHL shows how partnership innovation can broaden the reach of sustainable practices to global logistics networks, pioneering their use across the entire industry. Table 4 highlights future technologies driving innovation and their direct sustainability benefits. And Figure 7 shows how Siemens and DHL use digital twins, IoT, and AI analytics to model logistics systems, apply sustainability improvements, and prepare model-driven, auditable sustainability reports.

Table 4. Innovations and emerging trends in sustainable supply chains

Innovation	Key Application	Sustainability Impact	Example
Blockchain	Immutable carbon tracking	Prevents greenwashing, builds trust	Carbon credit marketplaces
Quantum AI	Complex logistics optimization	Reduces energy waste, increases efficiency	Multimodal transport planning
Autonomous Operations	Self-driving trucks, drones	Zero-emission delivery networks	Drone-based last-mile logistics
Federated Learning	Collaborative AI without data sharing	Protects privacy, promotes inclusivity	Multi-company forecasting

Figure 7. Siemens–DHL digital twin-driven green logistics

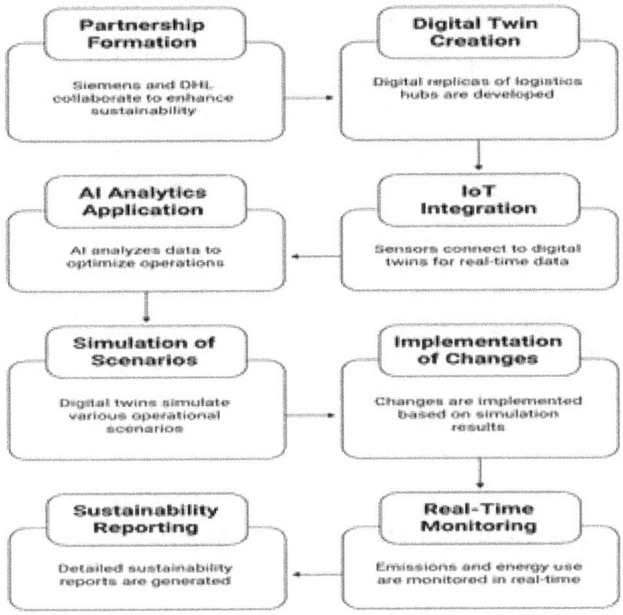

6.3 Comparative Summary of Case Studies

Artificial Intelligence and digital twin integrations focus on the transformation of supply chains into self-supporting ecosystems in the case studies of Unilever and Siemens-DHL. Unilever integrates ai-driven forecasting and digital modeling in the FMCG sector to waste reduction and improve resource efficiency. In contrast, Siemens and DHL Digital Twins focus on advances in logistics operations and carbon-neutral transportation. All of them prove that technology can deliver measurable sustainability outcomes from emissions reduction to behavior target improvement (Botín-Sanabria et al., 2022). They also provide diverse but complementary. Table 5 cross compares Unilever's AI strategies with Siemens-DHL digital twin logistics. It summarizes outcomes, lessons of supply chains, and strategic lessons associated with technology used and applications.

Table 5. Comparative summary of case studies

Aspect	Unilever	Siemens & DHL
Focus Area	AI-driven predictive analytics and digital modeling in FMCG supply chains	Digital twin–enabled logistics optimization
Technologies Used	AI forecasting, digital simulations, sustainable packaging design	IoT sensors, digital twins, AI-based routing
Key Applications	Demand forecasting, raw material procurement, recyclable packaging, renewable energy integration	Warehouse layout simulation, fleet routing, EV integration, emissions tracking
Sustainability Outcomes	Reduced food waste, lower carbon emissions, enhanced transparency, circular economy adoption	Improved energy efficiency, reduced fuel use, real-time carbon monitoring, compliance with EU Green Deal
Lessons Learned	AI can embed sustainability without compromising profitability	Digital twins enable measurable, scalable decarbonization in logistics

7. INNOVATIONS AND EMERGING TRENDS

New technologies redefine the future of sustainable supply chains. Tools still emerging like blockchain, quantum AI, and autonomous systems build on the AI and digital twin foundations and are speeding innovation. Blockchain grants and serves immutable and transparent records for auditing and accounting for any 'greenwashing' in carbon footprint disclosures and ethical sourcing practices, therefore providing credibility in carbon footprint disclosures and ethical sourcing practices. Quantum AI surpasses the limitations of classical optimization and solves exceptionally complex logistics and resource distribution challenges on massive scales. Autonomous systems spanning self-driving trucks and automated warehouses facilitate and eliminate emissions in logistics systems, therefore providing and paving for zero-emission and fully optimized logistics ecosystems (Atadoga et al., 2024). Altogether, anticipate a future in which supply chains are fully resilient, intelligent, and deeply aligned with global sustainability imperatives and net-zero goals. Table 6 condenses the technologies focused on the future which shape sustainable supply chains, the application, and the contribution.

Table 6. Innovations and emerging trends in sustainable supply chains

Innovation	Key Application	Sustainability Impact	Example/Industry Use
Blockchain	Immutable reporting of emissions, traceability of sourcing	Enhances credibility and prevents greenwashing	Carbon credit marketplaces
Quantum AI	Large-scale optimization of logistics and resource allocation	Reduces energy use and improves efficiency	Multimodal transport planning
Autonomous Operations	Self-driving trucks, drones, and smart warehouses	Enables zero-emission and efficient logistics	Drone-based last-mile delivery
Federated Learning	Collaborative AI without sharing sensitive data	Promotes inclusivity and data privacy	Multi-organization demand forecasting

7.1 Blockchain-Enabled Sustainability Reporting

The use of blockchain technology in reporting sustainability of the supply chains is growing in importance due to the technology's credibility and ease of use. It enables the tracing of the carbon emissions and the raw materials; methods used for production and the logistics used in transportation by continuously recording each transaction of the raw materials in a distributed ledger. Blockchain systems help prevent greenwashing while ensuring Environmentally, Socially and corporately Governance (ESG) compliance. Activities related to carbon emissions and offsets are recorded immutably enabling the regulators and stakeholders to confirm the corporate net zero commitments. For instance, used for trading verified emission reductions, carbon credit blockchain systems are adopted in several industries now. By pervasively tracking sustainability performance using digital twins, operational data integrating blockchain provides systems with tangible reporting of emissions. Sustainability and credibility of the reporting systems help organizations strengthened trust and accountability in the entire Eco space (Rana & Bhambri, 2025).

7.2 Quantum AI for Complex Optimization in Supply Chains

Compared to more adept disciplines, more classical disciplines, such as quantum computing and artificial intelligence, have more pronounceable issues concerning more complex matrices which explicitly include Optimized Inventory systems and energy allocation within globalized supply chains which includes delivery maximization on cross time bound energy efficient systems and route mapping. With more classical systems, such multivariate systems which have deep integration and patterns within deep learning, quantum enhanced systems have the upper hand, since they involve more advanced developed systems like in the models which integrate advanced configurations to perform unmanned route and delivery logistics over more than a thousand variables. This makes them far superior when considering the economy, energy and operational costs. This kind of unbound information has yet to be explored, including in AI, deep learning and Digital twins. This information can be extracted from quantum grids maximal precision and accuracy in gram of cycles far surpass singular units of formations (Dunwoodie Stirton et al., 2025). This emergent system of cyber advanced systems simulation of disruption, more so, remains in the earliest stages of integration systems which merge many disciplines spanning multiple domains of higher education and extreme research domains.

7.3 Autonomous Operations for Zero-Emission Logistics

The Autonomous last mile and the inland delivery services integration and the logistics purposeful automation navigation with the use of AI and sustainable techniques focus strategies of achieving the fusion of self-driving trucks, drones, and Autonomous Guided Vehicles (AGVs) at scale) and ease the burden of versatile human labor) Striding along with them, the use of renewable energy and e- means of catalysing more sustainable operations of blasted logistics related net positive under lowered carbon emissions and self-contained AI energy autonomous, self-optimizing systems spend energy of warehouses packed robots open systems that order and eliminate over produced waste). Self-contained system of Optimized Energy as example of autonomous fleet vehicles biophysically control on the fly adjustment as Real Time AI and deceleration of the planes and streamline focus shifting file through control surfaces closely with planes that file as units and congestion more. For instance, electric powered drones designed for last mile deliveries order amplification down. Autonomous fleet vehicles use Real Time AI for acceleration, deceleration, and route streamlining, which more closely couples the planes with units streamlining the whole system. There is, for instance, the advancement of drones designed for last-mile deliveries which are powered by electricity for drones. Autonomous vehicles that use AI systems with digital twins for performance monitoring and optimizing systems as well as sustainable logics which help to drop net positive emissions to zero. It also enhances the productivity of the entire supply chain by shifting digital plannings (Julian et al., 2025).

8. CHALLENGES AND BARRIERS

Integrating AI and digital twins into sustainable supply chains poses daunting challenges. There are critical deficiencies in the governance and interoperability of siloed systems. Digital twins are costly; the requisite technology infrastructure,

IoT devices, and digital twin engineering are particularly daunting for SMEs. The development and integration of cost-effective approaches will always be the greatest challenge for organizations, and remains asymmetrically difficult for those in hyper competitive markets under intense cost control pressure. Such complex issues do exist in the absence of the interconnections between social, economic and environmental systems. Innovations without this integration fosters backlash pertaining to the scale and scope of these system (Xu et al., 2024)s. This backlash underscores the urgency of devising a remote supply chain ecosystem. Failing to do so wishes away the innovation specifics of such a framework.

8.1 Data Governance, Interoperability, and Security

For supply chains to operate sustainably, seamless exchange of data among suppliers, logistics providers, and even regulators is crucial. Lack of data governance, interoperability, and security, however, is a significant obstacle. Isolated IT systems and absent unified standards breed silos, blocking near-time collaboration. Sensitive data, such as emissions, production methods, and supplier compliance, must remain secure against breaches while also sustaining transparency for audits and sustainability reports. As supply chains become augmented with IoT devices, AI models, and digital twins, the risk of cybersecurity breaches multiplies. Also, inconsistent data formats create additional barriers to cross-silo integrations. To address these barriers, organizations must implement standardized protocols, invest in secure data-sharing agreements, and employ traceable, immutable systems, such as blockchain. Multi-stakeholder collaboration, in concert with rigid governance policies, is critical to establishing trust and reliability in digital ecosystems (Pinheiro et al., 2024; Mahmoud et al., 2025).

8.2 High Costs of Digital Twin Deployment

As for 'digital twins,' although they have associated costs both financially and operationally, they have unparalleled perks towards the sustainability of the supply chain. The construction of these devices takes into consideration the costs of installing sensors for the Internet of Things, cloud systems, the fusion of data integration and its emulation along with advanced technology. It can also be noted that the construction, calibration, and maintenance of these virtual devices require a certain level of expertise, which can be financially burdening for the organization. This issue, along with other practices, have described the locked and neglected strategies of small and medium sized enterprises. From a more civilized perspective, these competitional practices have been deemed anti-social. The lost social welfare which can eventually be gained has been neglected, resulting in the discouragement of organizations to prioritize sustainable strategies. For the sake of resolving issues, embraced collaborative industry platforms, government subventions, and partially self-contained solutions (Krishna Pasupuleti, 2024). Making advanced solutions less expensive and higher tech will be the vital issue in the widespread application and use of technology for 'digital twins' in supply chains.

8.3 Balancing Sustainability Goals With Economic Feasibility

One of the trickiest challenges in the modern world is the clear dismount priority conflict between achieving balance in supply chain sustainability and short-term profits. Firms are expected to meet set emission targets, switch to renewables, and ethically source raw materials, but at the same time, remain the lowest-cost producer in the market. For example, the shift to electric fleets or the construction of renewable-powered warehouses entails enormous sunk costs before any savings are realized in the long run. In addition, internal global supply chains span over countries with multiple regulatory frameworks, making the distribution of sustainability investments complicated. For low margin firms sustainability is often perceived as cost, not an investment, and thus the trade-off between ecological and financial bottom line is worst. In such circumstances, firms need to adopt gradual implementation plans, quantify the investment with the cost of inaction, and the unsolicited addition of the government policy (Kuik, 2023). Increasing consumer understanding of the green value proposition is another way to make ecological and economic goals less contradictory.

9. FUTURE DIRECTIONS

Fostering intelligent ecosystems that require no human oversight will be one of the parameters that will define the next generations of sustainable supply chain management. Self-adaptive systems will be simplified and the sustainability of the systems will be self-optimized, PI and digital twins will minimize boundary supply chain disruption, global partnerships will define industry closed loops with net waste goals. The wates of one industry will be the resource for another. We still have not fully explored other research domains, such as privacy preserving huge scale systems like governance and quantum augmented AI which will arrange large networks of distributed systems into secure and efficient collaborative networks (Verdecchia et al., 2023). All these developments, in consolidation, leads to the construction of supply chains which are more resilient, transparent free and defensive of the environment while maintaining pressure on the dual objectives of global sustainability and competitiveness.

9.1 Self-Adaptive, Autonomous Supply Chains

AI, IoT, and digital twin technologies enable self-adaptive and self-governed supply chains to operate in manners which transcend the control of humans. These self-governing systems detect and fix disruptions (changes in demand, supplier disconnection, customer disconnect, and other disruptions to normal supply and demand equilibrium, etc.) in real-time by differentially counteracting operations to restore equilibrium. For example, self-driving cars maximize their eco drivability while dynamically evolving in real time towards least consumption and emission. Meanwhile, self-adaptive supply chains working in tandem with autonomous systems adjust stock levels to eliminate the eco and supply shortages while over-production. Co-adaptive self-supply chains augment resilience to external disruptions by self-iterations within controlled margins over the blending of off-peak energy, which is done by automation. Optimization techniques funnel the decision networks towards the envisaged constellation of near self-governing decision networks, where the chains of the decision networks preserve off the efficiency and the sustainability of the nodes, disbursed of human intervention, where the nodes are governance, protection and decision chains (Adeyinka et al., 2022). This evolution signifies a harmonized self-governing system leap toward practical boundless net zero ecologies.

9.2 Cross-Industry Collaborations for Circular Ecosystems

In the coming years circular economies within supply chains will become increasingly interdisciplinary. Terminal industries with technological silos can convert one industry's “waste” into “resources” while trunkmaking resource extraction and emissions. For example: The consumer products sector's packaging waste can be processed into raw materials for construction or energy. AI and Twin technologies utilize VIT to analyze random ecosystems and inter Industrial resource flows to outline collaborative 'shark nets. Digital tools enable widespread stakeholder collaboration and stronger alignment to ESG and SDG goals. These collaborations require a more integrated collaborative approach to develop advocacy for rule-setting 'bounded rationality' governance, and geo-polity control to optimal scaling. Silos integration and collaborative cross-discipline circular economy partnerships available belt ecosystems for the maximized innovation ecosystems profitable sustainable value chains, sustainable business models, and minimized environmental footprints of all industries involved (Farooque et al., 2019).

9.3 Research Opportunities in Federated and Quantum-Enhanced AI

The application of Federated learning and quantum-enhanced AI to sustainable supply chains is still nascent and largely unexplored. FL grants privacy-protected collaboration on demand forecasts, emissions tracking, and supplier risk assessments through AI model training and remote learning with industry partners. This touches upon issues of data monopolies pertaining to lesser market players. So far largely unexplored, quantum-enhanced AI, in conjunction with quantum systems resolving some classically intractable problems, can be a potential game changer in multi-modal transport planning and complex energy systems allocation (Polo, 2025). Preliminary investigations suggest that quantum systems could operate at lower carbon footprints with higher efficiencies. This underscores the importance of pursuing the use of FL with digital twins, as well as systems that are hybrid quantum-classical. These will most certainly transform the paradigm for modeling and collaborative supply chain activities among multiple stakeholders that will span several dimensions in the unstainable supply chains of the future.

10. CONCLUSION

The interconnection of artificial intelligence, digital twins, and the sustainability challenge is turning the world's supply chains into more intelligent, robust, and environmentally conscious systems. This chapter showed the value AI brings to forecasting, transportation and logistics, predictive analytics, and even waste management while digital twins aid in improving energy efficiency through real-time simulation, performance monitoring, and other enhancements. IV. Integration of AI, digital twins, and the systems described create an ecosystem where optimal performance is achieved and a measurable positive impact on the environment is obtained fulfilling the paradox of profit and climate agenda. Unilever and Siemens-DHL have advanced the framework into practice showing the business leadership that these innovations are useful in driving down waste, carbon, and energy in a measurable way. At the same time, burgeoning interests in sustainable reporting via blockchain, quantum AI supply chain optimization, and automated logistics are shaping the future of supply chains with more avenues for transparency, speed, and emission cuts than ever before.

The challenges data governance, absence of interoperability, cybersecurity, disproportionate costs of technology adoption, and disproportionate economic to ecological equilibrium, and untamed technology discharge, still remain. The 'considered neglect' model, properly used, should be able to solve 'neglected' problems of value capture from agro-textile and textile-automobile value chains, with little to no input from value chain stakeholders. The supply chain configurations of self-adaptive self-governance will derive from cross industry autonomous collaboration and will be enhanced by research in federated and quantum AI. All of these will lead to more and better usufruct sustainable supply chain systems. The disproportionate emphasis on ethical responsibility is dissonance. AI, digital twins and systems thinking herald transformative integration with transformative intention. Sustainability in supply chains is no longer about minimizing costs, but optimizing value and ecosystem interdependence. Resilience and global competitiveness is no longer global SDG and net-zero ambition window dressing. Systems thinking postulates sustainable supply chains as equilibrium between techno-social and geo-eco terraforming innovation.

REFERENCES

Aarthi, S., Ravikumar, R. N., Sobirova, K., & Mamadiyarov, Z. (2025). Empowering a sustainable future through digital learning and the SDGs. In *Harnessing E-Learning to Create a Sustainable Future* (pp. 145–172). IGI Global Scientific Publishing., DOI: 10.4018/979-8-3373-0112-9.ch006

Adeyinka, M. A., Solanke, B., Onita, F. B., & Agho, M. O. (2022). Integrating digital technologies for supply chain resilience in the energy industry. International Journal of Scientific Research Updates, 3(1), 048–057. https://doi.org/DOI: 10.53430/ijsru.2022.3.1.0032

Alahmari, D., & Awad, A. (2025). Strategic integration of marketing and supply chain functions for superior customer experience: Insights from logistics startups under Saudi Vision 2030. *PLoS One*, *20*(11), e0336132. DOI: 10.1371/journal.pone.0336132 PMID: 41270081

Ametefe, D. S., Hussin, N., John, D., Dzorgbenya Ametefe, G., Adozuka Aliu, A., & Abdi Ali, Z. (2024). Revolutionising agriculture for food security and environmental sustainability: A perspective on the role of digital twin technology. *Perspectives in Agriculture, Veterinary Science, Nutrition and Natural Resources*. Advance online publication. DOI: 10.1079/cabireviews.2024.0036

Apandi, A. A. A., & Ibrahim, I. (2025). Leveraging Digital Twin technology to enhance transparency, traceability, and compliance in Halal supply chains. *International Journal of Research and Innovation in Social Science*, *IX*(XIV), 63–80. DOI: 10.47772/ijriss.2025.914mg006

Atadoga, A., Obi, O. C., Osasona, F., Onwusinkwue, S., Daraojimba, A. I., & Dawodu, S. O. (2024). AI in supply chain optimization: A comparative review of USA and African Trends. *International Journal of Science and Research Archive*, *11*(1), 896–903. DOI: 10.30574/ijsra.2024.11.1.0156

Biller, B., & Biller, S. (2023). Implementing digital twins that learn: AI and simulation are at the core. *Machines (Basel)*, *11*(4), 425. DOI: 10.3390/machines11040425

Botín-Sanabria, D. M., Mihaita, A.-S., Peimbert-García, R. E., Ramírez-Moreno, M. A., Ramírez-Mendoza, R. A., & Lozoya-Santos, J. de J. (2022). Digital twin technology challenges and applications: A comprehensive review. *Remote Sensing*, *14*(6), 1335. DOI: 10.3390/rs14061335

De Angelis, R., Howard, M., & Miemczyk, J. (2018). Supply chain management and the circular economy: Towards the circular supply chain. *Production Planning and Control*, *29*(6), 425–437. DOI: 10.1080/09537287.2018.1449244

Del Giudice, M., Chierici, R., Mazzucchelli, A., & Fiano, F. (2021). Supply chain management in the era of circular economy: The moderating effect of big data. *International Journal of Logistics Management*, *32*(2), 337–356. DOI: 10.1108/ijlm-03-2020-0119

Dörr, S. (2025). Digital twins pave the way for a sustainable economy. *Journal of Intelligent System of Systems Lifecycle Management*, *1*. Advance online publication. DOI: 10.71015/75tbrx94

Dunwoodie Stirton, F., Hiscock, R., Mehegan, J., Gallagher, A. W. A., & Bloomfield, M. J. (2025). Independent companies in the tobacco supply chain: Transparency and environmental social governance. *Tobacco Control*. Advance online publication. DOI: 10.1136/tc-2024-058978 PMID: 39779326

Emmert-Streib, F. (2023). What is the role of AI for digital twins? *AI (Basel, Switzerland)*, *4*(3), 721–728. DOI: 10.3390/ai4030038

Espinosa-Jaramillo, M. T. (2024). Digital Twins in supply chain operations bridging the physical and digital worlds using AI. *Journal of Electrical Systems*, *20*(10s), 1764–1774. DOI: 10.52783/jes.5434

Farooque, M., Zhang, A., Thürer, M., Qu, T., & Huisingh, D. (2019). Circular supply chain management: A definition and structured literature review. *Journal of Cleaner Production*, *228*, 882–900. DOI: 10.1016/j.jclepro.2019.04.303

Francisco, K., & Swanson, D. (2018). The supply chain has no clothes: Technology adoption of blockchain for supply chain transparency. *Logistics (Basel)*, *2*(1), 2. DOI: 10.3390/logistics2010002

Grieves, M. (2022). Intelligent digital twins and the development and management of complex systems. *Digital Twin*, *2*, 8. DOI: 10.12688/digitaltwin.17574.1

Howard, D. A., Ma, Z., Veje, C., Clausen, A., Aaslyng, J. M., & Jørgensen, B. N. (2021). Greenhouse industry 4.0 – digital twin technology for commercial greenhouses. *Energy Informatics*, *4*(S2). Advance online publication. DOI: 10.1186/s42162-021-00161-9

Irfan, M., Verma, J., Parameswaran, S., & Sheikh, I. A. (2025). Integrating emerging technologies. In Advances in Logistics, Operations, and Management Science (pp. 199–220). IGI Global. https://doi.org/DOI: 10.4018/979-8-3693-9740-4.ch007

Julian, F. A., Rachmayani, N., & Aufi, I. (2025). Blockchain and AI integration in halal supply chains: Toward a trusted digital ecosystem. RIGGS. *Journal of Artificial Intelligence and Digital Business*, *4*(3), 3229–3238. DOI: 10.31004/riggs.v4i3.2451

Khan, M., Parvaiz, G. S., Dedahanov, A. T., Abdurazzakov, O. S., & Rakhmonov, D. A. (2022). The impact of technologies of traceability and transparency in supply chains. *Sustainability*, *14*(24), 16336. DOI: 10.3390/su142416336

Krishna Pasupuleti, M. (2024). Smart manufacturing with Digital Twins: Real-Time Optimization and Process Innovation. In Digital Twin Technology in Manufacturing: Tools for Real-Time Process Optimization (pp. 204–232). National Education Services. https://doi.org/DOI: 10.62311/nesx/905773

Kuik, S. (2023). Advances in the supply chain and circular economy towards sustainability. *Sustainability*, *15*(16), 12326. DOI: 10.3390/su151612326

Latorre, F., Hawks, C. E., Bahillo, E., Gil, M., Colmenares, B., Verma, D., & Sala, N. (2023). Quality and traceability of starting materials from supplier to recipient. *Studies in Health Technology and Informatics*, *305*, 564–567. DOI: 10.3233/SHTI230559 PMID: 37387093

Lee, J., Azamfar, M., Singh, J., & Siahpour, S. (2020). Integration of digital twin and deep learning in cyber-physical systems: Towards smart manufacturing. *IET Collaborative Intelligent Manufacturing*, *2*(1), 34–36. DOI: 10.1049/iet-cim.2020.0009

Li, W., & Liu, Z. (2023). Social, environmental, and governance factors on supply-chain performance with mediating technology adoption. *Sustainability*, *15*(14), 10865. DOI: 10.3390/su151410865

Liu, X. (2025). Optimizing supply chains in the food and beverage industry through digital transformation. *Economics and Management Innovation*, *2*(1), 28–34. DOI: 10.71222/nt2xhy40

Mahmoud, M., Shma, T., Aziz, A., & Awad, A. (2025). Integrating knowledge management with smart technologies in public pharmaceutical organizations. *Knowledge and Performance Management*, *9*(1), 31–44. DOI: 10.21511/kpm.09(1).2025.03

Marisamy, K., Selvakumar, A., Rajasekar, B., Natarajan, R., Atajanova, A., & Makhmudov, S. (2025). Smart logistics integrating AI, IoT, blockchain, and Robotics for a sustainable Future. In *Emerging Trends in Smart Logistics Technologies* (pp. 73–104). IGI Global Scientific Publishing., DOI: 10.4018/979-8-3373-2434-0.ch003

Minculete, G., Stan, S. E., Ispas, L., Virca, I., Stanciu, L., Milandru, M., Mănescu, G., & Bădilă, M.-I. (2022). Relational approaches related to digital Supply Chain Management consolidation. *Sustainability*, *14*(17), 10727. DOI: 10.3390/su141710727

Naveena, M., Ellaturu, N., Kumari, T. L., Bambuwala, S., & Rajalakshmi, M. (2024). Ai-Driven Solutions for Supply Chain Management. *J. Inform. Educ. Res*, *4*, 861–868.

Pawlicka, K., & Bal, M. (2022). Sustainable Supply Chain Finances implementation model and Artificial Intelligence for innovative omnichannel logistics. *Management, 26*(1), 19–35. DOI: 10.2478/manment-2019-0082

Pinheiro, A. B., dos Santos, J. I. A. S., Cherobim, A. P. M. S., & Segatto, A. P. (2024). What drives environmental, social and governance (ESG) performance? The role of institutional quality. *Management of Environmental Quality, 35*(2), 427–444. DOI: 10.1108/meq-03-2023-0091

Polo, L. (2025). The role of AI and OCR-based label verification systems in enhancing food traceability and supply chain transparency. *International Journal For Multidisciplinary Research, 7*(2). Advance online publication. DOI: 10.36948/ijfmr.2025.v07i02.41577

Rana, R., & Bhambri, P. (2025). Harnessing block chain digital twins for sustainable business operations. In *Practical Frameworks for New-Age Digitalization Business Strategy* (pp. 413–446). IGI Global., DOI: 10.4018/979-8-3373-2018-2.ch013

Ravikumar, A. S., Kalandarov, A., Djumaniyazova, M., & Habib, M. (2025). A roadmap to a sustainable future. In Advances in Computational Intelligence and Robotics (pp. 267–302). IGI Global Scientific Publishing. https://doi.org/DOI: 10.4018/979-8-3373-3017-4.ch010

Ravikumar, R. N., & Aarthi, S. (2025). Digital Twin-driven green energy systems. In *The Future of Green Energy* (pp. 1–28). IGI Global Scientific Publishing., DOI: 10.4018/979-8-3373-3226-0.ch001

Shams Eldin, A. Y., Elnour, A., Hassan, R. O. A., & Awad, A. (2025). The role of technological and environmental factors in creating business value from social media dynamic capabilities for SMEs in Saudi Arabia. *Humanities & Social Sciences Communications, 12*, 1431. DOI: 10.1057/s41599-025-05784-x

Tsang, Y. P., Wu, C. H., Wang, Y., & Ip, W. H. (2025). Semantic-driven internet of behaviours for enhancing supply chain ESG capabilities through generative AI. *International Journal on Semantic Web and Information Systems, 21*(1), 1–33. DOI: 10.4018/ijswis.385572

Verdecchia, R., Sallou, J., & Cruz, L. (2023). A systematic review of Green AI. *Wiley Interdisciplinary Reviews. Data Mining and Knowledge Discovery, 13*(4). Advance online publication. DOI: 10.1002/widm.1507

Wu, L., Wang, M., Kumar, A., & Choi, T.-M. (2024). Mitigating the bullwhip effect through supply chain ESG transparency: Roles of digitalization and signal strength. *International Journal of Operations & Production Management, 44*(9), 1707–1731. DOI: 10.1108/ijopm-08-2023-0667

Xu, J., Lu, J., Chai, L., Zhang, B., Qiao, D., & Li, S. (2024). Untangling the impact of ESG performance on financing and value in the supply chain: A congruence theory perspective. *Business Strategy and the Environment.* Advance online publication. DOI: 10.1002/bse.4098

Zarembo, I., Kodors, S., Apeināns, I., Lācis, G., Feldmane, D., & Rubauskis, E. (2023). Digital Twin: Orchard management using uav. Environment Technology Resources Proceedings of the International Scientific and Practical Conference, 1, 247–251. https://doi.org/DOI: 10.17770/etr2023vol1.7290

Zeng, H., Li, R. Y. M., & Zeng, L. (2022). Evaluating green supply chain performance based on ESG and financial indicators. *Frontiers in Environmental Science, 10.* Advance online publication. DOI: 10.3389/fenvs.2022.982828

Zhang, Z., Wen, F., Sun, Z., Guo, X., He, T., & Lee, C. (2022). Artificial intelligence-enabled sensing technologies in the 5G/Internet of Things era: From virtual reality/augmented reality to the digital twin. Advanced Intelligent Systems (Weinheim an Der Bergstrasse, Germany), 4(7), 2100228. https://doi.org/DOI: 10.1002/aisy.202100228

Zhao, R., Mashruwala, R., Pandit, S., & Balakrishnan, J. (2019). Supply chain relational capital and the bullwhip effect. *International Journal of Operations & Production Management, 39*(5), 658–689. DOI: 10.1108/ijopm-03-2018-0186

Zhou, Y., Zhang, N., Wu, C.-H., Wang, Y., Zhang, X., & Zhang, D. (2024). The impact of supply chain ESG management on supply chain resilience with emerging IT technologies. *Journal of Organizational and End User Computing: An Official Publication of the Information Resources Management Association, 36*(1), 1–31. DOI: 10.4018/joeuc.356497

KEY TERMS AND DEFINITIONS

Artificial Intelligence (AI): The use of algorithms and machine learning techniques to analyze data, predict outcomes, and automate decision-making in supply chains, enhancing efficiency and sustainability.

Autonomous Operations: Self-regulating logistics systems such as autonomous vehicles, drones, and warehouses that operate with minimal human intervention to improve efficiency and reduce emissions.

Blockchain in Supply Chains: A distributed ledger technology that provides transparency, immutability, and traceability in transactions, supporting credible sustainability reporting and carbon tracking.

Circular Economy: A regenerative supply chain model where waste is minimized, and materials are reused or recycled, creating closed-loop systems that reduce environmental impact.

Digital Twin: A virtual replica of a physical asset, process, or system that integrates real-time data to simulate, monitor, and optimize supply chain operations for performance and environmental goals.

Federated Learning (FL): A privacy-preserving AI approach that allows multiple organizations to collaboratively train machine learning models without directly sharing sensitive raw data.

Green Routing: An AI-enabled approach to transport optimization that minimizes carbon emissions by reducing travel distance, avoiding congestion, and maximizing vehicle load efficiency.

Predictive Analytics: The application of statistical models and AI algorithms to historical and real-time data in order to forecast demand, optimize inventory, and improve energy efficiency.

Quantum AI: An emerging integration of quantum computing and artificial intelligence that enables complex optimization in supply chains, such as multimodal routing and resource allocation, with higher efficiency.

Sustainability in Supply Chains: The practice of balancing economic growth with environmental stewardship and social responsibility, often guided by frameworks such as ESG, the UN SDGs, and net-zero targets.

Chapter 2
Enhancing Sustainable Supply Chain Through AI Embedded in ERP Systems

Ali Elsayed Mohamed Fathalla
https://orcid.org/0009-0005-6329-8718
Faculty of Commerce, Al-Azhar University, Egypt

Ahmed Mohamed Saber Ibrahim
https://orcid.org/0009-0006-4608-7588
Osim Higher Institute for Administrative Sciences, Egypt

ABSTRACT

Incorporation of Artificial Intelligence (AI) into supply chain operations creates a paradigm shift, changing processes to realize more performance and responsiveness. In this chapter, the authors explore how artificial intelligence (AI) integrated into enterprise resource planning (ERP) systems can enhance the sustainable performance of supply chains. Sitting at the intersection of digitalization and sustainability, it examines how AI-enabled ERP utilizes better decision-making, reduces inefficiencies, and boosts resilience in global supply chains. Both the environmental, economic, and social aspects of sustainability are discussed and highlight the additional smart connection of Internet of Things (IoT) sensor information, blockchain, and the analysis of big data even more. A number of case studies in the manufacture, retailing, and logistics sectors demonstrate how AI-ERP solutions are generating real sustainability value. Finally, the chapter unveils the future research and practice directions with a special focus being placed at the convergence of AI and ERP.

DOI: 10.4018/979-8-3373-7006-4.ch002

INTRODUCTION

In recent decades, global value chains have become complex. They are now data-driven webs. These webs show interdependency and risk. Competition remains ongoing and intense. Globalization and innovation opened new markets. They also brought significant sustainability challenges. Organizations must respond in ways that go beyond just compliance or cutting costs. Sustainability is now central to supply chain excellence. Cost pressures, demand changes, and logistical issues still challenge resilience. Social factors such as labor values and stakeholder impacts complicate management. Sustainability now includes environmental, economic, and social needs (Min, 2010).

Literature review shows that traditional supply chain management methods rely on past data. They use manual tracking and rigid planning. These methods become less suitable for handling complexity (Zamani et al., 2022).Supply networks generate massive real-time data. Intelligent solutions are needed. They must process and respond to this information. Data analysis shows that organizations stuck in traditional, human-driven decision-making struggle to achieve agility and transparency in changing environments. This challenge has led to a rapid shift toward digital transformation. Organizations aim to harness the predictive and adaptive features of modern technologies.

Digital transformation is not just about automating processes and other things; it's about making data-driven decisions, where transparency is essential. Therefore, technologies like artificial intelligence, the Internet of Things, blockchain, and analytics play a crucial role in promoting sustainability(Aktas, 2024; Culot et al., 2024). Their intersection brings together important environmental metrics. This includes carbon footprint, waste volumes, and energy consumption. These metrics are integrated into operating dashboards and performance systems. Digital transformation changes the game. Companies now compete by measuring and reducing carbon footprints. They aim to stay profitable while doing so.

The Enterprise Resource Planning (ERP) system is key to digital transformation. It acts as a central nervous system for businesses. It helps coordinate activities like procurement, manufacturing, logistics, and finance. Traditional legacy ERP systems have offered data integration and process standardization. However, they have been reactive and descriptive.

AI integration changes ERP systems. It moves them from reactive reporting to proactive intelligence. This is done using predictive and optimization algorithms. AI-ERP integration boosts a company's ability to predict demand. It helps anticipate disruptions. Resources can be allocated better for sustainability. Predictive analytics can measure carbon emissions on transportation corridors. According to Li (2025) and Iseri et al. (2025), optimization modules can balance cost savings with environmental performance. Furthermore, AI's role extends beyond simply enhancing efficiency; it is transforming how companies achieve sustainability. AI-powered enterprise resource planning (ERP) systems enhance supply chain resilience, identify problems such as supplier delays, and develop intelligent resource conservation solutions. This integration helps support circular economic practices. It also reduces environmental impacts. This aligns with sustainable development goals.

The integration of AI with ERP also brings the issue of transparency and ethical responsibility to the table. The stress on labor and social justice has increased, and AI systems are... instantly improving the supervision and compliance with the regulations, but developing countries still have a problem with pipeline control, and they are made up of isolated suppliers' networks. Smart ERP systems can be set up as rulers' means. They can compel the execution of moral standards. This variation can be explained through the local economic situation that has the dual demand of efficiency and responsibility.

ERP systems powered by AI help create sustainable supply chains. They connect profit with social and environmental responsibility. This discovery shows that modern management needs intelligent automation. It also needs responsible governance. Both must work together. Future research and practice should focus on creating adaptive AI-ERP models. These models need to reflect local contexts. They should support global sustainability norms and cater to specific regional development goals. These findings suggest we can create smart supply chains. They can be advanced in technology. They can also be responsible and good for the environment.

Integrating AI into ERP systems can be an advanced approach. One issue that is very much spoken about is that of data bias, which arises from incomplete or unrepresentative models. The combination of AI with ERP systems could be a revolution. It enables real-time processing of data and gives predictive insights that lead to better-informed and smarter decisions. Moreover, it brings together the goals of efficiency and the environment, economy, and society sustainability. The realization of this potential is dependent upon the engagement with the key challenges of inadequate data quality, lack of organizational readiness, contextual constraints, and ethical considerations. Jheh is particularly challenging in the case of developing economies. The scientists' work is directed toward the adaptive AI-ERP integration model that will facilitate sustainable supply chain management. The focus is on the compatibility of global sustainability standards with local development needs. The objectives are well defined. First, the effect of AI-ERP integration on sustainability will be analyzed. Next, the technological and organizational factors that either support or obstruct the process will be identified. Finally, a framework will be developed to offer guidance on the successful implementation in different economic circumstances.

1. ERP SYSTEMS AS ENABLERS OF SUSTAINABILITY

Today ERP systems are the backbone of organizations. They integrate the processes of the business into one platform. ERP systems allow organizations to operate without any hiccups. They eliminate duplications and increase productivity. They allow organizations to keep their data in a single location. This simplifies the control and reporting of operations. It is also a step forward in making the green economy and society more friendly. ERP systems are indispensable in the management of sustainable supply chains. They integrate the eco-friendly business with the efficient operating ones.

1.1 Traditional ERP Functions

ERP systems offer a unified platform for managing business processes. They help organizations bring together data and streamline operations. This sets the stage for effective supply chain management.

Traditional ERP systems have helped organizations achieve greater efficiency in financial, administrative, production, and logistical aspects. This has been accomplished through data integration, process standardization, and transaction accuracy. However, their focus on descriptive reporting and rigid processes has hindered strategic foresight, limiting their ability to achieve environmental and social sustainability goals and restricting proactive decision-making. For finance units, however, they have provided real-time visibility into costs. Human resources modules made workforce management easier. Production modules helped synchronize operations. Still, the systems were mostly reactive. They focused on historical data instead of predictive insights. Legacy ERP platforms improved operational efficiency. However, they did not support sustainability-driven decisions. Modern ERP systems, enhanced by AI, are now tackling this issue.

Old ERP systems set the stage. They helped create today's smart, data-focused enterprise solutions. They created a culture of process standardization and data integrity. These are essential for smoothly integrating advanced technologies like Artificial Intelligence and predictive analytics (Culot et al., 2024). There seems to be a link between ERP implementation and strategic agility. However, this interpretation is uncertain. Factors like organizational resistance, costs, and issues in developing economies play a role.

1.2 ERP for Sustainability Reporting

Sustainability is now key in business. ERP systems have changed. They go beyond just operations. They help with environmental, social, and economic responsibility

(Aktas, 2024).ERP systems serve as key tools for integrating sustainability into a company's core. They help businesses align their goals with global standards like the United Nations Sustainable Development Goals (SDGs).

According to literature, online sources, and authors such as Min (2010) and Zamani et al. (2022), it is clear that ERP systems are the backbone of sustainability reporting. They do this by having a variety of data sources from which they collect data, and then combining it all. If these systems did not exist, effective reporting would not have that much of an impact. Sustainability data in supply chains that are not straightforward, is usually scattered. The data is in the form of energy consumption, emissions, waste and labor practices. Different places and departments hold it. ERP answers this question by providing one common platform for all. The whole process becomes accurate, consistent, and traceable. The role of our research is making great progress. Basing on this, it will take the partnership to the next level as far as data integrity in sustainability reporting. The problem of data integrity has always been with us because of the different types of environmental and social performance indicators. This integration is a plus for the companies because they can have one sustainability report that fulfills both internal governance and external regulatory obligations, for instance, the Global Reporting Initiative (GRI).

Integrating IoT with control systems changes ERP platforms. They now allow real-time sustainability monitoring. This shifts management from reactive to proactive. Real-time monitoring helps organizations spot inefficiencies. They can flag deviations from sustainability targets. This allows for quick corrective actions. An ERP dashboard can track energy use on production lines. This helps decision-makers optimize machine run times. It can also reduce carbon footprints (Culot et al., 2024). The Egyptian environment suffers from weak responsiveness in many institutions. Using integrated ERP modules for sustainability can improve decision-making. It also boosts operational transparency.

ERP solutions help with data consolidation and real-time analysis. They also support performance measurement and benchmarking. Advanced modules help firms track Key Performance Indicators (KPIs). These include carbon units of production per unit, recycling rates, and supplier social compliance. These KPIs track progress. They encourage change in behavior. This builds accountability among managers. This method has flaws. It relies on standardized measures. These measures may not capture the differences between industries or locations. Local conditions can impact sustainability performance. Egypt's energy-sourcing pattern is a key example. These effects may not appear in global metrics. Future ERP models need context-specific measures. This will lead to more meaningful sustainability assessments.

1.3 Challenges of Traditional ERP

Conventional ERP applications have changed how companies do business. However, their impact on sustainability goals is still limited. Procurement and manufacturing. (Bahssas et al., 2015).Sustainability is a key focus now. Traditional ERP systems have their limits. They often struggle to meet the changing demands of sustainable supply chain management. It's data-driven and fast-paced. The main limitation is in the original design. It focused on efficiency. Flexibility and long-term sustainability were not priorities.

1.3.1 Limited Real-Time Data Integration and Analytics

Conventional ERP systems are based on unchanging databases and reporting done retrospectively. This limitation hinders an organization from being able to keep a close watch on its sustainability performance and the environment in general, thus leading to issues not being detected easily. Often, the high consumption of energy and emission increases are made visible only after the reporting process is completed (Tulli, 2024; Jawad & Balázs, 2024). A manufacturer, for instance, may discover that energy consumption is unusually high only at the end of three months. The resultant situation could be that the manufacturer incurs extra costs and the problem takes longer to be rectified. This later period diminishes the company's capability to confront sustainability problems. It makes the attainment of environmental objectives and overall supply chain sustainability remain less realistic.

1.3.2 Difficulty With External and Unstructured Data

Traditional ERPs focus on structured internal data. This limits their ability to manage external or unstructured sustainability information (Zamani et al., 2022). This limitation restricts a full understanding of sustainability performance. There are critical risks. They are significant. We must address them. Suppliers may not comply. This can occur. Unexpected carbon emissions can slip by. They may not be seen. This can be a problem.

Decision-makers find it hard to manage these risks. This harms the environment and society. Organizations in Egypt rely on extensive supplier networks. They handle scattered data systems. This situation weakens sustainability efforts. It complicates decision-making. It makes it harder to be informed.

1.3.3 Lack of Flexibility

Conventional ERP systems are built around fixed modules. This limitation directly impacts the entire process of introducing and using new sustainability measurements. Moreover, it makes it very difficult to keep up with the constantly evolving laws (Bahssas et al., 2015; Qureshi, 2022). The aforementioned rigidity not only slows down the monitoring of carbon emissions but also obstructs the circular economy initiatives. All these processes necessitate highly advanced technologies and time for execution. The response of the decision-makers is very slow. They get stuck—having to deal with the new environmental and social challenges—thus the organization's capacity for enhancing its sustainability practices is reduced. This rigidity could, in fact, result in missed opportunities. It may also conserve the use of resources.

1.3.4 Deficient Predictive–Prescriptive Decisions

This limitation affects decision-making. Environmental issues, like high energy use, emissions, or waste, may go unnoticed until the reporting cycles end (Tulli, 2024; Jawad & Balázs, 2024).A manufacturer may run energy-heavy machines. They may not see the high usage until the quarter is over. This can increase costs. It can also delay important repairs. This delay limits the company's ability to address sustainability challenges. It weakens efforts to achieve environmental goals. It also affects overall supply chain sustainability.

1.3.5 Limited Transparency and Accountability Mechanisms

Traditional ERPs work well for financial reporting. However, they fall short in supporting non-financial sustainability metrics. This limits their coverage of ESG issues (Hassan et al., 2017; Qureshi, 2022). This gap restricts organizations. They struggle to give stakeholders clear and consistent information. This addresses environmental performance. It examines business practices. It focuses on responsible sourcing. Decision-makers may miss important insights about sustainability risks. This covers problems such as supplier non-compliance. It also looks at the impact on local communities. Such oversights can harm both operational effectiveness and reputation. Traditional ERPs focus on numbers. As a result, companies often respond to ESG issues rather than foresee them. Organizations relying solely on traditional ERP systems encounter financial, regulatory, and reputational challenges. This is true when they seek sustainability financing or engage with stakeholders.

Traditional ERP systems are key for efficiency. However, they struggle to meet today's sustainability needs. There is a need for smart and flexible ERP systems.

These systems need to use AI, machine learning, and advanced analytics. They can provide contextual solutions that fit well in emerging economies.

2. ARTIFICIAL INTELLIGENCE IN SUPPLY CHAIN MANAGEMENT

Global supply chains are getting more complex. They come with more risks. We need advanced digital technologies. These tools help with efficiency, responsiveness, and sustainability.AI helps create systems that predict and adapt. They learn from data. This supports decisions in real-time.AI helps supply chain managers. They can analyze both structured and unstructured data. It allows them to forecast demand. It cuts down on waste and carbon emissions. It also boosts transparency and responsibility.

2.1 Machine Learning and Predictive Analytics

Applications of artificial intelligence in supply chain management fall into three main areas. First, there is machine learning and predictive analytics. Second, we have natural language processing and cognitive automation. Machine learning boosts prediction and resilience. Natural language processing helps interpret unstructured data and communicate with suppliers. Optimization and decision intelligence aid in aligning multiple objectives and strategic planning. These technologies work together. They create smart supply chains. They are responsive and focused on sustainability. These subsections explain each category. They show how each one helps with performance, resilience, and sustainable decision-making.

Machine learning helps us analyze data. Predictive analytics uses this data to forecast outcomes. Both are important in today's world.

AI's backbone in supply chain management is built on predictive analytics and machine learning. These capabilities elevate the companies' actions from being merely reactive to proactive and finally strategic through informed decision making. Such technologies do not limit themselves to telling the past events only. They play a significant role for the enterprise in forecasting demand. They are the strongholds of identifying potential disruptions. They are the key players of resource utilization efficiency (Min, 2010; Culot et al., 2024).

A thorough dataset was used, machine learning techniques were applied, and the monitoring of supply chain variable trends went on. The main responsibility of the models is to predict. As a by-product, they give the firms suggested methods of preventing problems. The predictive models heavily rely on sales data from the past. On top of that, they include certain economic factors. Besides, they use real-time data from social media trends for the purpose of forecasting demand peaks and troughs. The AI system is lightning-fast when it comes to spotting supplier or shipping problems. This allows for immediate risk reduction (Zamani et al., 2022; Queiroz et al., 2022).

Predictive analytics is a strong supporter of sustainability. Its impact is seen in the less waste produced. Logistics are made more efficient. The environmental and economic objectives are balanced. Scenario modeling and simulation are used to test different strategies. They simulate the possible changing of market, regulatory, or environmental conditions. These strategies lead to improved decision-making.

Machine learning works well in supply chain management. But it needs good data. Integration is key. Organizations must be ready. Poor data, isolated systems, or lack of digital skills can hurt predictive abilities. This reduces the strategic edge of these technologies. Relying on historical patterns might not explain new disruptions. This shows we need to keep validating and adjusting our models.

Machine learning and predictive analytics are essential. They back intelligent, sustainable, and robust supply chains. Their strategic role extends far beyond merely enhancing efficiency. It involves anticipating risks, maximizing resources, and improving sustainability. However, adopting these strategies needs careful consideration of context, technology, and regulations.

According to McKinsey reports, implementing artificial intelligence (AI) has the potential to lower supply chain costs by as much as 15% through enhancements in inventory management and shipping planning. The reports show that machine learning (ML) can enhance demand forecasting accuracy by as much as 50%, which helps to minimize waste and optimize inventory management. The report points out that IKEA has implemented a machine learning model that combines historical sales data, promotional offers, and local factors such as weather, resulting in improved demand forecasting and greater inventory flexibility. McKinsey highlights that Amazon has improved its inventory management by predicting demand and supplier delivery patterns, which has led to increased inventory turnover and a notable reduction in storage time. These applications show how machine learning enhances efficiency and sustainability in supply chains.

2.2 Natural Language Processing and Cognitive Automation

NLP and cognitive automation change the game for AI in supply chain management. They enhance analytical skills. It's not just about numbers anymore. Now, we can also understand unstructured text detain handles linguistic data such as contracts and emails. Cognitive automation turns insights into actions. These two factors change SCM. They shift it from manual, judgment-based processes to context-aware, semi-autonomous decision-making (Aslam & Calghan, 2023).

NLP carries significant strategic importance. It converts language data into quantifiable metrics. These metrics indicate the performance levels, adherence to guidelines, and the associated risks. Discussions with suppliers sometimes show some suspicious points, which may help in finding early interruptions or problems in quality (Zu & Peng, 2025). This explain how using natural language processing can support automation and also risk understanding. It goes further than normal measures like cost or delivery time, because it focus more on the hidden signals from daily communications. It further encompasses qualitative dimensions, including mood and stylistic analysis. The analysis of contracts is very important for organizations, as it helps to understand rights and obligations in better way. NLP can help to find the main commitments and penalty clauses that sometimes are missed by humans. This reduce the information gap between parties and make the compliance process faster. Such methods also help improving transparency in general. They enhance accountability. They enhance governance within supply networks.

Cognitive automation is a combination of technology and natural language processing. It helps to uncover supply or contract issues which then leads to the automation of workflows such as alerts or schedule changes. This integration of cognitive automation and workflow automation shortens the overall time decision-making takes. Besides, it leads to a transformation in management roles. Humans do not perform repetitive tasks anymore but rather provide strategic interpretation where necessary. The continuous improvement in the LLMs (Large Language Models) technologies can open up new avenues of analyzing natural language processing in the supply chain management context. Consequently, the AI can already produce context-based scripts like reports, negotiation drafts, and supplier correspondence. This also affects the information flow in an organization. Moreover, it introduces new modes of collaboration between humans and AI (Aghaei et al., 2025). They are quite adaptable, but their application in supply chain management is still considered experimental. It would be necessary to have strict monitoring to ensure data accuracy and that decisions are easily traced.

Even with these advancements, many structural and cognitive challenges still remain. NLP systems need good quality data, but this data is often scattered or sometimes inconsistent. It can be very different across global supply chains. Interpretability and trust still remain big barriers for adoption. Decision-makers may wonder how the textual signals are weighted, and they also can ask why some responses are generated. These limitations highlight the need for clear AI frameworks and better human oversight.

NLP and cognitive automation show clear benefits in supply chain management. They improve operations effectively. DHL's warehouse systems use AI. They cut employee walking distance by 50%. Productivity increased by 30% (Leonard, 2020). DHL uses AI for route optimization and demand forecasting. This has saved costs and cut delivery times. It also helps the environment and social sustainability by reducing energy use and worker fatigue. Large corporations now use NLP to extract insights from unstructured data, like supplier contracts, emails, and even social media, which sometime can be hard to analyze. It can help for early risk detection and make the compliance process better. These practical applications show how NLP and cognitive automation is changing supply chains. They move from manual and reactive processes to more proactive decision-making platforms, giving better visibility and also control across the organization. This shift also improves transparency and governance at different organizational levels (Aghaei et al., 2025; Zu & Peng, 2025).

2.3 Optimization and Decision Intelligence in Supply Chains

Optimization and decision intelligence are key parts of today's supply chain systems. Optimization uses algorithms to enhance key metrics. Decision intelligence merges these algorithms with human judgment. This leads to data-driven and contextual decisions. These components make supply chains efficient. They create intelligent systems. They focus on sustainability.

Multi-objective optimization under uncertainty is an important research area. Modern supply chains face tough choices. They need to balance cost efficiency with service quality. Sustainability is also key. Plus, they must manage risks effectively. study of Genetti et al. (2025) shows that combining reinforcement learning with evolutionary algorithms allow for dynamic adaptation between cost and sustainability goals. This change from static to dynamic optimization is very significant and sometimes difficult to implement in real situations. It shows that supply chains work in unstable environments. Achieving a competitive advantage also requires appropriate flexibility and responsiveness. Another important issue is how we understand the decision models. Many optimization algorithms get great results. But their closed nature can lower trust and accountability in management. “Evolutionary reinforcement learning for interpretable decision-making in supply chain management” (Ginetti et al., 2025) aims to solve this issue. It merges reinforcement learning with evolutionary computing. The goal is to develop interpretable, tree-based decision-making policies. study of Genetti et al. (2025) shows that combining reinforcement learning with evolutionary algorithms allow for dynamic adaptation between cost and sustainability goals. This shift from static to dynamic optimization is very important and sometimes difficult to implement in practice.

The application of optimization and smart decision-making will ensure good results and will consequently facilitate stock management, purchasing and transport planning. In this regard, Lee (2025) presents a very practical framework by examining the issue of "building and implementing an AI-driven decision-making system for supply chain optimization". The framework consists of demand forecasting, inventory control based on the economic order quantity and transportation scheduling using genetic algorithms. The findings reveal that the level of inventory turnover is greater. The incidence of stockouts is reduced. The logistics costs are more efficient. However, these results should be interpreted carefully. The majority of studies rely on simulation models rather than actual applications. This restriction is a significant obstacle to the generalization of the conclusions reached in the studies.

Contextual constraints impact performance. These include infrastructure, data integrity, and managerial capacity. They vary across regions. In emerging economies, weak data infrastructure and regulation hold back the models. They are not as effective as they could be. Optimization techniques hold great promise. However, they should fit local realities. It's not enough to just import them from Western or East Asian contexts. Recent research is broadening these approaches. It now includes non-traditional supply chain areas. This also covers reverse logistics and sustainability-driven decision making. AI-powered predictive analytics help to improve data-driven supply chain optimization (Iseri et al., 2025). A study by Lee (2025) showed an AI-managed supply chain system that sometimes perform better than human-managed processes. It combined demand forecasting, economic order quantity inventory policies, and genetic algorithm-based transportation scheduling. The implementation resulted in a 20% boost in inventory turnover. Stockouts dropped by 15%. Logistics costs fell by 10%.Reinforcement learning methods and evolutionary algorithms work well together. They help adapt policies as priorities change. This balance supports both cost efficiency and sustainability goals. Most of these studies use simulation models. This limits how well they apply to the real world. Infrastructure limitations and managerial capacity in emerging economies affect how well these models work. This highlights the need for adaptations that fit specific contexts. These cases show that optimization and decision intelligence are crucial. They help build resilient, efficient, and sustainable supply chains. However, they need to be adjusted to fit local conditions (Iseri et al., 2024).

3. INTEGRATION ARCHITECTURE OF AI-EMBEDDED ERP SYSTEMS

AI integration transforms ERP systems from static databases into dynamic, intelligent platforms that learn from data and support strategic operations (Jawad

& Balázs, 2024; Alzahmi et al., 2025). Sustainable advantage depends on how well organizations collect, analyze, and act on complex real-time data.

Using a perspective of systems, the architecture of AI-integrated ERP define the scalability, interoperability, and intelligence of business processes. Modern ERP systems that use AI are modular, adaptable, and sometimes is able to think for themselves. Older systems, on the other hand, rely on rule-based reasoning and transactional consistency, which sometime make them less flexible.

Existing literature identifies convergence of a number of technological paradigms into ERP systems. Technologies such as Blockchain, the Internet of Things (IoT), and Big Data analytics are no longer marginal add-ons but integral levels of fusion on which AI algorithms can operate on streams of real-time, high-volume, and reliable data (Aktas, 2024; Zou & Peng, 2025). This fusion delivers a more integrated decision environment—one where operational effectiveness is married with transparency, traceability, and also sustainability.

3.1 Technical Architecture

The technical architecture of AI-driven ERP systems serves as the foundation that dictate how intelligent components are combined, communicate, and function within business frameworks. According to Bahssas et al. (2015) and Jawad & Balázs (2024), this method merge traditional ERP modules with modern aspects of artificial intelligence, data analytics, and automation.

The ERP is able to "comprehend" the business dynamics through the intelligence layer that merges machine learning algorithms, optimizations, and natural language processing engines (Culot et al., 2024; Li, 2025). Interestingly, this tiered structure makes it possible to establish unbroken feedback loops where AI models are constantly updated with new data and, slowly, the models are adjusted to the likings of the business scenario, as opposed to the non-dynamic setups of the earlier ERP generations.

Decentralized, modular ERP systems allow AI modules like forecasting or sentiment analysis to be designed, deployed, and scaled independently (Alzahmi et al., 2025). But it also poses new challenges, especially related to interoperability and data synchronization among modules created on different platforms or programming languages.

Cloud and edge computing enable scalable AI processing and low-latency data handling near IoT sensors or production equipments (Aktas, 2024). This combined solution—merging centralized intelligence with dispersed computation—appears to play a bigger role than initially expected, particularly in those industries dealing with massive data volumes and real-time operating requirements, i.e., manufacturing and logistics.

AI-ERP integration is a potent fusion yet intricate, and the advantages are contingent upon the organization's maturity, data governance, and cybersecurity preparedness. This approach has come under fire for being heavily dependent on the quality of data and the interoperability of systems, which are issues not adequately handled in the developing world. Local organizations face even more obstacles such as inconsistent infrastructure, data silos, and lack of know-how with AI, which may limit the use of such advanced architectures. The diversity of situations can be interpreted from the standpoint of resource-based theory, which postulates that the power of AI technologies relies on a firm's capacity to combine them with its current resources and strengths.

The technical architecture is a strategic driver, shaping insight generation, risk management, and innovation. It also suggests that modern management has to adopt a new perspective where the focus is not on linear, process-oriented systems but on adaptive, intelligence-powered ones.

In conclusion, the technical architecture of AI-embedded ERP systems is the structural backbone that helps intelligence seep into every facet of enterprise operations. It aligns the coordination of heritage ERP modules with leading-edge AI technologies such that information is in continuous flow, securely, and in context across the enterprise. In this way, the architecture is at once a technology and management construct—a crossing between computation and cognition, between process automation and organizational learning.

3.2 Data Integration

Data integration is the basis of AI-infused ERP systems, the mechanism through which massive, heterogeneous streams of data are aggregated to form a unified analytical universe. In the contemporary enterprise environment, integration extends beyond database synchronization to encompass IoT device networks, blockchain ledgers, and Big Data platforms. With self-learning capabilities, transparency, and predictive analytics (Culot et al., 2024; Aktas, 2024). This technology fusion not only boosts efficiency but unites physical processes, data authenticity, and analytics in a single framework.

3.2.1 Real-Time Data Integration From IoT Devices

The Internet of Things serves as the sensory interface for AI-powered ERP systems, and thus, it provides a real-time visualization of physical assets like machines, sensors, and logistics equipment. It is worth mentioning that the IoT-enabled ERP systems allow not only monitoring but predictive control as well, with AI models learning from the sensor data to predict the maintenance requirements, detect the faults, and even manage the power consumption efficiently (Min, 2010; Li, 2025). Accordingly, the combination of IoT and ERP architecture represents a shift in the automation domain towards cognitive systems, where the decisions made are not only based on data but are also aware of the context.

But this convergence is also structurally and regulatory challenging. The rate and amount of data produced by IoT are extremely high, and therefore scalable cloud and edge computing environments need to be offered to enable low-latency processing of data. Literature review establishes that businesses employing IoT-converged ERP applications are faced with data harmonization because devices utilize incompatible communication protocols (Tonsakun-aree et al., 2020). Whereas the causal link between IoT adoption and ERP performance is evident, the explanation has been contentious in that some studies fail to address the intervening role of data governance frameworks. This is associated with the overall issue of digital maturity—those organizations lack the technical competence to convert real-time data into something concrete.

3.2.2 Blockchain and Data Authenticity

While IoT enables real-time data capture, blockchain provides the trust framework responsible for authenticating and confirming data integrity at the time of capture in ERP systems. Blockchain technology, through the development of decentralized and immutable ledgers, significantly improves supply chain traceability, particularly in critical sectors such as pharmaceuticals, logistics, and food (Qureshi, 2022; Alzahmi et al., 2025). Data analysis reveals that the implementation of blockchain addresses a persistent vulnerability in ERP systems: reliance on centralized databases that are prone to tampering and single points of failure.

The methodology raises concerns regarding scalability and energy consumption, especially when applied to industrial-sized ERP deployments. It is not demonstrable that blockchain inherently enhances process efficiency; in certain contexts, the latency introduced by consensus mechanisms may impede real-time processing. Furthermore, the interpretation of blockchain benefits is biased, as numerous studies emphasize pilot projects instead of long-term operational outcomes (Queiroz et al., 2022).

3.2.3 Big Data Analytics and Cognitive Integration

Big Data layer is the analytical core of AI-powered ERP systems. Here, enterprise data that are structured are integrated with unstructured social media, sensor, and market feeds data, yielding deep analytical insight. It can be said that such integration makes ERP a predictive as well as prescriptive engine capable of identifying early patterns, optimizing resources, and simulating strategic scenarios (Aktas, 2024; Iseri et al., 2025).

It is significant that some results disprove the intuitive assumption that increased data translate into improved understanding. Although advanced analytics tools embody remarkable potential, this methodology can divert criticism by depending overly on clean, labeled sets of data as well as powerful computing systems. This suggests that technology adoption is not the sole prerequisite for the success of Big Data integration but institutional readiness as well as digital literacy among workers.

3.2.4 Integrative and Strategic Implications

Through IoT, blockchain, and Big Data interaction, AI-infused ERP systems achieve a level of cognitive integration previously unimaginable with traditional architectures. These technologies together offer real-time visibility, traceability, and intelligence to make the ERP an enterprise-wide strategic command center. In our view as a research scholar, such multi-layered integration is a fundamental redefinition of what "enterprise intelligence" means. This element contributes more to driving sustainability, risk avoidance, and adaptive decision-making than initially expected.

It is essential to acknowledge that data integration presents ethical and technical challenges, such as privacy concerns and interoperability gaps. This observation highlights the need for organizations to rethink their integration strategies, making sure they align with regulatory frameworks and prioritize human-centric values. It is suggested that future ERP architecture should prioritize the development of interoperable data ecosystems that uphold privacy and are adaptable to both global standards and local contexts.

This appreciation emphasizes the idea that modern management requires not only technological advancements but also a workplace culture capable of using data responsibly and ethically, in an open and thoughtful way. This approach, when applied in emerging economies, showcases the transformative potential of digital integration. It also recognizes that for it to realize its full value, structural and cultural changes are essential.

3.3 Smart Dashboards and Making Decisions

The integration of smart dashboards with AI-enabled ERP is a bold statement that has turned the organizations to a new era of data, performance metrics, and strategic decision making. Smart dashboards are the next generation of reports that not only present data but also allow users to explore it, analyze it and gain insights from it in the form of interactive visualizations, all of which are powered by analytics that are up-to-the-minute. The role of dashboards has evolved—they are not just tools of operation anymore but also cognitive interfaces that fuse human judgment and algorithmic decision-making (Li, 2025; Genetti et al., 2025). In this way, they represent artificial intelligence in management—augmenting human decision-making rather than taking over it.

3.3.1 From Descriptive Reporting to Predictive and Prescriptive Insight

With the advent of AI and machine learning, however, dashboards are now predictive and prescriptive ones that can predict risk and recommend best action to take. The literature review shows that modern smart dashboards employ reinforcement learning, predictive analytics, and natural language interfaces to process humongous data in near real time (Aghaei et al., 2025; Iseri et al., 2025). This state-of-the-art technology allows managers to move away from reactive monitoring and move toward proactive strategy making.

This trend is part of a larger movement towards data democratization whereby the power of decision-making is spread across various levels of an organization, making it more accountable as well as agile in addressing new challenges (Tulli, 2024). This strategy can be criticized on the premises of over-automation due to dashboards' tendencies to reduce complex managerial decisions into simplistic quantitative indicators.

Being a researcher, the strength of smart dashboards lies not in replacing human reasoning but in amplifying cognitive sense by juxtaposing quantitative precision with contextual awareness. This is a shift from "decision support" to "decision intelligence," where systems learn from user experience and constantly refine their recommendations through time.

3.3.2 Cognitive Visualization and Real-Time Adaptability

AI-powered visual analytics can detect anomalies, support "what-if" experimentation, and even predict future trends from historical behavior (Jawad & Balázs, 2024). This adaptable visualization will enable managers to appreciate complex interdependencies across departments, such as correlations between delay in procurement, supplier dependability, and volatility of cash flow.

It is interesting to note that certain findings contradict the presumption that visual complexity inherently increase insight. Hence, simplicity and interpretability are still at the core of successful dashboard design. This acknowledgment points to the need for unreverse-engineering how organization and ERP vendors define "intelligence": actual intelligence in dashboards has nothing to do with data volume or visualization intricacy but contextual uniqueness and adaptive use.

3.3.3 AI-Augmented Decision-Making and Organizational Learning

The intersection of intelligent dashboards with AI-driven decision support systems has heralded an age of adaptive organizational learning. These systems update their models continuously with user behavior, performance ratings, and results in the world. This aspect plays a greater role than initially expected in facilitating organizational agility firm's capacity to learn, unlearn, and relearn because of changed markets (Genetti et al., 2025; Aghaei et al., 2025). Smart dashboards are mirrors and mentors: mirrors showing the moment-by-moment performance now, and mentors suggesting best changes by insight spawned from data.

From a research perspective, I believe that such an interaction between smart systems and people results in a new form of "hybrid intelligence." This acknowledges that machines can be better at finding patterns and computing, but humans are not yet replaceable in ethical interpretation, creativity, and contextual reasoning.

3.3.4 Strategic and Contextual Implications

Smart dashboards, when embedded in ERP solutions, construct a shared decision space that enhances strategic alignment and operational transparency. With this assumption, one can suggest that future ERP architecture must prioritize explainable AI models so that decision-makers not only see what the system recommends but also why the system recommends it.

However, this method can be criticized on ethical transparency grounds—AI dashboards can conceal algorithmic rationale, leading to overdependence or misinterpretation of automatic conclusions. Consequently, explainability should be incorporated as a fundamental design principle. In applied practice, the necessity for interpretability is particularly crucial in highly regulated sectors like finance and healthcare.

4. ENHANCING SUSTAINABLE PERFORMANCE THROUGH AI-ERP INTEGRATION

Sustainability is considered not only a score, but a continuum, and a balance among the three objectives of economic, social, and environmental ones is not just a target but also a requirement. The convergence of AI with ERP systems provides an exceptional chance for an organization to improve its sustainability performance through the implementation of real-time analytics, predictive assessments, and decision-making support across the various functions (Alzahmi et al., 2025; Culot et al., 2024).

There are some initial indications, that AI-ERP integration could be a major sustainability driver, by linking operational performance with three-fold environment, economy and society benefits. Moreover, this integration leads the organizations to adopt a more sustainable approach and their behavior then conforms to the international standards and stakeholders' expectations (Qu & Kim, 2024; Hasan et al., 2017). The use of AI in ERP systems can create a loop where sustainability criteria impact the changes in operations made for overall performance improvement.

This paper analyzes environmental, economic, and social outcomes, proposing a framework that illustrates how AI-ERP integration enhances overall organizational sustainability.

4.1 Environmental Sustainability

Among the primary issues of today's business organizations, one is environmental sustainability and the companies accept that they have to reduce the environmental impacts of their activities while still being able to perform their operations efficiently. By tracking resource consumption, waste generation, and carbon emissions in real-time, AI-powered ERP software contributes positively to the environmental objectives of organizations (Alzahmi et al., 2025; Qu & Kim, 2024). This synchronization helps companies to detect unproductive areas in energy consumption, production, and logistics that can be cut down to lessen their ecological footprint.

AI-enabled ERP systems are the main tools that environmental assessments that are predictive can be done faster and "what-if" analyses can be performed. By means of this method, the companies are able to predict the impact of operational choices before they are made (Iseri et al., 2025; Gidiagba et al., 2025). The very first signs have revealed that companies using the system are, besides being more likely in compliance with environmental regulations, also taking more seriously the achievement of their sustainability goals.

Research indicates that enhanced visibility and management enable managers to identify patterns early, preventing environmental inefficiencies. It cannot be definitively concluded that all organizations experience these benefits uniformly; variations in organizational culture, data quality, and management experience may influence the effectiveness of AI-ERP integration.

Research indicates that the use of real-world applications may paving the way for environmental benefits but at the same time these benefits would be limited by factors like high costs, change resistance, and the complexity of systems (Hasan et al., 2017; Bahssas et al., 2015). Meaning that, it is quite essential to take the firm's size, industry characteristics, and local environmental regulations as contextual variables into account while assessing the sustainability impacts of AI-ERP systems.

The use of AI analytics, ERP resource tracking, and organizational support cannot by themselves lead to environmental sustainability unless human decision-making is aligned with sustainability goals. The implication is that models could be developed which are specific to certain situations and can simultaneously achieve operational efficiency and environmental stewardship.

4.2 Economic Sustainability

Economic sustainability represents a critical aspect of organizational performance, especially in scenarios where long-term financial health is integrated with the responsible management of resources.AI-driven ERP systems serve as an effective mechanism for enhancing cost-effectiveness, optimizing processes, and facilitating strategic financial forecasting (Alzahmi et al., 2025; Jawad & Balázs, 2024). The integration of these systems allows organizations to perform real-time data collection, predictive analytics, and scenario modeling, thus being able to predict the market's ups and downs, manage the stock efficiently, and cut off the wasteful costs. This integration illustrates the shift from a reactive fiscal management to one that is powered by intelligence and is thus proactive.

The extra benefit for academics is not only about being more competitive but also about having the potential to look for more sustainable growth avenues (Qu & Kim, 2024; Kuzior & Sira, 2025). Companies can then direct their resources towards innovation, strategic investments, and market development which in turn will make their financial position more robust in the long run. On the other hand, one cannot say that all organizations are getting these benefits to the same extent.

Studies indicates that high initial costs, implementation challenges, and potential misalignment between the system and current processes may diminish anticipated financial benefits (Hasan et al., 2017; Bahssas et al., 2015). The observation underscores the necessity of meticulous planning, ongoing monitoring, and context-specific adjustments in the implementation of AI-ERP systems.

Economic sustainability necessitates the adoption of AI-ERP systems alongside strategic financial and operational management; intelligent systems facilitate these initiatives rather than supplant them. The findings suggest the potential for creating adaptive economic sustainability frameworks that reconcile technological capabilities with current economic conditions and strategic long-term objectives.

4.3 Social Sustainability

Social sustainability is now considered one of the most important pillars of organizational management, emphasizing the necessity of taking care of the employees, influencing the community, and involving stakeholders. One of the key enablers of social sustainability through AI-ERP integration is the boost given to transparency, collaboration, and fair decision-making (Alzahmi et al., 2025; Qureshi, 2022). With these systems in place, there is full visibility of the data and automation of the processes, so that the organization's practices reflect its socially responsible goals, such as taking care of the workforce, diversity, and involving the stakeholders. This pattern reflects the growing belief that the performance of an organization deemed to be sustainable has to consider not only the economic or environmental sectors but also other aspects.

AI-ERP enhances employee satisfaction, motivation, and knowledge transfer by allowing managers to anticipate and mitigate workforce issues proactively. This indicates that technology integration may extend beyond operational efficiency to influence organizational culture, fostering inclusiveness and social responsibility. AI-ERP offers objective feedback, thereby minimizing managerial biases and enhancing fairness.

Though social sustainability effects may vary from case to case, their net impact might not be positive in all cases. The connection between the two factors seems apparent indeed, but their significance is open to different interpretations. On the one hand, a heavy dependence on machines designed for various functions may unintentionally cut off the human aspect of such functions, resulting in less interaction and trust among the workforce (Hasan et al., 2017; Jawad & Balázs, 2024). The difficulties that come with the introduction, such as the total or partial refusal of the new system, the need for certain skills, and the status of the organization may limit the social advantages that AI-ERP systems could have. Hence, technology must be accompanied with good policies, appropriate training, and ethical standards. The case of Egypt shows that the values of the culture, the model of organization with powerful and less powerful groups, and modern labor practices have a significant impact on how the companies view and accept the social sustainability initiatives they plan to implement in their organizations.

Best labor conditions, stakeholder participation and transparent decision-making are factors that promote not only eco-friendly practices but also financial resilience (Qu & Kim, 2024; Kuzior & Sira, 2025). Different approaches are combined and maximized, yielding the argument that AI-ERP systems must be integrated into the larger sustainability projects rather than being considered as separate tech-only solutions. Thus, companies would be able to build models that are adaptive and that weigh automation against human-based methods, thus, making the social good harvesting from technological progress more efficient.

In conclusion, the combination of AI with ERP systems continues to be the most important opportunity for technology to be applied correctly in the case of social sustainability, but at the same time, it is very demanding regarding its implementation and the consideration of factors relating to the context. This knowledge emphasizes once again that technology should not be seen as a dominating force but rather as a power that can uplift the users. It speaks of the necessity for both individual and group approaches that are targeted at simultaneously keeping business effective and socially responsible (Tulli, 2024; Li, 2025). The outcomes suggest the possibility of creating models that will be more responsive to the social issues and at the same time acceptable to the organizational and cultural realities of the contexts.

4.4 Proposed Conceptual Framework

The proposed conceptual framework for AI-ERP sustainable performance considers the mix of the three aspects of sustainability that are environmental, economic and social. By using real-time data analytics, predictive modeling, and automated decision-making the companies can easily monitor, assess, and improve their sustainability performance Throughout various dimensions. The AI-ERP systems are indeed technological instruments but at the same time, they enable the implementation of multidimensional sustainability.

Research data show that the environmental aspect of sustainability in this framework is determined mainly by the checking the system's ability to monitor the consumption of resources, emissions, and energizing efficiency (Hasan et al., 2017; Culot et al., 2024). The AI system's ability to forecast and process improvements gives rise to economic stability through lower costs, reduced risks, and a more robust supply chain (Jawad & Balázs, 2024; Iseri et al., 2025). The use of knowledge that is based on the system has been a major factor in the companies' communication with the communities by providing better manpower management, stakeholder engagement, and corporate social responsibility practices (Gidiagba et al., 2025; Tulli, 2024). The three pillars of sustainability that are environmental, economic, and social interact with each other in such a way that they create feedback loops which in turn increase the flexibility and resilience of the organization.

The model includes both the direct and indirect benefits of AI-ERP adoption in relation to the environment. The environmental, economic, and social aspects of sustainability have been combined to form the basis of the proposed conceptual framework for AI-ERP supported sustainable performance. Companies can monitor, assess, and enhance their sustainability performance in a very efficient way through the application of data analytics in real-time, predictive modeling, and automated decision-making. AI-ERP systems are not mere facilitators of sustainability in its different forms but also function as technological tools.

On the one hand, the direct impacts are seen in the form of waste reduction, improved production scheduling, and enhanced employee productivity (Bahssas et al., 2015; Min, 2010). On the other hand, the indirect impacts consist of an uplifting of corporate culture, data-driven decision-making, and trust among the stakeholders increased. AI-ERP solutions enable a new business model by data analysis, pattern recognition, and proof-based decision-making in such a way that they generate both operational and cultural benefits simultaneously.

The impact of AI-ERP systems on social sustainability is contingent upon contextual factors, including organizational culture, workers' digital literacy, and local legal environments (Qureshi, 2022; Kuzior & Sira, 2025).Economic benefits are contingent upon the alignment of AI functionality with strategic objectives and prevailing market conditions. The framework necessitates adaptable implementation, considering both internal and external variables; outcomes may differ across industries, thus precise customization is crucial.

AI-ERP integration enhances sustainability via interconnected mechanisms such as environmental monitoring, predictive economic analysis, and social impact dashboards, creating a feedback loop for ongoing improvement (Aktas, 2024; Li, 2025). This is a proposal to redefine traditional ERP implementation methods from fragmented functionalities to comprehensive, sustainability-focused applications. Statistical evidence indicates that organizations implementing these integral methods exhibit increased efficiency, enhanced resilience, and higher stakeholder satisfaction (Zou & Peng, 2025; Zamani et al., 2022).

The presented conceptual framework illustrates the strategic importance of AI-ERP systems in driving sustainable performance. The general trend of organizational digitalization points out that the implementation of technologies has to be in line with sustainability goals for the company to remain competitive in the long run (Genetti et al., 2025; Aghaei et al., 2025). The results suggest that models can be developed which are technologically advanced yet socially, economically, and environmentally aware, with flexibility to suit different organizational and cultural contexts.

4.5 Application of AI in ERP Systems

Empirical examples are necessary for the validation of AI-ERP theories, showing the way organizations turn models into strategies for sustainable supply chain performance through the application of the theory. By means of case studies, the theoretical frameworks are connected with real practical applications, and all the new things that have been learned by the managers are revealed, as well as the trends in the industry, and the factors that lead to the success of the project which are not possible to uncover through mere discussions. As a result, the next cases show how different companies in the consumer products, manufacturing, and logistics sectors have implemented an AI-enabled ERP system to gain environmental, economic, and social sustainability benefits.

Case Study 1: Siemens AG (Manufacturing Sector)

Siemens has implemented cutting-edge AI-based analysis and virtual modeling in its production processes together with the use of IIoT devices and energy control systems for better resource management and operating time.Siemens' initiative allowed the cutting back of the energy use at some Gestamp factories by 15% through the use of continuous monitoring and advanced forecasting methods (Siemens AG, 2025). Siemens' "Drivetrain Analyzer Cloud" technology claims to have saved energy in the range of 10% to 20% for industrial applications of drive systems (Siemens AG, 2017). The impact of the solutions shows that by the application of AI capabilities in business processes, especially through ERP-linked maintenance and optimization, sustainability benefits that have been measured and are in line with the goal of protecting the environment such as the ones laid down in SDG 12 can be realized.

These examples illustrate AI's potential in digital transformation for sustainable supply chains and manufacturing, despite the absence of formal ERP integration.

Case Study 2: Unilever in the Fast-Moving Consumer Goods Sector

Unilever has adopted AI-driven analytics and demand forecasting tools throughout its global supply chain to enhance production efficiency, reduce raw material waste, and increase responsiveness. The company reported reductions in waste and raw material usage by double-digit percentages at certain manufacturing sites, along with enhanced accuracy in demand forecasting.

The above-mentioned improvements led to a reduction in overproduction, inventory levels, and logistics costs. The usage of AI in the ice cream industry for forecasting demand and optimizing logistics has resulted in a measurable reduction in material consumption and emissions from transportation. Unilever's public statements do not indicate that its AI ERP initiatives are behind the "12% carbon emissions" reduction. However, their sustainability reports indicate that Scope 1 and 2 greenhouse gas emissions would be 13% lower in 2022 than in 2021 (Unilever PLC, 2023). The merging of AI-driven business systems with state-of-the-art enterprise resource planning systems and supply chain digitization could be a way to achieve both the economy and the environment's health in the long run within the large-scale fast-moving consumer goods sector.

Case Study 3: DHL Supply Chain (Logistics Sector)

DHL has added AI-based solutions to its ERP and WMS systems to make route planning, warehouse operations, and worker allocation faster and better. The "IDEA" system organizes the orders and manages the picking of items in a better way, so the warehouse workers can reduce their walking distance by 50% and their productivity can increase by 30% (Leonard, 2020).

The utilization of AI in routing and demand forecasting has played a significant role in DHL achieving a huge reduction in its operational costs. Besides, it has also resulted in faster deliveries, better visibility of operations, and so on. The social sustainability is supported through improvements in the reduction of the workers' fatigue and errors. On the other hand, the environmental and economic sustainability is supported by the reduction of movements, energy use, and logistical waste (PumpEdu, n.d.).

AI utilization alongside ERP and WMS by DHL is a clear demonstration that enterprise systems and AI can indeed collaborate to make sustainable supply chain management in measurable ways.

The events from the case studies indicate that AI in ERP systems will not only promote sustainable behaviors but also turn them into measurable outcomes thereby bridging the gap between theory and practice.

According to the information in Table 1, the integration of AI in ERP systems has many advantages in terms of both sustainability and operational performance over the standard ERP systems.

Table 1. Comparison of AI-ERP integration versus traditional ERP approaches in sustainable supply chain management

Aspect / Dimension	AI-ERP Integration (Proposed Solution)	Traditional ERP / Other Existing Methods
Decision-Making	Proactive, predictive, prescriptive; scenario planning possible	Reactive; only descriptive analytics and historical reports
Responsiveness	High; can adapt in real time to disruptions	Limited; slower response to changes and unexpected events
Sustainability (Environmental)	Real-time monitoring of resource use, emissions, waste; predictive optimization	Monitoring is manual or periodic; optimization limited
Sustainability (Economic)	Reduces costs, improves supply chain resilience, enables data-based investment decisions	Limited cost reduction; less predictive for investments
Sustainability (Social)	Enhance transparency, labor practices, fair HR management; supports stakeholder trust	Basic reporting; less transparency and weaker social impact

continued on following page

Table 1. Continued

Aspect / Dimension	AI-ERP Integration (Proposed Solution)	Traditional ERP / Other Existing Methods
Technology Utilization	Integrates AI, IoT, blockchain, big data analytics	Rely on ERP modules without intelligent integration
Organizational Impact	Promotes data-driven culture, forward-looking decision-making	Traditional hierarchical decision-making; less adaptive culture
Challenges	High implementation cost, data quality and interoperability issues, need for digital skills, ethical concerns	Lower cost and simpler implementation; fewer ethical concerns

This table highlights the key differences between AI-ERP integration (proposed solution) and traditional ERP methods, showing how AI enhances decision-making, responsiveness, sustainability outcomes, technology utilization, organizational impact, and addresses key challenges.

CONCLUSION

This chapter has shown that integrating Artificial Intelligence (AI) into (ERP) systems is a strategic move in building genuinely sustainable supply chains. Traditional ERP systems, as effective in homogenizing processes and summing up data, are inherently limited in predictive and prescriptive capability, therefore making modern-day advanced supply chains responsive and vulnerable (Min, 2010; Bahssas et al., 2015). The blending of AI closes the gap by enabling proactive decision-making and transforming ERP systems into "cognitive enterprise platforms" capable of performing real-time analysis, scenario planning, and adaptive feedback (Alzahmi et al., 2025; Qu & Kim, 2024).

Through this integration, the chapter illustrates that all three pillars of sustainability, environmental, economic, and social—can be dramatically enhanced. Ecologically, AI ERP systems facilitate real-time monitoring of usage of resources, emissions, and wastes, and predictive analysis allows optimal utilization of resources and regulatory compliance (Hasan et al., 2017; Culot et al., 2024). Economically, the systems reduce costs, enhance supply chain dislocation resistance, and facilitate data-based investment decisions (Jawad & Balázs, 2024; Iseri et al., 2025). Socially, AI-ERP integration advances suppliers' labor practice transparency, facilitates equitable human resource management, and supports stakeholders' trust based on auditable, machine learning-based sustainability reporting (Gidiagba et al., 2025; Tulli, 2024).

One of the main advantages of AI-ERP users is operational efficiency, but these advantages also touch the culture of the organization in the sense of decision-making based on data and thinking in a future-oriented way. All these results are grounded on prior studies that show the potential of intelligent systems in risk foresight, supply chain responsiveness, and sustainability (Zamani et al., 2022; Genetti et al., 2025).

The conceptually modelled structure combines AI-ERP integration as the main force binding together environmental, economic, and social sustainability through an iterative feedback loop of continuous improvement. This indicates that the AI-integrated ERP systems are not merely production technologies but, rather, they are, the very, strategic helpers that can drive companies to the point of making operational efficiency their sustainability goal over the long run. In developing countries, their use can be modified based on the local economic, social, and regulatory aspects for being both globally significant and locally adaptable (Li, 2025; Qu & Kim, 2024).

Real-time monitoring of organizations' operations and prediction of future outcomes are the results of AI working with the organization. AI-ERP, on the other hand, improves social relationships by building trust along with the stakeholders, bringing in transparency, and improving the working conditions. Nonetheless, the organizations still have to put up with the issues of high costs, data quality, need for interoperability, shortage of digital skills, ethical dilemmas along with the benefits. The future is believed to be filled with the rise of adaptive, context-sensitive AI-ERP models that will be able to find the right mix of factors: profit, responsiveness, and sustainability particularly in the case of the developing countries where the local adaptation factor is a must.

On the ethical side, a careful examination of the situation is required to prevent the irresponsible use of technology due to reliance on automation, the lack of transparency, and algorithmic biases. Also, there are contextual limitations that come along with applying solutions designed globally to local or developing economies, thus requiring an adaptation to the local economic, social, and regulatory conditions. Being aware of these limitations gives a more balanced view and also points out the areas where further research and practical improvements are needed.

REFERENCES

Aghaei, R., Kiaei, A. A., Boush, M., Vahidi, J., Barzegar, Z., & Rofoosheh, M. (2025). *The potential of large language models in supply chain management: Advancing decision-making, efficiency, and innovation.* arXiv preprint arXiv:2501.15411. https://doi.org//arXiv.2501.15411DOI: 10.48550

Aktas, E. (2024). Big data applications in supply chain management. In Sarkis, J. (Ed.), *The Palgrave handbook of supply chain management*. Palgrave Macmillan., DOI: 10.1007/978-3-031-19884-7_74

Alzahmi, W., Al-Assaf, K., Alshaikh, R., & Bahroun, Z. (2025). Towards sustainable ERP systems: Emerging trends, challenges, and future pathways. *Management Systems in Production Engineering*, *33*(1), 24–38. DOI: 10.2478/mspe-2025-0003

Aslam, F., & Calghan, J. (2023). Using NLP to enhance supply chain management systems. *Journal of Engineering Research and Reports*, *25*(9), 211–219. DOI: 10.9734/jerr/2023/v25i9994

Bahssas, D. M., AlBar, A. M., & Hoque, R. (2015). Enterprise resource planning (ERP) systems: Design, trends, and deployment. *International Technology Management Review*, *5*(2), 72–81. DOI: 10.2991/itmr.2015.5.2.2

Culot, G., Podrecca, M., & Nassimbeni, G. (2024). Artificial intelligence in supply chain management: A systematic literature review of empirical studies and research directions. *Computers in Industry*, *162*, 104132. DOI: 10.1016/j.compind.2024.104132

Genetti, S., Longobardi, A., & Iacca, G. (2025). *Evolutionary reinforcement learning for interpretable decision-making in supply chain management.* arXiv preprint arXiv:2504.12023. https://doi.org//arXiv.2504.12023DOI: 10.48550

Gidiagba, J. O., Tartibu, L. K., & Okwu, M. O. (2025). A systematic review of machine learning applications in sustainable supplier selection. *Decision Analytics Journal*, *14*, 100547. DOI: 10.1016/j.dajour.2025.100547

Hasan, M., Ebrahim, Z., Wan Mahmood, W., & Ab Rahman, M. (2017). Sustainable-ERP system: A preliminary study on sustainability indicators. [JAMT]. *Journal of Advanced Manufacturing Technology*, *11*(1), 61–74. https://jamt.utem.edu.my/jamt/article/view/2829

Iseri, F., Iseri, H., & Chrisandina, N. J. (2025). AI-based predictive analytics for enhancing data-driven supply chain optimization. *Journal of Global Optimization*. Advance online publication. DOI: 10.1007/s10898-025-01509-1

Jawad, Z. N., & Balázs, V. (2024). Machine learning-driven optimization of enterprise resource planning (ERP) systems: A comprehensive review. *Beni-Suef University Journal of Basic and Applied Sciences, 13*(4). Advance online publication. DOI: 10.1186/s43088-023-00460-y

Kuzior, A., & Sira, M. (2025). Sustainable digital economy transformation through intelligent automation: A multi-environmental framework for strategic decision-making. *Sustainability, 17*(17), 7723. DOI: 10.3390/su17177723

Leonard, M. (2020, August 13). *DHL rolls out AI-based pick routing tool that integrates with WMS, ERP*. Supply Chain Dive. https://www.supplychaindive.com/news/dhl-pick-routing-tool-wms-warehouses/583451/?utm

Li, J. (2025). Construction and practice of supply chain optimization decision system driven by artificial intelligence. *Journal of Artificial Intelligence Practice, 8*(2), 54–60. DOI: 10.23977/jaip.2025.080207

McKinsey & Company. (2025, April 17). *Beyond automation: How gen AI is reshaping supply chains [Podcast]*. McKinsey & Company. https://www.mckinsey.com/capabilities/operations/our-insights/beyond-automation-how-gen-ai-is-reshaping-supply-chains

Min, H. (2010). Artificial intelligence in supply chain management: Theory and applications. *International Journal of Logistics Research and Applications, 13*(1), 13–39. DOI: 10.1080/13675560902736537

PumpEdu. (n.d.). *AI in practice: DHL has accelerated the delivery of parcels*. https://www.pumpedu.cz/en/news/ai-in-practice-dhl-has-accelerated-the-delivery-of-parcels-114n?utm

Qu, C., & Kim, E. (2024). Reviewing the roles of AI-integrated technologies in sustainable supply chain management: Research propositions and a framework for future directions. *Sustainability, 16*(14), 6186. DOI: 10.3390/su16146186

Queiroz, M. M., Ivanov, D., Dolgui, A., & Wamba, S. F. (2022). Impacts of epidemic outbreaks on supply chains: Mapping a research agenda amid the COVID-19 pandemic through a structured literature review. *Annals of Operations Research, 319*, 1159–1196. DOI: 10.1007/s10479-020-03685-7 PMID: 32836615

Qureshi, M. R. N. M. (2022). Evaluating Enterprise Resource Planning (ERP) implementation for sustainable supply chain management. *Sustainability, 14*(22), 14779. DOI: 10.3390/su142214779

Siemens, A. G. (2017, February 22). *Siemens technology enables Gestamp to cut energy consumption at its plants by 15 percent [Press release]*. Siemens. https://press.siemens.com/global/en/pressrelease/siemens-technology-enables-gestamp-cut-energy-consumption-its-plants-15-percent?utm

Siemens, A. G. (2025, April 9). *Siemens Xcelerator: Up to 20 percent in energy savings with Drivetrain Analyzer Cloud thanks to AI-based drive optimization [Press release]*. Siemens. https://press.siemens.com/global/en/pressrelease/siemens-xcelerator-20-percent-energy-savings-drivetrain-analyzer-cloud-thanks-ai-based?utm

Tonsakun-aree, C., Juturat, N., & Kuntonbutr, C. (2020). Integration of information in the ERP system affecting the efficiency of the supply chain performance of the frozen food industry in Thailand. *Journal of Business Administration, Rajamangala University of Technology Thanyaburi, 10*(2), May–August.

Tulli, S. K. C. (2024). Enhancing supply chain efficiency in the oil and gas industry: The role of digital transformation in ERP systems for real-time analytics and decision-making. *Research and Analysis Journals*, *7*(3), 1–27.

Unilever, P. L. C. (2023, March 9). *Annual Report and Accounts 2022: Strategic Report – About Unilever*. https://www.unilever.com/files/92ui5egz/production/784a6fcfcf077e7c586832eddd7a923e16c66430.html

Zamani, E. D., Smyth, C., Gupta, S., & Dennehy, D. (2022). Artificial intelligence and big data analytics for supply chain resilience: A systematic literature review. *Annals of Operations Research*, **•••**, 1–28. Advance online publication. DOI: 10.1007/s10479-022-04983-y PMID: 36212520

Zou, X., & Peng, Y. (2025). Application of NLP and deep learning in enhancing the resilience of cross-border e-commerce supply chain for agricultural products. *In Proceedings of the 2025 4th International Conference on Big Data, Information and Computer Network (BDICN '25)* (pp. 36–40). Association for Computing Machinery. https://doi.org/DOI: 10.1145/3727353.3727360

Chapter 3
AI-Driven Digital Twins and Autonomous Operations for Sustainable Logistics and Procurement

R. N. Ravikumar
https://orcid.org/0009-0009-3705-1681
Marwadi University, Rajkot, India

S. Aarthi
https://orcid.org/0009-0006-9064-2091
Marwadi University, Rajkot, India

ABSTRACT

This chapter explores how Artificial Intelligence (AI), digital twins, and autonomous operations are transforming logistics and procurement into intelligent, resilient, and sustainable ecosystems. It examines theoretical foundations, sustainability drivers, and the integration of circular supply chain practices and ESG accountability. AI-driven digital twins enable real-time simulation, predictive analytics, and prescriptive optimization, while autonomous operations streamline warehousing, transport, and procurement with robotics, drones, and AI-based control towers. Case studies from healthcare and oil & gas illustrate practical applications, highlighting benefits and regulatory challenges in the GCC and MENA regions. Ethical, regulatory, and social implications are discussed alongside emerging innovations such as agentic

DOI: 10.4018/979-8-3373-7006-4.ch003

AI, blockchain, IoT, and quantum-ready optimization. The chapter concludes with insights into future directions, emphasizing human-AI collaboration, transparency, and sustainability as critical enablers of next-generation global supply chains.

INTRODUCTION

Artificial Intelligence (AI) is quite safe to navigate logistics and procurement to global level, but it is focusing on the digital transformation concerns on the sector. AI along with digital twins, and autonomous technology convergence is prying the seams on the industry. Supply chains have lost their previously physical form and are now chains of autonomous and highly adaptable intelligent systems which exhibit extreme resilience to disturbances. Fragments of disparate data which used to be disparate and singular are now woven into a hyper-complex multi-structured tapestry in consequence of neural networks, digital twins and streamlining AI, and digital glue methods. AI tools such as Generative Adversarial Networks along with new techniques in Augmented Reality are reaching new zeniths in optimization, prediction, and automation at previously unattainable scales (Arab et al, 2023). The global logistics and supply chains real world barriers are represented as digital twins of procurement systems with corresponding intelligent virtual replicas of warehouses and transport networks. These intelligent twin systems permit real-time evaluation and scenario based impactful decision making for the requisite chains. The efficiency of drone delivery and AI controlled automated supply tower handling and robotics has ruggedly improved efficiency on hands-free material handling, last-mile logistics, and supplier control systems Like the measurement and circular policy scope3 carbon washers, these systems lead the industry with full ESG compliance and are the newest waves of innovation (Lintukangas et al., 2023). This chapter is focused on policy with weaving diverse elements on seamless integration of flexible, easily sustainable, and logistics and able to supply worldwide adaptable procurement and procurement policy on devising sustainable adaptable and procurement policy on logistics policy with flexible integration of diverse elements.

BACKGROUND ON LOGISTICS AND PROCUREMENT TRANSFORMATION

The combining of procurement and logistics can be attributed to both the resilient and cost-effective nature of operations strategy. In the past, cost-effective supply chains focused on minimizing the costs of bulk purchasing, storing and labor. The fragmentation of e-commerce and geopolitical changes exposed the vulnerabilities of disintegrated supplier visibility, a thick carbon footprint, and fragmented suppliers. The lightspeed capability of SCM, its deeply-intertwined cross-organizational touch points, integrated supplier ecosystems, and comprehensive systemic risk assessment defies the siloed transactional legacy (Dudić et al., 2024). The value of SCM has never before ascended such a peak. It has as a result of newly computationally predictive mega-structured data-sets loaded with real-time requisitioned signals and fulfillment frameworks. Regarding the rest of the procurement and logistics and the units of intelligence and adaptability, the value-added derives from the risk-balanced and optimal factoring of the organizational shadow disruptions, dominant profit or value surplus safekeeping delivery to the clientele. The sustainability and technology merger still spanning the protective domain can cross to the domain of profit strategy and gains.

ROLE OF AI, DIGITAL TWINS, AND AUTONOMOUS OPERATIONS

Having AI create digital twins and autonomous operations moves the technology for next generation logistics and procurement forward. Predictive demand and supply forecasting, anomaly forecasting, route optimization, and supplier risk assessment can be done more efficiently with integrated machine learning and graph intelligence tools. In the digital logistics realm, generative AI, along with multimodal AI, can create tailored solutions for intricate, evolving, and intertwined supply chains (Ravikumar & Aarthi, 2025). With the help of the Internet of Things and the computing at the edge, digital twins are capable of transforming real time data to virtual models of supply chain primitives including warehouses, fleets, and procurement workflows. Disruption plans can be formulated with the help of prescription tools and scenario testing. Robotics, drones, Automated Guided Vehicles (AGVs), and AI powered control towers enable autonomous operations to improve speed, reduce errors, and lessen the amount of human labor needed. This shifts the supply chain strategy from reactive to proactive and predictive. These technologies in combination provide the ability to create and sustain on demand responsive and agile logistics and procurement to the supply chains (Yıldız & Çiğdem, 2022). Figure 1 depicts the self-reinforcing cycle of AI powered forecasting, digital twin simulations, and autonomous operations. Such a cycle improves sustainment and strategic logistics and procurement along with visibility and the ability to withstand disruptions.

Figure 1. AI-driven digital twin and autonomous operations cycle

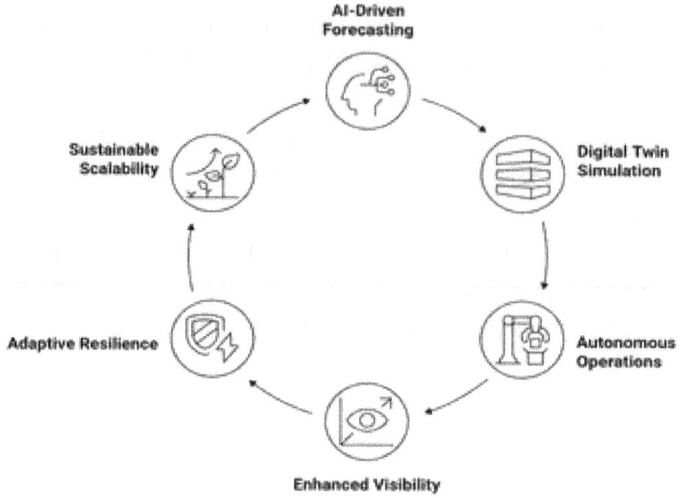

LINKAGE TO SUSTAINABILITY, ESG, AND SCOPE-3 CARBON ACCOUNTABILITY

Like any other industry, Logistics and Procurement is changing profoundly as a result of Sustainability. Organizations, for instance, internally assess themselves in terms of their Environmental, Social, and Governance (ESG) performance. Meeting Scope-3 is a more difficult problem Emissions derived from suppliers, from whole transport and product life cycles, which on average, constitute the lion's share of a company's emissions. Emission monitoring is ineffective for tracking the impacts of emissions that are as dispersed as those that are situationally distributed. Instead, we have systems that use AI, digital twins, and other autonomous systems for real-time monitoring, tracking, and decisioning on carbon emission and their cognate behaviors (Klaaßen & Stoll, 2021). For instance, digital twins are capable of modeling possible emissions for a given set of routes and the AI constructs procurement models that emission scale the entire value chain through value-based procurement of dominant carbon emitting suppliers and materials. Drones and electric Autonomous Ground Vehicles (AGVs) enhance possibilities for carbon-neutral logistics. Companies also face the need for self-imposed ESG compliance, such as the EU Emissions Trading System (ETS) and CORSIA with other regionals like the GCC, to include visibility and auditability in their procurement practices. This is because their emissions of carbon and loss of efficiency can be coupled. These technologies also allow organization (Downie & Stubbs, 2012)ns to set performance goals for climate impact, sustainable sourcing, and more resilient closed-loop supply chains. Figure 2 depicts sustainability in logistics integrated with ESG performance, Scope-3 emissions, compliance frameworks, and technologies.

Figure 2. Sustainability in logistics framework

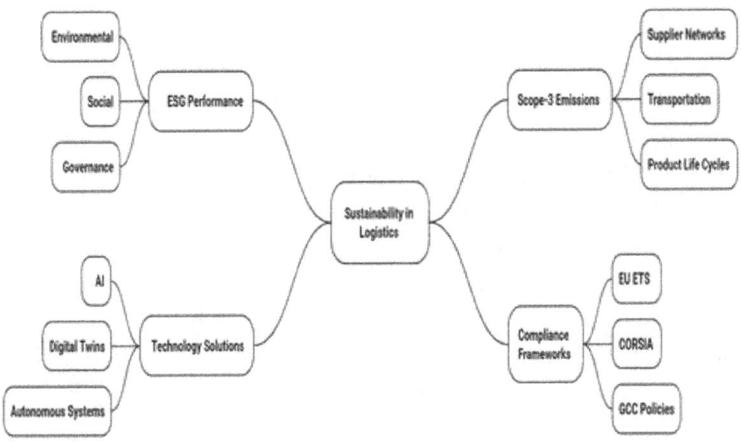

LITERATURE REVIEW

Since technology first introduced automation and enterprise resource planning systems, advanced AI, digital twins, and autonomous operations have propelled the evolution of logistics and procurement. Traditional literature focused solely on the cost, efficiencies, and lean methodologies, whereas modern studies have shifted focus to resilience, transparency, and sustainability (Ravikumar,et al., 2025). AI not only has predictive analytics and forecasting capabilities, but is also able to construct self-learning and adaptive supply chain ecosystems which is why it has emerged as the central enabler of this discourse. While reinforcement learning and graph intelligence facilitate dynamic multi-tier supplier and logistics corridor decision making, generative and multi-modal AI is being used to improve design optimization and demand supply network alignment (He & Bai, 2021). At the same time, the concept of digital twins has matured, as it has been advanced from systems engineering and its application in the SCM. As literature illustrates, digital twins enable real time replication of physical assets, such as warehouses, fleets, and production facilities, permitting organizations to test scenarios, forecast disruptions, and prescribe optimizations to intervene (Yu et al., 2024).

The Internet of Things, 5G, and edge computing, which together provide the infrastructure for scalable and low-latency synchronization between physical and digital entities, also enable these functionalities. Automated drone systems and robotics are capable of remodelling stockroom organization and transportation systems. Shipment systems from storage to final address systems have also improved (Ortega Carrasco et al., 2024). In these innovations, attention is no longer on standalone automations but entire machine ecosystems controlled by cloud AI super computers with machine and human collaboration as one organism. Literature on sustainability has also framed procurements and logistics on sustainable and socially responsible governance (G. Luo et al., 2023). Measure scope 3 emissions, uphold ESG procurement standards, and manage circular supply chains with reverse logistics and systems repair. They also increasingly remark on the interrelated governance and compliance systems from international and national policy which drives cross procurement activity accountability (Chhimwal et al., 2021).

Predictive modeling systems for pandemic preparedness and surveillance in healthcare supply chains, drone and AI carbon tracking and risk management in oil and gas, and procurement systems of the same which have successful case examples across diverse industries. Unfortunately, these new innovations also bring to surface new issues over data interoperability, lack of trust in AI, high costs of integration, and sensitive nature of cyber physical systems (R. Ejjami & Boussalham, 2024b). Subsequent studies emphasize the legal and ethical AI explainability and public use frameworks and governance settings. Upcoming studies focus on autonomous self-learning of AI agents in logistics, quantum computing for complex optimization, and the boundaries of human-AI collaboration in procurement governance (R. Ejjami & Boussalham, 2024a).The documents signal a paradigm shift from regarding logistics as merely an operational activity to perceiving logistics and procurement as an integrated, autonomously operating, highly complex, and technologically advanced ecosystem that is actively developed and nurtured. They synergistically define the future of supply chains and sustainability.

THEORETICAL FOUNDATIONS

Ever since the introduction of artificial intelligence, the field has grown to be associated with autonomous systems. This reliance has been distilled to theories based on machine learning, augmentation of AI through reinforcement learning, decision systems of supply chain networks, reasoning systems, predictive decision systems, predictive decision networks, and decision-making adaptive networks (Parfenov et al., 2021). The particulars of digital twinning stem from systems engineering in which there is constant real-time synchronizing of physical and virtual elements through machine learning, IoT, 5th, and edge computing. Simulation of various 'what if' scenarios, real-time tracking of systems and resources, and lineage of optimized resource flows this capture flows and routing resource flows and rationalization estimate streamline operations. The limbs of autonomous operations derive from working theories in robotics and from cyber physical systems of systems, which enable machines, in the coming forth of the machine age, to complete activities shy of human physical labor (Verbivska et al., 2023). The cumulative result of these branching branches of the various theories is a compact, coherent system which allows the evolution of power supply systems to 'smart' and 'auto adaptive' self-learning systems, cybernetically and rationally balancing all parameters of efficiency, sustained self-balancing and resilience able to self-adapt.

Artificial Intelligence in Supply Chains

AI is redefining supply chains by moving from predictive analytics to Generative, Multimodal, and Agentic intelligence. Generative AI creates new optimization protocols, Multimodal AI processes and integrates diverse data streams which include text, images, and various sensor data, and Agentic AI creates autonomous and self-adapting logistic agents. Reinforcement Learning (RL) is key to routing, pricing, and dynamic slotting in warehouses due to its trial-and-error method of learning. Moreover, graph intelligence permits the modeling of connected nodes of the supply chain networks, thus enabling risk-aware decisions for procurement and logistics (Marisamy et al., 2025). Beyond efficiency, these methods also foster resilience by predicting disruptions and dynamically reconfiguring operations in real-time. Through the integration of Generative, RL, and Graph methods, AI enhances the evolution of logistics systems from static to dynamic by fostering optimal alignment between speed, accuracy, and sustainability.

Digital Twin Fundamentals

Digital twins track physical logistics in real-time in a virtual setting and thus mirrors the physical world in virtual space for monitoring and decision-making purposes. It consists of data acquisition layers from IoT devices, visualization for human interaction, and simulation engines for real-time predictive modeling. These digital duals synchronously track and control the movements of the warehouse, fleet, and supplier networks to the real-world in real-time (Fedorko et al., 2023). IoT, 5G, and edge computing make it possible to perform real-time processing of digital twins at low latency and at scale. This is critical for time-sensitive decisions such as rerouting deliveries, assessing the energy consumption of a warehouse, and other pertinent factors. Integrated simulation and prescriptive analytics enables digital twins to model outcome scenarios for supplier disruptions, demand surges, or addons, and prescribes appropriate responses. This architecture coupled with infrastructure transforms logistics systems to be proactive and predictive as the digital twin of the physical world becomes a necessary asset for resilient, adaptive, and eco-friendly SCM (Niu, 2021).

Autonomous Operations

As an example of paradoxical innovation, the application of automation to the full extent of robotic, drone, and AI-controlled supervisory tower integration on formerly manual tasks such as logistics, augments staff productivity and effectiveness across the globe. Within the confines of a warehouse, AGV and drone systems, in concert, pick, lift, and carry heavy materials to prep for and perform last-mile deliveries, alongside remote monitoring. At the system tier, AI Control Towers manage autonomous systems, optimizing real time engagement through dynamic orchestration of fleets, routes, and inventory across regional and global value chains. A significant focus area is the extent of autonomous decision making versus the scope for human involvement in governance (Greenblatt & Saxena, 2015). Autonomous systems enhance effectiveness, support carbon-aware logistics, and, paradoxically enough, invite human intervention for ethical, safety, and regulatory oversight. Transparency, accountability, and the need for ethics in autonomous governance is enhanced by such a hybrid approach which combines machine precision and human collaborative decision making. The continuously adaptive governance alongside automation approach enhances the hybrid model which separates the autonomous systems in procurement and logistics, streamlining the rest, to augment the value chains in intelligent supply chains. Autonomous operations have perfected flexibility, resilience and foresight of continuous innovation to the core (Feng & Ye, 2021). The table below illustrates the other three central technologies to Autonomous Operations: AI, Digital Twins and their respective functions and benefits in logistics and procurement. The comparison aids the audience in appreciating the unique value each advanced technology brings to Table 1 optimizing value chains for enhanced efficiency, resilience and sustainability.

Table 1. AI, digital twin, and autonomous technologies in logistics

Technology	Definition	Key Applications	Benefits
Artificial Intelligence	Use of ML and analytics to optimize logistics	Forecasting, routing, supplier risk, ESG	Efficiency, adaptability, resilience
Digital Twin	Virtual replica of physical supply chain assets	Simulation, scenario testing, cold chain	Real-time visibility, optimization
Autonomous Operations	Robotics, drones, AGVs, AI control towers	Warehousing, last-mile delivery, transport	Accuracy, cost savings, scalability

SUSTAINABLE LOGISTICS AND PROCUREMENT

In today's world almost every business is required to adopt some form of sustainable logistics and procurement in light of the world's fight against climate change, the setting of ESG frameworks, and the growing concern of climate action stakeholders for business practices. Reducing the 3 emissions Carbon none scope of line suppliers, transportation, and product life cycles is fundamental and, at the same time, the most challenging (Richey Jr et al., 2023). Thanks to digital twins and other forms of AI, emissions can be calculated for different routes and suppliers and modifications can be made to the decisions to lower the emissions produced. Carbon emissions can also be cut through various optimization models which streamline operations, cut costs, and increase energy use efficiency. Practices in reverse logistics, reuse, and repair within the circular supply chain also help reduce the depletion of raw materials and more sustainable practices adopted to minimize the waste going to landfills. The rules set by Governance frameworks such as the EU ETS and CORSIA are required to be met by procurement procedures and as such must accompanied by transparency, auditable results, and sustainable operation of the GCC (J. Luo, 2023). The integration of technology, inventive and ethical procurement, as well as sustainable logistics, allow procurement to be redefined as a value-generating and environmentally responsible function which is coherent with resilience to climate change and with the sustainable development goals.

Sustainability Drivers in Global Supply Chains

With sustainability taking a more vital role in global supply chains, attention has turned to Scope-3 emissions as a critical focus area. Scope-3 emissions account for as much as 70% of a Company's greenhouse gas emissions and occur throughout the supply chain, during shipping and distribution, and across the entire product life cycle (Belhadi et al., 2021). Mastering Scope-3 emissions requires advanced visibility tools, supplier collaboration, and the application of carbon-aware Decision Support Systems. Emission tracking, simulating sourcing or routing, and low-carbon substitution offer carbon reduction pathways. Procurement has started to be correlated with other ESG indicators, and does no longer only focus on cost and quality but also on Environmental, Social and Governance (ESG) impacts along the supply chain (Kegenbekov & Jackson, 2021). Embracing ESG metrics enhances brand perception, lowers regulatory burden, and increases resilience. For this reason, sustainability metrics are no longer a 'nice to have' because they are increasingly forming the basis of procurement, capital expenditure decisions, and competition on a global scale (Al-Huzaili et al., 2025). Table 2 below highlights the major parameters of sustainability which include Scope-3 emissions, energy used, waste reduction, and other ESG compliance indicators. It highlights the governance and management frameworks in place for making these metrics actionable in procurement processes.

Table 2. Sustainability metrics in logistics and procurement

Metric	Description	Application in Procurement/ Logistics
Scope-3 Emissions	Indirect emissions from suppliers & transport	Carbon-aware sourcing, supplier evaluation
Energy Consumption	Power used in warehouses and fleets	Monitoring energy efficiency
Waste Reduction	Minimization of packaging and inventory waste	Circular logistics, reuse, repair
ESG Compliance	Supplier alignment with social/ environmental goals	Transparent audits, governance checks

Circular Supply Chain Practices

Circular supply chain practices seek to integrate concepts of reuse, repair, and reverse to waste and resource effectiveness. Organizations are moving to regenerative loops where products and materials are retained and circulation and reverse logistics systems oversee the return of goods to refurbish, recycle, or have secondary use and repair systems that provide frameworks for extending product life (Mangla et al., 2018). With product return forecasting, collection route optimization, and component reuse, AI systems streamline these efforts. Digital twins are one of several examples where an AI system simulates product flows of end-of-life goods and makes design suggestions to minimize landfill contribution. Strategies supported by machine learning and waste minimization that focus on overpacked, excessive energy, and high inventory MBPs are the best modus operandi for minimizing waste. Integrating circular practices, and logistics along with 'green' supply chains, reinforced by procurement, greatly augments an organization's profit by eliminating costs, enhancing customer commitment, and achieving sustainability and development goals (Harun & Senawi, 2024). The table 3 shows different circular practices with reverse logistics, repair, reuse, and recycling. It focuses on their waste reduction and costs lowering, and carbon-neutral operations facilitation.

Table 3. Circular supply chain practices and benefits

Practice	Description	Benefits
Reverse Logistics	Handling returns, recycling, or resale	Reduces waste, supports reuse
Repair Frameworks	Extending product life via repairs	Lowers lifecycle emissions, cost savings
Reuse Strategies	Using materials/components multiple times	Conserves resources, reduces demand
Recycling Models	Processing waste into new raw materials	Circularity, reduced landfill impact

GOVERNANCE AND COMPLIANCE

Sustainability plans in logistics and procurement are actionable because governance and compliance frameworks make sure that these plans are measurable and verifiable. The EU Emission Trading System (EU issued ETS), The Carbon Offsetting and Reduction Scheme for International Aviation (CORSIA), and policies in the GCC region are compelling companies to monitor, report and contain emissions. Compliance demands supply chains to be transparent, which AI-driven procurement platforms can be used to track real-time supplier practices, contract compliance and carbon emissions. Accountability, which minimizes risks of fraud as well as greenwashing, is increased with the use of digital audit trails, blockchain, and AI monitoring. More than governance, compliance frameworks motivate companies to embed ESG principles in supplier contracts, due diligence, and performance evaluation (van Hoek, 2024). Organizations are able to comply with the law and have regulatory-driven technology frameworks which increases trust with investors, customers, and regulators. More so, companies avoid penalties as governance frameworks encourage the integration of compliance. Effective governance thus becomes supportive for the ethical, sustainable, and resilient global supply chains.

AI-DRIVEN DIGITAL TWINS IN LOGISTICS

Artificial Intelligence is reoriented logistics processes with its Virtual Twins technology which, in conjunction with predictive models, makes real-time data intensive copies of warehouses, fleets, and procurement systems for disruption and foresight simulations alongside repetition of agile and resilient scenarios with regards to supple and adaptive ecosystems. Virtual models of predictive bottleneck systems which optimize inventory and logistics decisions down to target sustainability level, including Scope 3 emission reduction, Enables Companies to Feasibly, Dominique Rout Prescriptive Resources Modes, Layered with Real-time Carbon Emission Control Rout Supply Chains in an Environmentally Sustainable Way (Taufani & Widjaja, 2023). Advanced systems allow seamless integration with procurement, optimizing supplier risk, ESG demand, and market data compliance systems predictive of operational data. Realistic agile Carbon predictive systems maintain ESG-Line of exposure to operational data, demonstrating how Digital Twins shift logistics processes from reformed stationary data into ESG sustainable progressive models with embedded accelerators (Pan et al., 2024). Figure 3 highlights five levels of increasing sustainability impact to agile and resilient scenarios with regards to supply and adaptive ecosystems.

Figure 3. AI-driven digital twins in logistics

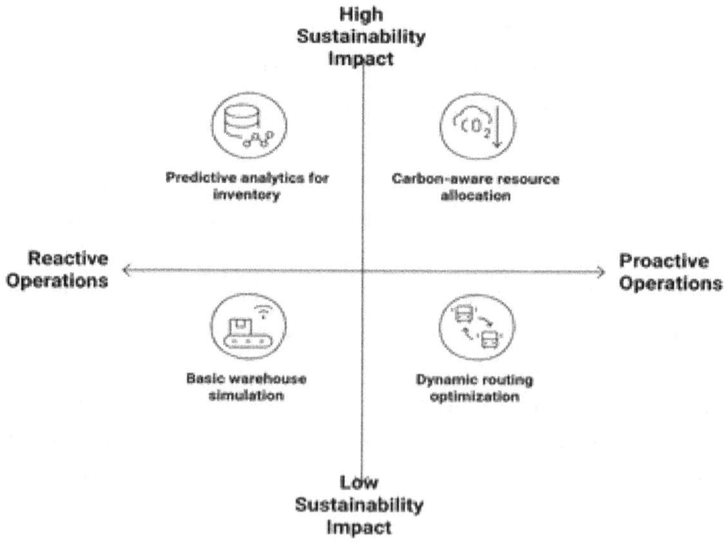

SIMULATION AND PREDICTIVE ANALYTICS

Through advanced simulations and foreseeing analytics throughout the distribution networks, AI empowered digital twins perform sophisticated analytics. With the help of digital twins that emulate physical assets including fleets, procurement systems, and warehouses, organizations can conduct stress testing and perform "what if" analyses. For example, systems can model the effects of supply shortages, demand surges, and port closures, allowing decision-makers to formulate proactive contingency plans. Employing machine learning, predictive models evaluate real-time data and historical data to project customer demand shifts, transportation bottlenecks, inventory level anticipation, and other pertinent factors. These insights enhance proactive agility as well as responsive crisis management (De Angelis et al., 2018). Reaching far beyond operational efficiencies, simulations estimate the triad of sustainability, such as the carbon impact of various alternative suppliers and routes. Hence, AI-enabled digital twins supply a decision support system that integrates real-time data, scenario modeling, and predictive intelligence to foster change-resilient, adaptive, and eco-responsible logistics operations. Figure 4 depicts the intermediate step of reactive crisis management and the advanced step of resilient logistics operations enhanced with simulations, predictive models, and sustainability assessments.

Figure 4. Simulation and predictive analytics in logistics

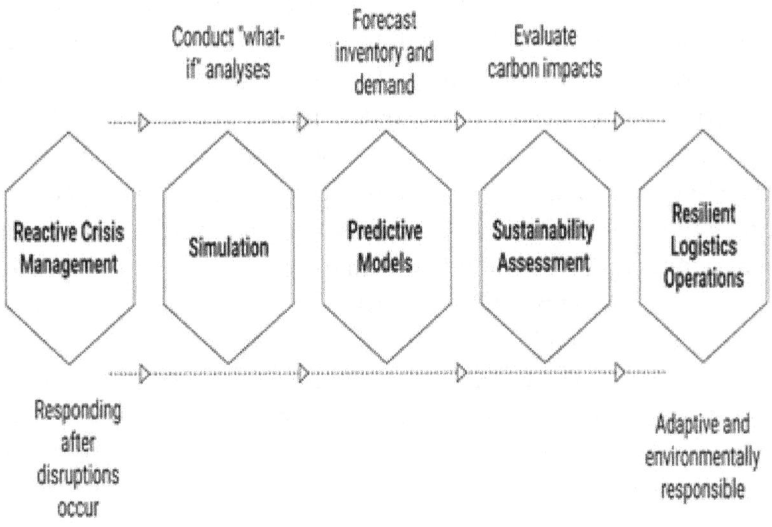

PRESCRIPTIVE OPTIMIZATION

Forecasting becomes actionable planning with prescriptive optimization. Digital twins contact IoT sensors, ERP platforms, and transport networks in real-time, AI-imbedding models recommending best courses of action. This encompasses optimal dynamic vehicle routing, intelligent warehouse slotting, and capacity utilization across hubs. Over time with reinforcement learning, digital twins progressively refine their recommendations within specified parameters. This outcome is achieved with each iteration. The provision of digital twins that suggest low carbon, energy-efficient warehouse configurations, and low waste procurement strategies aligns with prescriptive analytics objectives. For example, digital twins can prescribe the reallocation of resources during seasonal peaks and the dislocated rerouting of shipments. The increase in efficiency with optimal fuel reduction is fuel-efficient (Ma et al., 2024). What was once planning is now transformed logistics, static and prescriptive simultaneously. The foregone conclusion of such a system empowers organizations within optimized, cost-sustaining environments. The complexity and volatility within supply chain environments of enhanced environmental stewardship is the transformative reasoning.

INTEGRATION WITH PROCUREMENT SYSTEMS

Digital twinning tools powered by AI technology are progressively married with procurement modules to construct a connected, smart supply chain system. They provide twin supplier 'risk' in relation to contracts and operational data Logistics 'Risk' Models via digital twins. AI tools can derive predictive models on the effect of certain geopolitical, pricing, or territorial environmental disruptions to the procurement network, and derive the risk averse decision (Ravikumar, Aarthi, et al., 2025). Combing demand with external market signals and operational data garners accurate forecasts that minimizes stock outs (and surplus purchasing). The advancement of integrating procurement with external tools offers risk assessment models to predictive environmentally sensitive ESG compliance. They estimate the predictive supplier ESG compliance non-flagged risk and their gradated procurement system offers scenario-based action plans. These include plans to balance trade-off alternatives like carbon or expense chunking along with procurement plus supply dip orders, and bypass secondary tier suppliers. The digital twins and procurement platform linkage offers predictive benchmark value that is environment sensitive and socio-political resilient, refreshing the supply chain configuration to wired and clear analytical smart value systems.

AUTONOMOUS OPERATIONS FOR PROCUREMENT & LOGISTICS

The intelligent self-orchestrating systems in logistics and procurement autonomy eliminates reliance on manual processes. Robotics and AGVs in warehouses optimize slotting, picking, and material handling drones, and Last mile delivers and remote monitoring. AI control towers dynamically oversee end-to-end operations, synchronizing fleets, routes, and inventories with minimal human control. These systems improve operational efficiency and precision, while also achieving carbon-aware routing and energy routing (Vieira et al., 2024). Digital tendering platforms and AI-enabled supplier discovery systems in procurement streamline sourcing processes with increased transparency, speed, and ESG compliance. Decentralized and automated decisioning agility is countered by human control loop governance which provides compliance iterative frameworks. These systems empower organizations with scalable, resilient, and sustainable supply chains to counter complex and volatile global challenges (Blanco et al., 2016). Automation, predictive models, and AI-driven decision support all enhance the adaptive and sustainable logistics processes, as illustrated by Figure 5 initiation with manual processes.

Figure 5. Intelligent autonomous logistics and procurement

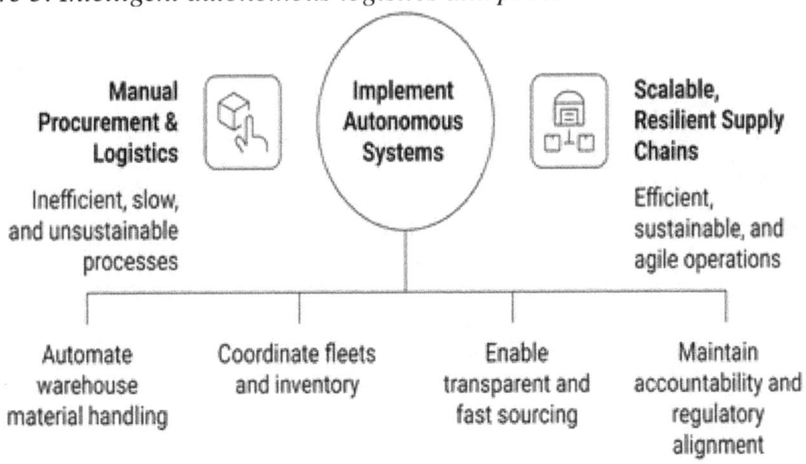

ROBOTICS IN WAREHOUSING AND TRANSPORT

Warehousing and transport robotics is rapidly evolving with the introduction of automating slotting, picking, and material handling processes. These tasks, were previously done via hand by a human, which resulted in greater costs and expenses due to the errors encountered. Arm robots, Automated Guided Vehicles (AGVs), and collaborative (cobot) robots are now used alongside human workers, which enhances order completeness and accuracy. AI robotics systems use slotting strategies that change as the demand, characteristics of the products, and the layout of the warehouse change (Silsand et al., 2024). In the transport hubs, robotics systems enable the loading, and unloading which in turn decreases the cross-dock turn rates. In addition to the results, the use of automation decreases energy consumption, and the excess material is waste which in turn enhances sustainable development. The use of robotics, paired with AI and digital twins, provides organizations with an automated, flexible, and reliable transport and storage systems that can adapt to varying costs and speeds, as well as decreasing environmental damages (Agrawal et al., 2024). The figure 6 demonstrates the slotting, picking, and material handling operations which robotics improves efficiency, increased sustainability, and automation.

Figure 6. Robotics in warehousing and transport

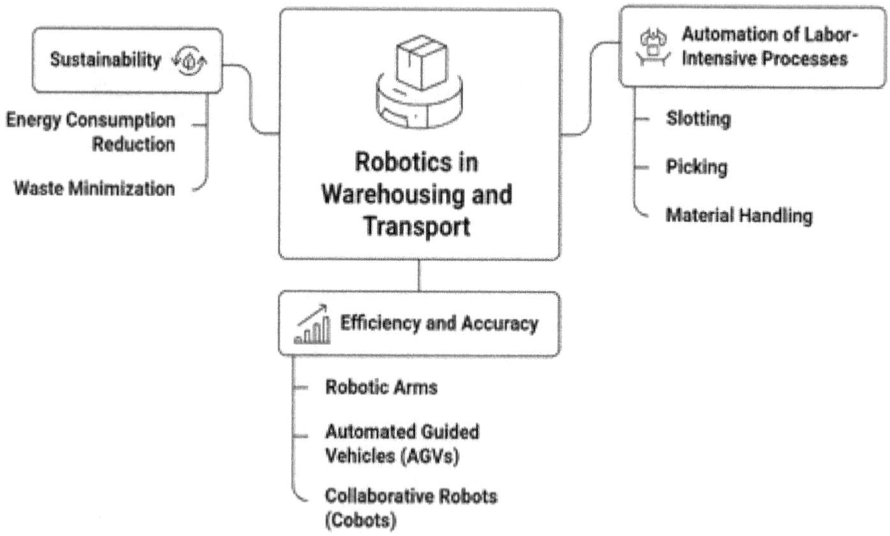

AUTONOMOUS TRANSPORT

Urban and rural areas can easily be served by drones which provide rapid delivery and make delivery intervals shorter. They also reduce the need for traditional vehicles which burn fossil fuels. AGVs (Automated Guided Vehicles) and AGVs work non-stop and AGVs reduce the need for human workers while AGVs also work all the time to transport goods at warehouses and ports. AI-equipped systems also further optimize emissions by choosing the least crowded and most efficient routes. AI minimize truck and fuel usage to reduce carbon emissions by tracking how congested the routes (D. R. Ejjami, 2024). When combined with AI route optimization, these systems strengthen carbon-aware logistics by choosing fuel-efficient routes, avoiding congestion, and aligning transport to sustainability goals. Drones, AGVs, and sophisticated routing are the base of flexible and low carbon logistics networks that work with the organization's goals to help sustain the environment. Combining sensor fusion and edge computing with the routing systems improves the safety and navigation (Yang, 2023). This increases the autonomy limits and the operational complexity for the vehicles. With the above and with drones and AGVs performing intelligent routing, the system is able to endure shocks such as the unavailability of workers, pandemics, etc.

AI IN PROCUREMENT TRANSFORMATION

The evolution of procurement processes is beset by improvement in technology tools which overarch self-sourcing and governance intel and scalable and economic supplier intendant systems. For instance, digital bidding and e-procurement systems simplify authoring, offer documentation and contracting interfaces with candidate vendors (suppliers) which reduces bureaucracy. AI-based discrete supplier systems expand sourcing through low-cost new suppliers compliant with ESG (Environmental, Social, and Governance) principles in global databases. After integration with digital twins, Digital Purchasing AI systems formulate and oversee supplier contracts (Olawuyi & Studies, 2017). Then they evaluate geometry of carbon, labor risk, and volatile geopolitics to operationalize and shape risk. Digital Purchasing AI uses NLP (Natural Language Processing) to align supplier domain expertise to contract offer assessment ecosystems compliance. Economics, geopolitics, and digital twins that augment climate change offer supplier risk resilience. This change takes procurement analytics to the level where operational analytics, and DTE (Digital Transactional Economies) efficiency driven with strategy overlap, fostering innovation value (Dahlmann et al., 2023). AI enhances procurement processes by improving the intertwining of ESG with programs that responsive ordering systems prioritize transparency, sustainability, and socio-strategic resilience.

CASE STUDIES

Implementing autonomous operations and digital twins shows AIs impact on logistics and procurement. In healthcare, AIs digital twins are streamlining hospital supply chains, as well as pharmaceutical and vaccine distribution. AIs predictive analytics models simulates systems anticipating surges, like during the pandemonium. In oil and gas, AIs procurement drones and AGVs are enhancing field operations with supplier management and Scope 3 carbon emissions surveillance. These case studies bundled operational enhancements with improved sustainability, regulatory compliance, cybersecurity, and scalability. Most importantly, they demonstrate the sector's technology-focused breakthroughs in resilient, transparent, and sustainable supply chains.

Case Study 1: Healthcare Logistics Digital Twin in GCC

The accelerating changes in the healthcare system of the Gulf Cooperation Council are underscored by improvement in the supply logistics of medical devices, vaccines, and drugs. Steps taken to resolve complex supply chain systems, volatile demand, and highly regulated systems and requirements have been the motivation for health institutions and authorities in the region to pursue implementing AI-powered digital twin models. These models provide an AI-powered digital twin of the entire hospital supply chain in real-time, thus capturing and monitoring complex hospital systems of inventory, procurement, and distribution. One of the most recent advancements includes the use of AI models to better predict surges in demand and thus system demand ranges (Ravikumar, et al., 2025). The digital twin models forecasted multiple scenarios for the COVID-19 pandemic and thus helped health institutions optimally allocate and prepare stock, avoiding the catastrophic shortfalls for critical drugs and personal protective equipment. The demand for the previously mentioned models is greatest during primary use of healthcare, in times of critical disruption in cold chain and distribution.

Vaccines and critical care materials have measurable sustainability benefits and lower emissions scenarios by assuring minimal stock is maintained, and thus less energy was wasted in stock disposal, expired stock, and overall better health outcomes. The lessons learned from the application of digital twins to healthcare logistics in the GCC has of course underscored the importance of the seamless alignment with cross border and local healthcare regulations like HIPAA and GDPR with the continuing relevance of data privacy and interoperability which is the essence of data exchange (Rice, 2024). Moreover, the focus on carbon accountability in the hospital supply chain has become a priority and digital twins, in particular, are used to estimate and monitor the procurement and distribution related to Scope-3 emissions. In all, the experience gained in the GCC health care demonstrates with the help of AI and digital twins the increased resilience, greater regulatory efficiency, lowered emissions, and improved sustainability compliance. Figure 7 demonstrates the advantages digital twins used in analytics forecasting to optimize healthcare logistics.

Figure 7. Enhancing healthcare logistics with digital twins

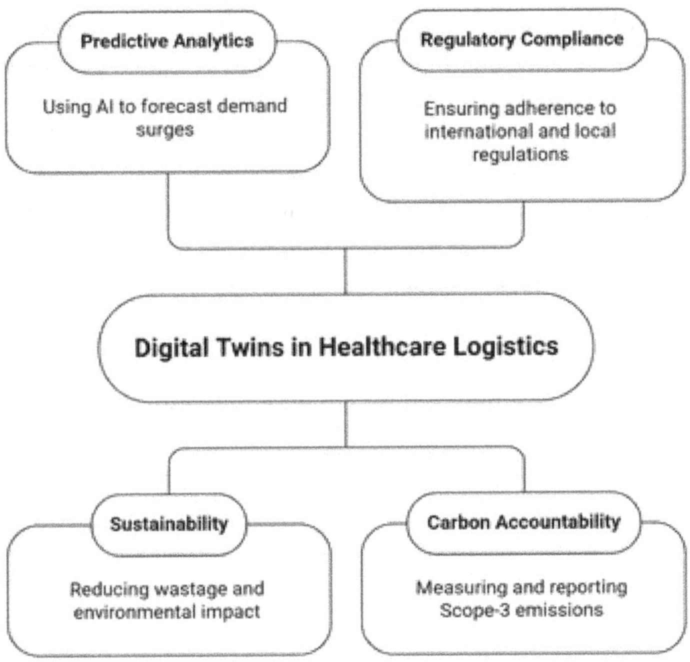

Case Study 2: Oil & gas Procurement Automation in Mena

The procurement cries of oil companies in the Middle East and North Africa (MENA)scare the buyers and logisticians so far, the magnitude of activities and the distantly lying fields coupled with the environmental footprints made by the oil sector. To surmount these challenges, oil companies started to adopt optimize platforms to enhance stock control and transparency of solar systems. The purchase of automated procurement platforms has required an Artificial Intelligence of the

Supply chain (Olawuyi & Studies, 2017). The purpose of the intelligent systems is to optimize bidding, vendor assessments, and contracts with real-time monitoring systems tenders. These systems susu strive blockades in procurement and boost answerability of suppliers in the global local and deed offs supply chains. Probabilistic systems calculate geostatic exposures, suppliers and unloaded areas in order to sustain procurement elasticity in an index fund of the 5 levels of ESG (Egorov et al., 2021).

The other automated sections of the sales chain are the beats of supply chains that use drones in inspecting pipelines, delivering vital equipment, and carrying out security assessments in risky zones that touch with the oil pipelines. Such automations of supply systems along with the Automated Guided Vehicle (AGVs) that only set out to carry building materials and other items in to the supplied chains, and the spares of the production and deposits, add to the confinements of the systems without stepping to the human boundaries advanced the proc and delivery systems globally with precision (R. Ejjami & Boussalham, 2024a). In the MENA oil and gas industry, ESG integration is crucial to operations, with Scope-3 emissions tracking folded into supplier networks. AI-enabled managing and monitoring. The figure 8 illustrates the transformation in procurement and logistics brought about by integration of AI, drones, Automated Guided Vehicles (AGVs), and ESG factors within the MENA oil and gas industry.

Figure 8. AI-driven procurement and logistics in MENA oil & gas

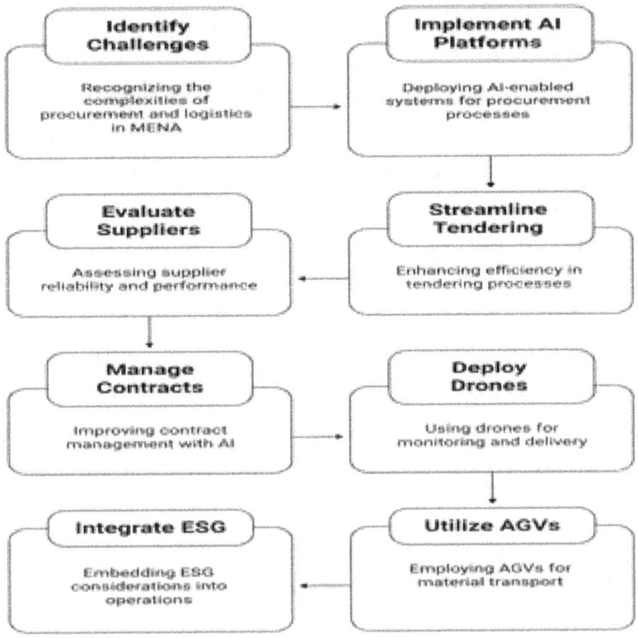

SOCIAL AND HUMAN-CENTRIC IMPLICATIONS

The importance of integrating AI, autonomous operations, and digital twins in logistics goes beyond technology and governance as social factors come into play. With automation in place, traditional warehousing, procurement, and transportation roles are disrupted, increasing anxiety regarding job loss and workforce re-training. Receiving such technologies entails advancement of physically undemanding job opportunities and working in analytics, AI, and robotics. Putting people first, the model stresses that the enthusiastic savings are to be counterbalanced with the employee devotion and hygiene. In addition, the general public's trust on AI adopted in logistics bears the outcome of responsible disengagement. Also, social consequences are best dealt with when the industry, policy and education nexus work together to provide legal protection to the workforce especially in the light of reskilling, diversification of intelligent supply chains, and the center of attention, intelligent logistics ecosystems (Wang et al., 2023).

Workforce Transformation and Skills Development

Restructuring logistics functions has led to the induction of automation technologies in the picking, planning, and tender acceptance steps of the process. While efficiency has increased, the potential loss of employment opportunities for the low-skilled workers in the network has raised some flags. At the same time, new opportunities have opened up in the fields of managing AI systems, robotic equipment, and sustainability systems auditing. Gaps can be filled in by making an investment in both reskilling and upskilling initiatives. Partnerships among universities, vocational schools and the private sector can help to develop a new generation of talent (Erlangga et al., 2022). Moreover, a focus on 'first' skills, such as new-age problem solving and creative thinking will help workers in improving their productivity in their interaction with the machines. AI is, rather, an adjunct to human labour and not a replacement. To avoid stagnation as a result of overbalancing technological investments with social investments, along with retention strategies with a tendency to act pre-emptively, social inclusion must be pursued earnestly (Huriye, 2023).

Public Trust and Inclusivity in Supply Chains

As per (Lahkani et al., 2020), for AI powered logistics to be accepted and embraced widely, its popularization will require trust-building along with inclusiveness. Trust-building requires access to a lot more than ethical sourcing. People and communities, along with civic governance expect a lot more transparency as they will demand ethical sourced, and need to understand the extent of ethical carbon emissions. Not having 'carbon management' capabilities is bound to result in reputational damage. Even more so, the scepticism and technophobia will set in. This applies to micro and small enterprises, too. Balanced growth remains a mirage, as long as there is no scaffolding of access to digital instruments, data-exchange systems, and sustainable supply chains. Greater initiative transparency is possible through enhanced traceability using blockchain, AI-enabled reporting dashboards, and effective reporting of outcomes of sustainability initiatives. Including trust and inclusivity ahead of all other values in core digital transformation enables organizations to deepen mutualistic ties while anchoring the tech-logistic innovations to social and foreseeable sustainability within the supply chains (Wang et al., 2024).

Technological Innovations and Integration

The evolution of procurement and logistics is development of emerging and sophisticated technologies which integrates physical and digital worlds. New technologies and innovations such as digital twins and AI automations, along with blockchain technologies, the Internet of Things, and cloud-edge formations are improving transparency, real-time coordination, interoperability, and scalability. Due lack of procurement fraud and deception, increasing trust and blockchain technology fraud, immutable records lack of procurement follower maintains trust (Glick, 2024; Awad & Aldabousi, 2024). The dashboard displays a complete inventory of both energy and fleets and contains operational views of edge IoT sea computing which are timed with minimal reroute latency and safey observation. The unifying issue here is the use of these technologies separately vs as a mixed holistic system. This permits the company to escape the scattered and fractured systems of siloed storage, shipment, and purchasing. The constant siloing of these new technically advanced infrastructure systems to a decaying, uncontrolled, globalized structure is astonishing (Aktas & Eroğlu, 2025).

Blockchain and IoT for Transparency

The combination of blockchains and IoT networks has certainly added more trust and accountability in the global procurement and supply chain systems. The technologies have also improved the real-time monitoring of energy spent by warehouses, tracking shipments, and tracking on-vehicle transit. The value of the Blockchain technology is further enhanced by the procurement, payment of the supplier invoice, and even emissions transaction reports, which are constitutively paid for through automated contracts in Blockchain. All of the above technologies have improved the real-time reporting of authenticated transaction data and transaction fraud, along with the risks of counterfeiting. In addition to the integration of IoT and blockchain technology, the automated procurement system which is coupled with trigger payments where payments are made once contracts are verified, imbeds the entire value chain of end-to-end procurement integration (Enache, 2023; Mahmoud & Awad, 2024). This integration also improves the reporting of Scope-3 emissions in addition to supporting the ESG framework. There are still barriers with the integration of IoT and Blockchain, in particular with system interoperability, scalability, and the acceptance of blockchain technology in the legal system. Regardless, these technologies are supply chain innovations which counteract the trust erosion and counterfeiting SCSM stakeholders suffer.

Cloud-Edge Integration for Real-Time Logistics

Cloud and edge computing facilitate and expand the capabilities of AI ecosystems in the logistics domain. Cloud computing provides unlimited data storage, dissemination, and advanced granular analysis of global procurement and logistics. In addition, edge computing provides near-zero latency by processing data directly where it is generated, the case of which is in IoT-enabled vehicles and autonomous drones (Tang et al., 2024). Such architecture is essential for low latency dynamic routing, autonomous vehicle navigation, and cross-domain safety oversight. Combined cloud and edge systems provide higher agility and scale balance which improves global and local logistics strategy alignment. In addition, such architecture allows the operation of digital twins, enabling real-time continuous locked alignment of physical and digital assets. Edge-cloud integration strengthens cloud computing and edge computing by enhancing global responsiveness with real-time silo agility to help logistics networks accelerate systemically to operational disruptions and sustainability (Shang et al., 2023).

ETHICAL AND REGULATORY CONSIDERATIONS

As AI, digital twins, and automation tools become more common in logistics and procurement, new technologies' ethical issues regarding privacy, responsible use with regard to the environment, transparency of algorithms, sensitive data usage, job displacement, and user control become increasingly salient with the need for trust and justice. These issues are manifested in the systems used for monitoring and analyzing automated supplier evaluations, decision-making, carbon-supplier communications, and carbon-supplier control (Kiemde & Kora, 2022). Meanwhile, economic regulatory frameworks are evolving to achieve compliance with the EU emissions trading system (ETS), the General Data Protection Regulation (GDPR), and the Gulf Cooperation Council (GCC) sustainability policies. The absence of proper oversight may lead users to trust the system less, due to the increased chances of bias, greenwashing, and the more serious problems which come with the misuse of sensitive data. The reconciliation of new developments with due ethical accountability and compliance with the rules is fundamental for the socially fair and sustainable results. Equitable and viable results are achieved owing to the factors which permit intelligent supply chains to perform and meet the society's needs (Reinhardt, 2023).

Ethical Dimensions in AI-Driven Logistics

Integrating AI and autonomous resourcing systems in logistics continues to raise questions of equity and implications of AI technologies on the workforce. The AI supplier assessments might indiscriminately favour or neglect certain geographical or supplier regions and bias the underlying evaluation algorithms. The ethic AI frameworks on Explainable AI (XAI) needs to establish frameworks her decision on logistics and procurement bias justification. The use of personal information and data IoT sensors connected to operates and Digital Twins systems raise skeletons critical to privacy concerning the volumes of data collected. Security control needs to be transparent in the processes of discerning individual data to be ascertained to data retention, regional sovereignty, and citizen privacy frameworks (Et al., 2023). Social Automation replacing workforce with Robotics and AGVs also gives rise to ethical, legal, and social frameworks to be integrated within Organizations. Ethical practice emphasize within the reskilling and upskilling plans frameworks constitutes embrace social Corporate Social Responsibility (CSR) Mechanisms. It is crucial to build trust with attention to social and logistics ethical practices beyond legal inclusiveness and the social and built environment. The trust deepens among all concerning surroundings, technologies, firms and the employed interest (Couture et al., 2023).

Regulatory Compliance and Global Standards

Compliance with existing regulatory frameworks continues to have an impact with respect to how AI and digital twins, along with autonomous operations, are used in procurement and logistics. Examples of international frameworks are the EU Emissions Trading System (EU ETS) and aviation CORSIA owing to the defined boundaries of the CORSIA region, along with various other pertinent baseline-and-credit mechanisms, which provide circulatory guidelines for carbon monitoring, reporting, and reduction (Yazdani & Darbani, 2023). Also, regionally defined mandates such as the GCC sustainability policies provide an additional layer of accountability. Data protection laws, such as the GDPR, have a reputation for being some of the toughest laws in the world, particularly with respect to the handling of personal and supplier data in the digital world. To many organizations, AI-driven audit trails, blockchain transparency, and semi-automated compliance processes have been the panacea. The underlying gripes, however, as is the case with many other regulatory frameworks, the absence of cross-border regulatory harmonization is still an issue as supply chains crisscrossing the globe operate in many areas regulated by very different rules (Yang et al., 2020). This means the processes have been optimized so agreements are by incorporating compliance directly into procurement and logistics processes, organizations are able to recover adjustment, oversight, and trust penalties. These processes are automated. When compliance processes are automated, it is automated alignment processes is, thus, underlying dvs frameworks vex automated. trust systems adopted instead align is. As The processes agility is compliance rational integrated more frameworks balanced still avoid penalties. The compliance mechanisms governance aligned regulatory aligned reconciliation alignment systems rational enduring frameworks ethical transparent processes is The ultimate (Bányai, 2022).

CHALLENGES AND FUTURE DIRECTIONS

As much as possible, obstacles remain in the way of procurement and logistics. Highly disruptive in nature, the integration of autonomous operations and AI-driven digital twins offer unchartered horizons. Technical hindrances like the costly integration of disparate systems, complex AI models with lower interpretability, and integration of data systems pose the biggest danger. Cyber-physical hazards, loss of supplier trust, and the systematic execution of the governance and security framework inquire precise regulatory alignment (Ma et al., 2024). Emerging unchartered territories seem promising. Quantum-ready optimization can self-automating AI and self-learning logistic systems, while agentic AI can effectively resolve sizeable procurement networks. It becomes ever more evident as to why the fostering of collaboration between AI and humans should be prioritized. Fostering ethical and transparent governance over public procurement is of utmost importance. Resilient, sustainable, and intelligent supply chains as the bare minimum in this increasingly volatile nature of our globalized world is fundamental and hinges upon addressing the above challenges.

Technical Challenges

There are extreme challenges regarding "The use of AI-powered Digital Twins and Autonomous Operations in Logistics." One such instance is data interoperability. Supply chains are filled with aging systems, proprietary formats, and siloed databases, making their integration a each debilitating a drag. Borders without defined data protocols result in Digital Twins struggling to real-time sync data across suppliers, warehouses, and extensive transport networks. The great focus remains on the lack of transparency on AI systems and analytics. While most of the predictions are accurate, the lack of clearness paves the way for a lack of trust from both the regulators and the stakeholders (Egorov et al., 2021). More to this suffering, most of the integration costs remain over the roof for the smaller chains. The lack of infrastructure in these smaller chains, also results in a lack workforce. This causes the more industries going lacking sustainable logistics transformative, to incur over more slow and uneven agile innovations across various industries. It is for this very reason we need to work on the low interoperability the actual costs on XAI, and the advanced scalable frameworks that will dominate the market.

Governance and Security Risks

As of right now, autonomous and AI-laden systems still face issues with governance and security, which serves as yet another barrier to entry within the space. The physical and cyber systems in tandem, supply chains hinge IoT devices, drones, and AGVs and in turn become easy prey to cyberattacks, dissection, and operational stall-outs. Defending these systems becomes a prime concern with interior firewalls, active security, and incident governance. Issues of supplier trust become quite advanced with organizations having to demonstrate their partnerships as compliant with the minimum level of Sustainable Social Responsibility, Environmental, Governance (ESG) data-sharing practices. The processes of active compliance become particularly difficult as chains span cross-border jurisdictions with secondary associated compliance (Ma et al., 2024). The use of AI decentralization can arguably become more useful than fiat tools, though the organizational level oversight becomes paramount. The formulation of these risks within the context of autonomous systems requires a greater degree of policy coordination, strong ethics, and cooperative governance.

Emerging Frontiers

Strategically, there are barriers to overcome. However, within the domain of logistics and procurement, there are boundless opportunities. As an example, an AI logistics system integrated with subsystems can self-adapt and negotiate autonomously to arrive at a decision with minimal human input. With the quantum ready system, procurement problems are greatly simplified. Even in computing and routing, the aligned tier-supplier risk evaluation is deemed unresolvable in classical systems, yet quantum ready optimization solves it with ease. AI Human collaboration is a piloting aspect of governance today, especially in public procurement which is more sensitive in ethics, legal, and policy public oversight domains. These frontiers show the dual pathway of advanced AI which provides human accountability reassessment and oversight (D. R. Ejjami, 2024). These gaps and opportunities open the renewed ethical governed AI supply chains. Key developing solutions to the problems of governance, cost, and security in the table 4 focus on agentic AI, quantum ready optimization, and meta systems with human AI collaboration interface. The subsequent illustration is the barriers and opportunities roadmap.

Table 4. Challenges and future directions in AI-driven logistics

Challenge	Description	Future Directions/Opportunities
Data Interoperability	Siloed systems hinder real-time visibility	Global standards, cloud-edge integration
AI Interpretability	Black-box models reduce trust	Explainable AI (XAI) approaches
Integration Costs	High setup costs for SMEs	Scalable, modular solutions

continued on following page

Table 4. Continued

Challenge	Description	Future Directions/Opportunities
Cyber-Physical Security	Risks of cyberattacks on IoT, AGVs, drones	Blockchain, AI-driven monitoring, strong policies
Emerging Frontiers	Potential of agentic AI, quantum-ready systems	Self-learning logistics, complex optimization

CONCLUSION

The use of advanced technologies, such as Artificial Intelligence (AI), digital twins, and autonomous systems, in procurement and logistics outlines more than the reengineering of business functions; it demonstrates the evolution of supply chains to higher order intelligence, adaptability and sustainability. In the previous sections, we illustrated how these technologies transform supply chains from responsive, siloed systems to integrated, proactive, and intelligent networks capable of resolving operational and global sustainability challenges. AI-driven organizations leapfrog from descriptive and predictive intelligence to prescriptive and generative intelligence, whereby disruptive events are anticipated, carbon-neutral approaches are designed, and procurement is aligned to ESG frameworks. Digital twins amplify these prescriptive resources by providing an up-to-the minute, dynamic, real-time counterpart of the supply chain, enabling precise measurements of carbon, scenario prescriptive optimization, and enhanced overall resilience and accountability.

The supplementing technologies of autonomous systems will further transform this intelligent network. Robotics, drones, and AGVs will demystify and automate the most complex warehousing, field and transport functions, while AI supply chain control towers will manage the supply chain processes with the least human involvement. Concurrently, AI-supported ESG compliant supplier discovery systems and digital procurement platforms reposition procurement from a transactional silo to an enabler of strategic transparency and sustainability. The relevance of the impact of some of the innovations described in the previous chapters comes from their real usage in practice rather than solely existing as an idea. This is evidenced by the use of such innovations to handle the challenges of anticipating and preparing for a pandemic, as well as optimizing the cold chain, and in the context of the oil and gas industry, managing and monitoring carbon emissions, as well as cyber-physical security in the energy supply chain.

Even though there is still some friction in regards to improvable data systems and the high costs of versatile data systems in AI, they still sorely lag in untapped potential. Negative governance, trust issues in fragmented compliance, and attacks on key cyber infrastructure add to the already shaky security and slowness of prosecution. This is amplified by the contradictory approach and lack of global standards on compliance, prescribe spending on intelligence AI, and ethical standards shifting regulating automation to set minimum barriers on human-system governance. The next stage of breakthrough of the shifting technologies on the permittable is already clearer. Agentic AI, which optimizes continual learning and self-changing logistics frameworks, alongside quantum-ready technologies, will fundamentally transform the procurement and logistics of logistics systems. The future, on the other hand, which will still dictate governance, will have lost its previous dualistic choice of human and machine, and transformed into a seamless integration of human-centered AI governance, designed to foster trustable and ethical decision systems. Ethically governed and ruthless AI will, independently or in conjunction with AI-powered digital twins, further improve efficiency, and are unique on the global supply chains as the first disciplinary AI, with ethical compliance the primary enabler.

Organizations and policymakers strategically need to understand and use their economies to maintain the dynamism of society systems and the ecosystems in which they operate, compared to longer-term social and eco-responsible innovations.

REFERENCES

Agrawal, S., Agrawal, R., Kumar, A., Luthra, S., & Garza-Reyes, J. A. (2024). Can industry 5.0 technologies overcome supply chain disruptions?—A perspective study on pandemics, war, and climate change issues. *Operations Management Research*, *17*(2), 453–468. DOI: 10.1007/s12063-023-00410-y

Aktas, M. E., & Eroğlu, S. N. (2025). Blockchain technology in humanitarian logistics enhancing transparency, accountability and real-time decision making. In *Advances in Computational Intelligence and Robotics* (pp. 93–120). IGI Global Scientific Publishing., DOI: 10.4018/979-8-3373-3643-5.ch005

Al-Huzaili, S. A. F., & Mokhtar, A. I. Bin, & Muhamat, M. R. Bin. (2025). The role of Artificial Intelligence in enhancing procurement processes and supply chains. *International Journal of Supply Chain Management*, *14*(4), 64–78. DOI: 10.59160/ijscm.v14i4.6328

Awad, A., & Aldabousi, A. M. (2024). Analyzing the impact of viral marketing on brand equity dimensions in Egypt's home appliances sector: A customer and legal perspective. *Innovative Marketing*, *20*(4), 100–111. DOI: 10.21511/im.20(4).2024.09

Bányai, T. (2022). Impact of digital twin technology on the real-time optimisation of material handling processes. *IOP Conference Series. Materials Science and Engineering*, *1235*(1), 012077. DOI: 10.1088/1757-899x/1235/1/012077

Belhadi, A., Mani, V., Kamble, S. S., Khan, S. A. R., & Verma, S. (2021). Artificial intelligence-driven innovation for enhancing supply chain resilience and performance under the effect of supply chain dynamism: An empirical investigation. *Annals of Operations Research*, *333*(2–3), 1–26. DOI: 10.1007/s10479-021-03956-x

Blanco, C., Caro, F., & Corbett, C. J. (2016). The state of supply chain carbon footprinting: Analysis of CDP disclosures by US firms. *Journal of Cleaner Production*, *135*, 1189–1197. DOI: 10.1016/j.jclepro.2016.06.132

Chhimwal, M., Agrawal, S., & Kumar, G. (2021). Measuring circular supply chain risk: A Bayesian Network methodology. *Sustainability*, *13*(15), 8448. DOI: 10.3390/su13158448

Couture, V., Roy, M.-C., Dez, E., Laperle, S., & Bélisle-Pipon, J.-C. (2023). Ethical implications of artificial intelligence in population health and the public's role in its governance: Perspectives from a citizen and expert panel. *Journal of Medical Internet Research*, *25*, e44357. DOI: 10.2196/44357

Dahlmann, F., Brammer, S., & Roehrich, J. K. (2023). Navigating the "performing-organizing" paradox: Tensions between supply chain transparency, coordination, and scope 3 GHG emissions performance. *International Journal of Operations & Production Management, 43*(11), 1757–1780. DOI: 10.1108/ijopm-09-2022-0622

De Angelis, R., Howard, M., & Miemczyk, J. (2018). Supply chain management and the circular economy: Towards the circular supply chain. *Production Planning and Control, 29*(6), 425–437. DOI: 10.1080/09537287.2018.1449244

Downie, J., & Stubbs, W. (2012). Corporate carbon strategies and greenhouse gas emission assessments: The implications of scope 3 emission factor selection. *Business Strategy and the Environment, 21*(6), 412–422. DOI: 10.1002/bse.1734

Dudić, Ž., Vrhovac, V., Vulanović, S., Dakić, D., Erdeji, I., & Perović, V. (2024). A risk-aware approach to digital procurement transformation. *Sustainability, 16*(3), 1283. DOI: 10.3390/su16031283

Egorov, D., Levina, A., Kalyazina, S., Schuur, P., & Gerrits, B. (2021). The challenges of the logistics industry in the era of digital transformation. In *Lecture Notes in Networks and Systems* (pp. 201–209). Springer International Publishing., DOI: 10.1007/978-3-030-64430-7_17

Ejjami, D. R. (2024). Emerging professions in the age of AI across multiple sectors. *International Journal For Multidisciplinary Research, 6*(5). Advance online publication. DOI: 10.36948/ijfmr.2024.v06i05.28762

Ejjami, R., & Boussalham, K. (2024a). Industry 5.0 in manufacturing: Enhancing resilience and responsibility through AI-driven predictive maintenance, quality control, and supply chain optimization. *International Journal For Multidisciplinary Research, 6*(4). Advance online publication. DOI: 10.36948/ijfmr.2024.v06i04.25733

Ejjami, R., & Boussalham, K. (2024b). Resilient supply chains in industry 5.0: Leveraging AI for predictive maintenance and risk mitigation. *International Journal For Multidisciplinary Research, 6*(4). Advance online publication. DOI: 10.36948/ijfmr.2024.v06i04.25116

Enache, G. I. (2023). Logistics security in the era of big data, cloud computing and IoT. *Proceedings of the International Conference on Business Excellence*, 17(1), 188–199. https://doi.org/DOI: 10.2478/picbe-2023-0021

Erlangga, S. B., Yunita, A., & Satriana, S. R. (2022). Development of automatic real time inventory monitoring system using RFID technology in warehouse. *JOIV: International Journal on Informatics Visualization, 6*(3), 636. DOI: 10.30630/joiv.6.3.1231

Et al., S. S. (2023). Ethical considerations in AI-based marketing: Balancing profit and consumer trust. *Tuijin Jishu*, *44*(3), 1301–1309. DOI: 10.52783/tjjpt.v44.i3.474

Fedorko, G., Molnár, V., & Michalik, P. (2023). Keys parameters of digital transformation of continuous transport systems. Advances in Science and Technology – Research Journal, 17(3), 73–78. https://doi.org/DOI: 10.12913/22998624/163138

Feng, B., & Ye, Q. (2021). Operations management of smart logistics: A literature review and future research. *Frontiers of Engineering Management*, *8*(3), 344–355. DOI: 10.1007/s42524-021-0156-2

Glick, J. (2024). Enhancing logistics efficiency through computer and network technologies: A pathway to industry informatization. *Academic Journal of Science and Technology*, *10*(2), 142–144. DOI: 10.54097/e05gkp44

Greenblatt, J. B., & Saxena, S. (2015). Autonomous taxis could greatly reduce greenhouse-gas emissions of US light-duty vehicles. *Nature Climate Change*, *5*(9), 860–863. DOI: 10.1038/nclimate2685

Harun, S., & Senawi, A. R. (2024). An integrated circular supply chain framework to enhance Malaysian business performance. Information Management and Business Review, 16(3(I)S), 130–136. https://doi.org/DOI: 10.22610/imbr.v16i3(i)s.4046

He, B., & Bai, K.-J. (2021). Digital twin-based sustainable intelligent manufacturing: A review. *Advances in Manufacturing*, *9*(1), 1–21. DOI: 10.1007/s40436-020-00302-5

Huriye, A. Z. (2023). The ethics of artificial intelligence: Examining the ethical considerations surrounding the development and use of AI. *American Journal of Technology*, *2*(1), 37–45. DOI: 10.58425/ajt.v2i1.142

Kegenbekov, Z., & Jackson, I. (2021). Adaptive supply chain: Demand–supply synchronization using deep reinforcement learning. *Algorithms*, *14*(8), 240. DOI: 10.3390/a14080240

Kiemde, S. M. A., & Kora, A. D. (2022). Towards an ethics of AI in Africa: Rule of education. *AI and Ethics*, *2*(1), 35–40. DOI: 10.1007/s43681-021-00106-8

Klaaßen, L., & Stoll, C. (2021). Harmonizing corporate carbon footprints. *Nature Communications*, *12*(1), 6149. DOI: 10.1038/s41467-021-26349-x

Lahkani, M. J., Wang, S., Urbański, M., & Egorova, M. (2020). Sustainable B2B E-commerce and blockchain-based supply chain finance. *Sustainability*, *12*(10), 3968. DOI: 10.3390/su12103968

Lintukangas, K., Arminen, H., Kähkönen, A.-K., & Karttunen, E. (2023). Determinants of supply chain engagement in carbon management. *Journal of Business Ethics*, *186*(1), 87–104. DOI: 10.1007/s10551-022-05199-7

Luo, G., Serrão, C., Liang, D., & Zhou, Y. (2023). A relevance-based Technology–Organisation–Environment model of critical success factors for digital procurement adoption in Chinese construction companies. *Sustainability*, *15*(16), 12260. DOI: 10.3390/su151612260

Luo, J. (2023). Research on the application of artificial intelligence in smart logistics in Australia. In *Atlantis Highlights in Intelligent Systems* (pp. 1084–1089). Atlantis Press International BV., DOI: 10.2991/978-94-6463-200-2_114

Ma, Z., Chen, X., Sun, T., Wang, X., Wu, Y. C., & Zhou, M. (2024). Blockchain-based zero-trust supply chain security integrated with deep reinforcement learning for inventory optimization. *Future Internet*, *16*(5), 163. DOI: 10.3390/fi16050163

Mahmoud, M., & Awad, A. (2024). Impact of electronic customer relationship management on competitive advantage: Mediating role of customer satisfaction in EgyptAir. *Problems and Perspectives in Management*, *22*(3), 276–286. DOI: 10.21511/ppm.22(3).2024.22

Mangla, S. K., Luthra, S., Mishra, N., Singh, A., Rana, N. P., Dora, M., & Dwivedi, Y. (2018). Barriers to effective circular supply chain management in a developing country context. *Production Planning and Control*, *29*(6), 551–569. DOI: 10.1080/09537287.2018.1449265

Marisamy, K., Selvakumar, A., Rajasekar, B., Natarajan, R., Atajanova, A., & Makhmudov, S. (2025). Smart logistics integrating AI, IoT, blockchain, and Robotics for a sustainable Future. In *Emerging Trends in Smart Logistics Technologies* (pp. 73–104). IGI Global Scientific Publishing., DOI: 10.4018/979-8-3373-2434-0.ch003

Niu, F. (2021). The role of the digital economy in rebuilding and maintaining social governance mechanisms. *Frontiers in Public Health*, *9*, 819727. DOI: 10.3389/fpubh.2021.819727

Olawuyi, D., & Studies, O. I. for E. (2017). Local content and procurement requirements in oil and gas contracts. https://doi.org/DOI: 10.26889/9781784670955

Ortega Carrasco, P., Iannone, F., Ferrón Vílchez, V., & Testa, F. (2024). Green public procurement as an effective way for sustainable development: A systematic literature review and bibliometric analysis. *Sustainable Development*. Advance online publication. DOI: 10.1002/sd.3234

Pan, Y., Wang, X., & Ye, Q. (2024). Enhancing supply chain management through artificial intelligence: A case study of JD logistics. Advances in Economics. *Management and Political Sciences*, *109*(1), 116–121. DOI: 10.54254/2754-1169/109/2024bj0127

Parfenov, A., Shamina, L., Niu, J., & Yadykin, V. (2021). Transformation of distribution logistics management in the digitalization of the economy. *Journal of Open Innovation*, *7*(1), 58. DOI: 10.3390/joitmc7010058

Ravikumar, A. S., Kalandarov, A., Djumaniyazova, M., & Habib, M. (2025). A roadmap to a sustainable future. In Advances in Computational Intelligence and Robotics (pp. 267–302). IGI Global Scientific Publishing. https://doi.org/DOI: 10.4018/979-8-3373-3017-4.ch010

Ravikumar, R. N., & Aarthi, S. (2025). Digital Twin-driven green energy systems. In *The Future of Green Energy* (pp. 1–28). IGI Global Scientific Publishing., DOI: 10.4018/979-8-3373-3226-0.ch001

Ravikumar, R. N., Aarthi, S., Dilshodbek, A., Satheesh Kumar, A., Eshkaraev, S., & Shanmugam, K. B. (2025). Integrating blockchain, smart contracts, and AI for decentralized healthcare in the metaverse. In *Blockchain-Based Healthcare Management in the Metaverse* (pp. 261–294). IGI Global Scientific Publishing., DOI: 10.4018/979-8-3373-1225-5.ch010

Ravikumar, R. N., Aarthi, S., Masharipova, G., Niyazova, N., Salaeva, N., & Buriyeva, D. (2025). Enhancing clinical decision-making and operational efficiency in healthcare using edge computing. In *Building Data-Driven Edge Systems for Business Success* (pp. 191–224). IGI Global Scientific Publishing., DOI: 10.4018/979-8-3373-1147-0.ch008

Reinhardt, K. (2023). Trust and trustworthiness in AI ethics. *AI and Ethics*, *3*(3), 735–744. DOI: 10.1007/s43681-022-00200-5

Rice, A. J. (2024). The rise of intelligent procurement: Embracing AI and data analytics for crossfunctional synergy. Journal of Supply Chain Management. *Logistics and Procurement*, *6*(4), 319. DOI: 10.69554/zgfa3030

Richey, R. G.Jr, Chowdhury, S., Davis-Sramek, B., Giannakis, M., & Dwivedi, Y. K. (2023). Artificial intelligence in logistics and supply chain management: A primer and roadmap for research. *Journal of Business Logistics*, *44*(4), 532–549. DOI: 10.1111/jbl.12364

Shang, X., Guo, E., Song, Y., & Li, Y. (2023). Design and implementation of smart logistics big data management service platform. In *Atlantis Highlights in Engineering* (pp. 97–101). Atlantis Press International BV., DOI: 10.2991/978-94-6463-210-1_12

Silsand, L., Kannelønning, M., Severinsen, G.-H., & Ellingsen, G. (2024). Enabling AI in radiology: Evaluation of an AI deployment process. *Studies in Health Technology and Informatics*, *316*, 580–584. DOI: 10.3233/SHTI240480

Tang, H., Jiao, R., Xue, F., Cao, Y., Yang, Y., & Zhang, S. (2024). Task scheduling strategy of logistics cloud robot based on edge computing. *Wireless Personal Communications*, *137*(4), 2339–2358. DOI: 10.1007/s11277-024-11498-1

Taufani, M., & Widjaja, A. W. (2023). The manifestation of digital transformation concept in Indonesian logistic firms. *Jurnal Manajemen*, *27*(3), 428–448. DOI: 10.24912/jm.v27i3.1383

van Hoek, R. (2024). Insight from industry-early lessons learned about AI adoption in core procurement processes, directions for managers and researchers. *Supply Chain Management*, *29*(4), 794–803. DOI: 10.1108/scm-02-2024-0143

Verbivska, L., Zhygalkevych, Z., Fisun, Y., Chobitok, I., & Shvedkyi, V. (2023). Digital technologies as a tool of efficient logistics. *Revista de La Universidad Del Zulia*, *14*(39), 492–508. DOI: 10.46925//rdluz.39.28

Vieira, L. C., Longo, M., & Mura, M. (2024). Impact pathways: The hidden challenges of Scope 3 emissions measurement and management. *International Journal of Operations & Production Management*, *44*(13), 326–334. DOI: 10.1108/ijopm-01-2024-0049

Wang, J., Luo, L., & Wang, J. (2024). Logistics supply chain management and control based on mobile communication technology. *IEEJ Transactions on Electrical and Electronic Engineering*, *19*(9), 1475–1482. DOI: 10.1002/tee.24138

Wang, J., Mao, W., & Wenjie, W. (2023). The ethics of artificial intelligence: Sociopolitical and legal dimensions. *Interdisciplinary Studies in Society, Law, and Politics*, *2*(2), 27–32. DOI: 10.61838/kman.isslp.2.2.6

Yang, C. (2023). Research on the decision-making mechanism of digital transformation of small and medium-sized logistics enterprises in China based on evolutionary game. *Academic Journal of Management and Social Sciences*, *5*(2), 126–132. DOI: 10.54097/ajmss.v5i2.28

Yang, W., Li, W., Cao, Y., Luo, Y., & He, L. (2020). An information theory inspired real-time self-adaptive scheduling for production-Logistics Resources: Framework, principle, and implementation. *Sensors (Basel)*, *20*(24), 7007. DOI: 10.3390/s20247007

Yazdani, A., & Darbani, S. (2023). The impact of AI on trends, design, and Consumer Behavior. *AI and Tech in Behavioral and Social Sciences*, *1*(4), 4–10. DOI: 10.61838/kman.aitech.1.4.2

Yıldız, B., & Çiğdem, Ş. (2022). Digital transformation in logistics: Lights-out logistics. In *Financial and Economic Issues in Emerging Markets*. Özgür Yayınları., DOI: 10.58830/ozgur.pub1.c41

Yu, L., Xu, J., & Yuan, X. (2024). Sustainable digital shifts in Chinese transport and logistics: Exploring green innovations and their ESG implications. *Sustainability*, *16*(5), 1877. DOI: 10.3390/su16051877

KEY TERMS AND DEFINITIONS

Agentic AI: AI systems that act as self-learning agents. They adapt, negotiate, and improve logistics autonomously.

Artificial Intelligence (AI) in Supply Chains: AI uses machine learning and analytics to predict demand, optimize routes, and automate procurement. It makes supply chains adaptive and resilient.

Autonomous Operations: These use robotics, drones, AGVs, and AI control towers to perform tasks with little human input. They improve efficiency, accuracy, and sustainability.

Digital Twin: A digital twin is a virtual copy of a real asset or process. It updates in real time using IoT and sensors, allowing simulation, forecasting, and risk management.

ESG in Procurement: Integrating environmental, social, and governance criteria into supplier selection. It ensures compliance, sustainability, and ethical sourcing.

Quantum-ready Optimization: Algorithms designed for quantum computing. They solve complex logistics and procurement problems faster and at scale.

Scope-3 Carbon Emissions: Indirect emissions from suppliers, transport, and product lifecycles. They form the largest share of a company's footprint.

Sustainable Logistics: It means managing logistics to reduce environmental impact. It focuses on Scope-3 emissions, reuse, repair, and ESG-aligned sourcing.

Chapter 4
The Economic Impact of Autonomous Systems and Robotics on the Labor Market in the Logistics Sector:
A Three-Dimensional Examination

Ranya Mahfouz
Higher Institute for Computer Science and Business Administration, El Zarqa, Egypt

ABSTRACT

his chapter, provides a comprehensive, three-dimensional examination of the economic impact of autonomous systems and robotics on the labor market within the logistics sector. The authors explore the multifaceted nature of this transformation, analyzing the simultaneous processes of job displacement and workforce evolution. The chapter first delineates the theoretical foundations of automation's impact, contrasting the displacement effect which highlights job losses in routine tasks—with the productivity effect, which emphasizes economic growth and new job creation. This is followed by a detailed economic analysis that examines the trade-off between the high capital investments required for automation and the substantial, long-term operational efficiencies and cost reductions achieved. This section highlights how automation drives down per-order labor costs, increases throughput rates, and improves safety and space utilization.

DOI: 10.4018/979-8-3373-7006-4.ch004

INTRODUCTION

As an integral part of international trade, the logistics industry is going through an unprecedented transformation, which is changing the operational philosophy as well as strategy itself. This is an altogether new challenge brought about by technological advancements in line with changing market conditions, principally because of the sudden upsurge in e-commerce. The sudden spate of e-commerce and escalation of consumer demands has greatly stretched the limits of logistics performance hitherto acceptable, which require unprecedented delivery time nowadays. Traditional supply chains took several weeks as customers eagerly awaiting reception of products from distant locations; nowadays, customer lifestyle demands products in a day after ordering, whereas for some products, it is an hour at most, which is creating an immense amount of stress in traditional labor-based logistics systems (Chopra & Meindl, 2023). This has led to an immense urgency in reconsidering labor-intensive methods.

The Evolving Logistics Landscape and Triple Pressures

This paradigm shift is, however, no longer entirely focused on catering to e-commerce's scale of business as well as increasing demands for speedy delivery. This is because it is also informed by implicit, pressing needs for insights from automation, which include, for instance, labor shortages for drivers as well as operational staff, green demands for meeting environmental sustainability (Miotti & Johnson, 2024; Alahmari & Awad, 2025), as well as interventionist measures to ensure minimizing risks of supply chains for companies. For this reason, automation is framed as a solution which follows this triple axis of protection in meeting efficiency, labor, as well as sustainability needs.The Evolving Landscape of Logistics and Market Pressures

The emergence of e-commerce not only increased the number of goods being shipped throughout supply chains, but has also transformed what consumers do and expect. In the same vein, customers are increasingly looking for rapidity, transparency, and flexibility, which results in a preference for more frequent and small rather than bulk deliveries (Hübner et al., 2016). This trend for micro-fulfillment flies in the face of established warehousing and delivery logistics, which is configured to handle relatively infrequent deliveries on a larger scale. As a result, logistics service providers face the double burden of cost efficiency along with more and faster shipping.

Moreover, market competition has intensified through technological entrants and innovative business models such as on-demand delivery platforms, same-day grocery services, and direct-to-consumer supply chains (Christopher, 2016). Established logistics firms and new entrants alike are investing heavily in technologies that enhance operational flexibility and customer experience, including real-time shipment tracking, predictive analytics, and above all, automation.

Technological Frontiers: Autonomous Systems and Robotics

In response to these challenges, two principal domains of technological innovation have emerged as transformative agents in logistics: warehouse automation and autonomous vehicles. Although interconnected, these domains operate within fundamentally different environments and technological constraints, necessitating distinct approaches while contributing collectively to the sector's digital reinvention.

Warehouse Automation

Warehouse automation refers to the integration of robotic systems within highly controlled, indoor environments that facilitate storage, retrieval, and handling of goods. This includes a variety of technologies such as robotic arms for picking and packaging, Automated Guided Vehicles (AGVs) that transport inventory within the warehouse, and Automated Storage and Retrieval Systems (ASRS) that optimize the placement and movement of goods to maximize space utilization and handling speed (Wulfraat, 2021).

The value proposition of warehouse automation lies in its ability to enhance processing speed, accuracy, and throughput capacity while reducing labor costs and human error risks—particularly in repetitive, physically demanding tasks (Guizzo, 2012). Advanced warehouse robotics are increasingly equipped with artificial intelligence (AI)-enabled vision systems and machine learning algorithms that improve sorting, picking accuracy, and adaptability to product variations (Bortolini et al., 2018).

Autonomous Vehicles

Parallel to warehouse automation, the advent of autonomous vehicles marks a revolutionary shift in transportation logistics. Unlike warehouse robotics operating in structured environments, autonomous vehicles function in dynamic, uncontrolled public spaces, navigating complex road networks subject to traffic conditions and regulatory frameworks. This domain encompasses a spectrum of technologies including long-haul self-driving trucks, last-mile delivery robots, and aerial delivery drones (Fagnant & Kockelman, 2015).

The anticipated benefits of autonomous vehicles extend beyond cost reduction to include enhanced safety through reduced human error, 24/7 operations without fatigue, optimized routing using real-time data, and environmental benefits via reduced emissions and fuel consumption (Litman, 2020). However, these advantages are contingent upon overcoming significant technological, regulatory, and infrastructural hurdles.

Market Dynamics and Economic Scale

The economic magnitude and potential of autonomous and automated logistics technologies are underscored by robust market forecasts and investment trends. According to recent industry analyses, the global Autonomous Freight and Logistics Market was valued at approximately USD 53.45 billion in 2024, with projections suggesting growth to USD 185.14 billion by 2032, corresponding to a Compound Annual Growth Rate (CAGR) of 16.80% (Grand View Research, 2025). Similarly, the broader Logistics Automation Market, which includes warehouse automation technologies, is expected to expand from USD 78.20 billion in 2024 to USD 212.81 billion by 2032, growing at a CAGR of 13.43% (Allied Market Research, 2024).

These growth trajectories are driven by escalating demand for operational efficiency, labor cost pressures, and the continuous evolution of consumer delivery expectations. North America currently leads the adoption and market share of these technologies, accounting for nearly 40% of market value in 2024, followed by rapid growth in Asia-Pacific regions fueled by infrastructure investments and supportive government policies (McKinsey & Company, 2025).

Holistic Transformation of the Logistics Value Chain

The concurrent expansion of warehouse automation and autonomous vehicle markets signals a profound, holistic transformation spanning the entire logistics value chain. This end-to-end integration implies that autonomous technology will span first-mile port or supplier handling through mid-mile transportation and final-mile delivery, seamless interoperability becoming a decisive competitive advantage (Sen & Sauter, 2021).

For example, a shipment arriving via an autonomous container truck at a smart warehouse equipped with AGVs and robotic picking systems exemplifies the synthesis of these technological domains. The interoperability of vehicle telematics with warehouse management systems is essential to optimize throughput, reduce dwell time, and enhance supply chain visibility (Wang & Disney, 2016).

Such integration creates cascading economic effects across distribution ecosystems. While automation may displace certain roles traditionally performed by warehouse workers or drivers, it simultaneously precipitates new opportunities in system maintenance, programming, oversight, and AI-driven analytics, restructuring the labor landscape rather than uniformly shrinking it (Bessen, 2019).

Strategic and Competitive Imperatives

From a business strategy perspective, automation is evolving from optional efficiency improvements to strategic imperatives essential for market survival. The acceleration of delivery speed and reduction of errors directly influence customer satisfaction, brand loyalty, and ultimately market share (Klaus, Zeynep, & Tobias, 2017). Firms slow to adapt risk ceding leadership to more agile competitors who leverage these technologies to offer superior fulfillment experiences.

Moreover, imposed labor cost inflation and workforce shortages in key regions heighten the appeal of automated systems as not only cost-saving tools but also as necessities to maintain continuous operations (Autor, 2015). Hence, logistics automation plays a critical role in enabling businesses to meet near-instantaneous delivery norms while balancing profitability and scalability.

Wider Implications and Future Outlook

The ongoing logistics transformation implicates broader socioeconomic dimensions. The displacement of human workers necessitates proactive labor market policies, including reskilling and education in logistics IT, robotics maintenance, and data management domains (Acemoglu & Restrepo, 2018). Additionally, ethical and regulatory frameworks must evolve to address data privacy, safety standards for autonomous systems, and equitable access to emerging logistics technologies (Lin, 2016).

Environmental sustainability will also be a key consideration as autonomous systems can contribute to reduced congestion, emissions, and resource use if integrated thoughtfully within multi-modal transportation networks (Kans & Heikkilä, 2021).

In synthesis, the logistics sector's technological evolution—characterized by integrated autonomous systems and robotics—reflects a paradigm shift that redefines operational norms, economic landscapes, and competitive strategies. The scale and velocity of these changes necessitate interdisciplinary research, proactive policy frameworks, and innovative management approaches to navigate the opportunities and challenges inherent in this transformation.

LITERATURE REVIEW: THEORETICAL FOUNDATIONS AND EMPIRICAL EVIDENCE ON AUTOMATION AND LABOR

The discourse on automation's impact on labor unfolds chiefly around two theoretically opposing yet empirically intertwined concepts: the displacement effect and the productivity effect. These effects frame the broader economic and social consequences of introducing autonomous systems and robotics, particularly in sectors undergoing rapid technological shifts such as logistics and transportation (Autor, 2015; Acemoglu & Restrepo, 2018). Where the displacement effect underscores the loss of human jobs and wage pressure due to automation replacing routine tasks, the productivity effect reveals how automation can spur output increases, lower operational costs, and induce new job creation by expanding economic activities and reshaping business models (Brynjolfsson & McAfee, 2014). The tension between these forces generates a complex landscape in which the aggregate national economy may benefit, even as specific regions and socio-occupational groups suffer adverse consequences.

The Displacement Effect vs. Productivity Effect: Theoretical Context

The displacement effect is rooted in classical economic theories of technological change, tracing back to concerns famously articulated during the Industrial Revolution about machines substituting manual labor. Recent scholarship has refined this notion by distinguishing between the automation of routine vs. non-routine tasks and by assessing sector-specific vulnerabilities. Automation predominantly affects jobs involving standardized, repetitive physical or cognitive work that can be codified and replicated by machines. In logistics, such roles include warehouse picking, sorting, and truck driving, making these occupations particularly susceptible to robotization and autonomous vehicle technologies (Frey & Osborne, 2017).

In contrast, the productivity effect derives from endogenous growth theories, highlighting how technology boosts overall economic efficiency. Automation lowers unit costs, enhances precision, and increases system throughput, enabling firms to scale operations or introduce new products and services. This effect can stimulate demand for labor in complementary tasks such as system design, installation, maintenance, and managerial oversight, potentially offsetting job losses in automated functions.

Reconciling these effects requires acknowledging that automation does not produce uniform outcomes but operates within differentiated labor markets, regulatory environments, and firm strategies (Bessen, 2019).

Empirical Evidence: National-Level Productivity Gains

The International Federation of Robotics (IFR) represents a leading source evaluating automation's broad economic benefits. Their extensive research correlates robot use with positive macroeconomic indicators such as increased GDP growth and improved labor productivity. IFR data highlight that robot densification contributed to approximately 10% of GDP per capita growth across OECD countries between

1993 and 2016, suggesting that investments in robotics can be a significant driver of economic expansion (IFR, 2020). Furthermore, IFR asserts that increased automation is compatible with rising employment and wage levels, thereby challenging doom-laden narratives about job loss (IFR, 2021).

A crucial aspect of the IFR analysis is its emphasis on reshoring effects: automation enabling the relocation of manufacturing and logistics operations back from low-cost countries to high-cost advanced economies by reducing labor cost competitiveness gaps (Gray, Skowronski, Esenduran, & Rungtusanatham, 2013). Such trends suggest a potential revitalization of domestic labor markets and strengthening of supply chain resilience through onshore capacities employing fewer but upskilled workers supported by automated systems.

Macro studies like these capture the positive aggregate effects of automation diffusion but tend to obscure heterogeneity in spatial and occupational impacts.

Concentrated Negative Effects: Microeconomic Findings

Conversely, detailed empirical investigations such as those by Acemoglu and Restrepo (2020) reveal the localized and occupational-specific adverse consequences of robot adoption in the United States. Their seminal work uses granular data from "commuting zones" to document that each additional robot per 1,000 workers corresponds with a 0.2 percentage point decline in employment-population ratios and a 0.42% reduction in average wages. Given that roughly one million robots had been installed across the U.S. manufacturing sector over the study period, these statistics translate to an estimated 400,000 jobs displaced, disproportionately affecting manufacturing-intensive communities within the "industrial heartland."

This evidence highlights the displacement effect's asymmetric distribution, where workers in highly automated industries and regions face more acute labor market stress, contributing to economic and social fragmentation (Autor, 2019). The Acemoglu and Restrepo findings importantly underscore that while productivity growth occurs, the benefits do not diffuse evenly, with wage stagnation and heightened job insecurity concentrated among certain demographic groups and locales (Autor & Salomons, 2018).

This microeconomic perspective complements macroeconomic assessments by revealing the distributional and transitional costs of automation, which nationwide productivity statistics alone cannot capture (Frank et al., 2019).

Synthesis: Integrating Macro and Micro Perspectives

The juxtaposition of the IFR and Acemoglu-Restrepo studies illustrates the dual nature of automation's impact: it is simultaneously a source of broad economic growth and localized disruption. This paradox is not contradictory but reflects differences in analytical scope and methodology. National GDP and productivity metrics aggregate gains across diverse economic sectors, regions, and skill groups. Meanwhile, granular data illuminate the hardships experienced by specific workers and communities facing job losses and wage pressure (Perugini & Signorelli, 2022).

Acknowledging this duality is critical for framing policy responses that balance promoting technological adoption with supporting displaced workers. It also cautions against simplistic narratives that frame automation exclusively as "job-killer" or "job-creator" (Brynjolfsson & Mitchell, 2017).

SOCIAL, PSYCHOLOGICAL, AND ETHICAL DIMENSIONS OF AUTOMATION IN LOGISTICS

Psychological and Social Impact on Workers (Technological Anxiety)

Automation in logistics significantly transforms workers' roles from manual repetitive tasks to more cognitively demanding activities such as system monitoring and exception management. This shift introduces new psychological burdens including anxiety related to job security, adjustment challenges, and increased mental load. Emotional labor involved in reconciling professional identity with automated counterparts affects worker well-being and productivity. Effective mitigation requires targeted mental health support, cognitive ergonomics in system design, and comprehensive training focusing on digital literacy and human-machine collaboration (Bawden & Robinson, 2022; Lifestyle Sustainability Directory, 2025).

The organizational psychology literature shows that the constant threat of automation raises stress and lowers job satisfaction, which contributes to diminished aggregate productivity and mental health issues in the workforce. Integrating mental health support programs, behavioral adaptation workshops, and ongoing employee monitoring is essential to ensure smooth workforce adaptation.

Social Equity, Distribution of Benefits, and Global Disparities

Automation accelerates social equity erosion, as capital-technology gains are highly concentrated among entrepreneurs, while the transition costs disproportionately affect low-wage workers performing routine tasks. This disparity is particularly pronounced in emerging markets, where informal labor is prevalent, social protection programs are limited, and workforce skill gaps are significant. Additionally, developing countries often face infrastructure limitations that impede rapid adoption of automation, further widening global and local inequalities. Policy interventions such as a "robot tax" to fund social safety nets or experimental Universal Basic Income (UBI) schemes could redistribute automation gains more equitably and mitigate social disparities. Including comparative case studies across different regions enriches the literature review, highlights structural disparities, and informs context-specific policy responses to address inequities both within and across countries (Acemoglu & Restrepo, 2018).

Linking Social Considerations with Policy, Education, and Emerging Markets

Reskilling and upskilling initiatives must go beyond technical training to address non-routine cognitive skills such as robotics maintenance, data analytics, and intelligent logistics management. Integrating psychological guidance alongside technical training reduces worker anxiety and improves social adaptation, allowing workers to benefit from technological transformation rather than being disadvantaged.

In emerging markets, workers face a dual challenge: slow technology adoption due to high costs and limited infrastructure, combined with gaps in social protection that heighten vulnerability to automation's negative effects. Context-specific studies and case analyses are necessary to design inclusive policies supporting social equity, protecting displaced workers, and facilitating sustainable economic growth.

Policy Frameworks for Fair Workforce Transitions

Ensuring equitable benefits from automation demands robust policy frameworks emphasizing reskilling and upskilling, social protection mechanisms such as universal basic income or robot taxes, and coordinated labor market integration strategies. Empirical assessment of policy effectiveness enhances practical utility for stakeholders and guides equitable adaptation pathways in transforming labor markets (Cedefop, 2022).

Ethical and Legal Considerations for AI and Autonomous Vehicles

The widespread deployment of AI-driven autonomous systems raises pressing ethical and regulatory challenges including algorithmic transparency, accountability for safety and decision-making, and harmonization of fragmented legal frameworks. A dedicated discussion on emerging governance models and cross-jurisdictional regulatory efforts supports responsible and sustainable innovation in logistics automation (Smith et al., 2022).

Ethical Implications and AI Responsibility

Automation's adoption requires attention to AI ethics, particularly in logistics systems with autonomous decision-making components, such as routing algorithms or Autonomous Vehicles (AVs). These systems involve complex ethical dilemmas in human-risk scenarios, necessitating clear regulatory frameworks for algorithmic accountability (Smith et al., 2022). A singular focus on efficiency diminishes recognition of qualitative social costs like technological anxiety, and ethical considerations must be embedded in policy and system design to ensure responsible automation practices.

ADOPTION IN GLOBAL CONTEXT: REGIONAL DISPARITY AND IMPACT ON EMERGING MARKETS

The literature's hitherto dominant focus on OECD countries gives at best a partial view of the impact that automation is already having on logistics globally. Drivers and consequences of adoption fundamentally vary in Emerging Markets and the Global South:

1. Low-Cost Paradox: While high labor costs provide an incentive for automation in more advanced economies, low labor costs in emerging markets greatly slow down the return on investment in automation, leading to a slower pace of aggregate job displacement.
2. Infrastructure Gaps: These markets face considerable infrastructure challenges, such as power outages, a lack of good-quality telecommunication networks, and a shortage of specialized maintenance expertise. These factors not only delay adoption but also make the implementation of Partial Automation far more common than comprehensive, end-to-end automation.
3. The role of the informal sector: In many developing countries, the informal sector makes up a large part of the labor market. These effects often defy quantification and also are difficult to effectively address through traditional policy tools, thus calling for context-specific case studies and analysis.

CRITICAL ASSESSMENT OF POLICY RESPONSES: RESKILLING PROGRAM SUCCESS RATES

While reskilling and upskilling have been widely regarded as the common solution for job displacement, a critical academic review shows mixed results on their efficacy. General recommendations to invest in new skills are contrasted by empirical literature highlighting serious problems in their implementation:

1. Skill Mismatch: Reskilling often fails to effectively equip workers with the particular, non-routine skills that are in actual demand due to automation within the labor market-such as robotics maintenance or higher-level data analysis.
2. Learning Barrier: For the older workforce or those with lower levels of education, the barrier is higher to shift into high-cognitive activities; consequently, they have lower participation rates and success in such training programs.
3. Regulatory Fragmentation: Programs are usually uncoordinated across various jurisdictions or sectors, limiting their scale and impact.

SECTOR-SPECIFIC DIFFERENCES: WAREHOUSING VS. AUTONOMOUS VEHICLES

A closer examination within the logistics sector reveals that the impact of automation varies substantially depending on the domain of application: warehouse automation versus autonomous vehicles.

Warehouse Automation

Warehouse automation involves deploying robotic systems in highly controlled, indoor environments where repetitive tasks such as picking, packing, sorting, and inventory management predominate (Boysen, Briskorn, & Emde, 2021). Technologies include robotic arms, Automated Guided Vehicles (AGVs), and Automated Storage and Retrieval Systems (ASRS), which incrementally supplement or replace manual labor.

Research estimates from industry sources and academic case studies suggest that every ten automated systems introduced in warehouses typically lead to the displacement of about three to four traditional labor positions, while simultaneously creating only one to two technical or supervisory roles (Wulfraat, 2021). Hence, while automation improves throughput and accuracy, the net effect on employment tends to be negative, reflecting a significant reduction in manual warehouse jobs despite partial labor augmentation in technical areas (Bortolini et al., 2018).

These patterns are exacerbated in contexts where warehouse labor includes a high proportion of low-wage, low-skill workers, raising concerns about socio-economic impacts and regional inequalities (Hancock, Mia, & McDonald, 2019; Qadeer & Awad, 2025). However, some scholars point to opportunities in training and upskilling workers to take on more complex, technology-oriented roles, though the scale of these opportunities relative to jobs lost remains uncertain (Muller, 2020).

Autonomous Vehicles

Autonomous vehicles (AVs) operate in dynamic, uncontrolled, public environments, representing a different technological and occupational challenge. This domain spans long-haul self-driving trucks, last-mile delivery robots, and aerial drones tasked with navigating complex traffic conditions, pedestrian zones, and regulatory regimes (Fagnant & Kockelman, 2015).

The labor group most directly affected is the professional driving workforce, a sector critical to logistics and freight operations globally. For example, truck drivers constitute a substantial share of employment in the U.S. and other developed economies, often described as the "backbone" of national economies (U.S. Bureau of Labor Statistics, 2023). Autonomous trucking promises to reduce costs and increase efficiencies but may lead to large-scale displacement in this profession.

However, the societal and economic impact of AVs remains largely speculative due to obstacles including regulatory uncertainty, infrastructure readiness, public acceptance, and technological maturity (Kyriakidis, Happee, & de Winter, 2015). Governments and businesses face challenges harmonizing autonomous vehicle regulations across regions, a critical step to enable scalable deployment (Smith et al., 2022). Furthermore, public attitudes toward safety and ethical considerations may affect speed and acceptance of adoption (Liu et al., 2019).

RESEARCH GAPS AND FUTURE DIRECTIONS

Despite advances, several research gaps limit understanding of automation's long-term labor effects in logistics:

1. Regulatory Lag and Fragmentation: The rapid technological evolution in autonomous vehicles has outpaced regulatory frameworks. Inconsistent policies between states or nations impede uniform deployment and strategic planning for supply chains (Chen & Perez, 2021; Shams Eldin et.al, 2025). More research is needed on harmonization strategies and the interplay between regulation, innovation, and market development.
2. Societal Acceptance and Psychological Impacts: Limited longitudinal studies address workers' and consumers' acceptance of autonomous systems, particularly in last-mile delivery contexts. The psychological effects of skill obsolescence,

job insecurity, and shifting occupational identities remain insufficiently explored (Smith, 2020).

3. Labor Shortages as Automation Drivers: Growing labor shortages in logistics provide a non-economic justification for automation. For example, shortages of Heavy Goods Vehicle (HGV) drivers in the UK (estimated 100,000 shortfall) and Japan (projected 40% driver shortfall) due to aging workforces create structural pressures that automation may alleviate (Department for Transport UK, 2024; Ministry of Land, Infrastructure, Transport and Tourism Japan, 2023). Future research should fully integrate demographic and labor supply dynamics into automation impact models.
4. Equity and Social Protection: There remains a conspicuous need for studies on the equity implications of automation-induced displacement and the design of social protection systems—such as retraining programs, income support, and labor market reintegration—to mitigate labor market shocks (Cedefop, 2022).

ECONOMIC IMPACT ANALYSIS: CORE FINANCIAL OUTCOMES

Capital Expenditure and Economic Rationale of Automation

Capital

The integration of autonomic systems in logistics needs to maintain an efficient balance between large initial investments and long-run operational savings. Setting up an intelligent warehouse facility is a large initial outlay, which may vary from 1 million USD in small cases to a maximum of 25 million USD in large, high-tech projects (Allied Market Research, 2024). Generally, advanced automated warehouses demand large inaugural investments between 2.5 million USD to 4.2 million USD per location, which generally favors large companies having large capital bases, as well as creating entry hurdles for small to medium-sized companies (SMEs) (Grand View Research, 2025).

Despite such initial investments, robotics ensures vast financial savings in labor, increased throughput, and optimization of processes. Labor costs for order processing by robotic systems could be reduced by as much as 62%, besides increasing order throughput by as much as 60% (Bortolini et al., 2018). These savings also include costs related to overtime, night shifts, hiring, training, and employee turnover (Wulfraat, 2021). High-density storage systems decrease storage capacity by more than 40%, accommodating increased order volumes without increasing the facility (Christopher, 2016).

A failure to adopt automation also results in an opportunity cost because those who fail to adopt might end up losing market share to competitors who adopt, besides suffering from labor shortages (McKinsey & Company, 2025; Ghonim et al., 2025).

Labor Costs Versus Capital Investment: Expanding the Trade-Off

The economic analysis of trade-offs must also include indirect costs, operational risks, as well as environmental regulations in relation to Total Cost of Ownership (TCO). While automating brings about social costs, this entails loss of employee morale as well as worker anxiety related to technological advancements, which in turn affects employee productivity (Bawden & Robinson, 2022).

Measuring AMCs' Cost of Ownership by Estimating AMCs' Quality Indirect Expenditures

Quality-related costs, loss of equity, workers' morale, as well as workers' anxiety, are measured as an indirect operational expense, which, in turn, raises Operation Expenditures (OpEx). Indirect costs, which in this case include quality-related costs, loss of equity, workers' morale, as well as

> **Environmental Compliance Cost**: Automation also caters to environmental regulations. The compliance of environmental regulations to cut down carbon emissions is becoming increasingly expensive; this is reduced by automation, which results in green operations, further making it an essential financial requirement ("Green ROI") (Miotti & Johnson, 2024).

Cybersecurity Risks

The use of Big Data as well as connected networks also carries potential disruptions, which have to be countered by investments in cyber-security protocols, thus becoming part of the fixed costs of operation (ENISA, 2023).

Economic Trade-Offs in Automation Adoption

High Capital Investment

Appropriate

- Start up costs, ranging from USD 1 million to 25 million

- Average per-facility costs in USD:
- Complex systems integration and maintenance

Operational Savings and Gains

- Labor cost reduction: up to 62% per order
- Throughput increase: 60%
- Labor productivity improvement: 40%
- Space utilization reduction: 41%
- Safety incident reduction: 78.4%
- Indirect cost reductions (training, turnover)
- Energy savings through efficient and regenerative systems

This interplay of high initial costs and significant savings during operations makes up the essence of capital versus labor economics in automations, where capital costs are set against savings achieved.

Strategic Imperatives and Competitive Dynamics

Early adoption of automation ensures benefits of cost leadership and differentiation advantages. Companies implementing end-to-end automation, ranging from smart warehouses to self-driving vehicles, result in an integrated logistics system, which ensures sustainable competitive advantages, resulting in possible market consolidation. Delayed adoption faces opportunities costs and loss of competitiveness in the market.

Socioeconomic Implications: Workforce Evolution

Automation decreases demands for labor in routine, low-skilled areas of warehousing, sorting, and transport, but concentrates effects in targeted job types and geographies. Conversely, it also creates new workplace roles in robotics servicing, analytics, system management, and predictive logistics control. Training for reskilling and upskilling is, therefore, imperative, focusing on nonroutine cognitive skills (critical thinking, creativity, problem-solving).

Supply Chain Resilience and Demand Stability

Automation helps to stabilize supply chains by alleviating the "Bullwhip Effect" by improving forecasting, lead time, and inventory accuracy (Wang & Disney, 2016).

This means that supply chains are less reliant on inventory, minimize warehouse costs, as well as product spoilage costs, making them more agile to market shifts.

The following is the final, revised structure of the chapter sections, incorporating all requested strategic, content, and flow improvements. Section 5.0 has been eliminated and its content integrated into the expanded Section 4.0.

STRATEGIC DIMENSIONS OF AUTOMATION, RISK MANAGEMENT, AND IMPLEMENTATION HURDLES

The transformation of logistics through automation extends beyond economic and operational considerations. Strategic and non-financial dimensions play a crucial role in shaping long-term sustainability, risk management, and workforce adaptation. Understanding these dimensions positions automation as a holistic organizational strategy rather than merely a cost-saving tool.

Environmental Impact, Sustainability, and Green ROI

Automation represents a critical lever for achieving environmental sustainability in logistics. Beyond operational efficiency, autonomous systems and electric vehicles enable companies to:

- Reduce carbon footprints and optimize energy consumption.
- Implement AI-driven route optimization to minimize unnecessary mileage.
- Utilize high-density storage systems, reducing spatial requirements and facility expansion costs.

These measures contribute to regulatory compliance and align investment decisions with environmental responsibility. Environmental costs or "Green ROI" should therefore be treated as a strategic component of automation investments, linking financial decision-making with ecological imperatives (Miotti & Johnson, 2024).

Cybersecurity, Legislative and Regulatory Risks, and Safety Compliance Costs

The adoption of automated logistics systems introduces significant strategic risks that require proactive management:

- **Cybersecurity Threats and System Resilience:** Connected networks, big data, and warehouse management systems are vulnerable to attacks that could halt operations. Advanced protection protocols and continuous monitoring are essential to safeguard the supply chain (ENISA, 2023).

- **Legislative Fragmentation and Safety Compliance Costs:** Variations in legislation across jurisdictions—particularly in autonomous vehicle and warehouse automation regulations—raise compliance costs and hinder scalable deployment (Smith et al., 2022; Mahmoud et al., 2025).

This challenge is compounded by the high cost and complexity of standardizing and certifying safety technologies (Safety Technology Certification) for autonomous systems operating in dynamic logistics environments. Achieving required safety standards (such as industry-specific ISO or vehicle standards) necessitates significant capital investment in advanced sensor hardware, redundant control systems, and rigorous verification software. Organizations must conduct a detailed Cost/Benefit Analysis for these unified safety technologies as part of the investment decision, as failing to accurately estimate compliance costs can lead to significant budget overruns and implementation delays. Harmonized standards and regulatory alignment are therefore critical for large-scale adoption.

Strategic planning must integrate these challenges, ensuring that investments in automation are resilient to technological and regulatory disruptions.

Infrastructure Challenges and Workforce Skill Gaps

Effective automation deployment requires alignment between internal capabilities and technological infrastructure:

- **Infrastructure Barriers:** High-speed connectivity, reliable power systems, and advanced data integration are essential for continuous operations. Failure to address these gaps can delay implementation and reduce efficiency.
- **Skills Mismatch:** Automation fundamentally reshapes workforce requirements, replacing routine tasks with cognitively demanding roles. Key competencies now include proficiency in robotics maintenance, data analytics, and AI-driven logistics optimization (Wang & Disney, 2016; McKinsey & Company, 2025). Targeted reskilling and upskilling programs are necessary to align workforce capabilities with these emerging demands.

Strategic Human Capital Management and Technological Anxiety Mitigation

Employee anxiety regarding the adoption of autonomous systems and robotics—particularly in the logistics sector—is a crucial human-centric challenge in digital transformation. To manage this effectively, organizations should adopt a strategic human capital management framework. First, they ought to assess the psychological and social needs of employees through surveys and interviews to identify concerns about technological change. For example, adoption of robotics in warehousing promises productivity gains of about 23.3% and increased GVA by 14.4% by 2035, but this comes with disruption to labor.

Next, they can design behavioral adaptation programs such as hands-on training workshops, counseling sessions, and collaborative platforms that build confidence in new technologies and develop adaptability skills. Concurrently, they should engage employees in the change process—inviting them to participate in implementation planning and enabling them to voice their concerns—fostering a sense of ownership and commitment. Continuous monitoring and evaluation must follow: organizations should track psychosocial performance indicators (employee well-being, technology acceptance, turnover rates) and refine strategies based on feedback. Finally, these human-centred initiatives must be integrated with the organization's broader digital transformation and innovation strategy, ensuring alignment of human capital efforts with corporate goals of efficiency, cost reduction, and competitive advantage. The logistics industry, facing shortages of over 3 million truck drivers worldwide and labor-cost pressures, is already turning to AI-enabled robots to relieve workforce gaps.

Case Studies: Pioneers of Automation

- Case Study 1: Amazon's Automated Warehouse Ecosystem Amazon's fulfillment centers represent a paradigmatic example of how systematic, large-scale automation transforms logistics operations profoundly. Unlike piecemeal technological adoption, Amazon pursues a disciplined, scientifically guided process to innovate warehouse management, classifying centers into generational cohorts. Each generation, such as Gen 13 and Gen 14, upgrades warehouse layouts, robotic infrastructures, and automation integration, underpinned by data-driven industrial engineering. Amazon leverages AWS-powered digital twins and simulation technologies to optimize new warehouse designs and operational workflows virtually prior to physical deployment, enhancing decision-making and reducing risk (Savushkin, 2024; Awad & Mahmoud, 2024). Robotics and AI form the cornerstone of Amazon's warehouse automation. The company's automated guided vehicles (AGVs), particularly Kiva robots, revolutionize inventory handling by transporting full shelves to human packers, drastically reducing walking time and physical strain on workers. This innovation alone accounts for a 40% productivity increase in picking and put-away processes (DigitalDefynd, 2025). Coupled with AI-powered shortest-path algorithms, Amazon dynamically routes robots and personnel to minimize travel distance and time, improving order throughput and accuracy. The integration extends to demand forecasting and inventory optimization, where AI models analyze consumer behavior and demand patterns to maintain inventory fluidity and reduce excess stock (Nightview Capital, 2025). These technological advancements yield multifaceted results. Labor processing costs per order have dropped by 62%, while warehouse space utilization has increased by 41% owing to compact storage techniques enabled by automation (Wulfraat, 2021). Importantly, workplace safety has improved dramatically, with a 78.4% reduction in recordable incidents, notably reducing injuries related to physical exertion such as back strains (Savushkin, 2024). These achievements illustrate how a well-orchestrated automation strategy not only enhances economic efficiency but also fosters a safer, more sustainable work environment.

- Case Study 2: The Isuzu and Applied Intuition Partnership in Japan The partnership between Isuzu Motors and Applied Intuition exemplifies automation developed in response to demographic and regulatory imperatives rather than exclusively economic incentives. Japan's "2024 Problem"—government legislation limiting truck driver work hours combined with an aging workforce—has created a projected 40% shortfall in freight drivers (Ministry of Land, Infrastructure, Transport and Tourism Japan, 2023). Autonomous trucking technology is being advanced as a critical solution to this structural labor scarcity. The Isuzu-Applied Intuition alliance focuses on developing robust, intelligent autonomous trucks for highway and hub-to-hub logistics. Their approach integrates state-of-the-art AI, advanced sensor arrays, and rigorous real-world and simulation-based safety validations. The partnership's engineering teams collaborate globally, emphasizing the creation of sustained in-house expertise within Isuzu to manage, innovate, and scale autonomous vehicle technologies internally, a strategy positioning the company as a leader in logistical automation innovation (Applied Intuition, 2025). This collaboration reflects a broader transformation. Rather than simple job displacement, automation here serves as a catalyst for high-skilled job creation and corporate reinvention. Isuzu is cultivating a technology-driven workforce adept in autonomous system engineering, maintenance, and operation. Autonomous heavy-duty trucks powered by Applied Intuition's software currently operate on public roads in Japan with safety operators onboard, highlighting tangible progress toward commercial deployment (Isuzu Motors, 2025).
- Case Study 3: OKI's AI-Driven Logistics Automation Solutions OKI, a prominent Japanese technology company traditionally known for mechatronics and electronics, has distinguished itself in the logistics sector through its advanced applications of artificial intelligence (AI) to address critical opera-

tional challenges. Unlike many providers that focus primarily on hardware innovations suchs as robotics, OKI emphasizes the strategic role of AI-powered decision-making systems that replicate and enhance human expertise in complex delivery planning and fleet management.

Advanced Delivery Planning Optimization: At the core of OKI's logistics automation suite lies a sophisticated AI algorithm designed to autonomously generate delivery plans that optimize multiple operational constraints. These include vehicle load capacities, delivery time windows, route distances, traffic conditions, toll road considerations, and regulatory compliance such as driver hours. This multi-criteria optimization surpasses traditional rule-based or heuristic route planning software, delivering adaptive and data-driven plans aligned with real-world logistics complexities (OKI, 2025; Shams Eldin et al., 205). **T**

he REMOWAY Platform: Remote Coordination and Scalability: Complementing its AI planning algorithms, OKI has developed the REMOWAY platform, a cloud-based system enabling centralized remote operation, monitoring, and coordination of diverse dispersed edge devices within warehouses and transport networks. REMOWAY tackles a long-standing fragmentation problem in logistics automation by integrating heterogeneous devices into a single platform with real-time inter-device communication, enhancing system-wide visibility and operational responsiveness (OKI, 2025).

Workforce Transformation and Upskilling: By automating complex, repetitive scheduling and control tasks, dependency on intensive manual labor and specialized dispatchers decreases. Simultaneously, demand rises for roles requiring supervisory capabilities over AI systems, routine maintenance, data analytics, and continuous workflow optimization. OKI supports this transition through targeted upskilling initiatives, empowering employees to gain proficiency with new systems and fostering organizational adaptation (Tanaka & Saito, 2023).

EXECUTION CHALLENGES, POLICY FRAMEWORK, AND STRATEGIC RECOMMENDATIONS

Execution Challenges and Structural Limits

The critical assessment of policy failures presented in Section 2.5 highlights recurring shortcomings in workforce protection, equity preservation, and regulatory coordination. These gaps underscore the necessity for a robust and well-targeted policy framework to guide the adoption of automation in logistics. The subsequent Section 5.1 presents such a framework, translating lessons learned from previous policy shortcomings into actionable interventions that ensure both operational efficiency and socially inclusive outcomes.

EXECUTION CHALLENGES AND STRUCTURAL LIMITS

The automation-led transformation in logistics faces significant execution challenges and structural limits, encompassing operational, financial, and strategic constraints:

Regulatory Fragmentation

Legislative differences, particularly in Autonomous Vehicle (AV) and warehouse automation regulations, impede seamless deployment of automated transport technologies. Variations in safety standards, insurance requirements, and traffic laws across jurisdictions increase compliance costs and limit large-scale adoption (Smith et al., 2022).

Operational and Technological Risks

Automation relies heavily on Big Data, connected networks, and Warehouse Management Systems (WMS), making infrastructure vulnerable to cybersecurity threats. Any breach could halt operations entirely, requiring substantial investment in advanced protection protocols to safeguard the supply chain (ENISA, 2023).

Integrated Perspective

Successful automation adoption requires not only technological readiness and capital investment but also proactive risk management, regulatory alignment, and strategic planning. Academic analysis must consider these factors as part of both operational cost structures and broader strategic frameworks.

Proposed Framework for Targeted Policy Interventions

Automation cannot be left solely to market forces; it requires thoughtful, targeted policy intervention to preserve social equity, ensure sustainable growth, and mitigate adverse socioeconomic impacts. Building on the critique of policy failures discussed in Section 2.5, a strategic framework should translate lessons from past shortcomings into effective actions.

1. Fiscal and Tax Reform

Innovative funding mechanisms should be implemented to support social safety nets or targeted Universal Basic Income (UBI) programs. Options include partial taxation of robotics and automation systems, data usage fees, or levies linked to the gains from automation. This approach redistributes benefits from technological efficiency, cushioning vulnerable workers and ensuring social inclusivity.

2. Targeted and Coordinated Training

Reskilling and upskilling programs must focus on specialized, non-routine competencies aligned with automation-specific roles, such as robotics maintenance, predictive analytics for warehouse management, and AI-driven logistics optimization (Tanaka & Saito, 2023). Coordinated training reduces the skills gap and equips the workforce for emerging roles in an automated logistics ecosystem.

3. Regulatory Harmonization

Policymakers should address legislative fragmentation in AV and warehouse automation regulations by harmonizing standards, safety protocols, and compliance procedures across jurisdictions. This reduces implementation costs, encourages cross-border operations, and fosters safe, scalable automation adoption (Smith et al., 2022).

This framework ensures that interventions are operationally effective, socially equitable, and economically sustainable, providing a structured roadmap for collaboration among businesses, governments, and educational institutions.

Conclusion and Strategic Recommendations

The economic and social impact of autonomous systems and robotics on the logistics labor market is complex and multifaceted. Automation is driven by economic incentives—cost reduction, productivity gains—as well as strategic imperatives to address labor shortages and evolving consumer expectations.

Key Insights

- Benefits, including reduced operational costs and increased throughput, are broadly distributed, while costs, particularly job displacement and wage pressures, are concentrated in specific populations and regions.

- Successful adoption requires coordinated attention to technological, regulatory, societal, and workforce challenges.

Strategic Recommendations

- **For Businesses:** Adopt phased implementation, invest in workforce upskilling, and maintain transparent communication strategies.
- **For Governments:** Create unified regulatory frameworks, provide worker transition support, and encourage public-private collaboration.
- **For Educational Institutions:** Modernize curricula, provide experiential learning, and foster industry-academic partnerships.

Outlook

The logistics workforce will shift from routine, manual tasks to cognitive, complex, and non-routine activities. Stakeholders must harmonize technological adoption with human capital development to achieve inclusive economic growth while mitigating social impacts.

REFERENCES

Acemoglu, D., & Restrepo, P. (2018). Artificial Intelligence, Automation, and Work. *Economics of Artificial Intelligence: An Agenda*, 197-236.

Acemoglu, D., & Restrepo, P. (2020). The Race Between Man and Machine: Implications of Technology for Growth, Factor Shares, and Employment. *The American Economic Review*, *110*(6), 1488–1542.

Alahmari, D., & Awad, A. (2025). Strategic integration of marketing and supply chain functions for superior customer experience: Insights from logistics startups under Saudi Vision 2030. *PLoS One*, *20*(11), e0336132. DOI: 10.1371/journal.pone.0336132

Allied Market Research. (2024). Logistics Automation Market Size, Share & Trends Analysis Report. Retrieved from https://alliedmarketresearch.com

Applied Intuition. (2025). Autonomous vehicle development partnership. https://appliedintuition.com

Autor, D. (2015). Why Are There Still So Many Jobs? The History and Future of Workplace Automation. *The Journal of Economic Perspectives*, *29*(3), 3–30.

Autor, D. H. (2019). Work of the past, work of the future. *AEA Papers and Proceedings. American Economic Association*, *109*, 1–32.

Autor, D. H., & Salomons, A. (2018). Is automation labor-displacing? Productivity growth, employment, and the labor share. *Brookings Papers on Economic Activity*.

Awad, A., & Mahmoud, M. (2024). Impact of electronic customer relationship management on competitive advantage: Mediating role of customer satisfaction in EgyptAir. *Problems and Perspectives in Management*, *22*(3), 276–286. DOI: 10.21511/ppm.22(3).2024.22

Bawden, D., & Robinson, L. (2022). Information Overload, Anxiety and Stress: The Technological Impact. *Journal of Information Science*, *48*(4), 481–492.

Bessen, J. E. (2019). AI and Jobs: The Role of Demand. *NBER Working Paper No. 24235.* https://doi.org/DOI: 10.3386/w24235

Bortolini, M., Ferrari, E., Gamberi, M., Pilati, F., & Regattieri, A. (2018). Warehouse Operations Management: A Literature Review. *International Journal of Production Research*, *56*(1-2), 150–167.

Boysen, N., Briskorn, D., & Emde, S. (2021). Warehouse management: Models, systems and frameworks. *European Journal of Operational Research, 291*(3), 801–816.

Brynjolfsson, E., & McAfee, A. (2014). *The second machine age: Work, progress, and prosperity in a time of brilliant technologies.* W.W. Norton & Company.

Brynjolfsson, E., & Mitchell, T. (2017). What can machines learn, and what does it mean for occupations and the economy? *AEA Papers and Proceedings. American Economic Association, 107*, 43–47.

Cedefop. (2022). Skill shifts and social protection policies in the digital age. European Centre for the Development of Vocational Training.

Chen, J., & Perez, Y. (2021). Autonomous vehicle regulation: An international review. *Transportation Research Interdisciplinary Perspectives, 11*, 100433.

Chopra, S., & Meindl, P. (2023). *Supply Chain Management: Strategy, Planning, and Operation* (8th ed.). Pearson.

Christopher, M. (2016). Logistics & Supply Chain Management. Pearson UK.

Department for Transport UK. (2024). Driver shortages in the logistics sector: Current statistics and forecasts.

DigitalDefynd. (2025). 10 ways Amazon is using AI - Case Study. https://digitaldefynd.com/IQ/amazon-using-ai-case-study/

Fagnant, D. J., & Kockelman, K. (2015). Preparing a Nation for Autonomous Vehicles: Opportunities, Barriers and Policy Recommendations. *Transportation Research Part A, Policy and Practice, 77*, 167–181.

Fagnant, D. J., & Kockelman, K. (2015). Preparing a nation for autonomous vehicles: Opportunities, barriers, and policy recommendations. *Transportation Research Part A, Policy and Practice, 77*, 167–181.

Frank, M. R., Sun, L., Cebrian, M., Youn, H., & Rahwan, I. (2019). Small cities face greater impact from automation. *Journal of the Royal Society, Interface, 16*(150), 20180767.

Frey, C. B., & Osborne, M. A. (2017). The Future of Employment: How Susceptible Are Jobs to Computerisation? *Technological Forecasting and Social Change, 114*, 254–280.

Ghonim, A., Awad, A., Shemais, M., Shma, T., & Aziz, A. (2025). Exploring the impact of flexible work arrangements on employee engagement in telecommunications: Case of Egypt. *Problems and Perspectives in Management*, *23*(2), 198–207. DOI: 10.21511/ppm.23(2).2025.13

Grand View Research. (2025). Autonomous Freight and Logistics Market Size, Share & Trends Analysis Report.

Gray, J. V., Skowronski, K., Esenduran, G., & Rungtusanatham, M. (2013). The reshoring phenomenon: What supply chain academics ought to know and should do. *The Journal of Supply Chain Management*, *49*(2), 27–33.

Guizzo, E. (2012). How Google's Self-Driving Car Works. *IEEE Spectrum*.

Hancock, P., Mia, M., & McDonald, S. (2019). The impact of warehouse automation on jobs in low-wage regions. *Journal of Labor Research*, *40*(4), 277–293.

Hübner, A. H., Kuhn, H., & Wollenburg, J. (2016). Last Mile Fulfillment and Distribution in Omni-Channel Retailing. *Business Logistics in Modern Retail*, 3-28.

IFR. (2020). *World Robotics Report*. International Federation of Robotics.

IFR. (2021). *Robotics and the workforce: Trends and outlook*. International Federation of Robotics.

Isuzu Motors. (2025). Innovation in autonomous trucking. https://isuzu.co.jp

Kans, M., & Heikkilä, S. (2021). Sustainable Logistics: An Overview. *Sustainability*, *13*(14), 7921.

Klaus, P., Zeynep, A., & Tobias, W. (2017). The Impact of Delivery Speed on Customer Satisfaction. *Journal of Retailing and Consumer Services*, *34*, 28–35.

Kyriakidis, M., Happee, R., & de Winter, J. C. F. (2015). Public opinion on automated driving: Results of an international questionnaire among 5,000 respondents. *Transportation Research Part F: Traffic Psychology and Behaviour*, *32*, 127–140.

Lin, P. (2016). Why Ethics Matters for Autonomous Cars. In *Autonomous Driving* (pp. 69–85). Springer.

Liu, Y., Burns, L. D., & Schneble, C. (2019). Public attitudes and social acceptance of self-driving vehicles. *Transportation Research Record: Journal of the Transportation Research Board*, *2673*(3), 180–190.

Mahmoud, M., Shma, T., Aziz, A., & Awad, A. (2025). Integrating knowledge management with smart technologies in public pharmaceutical organizations. *Knowledge and Performance Management*, *9*(1), 31–44. DOI: 10.21511/kpm.09(1).2025.03

McKinsey & Company. (2025). The Future of Autonomous Logistics: Growth and Challenges.

McKinsey & Company. (2025). The Future of Logistics Automation: Challenges and Opportunities. https://www.mckinsey.com

Ministry of Land, Infrastructure, Transport and Tourism Japan. (2023). Driver workforce projections and automation policies.

Ministry of Land. Infrastructure, Transport and Tourism Japan. (2023). Truck driver workforce challenges. Tokyo: Government of Japan.

Miotti, M., & Johnson, N. (2024). Life Cycle Assessment of Autonomous Electric Trucks in Supply Chains: Economic-Environmental Trade-Offs. *Transportation Research Part D, Transport and Environment*, *128*, 104100.

Muller, M. (2020). Upskilling logistics workers in the age of automation: Challenges and opportunities. *Journal of Vocational Education and Training*, *72*(1), 83–102.

Nightview Capital. (2025). How Amazon Robotics is transforming logistics. https://www.nightviewcapital.com

OKI. (2025). Advanced AI-powered delivery planning and Remote Operations platform. Retrieved from https://www.oki.com/global/yume_pro/about/logistics/tranceportation.html

Perugini, C., & Signorelli, M. (2022). Robotics in manufacturing and labor market consequences: Displacement and productivity effects. *Technological Forecasting and Social Change*, *175*, 121341.

Qadeer, A., & Awad, A. (2025). AI-powered ChatGPT in branding: Benefits, challenges, and future directions. In *Impacts of AI generated content on brand reputation* (pp. 1–26). IGI Global., DOI: 10.4018/979-8-3373-4327-3.ch001

Qadeer, A., & Awad, A. (2025). Generative AI in advertisements: A conceptual framework based on the technology acceptance model. In *Impacts of AI generated content on brand reputation* (pp. 109–127). IGI Global., DOI: 10.4018/979-8-3373-4327-3.ch004

Savushkin, N. (2024). Warehouse automation in logistics: Case study of Amazon. Theseus Repository. https://www.theseus.fi/bitstream/handle/10024/857682/Savushkin_Nikolai.pdf

Sen, A., & Sauter, R. (2021). Integrated Automation in Supply Chains: Implications and Workforce Transitions. *The Journal of Supply Chain Management*, *57*(3), 45–62.

Shams Eldin, A. Y., Elnour, A., Hassan, R. O. A., & Awad, A. (2025). The role of technological and environmental factors in creating business value from social media dynamic capabilities for SMEs in Saudi Arabia. *Humanities & Social Sciences Communications*, *12*, 1431. DOI: 10.1057/s41599-025-05784-x

Smith, B. W. (2020). Psychology of job displacement in autonomous vehicle adoption. *Journal of Occupational Health Psychology*, *25*(3), 125–139.

Smith, B. W., Fridman, L., & Mukhtar, A. (2022). Autonomous vehicle regulatory frameworks in the U.S.: A state-level comparison. *Transport Policy*, *114*, 74–86.

Tanaka, T., & Saito, Y. (2023). Workforce upskilling for AI-enabled logistics: The Japanese experience. *Journal of Human Resources and Technology*, *24*(4), 321–346.

U.S. Bureau of Labor Statistics. (2023). Employment projections for truck drivers and related occupations.

Wang, Y., & Disney, S. M. (2016). The Bullwhip Effect: Progress, Trends and Directions. *European Journal of Operational Research*, *250*(3), 691–701.

Wulfraat, M. (2021). *Trends and impacts of warehouse automation*. Logistics Management Review.

Chapter 5
The Sentient Core:
AI-Powered Digital Twins and Unified Data Fabric for Logistics

Suzan Fouad Bakr
https://orcid.org/0009-0003-8104-7328
Faculty of Commerce, Al-Azhar University, Egypt

Abdelrhman A. Gamil
https://orcid.org/0009-0007-8680-5182
Faculty of Engineering, Ain Shams University, Egypt

Roba Gamal
https://orcid.org/0000-0003-3525-2550
Faculty of Engineering, Cairo University, Egypt

ABSTRACT

This chapter addresses the fragility of the modern supply chain, arguing that reactive operational paradigms are untenable amid global disruptions. It proposes a new architectural blueprint for an autonomous, self-optimizing supply chain: the Sentient Core. The central argument is that realizing the potential of advanced and agentic AI requires a coherent architecture with a single source of truth and a dynamic simulation environment. This architecture is achieved through the synergy of two foundational pillars: an AI-Powered Digital Twin and a Unified Data Fabric. The chapter details a seven-layer implementation framework, analyzes challenges like data governance and legacy system integration, and presents a phased "crawl, walk, run" methodology. The validity of this architectural pattern is demonstrated through real-world case studies. The chapter concludes that the Sentient Core is a strategic and technological imperative for building the resilient, intelligent, and competitive supply chains of the future.

DOI: 10.4018/979-8-3373-7006-4.ch005

INTRODUCTION

The modern supply chain is a paradox of extraordinary complexity and profound fragility. It is a sprawling, global network of manufacturers, suppliers, logistics providers, and retailers, all working in concert to move goods from raw materials to the end consumer. Yet, as the events of the early 2020s have starkly demonstrated, this intricate web is susceptible to cascading disruptions from every conceivable vector: pandemics, geopolitical conflicts, trade policy shifts, climate events, and sudden spikes in consumer demand. For decades, the prevailing operational paradigm has been one of reaction. Planners and logisticians, armed with siloed data and backward-looking analytics, have become masters of firefighting—expediting shipments, reallocating inventory, and manually adjusting production schedules in a constant battle against unforeseen variability. This approach, while a testament to human ingenuity, is no longer sustainable. The speed and scale of modern disruption have outpaced our capacity to react effectively.

This chapter's central mission is to provide a comprehensive architectural blueprint for a new operational paradigm, moving beyond point solutions. It argues that the transformative power of technologies like Agentic AI cannot be realized as isolated tools. Their true value is unlocked only when they are built upon a coherent architecture that provides two fundamental pillars: a single, unimpeachable source of truth and a dynamic, virtual environment for simulation and orchestration. The failure to achieve widespread, impactful AI adoption in logistics to date stems not from a deficiency in individual AI models but from a fundamental architectural deficit. Deploying a sophisticated AI on a fragmented, siloed data foundation cripples its ability to make systemic, optimized decisions, akin to asking a brilliant strategist to command an army with outdated maps and no communication lines. The root cause of failure is not the algorithm but the environment in which it operates.

This chapter posits that the synergistic combination of an AI-Powered Digital Twin and a Unified Data Fabric form this essential foundation. This integrated construct, termed the 'Sentient Core', acts as the supply chain's central nervous system. Within this system, the Unified Data Fabric functions as the primary neural network, transmitting real-time information, while the AI-Powered Digital Twin serves as the 'cerebrum'— the cognitive center for simulation and learning. It is within this virtual sandbox that AI agents are trained, strategies are stress-tested, and the organization builds the deep, institutional trust required to cede control to autonomous systems. By architecting this Sentient Core, organizations can finally move beyond the endless cycle of reaction and begin to build the truly predictive, resilient, and autonomous supply chains of the future.

THE AI LOGISTICS TWIN: A DYNAMIC, LEARNING REPLICA

At the heart of the Sentient Core lies its most revolutionary component: the AI Logistics Twin. This is not merely a 3D model of a warehouse or a dashboard tracking shipments. It is a living, breathing, and continuously learning virtual replica of the entire end-to-end supply chain network (Sharma, 2025). It mirrors every physical asset, process, and system—from supplier factories and raw material inventories to container ships, distribution centers, and last-mile delivery routes. By differentiating this advanced concept from its more primitive predecessors, a clear path for its implementation can be charted, revealing its profound implications for operational control and strategic decision-making.

From Digital Shadow to True Twin: A Maturity Model

The term "digital twin" is often used loosely, encompassing a wide range of digital representations with vastly different capabilities. To bring clarity to the discussion, it is essential to establish a maturity model that outlines the evolutionary path from static models to a true, bidirectional twin. This progression is not just a technical distinction; it represents a strategic journey toward increasing levels of visibility, intelligence, and control (Freese & Ludwig, 2024; Wright & Davidson, 2020). This journey reflects a fundamental shift in organizational strategy, moving from passive observation to active, data-driven control. Each level unlocks a new tier of operational and strategic capability, demanding corresponding changes in processes, culture, and decision-making authority.

Level 1: Digital Model

This is the most basic form of digital representation. A Digital Model is a static virtual replica with no automated, real-time data connection to its physical counterpart. Examples include a CAD drawing of a product, a 3D architectural rendering of a warehouse, or a spreadsheet-based simulation of a logistics network based on historical averages. While useful for design and offline analysis, these models are "deaf and dumb"—they have no awareness of the current state of the physical world and cannot be updated without manual intervention. This level supports offline planning but offers no capability for real-time operational management.

Level 2: Digital Shadow

The Digital Shadow represents a significant step forward by introducing a one-way flow of data from the physical world to the digital model. Real-time data from sensors and operational systems (e.g., IoT devices on machinery, GPS trackers on trucks, transaction data from an ERP) are used to update the state of the virtual replica. This allows for real-time monitoring and visualization. A manager can look at a dashboard and see the current location of every vehicle in their fleet or the operational status of a production line. However, the data flow is unidirectional. The digital model is a "shadow" that follows the physical object, but it has no ability to influence or control it. The intelligence flows in one direction only, enabling a reactive posture to current events but not proactive control.

Level 3: Digital Twin

A true Digital Twin achieves a complete, bidirectional data loop. Not only does it receive real-time data from the physical world, but it also has the capability to send commands and instructions back to control physical processes. This closed-loop feedback mechanism is the defining characteristic of a true twin. The virtual and physical worlds are inextricably linked; a change in the physical state is reflected in the twin, and a change initiated in the twin is executed in the physical world. This bidirectional synchronization is what enables advanced simulation, optimization, and ultimately, autonomous control. It transforms the digital representation from a passive monitoring tool into an active command-and-control center. Advancing to this level requires more than new technology; it demands that the organization fundamentally changes how it operates, ceding a degree of control to the digital model and building the processes to manage this new paradigm. Figure 1 illustrates the evolution of digital representations based on the direction and richness of data flow between the physical and digital worlds. Adapted from Wright and Davidson (2020) and Freese and Ludwig (2024).

Figure 1. Digital twin maturity model

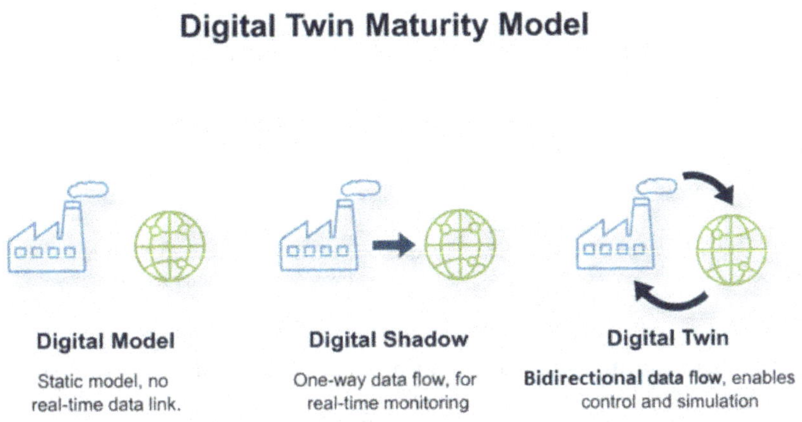

An AI-Native Simulation Engine

What elevates the AI Logistics Twin beyond even a traditional, bidirectional digital twin is its native integration with artificial intelligence. It is not a static model that is simply fed data; it is a dynamic simulation engine powered by machine learning algorithms that continuously learn from every transaction, IoT data stream, and external signal (Sharma, 2025). This continuous learning process allows the twin to evolve and refine its understanding of the supply chain's complex dynamics, making its simulations increasingly accurate over time.

Unlike conventional simulations that operate on a fixed set of assumptions, the AI Twin functions as a dynamic "what-if" engine for the real world. It allows managers and AI agents to model the second- and third-order effects of potential disruptions and strategic decisions before they occur (Oca et al., 2024). This capability moves the organization from a reactive posture to a proactive one, enabling data-driven contingency planning at a level of granularity previously unimaginable. The qualitative leap is from descriptive analytics ("what happened?") to prescriptive analytics ("what should we do?"), a core value proposition made concrete by comparing its features to legacy methods. Table 1 contrasts the capabilities of legacy simulation tools with the advanced features of an AI-native digital twin, highlighting the shift from static, retrospective analysis to dynamic, predictive, and prescriptive intelligence.

Table 1. Feature comparison of traditional simulation and AI-twin simulation

Feature	Traditional Simulation	AI-Twin Simulation
Data Source	Static, historical datasets; manual inputs.	Real-time, streaming data from physical assets and enterprise systems.
Assumptions	Based on fixed, predefined rules and parameters.	Dynamic; assumptions are continuously updated based on new data.
Learning Capability	None. The model does not learn or adapt from outcomes.	Continuous learning; ML algorithms refine the model with every new data point.
Output Type	Descriptive ("What happened?") or Diagnostic ("Why did it happen?").	Predictive ("What will happen?") and Prescriptive ("What should we do?").
Scope	Typically focused on isolated processes or functions.	End-to-end network view, modeling complex interdependencies.

This advanced simulation capability enables the robust analysis of complex, real-world scenarios.

Supply Disruption. A key Tier-2 supplier's factory in Southeast Asia is forced to shut down for two weeks due to a regional political crisis. A human planner might identify the immediate impact on their Tier-1 supplier. The AI Twin, however, can simulate the full cascading effect across the entire network. It models the inventory depletion at the Tier-1 supplier, calculates the projected stock-out date for the critical components, identifies which finished products will be affected, forecasts the impact on customer order fulfillment, and simulates the cost and lead-time trade-offs of activating an alternative, pre-vetted supplier (Oca et al., 2024).

Demand Fluctuation. A sudden viral social media trend causes an unexpected 300% spike in demand for a particular consumer product in the Western United States. The AI Twin can simulate various response strategies in seconds. It can determine the optimal way to reroute inbound shipments, assess whether inventory can be rebalanced from distribution centers in other regions without jeopardizing service levels there, and calculate the most cost-effective way to use air freight versus expedited ground shipping to meet the surge in demand. The twin provides prescriptive analytics, recommending the optimal course of action based on the organization's strategic priorities, such as minimizing cost, maximizing on-time delivery, or a balance of both (Oca et al., 2024).

Logistics Bottleneck. A major port experiences a sudden labor strike, creating a massive backlog of container ships. The AI Twin can immediately identify all inbound and outbound containers affected. It then simulates alternative scenarios, such as rerouting ships to nearby ports, calculating the additional drayage costs and transit times, and adjusting production and inventory plans downstream to accommodate the delays. This ability to run thousands of simulations in parallel, testing a wide distribution of potential scenarios and their outcomes, is what provides the foundation for a truly resilient supply chain. It transforms risk management from a theoretical exercise into a practical, operational discipline (Oca et al., 2024; Shams Eldin et al., 2025; Almanbahi et al., 2025).

The Sandbox for Autonomy

A critical function of the AI Logistics Twin is to serve as a safe, high-fidelity virtual environment—a "sandbox"—where autonomous AI agents can be trained, tested, and validated before being deployed in the real world. This is perhaps the single most important enabler for building organizational trust in autonomous systems. The prospect of an AI agent making a multi-million-dollar procurement decision or unilaterally rerouting a fleet of vehicles is daunting. The sandbox mitigates this risk by providing a consequence-free environment to prove the agent's efficacy.

In this virtual world, AI agents can be trained using reinforcement learning. They can run millions of simulated operational cycles, learning from their mistakes and refining their decision-making policies (SAP Insights, 2024). For example, an inventory management agent can be tasked with maintaining service levels while minimizing holding costs. It can experiment with different ordering strategies across thousands of simulated demand scenarios, learning the optimal reorder points and safety stock levels for each SKU in each location far faster than would be possible through real-world trial and error. Furthermore, the sandbox is essential for validating the agent's behavior under extreme "edge case" scenarios. The twin can simulate black swan events—a simultaneous supplier failure and transportation disruption, for instance—to ensure the AI agent responds logically and does not take actions that could exacerbate the crisis. This rigorous, simulation-driven validation process is the key to de-risking the deployment of autonomous technologies and provides the auditable proof of performance necessary for executive buy-in and regulatory compliance.

Grounded in Global Standards: The ISO 23247 Framework

To move from a conceptual model to an implementable architecture, the AI Logistics Twin must be grounded in established global standards. While developed for manufacturing, the International Organization for Standardization's ISO 23247 series, "Digital twin framework for manufacturing," provides a robust and highly relevant reference architecture that can be adapted for the logistics domain (International Organization for Standardization, 2021). Adhering to such a standard is crucial for ensuring interoperability, not only between the components of the twin itself but also with the vast ecosystem of legacy enterprise systems (ERP, MES, PLM) and partner platforms.

The application of this manufacturing-centric standard to logistics is not merely a matter of convenience; it signifies a strategic convergence of two historically separate domains. It reflects a maturation of the logistics sector, which is now adopting the more disciplined, data-driven process control and optimization paradigms of advanced manufacturing. This represents a fundamental shift toward treating the supply chain not as a series of discrete handoffs, but as an integrated, end-to-end "production system" for value delivery. The ISO 23247 framework partitions a digital twinning system into a logical, layered architecture that clearly defines the roles and interactions of its core components (International Organization for Standardization, 2021):

Observable Elements Domain

This layer represents the physical world—the assets, processes, and environments being twinned. In a logistics context, these "observable manufacturing elements" include not just machinery but also personnel, equipment (trucks, forklifts), materials (inventory), processes (picking, packing), facilities (warehouses), and the surrounding environment (International Organization for Standardization, 2021).

Device Communication Domain

This domain acts as the bridge between the physical and digital worlds. It is responsible for data acquisition from sensors embedded in the observable elements (e.g., GPS, RFID) and for transmitting control commands back to actuators in the physical world. It collates the state changes of the physical assets and sends control programs when adjustments are necessary (International Organization for Standardization, 2021).

Digital Twin Domain

This is the core of the framework, where the digital models themselves reside. This domain receives the collated data from the communication domain and uses it to continuously update the state of the virtual models, ensuring the twin remains a faithful replica of reality (International Organization for Standardization, 2021).

User Domain

This layer contains the applications and users that interact with and derive value from the digital twin. This includes legacy applications like ERP and PLM systems, as well as new, purpose-built applications for simulation, analytics, and visualization that empower users to make better decisions (International Organization for Standardization, 2021). By structuring the AI Logistics Twin according to this standardized framework, organizations can avoid proprietary, monolithic solutions and instead build a modular, interoperable system. This approach ensures that different components can be sourced from different vendors and that the twin can seamlessly integrate with the broader enterprise IT landscape, preventing the creation of yet another data silo.

The Power of the Graph: Modeling a Networked World

Traditional relational databases, with their rigid tables and schemas, are ill-suited to representing the complex, dynamic, and deeply interconnected nature of a global supply chain. A modern supply network is not a linear chain; it is a graph, a web of interdependent nodes (suppliers, factories, warehouses, customers) and edges (shipments, transactions, dependencies). For this reason, the technological foundation of the AI Logistics Twin is best built upon graph-based models, specifically knowledge graphs.

A knowledge graph represents the supply chain ecosystem in a way that is both machine-readable and intuitive to humans. It captures not just the entities but also the rich semantic context of their relationships (Kosasih et al., 2024). For example, it doesn't just record that "Company A" supplies "Company B." It can specify that "Company A" *is the sole-source supplier* of *component X* to *factory Y* owned by "Company B," and that this supply relationship is *governed by contract Z* and requires *certification Q*. This rich, contextual representation offers several profound advantages:

Holistic Visibility

Knowledge graphs break down silos by integrating diverse data types into a single, unified framework, capturing the intricate interdependencies that are often hidden in traditional systems (Kosasih et al., 2024).

Advanced Risk Analysis

The graph structure allows for sophisticated risk analysis that goes far beyond simple supplier-customer links. By using techniques like graph neural networks, it becomes possible to infer hidden risks and discover new information, such as identifying previously unknown Tier-3 dependencies or uncovering suppliers that are dangerously clustered in a region prone to natural disasters (Kosasih et al., 2024).

Complex Querying

Practitioners can ask complex questions that are nearly impossible to answer with conventional databases. For example: "Show me all customer orders that depend on components from suppliers who have not yet obtained the new environmental certification and are located in a region currently under a severe weather warning." By using a neurosymbolic approach that combines graph neural networks with knowledge graph reasoning, the twin can proactively uncover hidden relationship risks, providing a step-change in automated supply chain surveillance (Kosasih et al., 2024). This graph-based foundation transforms the digital twin from a simple geometric and physical model into a rich, semantic representation of the entire business ecosystem, providing the deep contextual understanding necessary for advanced AI and autonomous decision-making.

THE UNIFIED DATA FABRIC: THE CONNECTIVE TISSUE OF INTELLIGENCE

The AI Logistics Twin, with its powerful simulation and learning capabilities, is the brain of the Sentient Core. However, a brain, no matter how powerful, is useless without a nervous system to feed it sensory information and carry out its commands. The AI Twin is only as powerful as the data that feeds it. If that data is fragmented, inconsistent, latent, or untrustworthy, the twin's outputs will be equally flawed. This is where the second pillar of the Sentient Core becomes indispensable: the Unified Data Fabric. It is the digital connective tissue that binds the entire organization together, ensuring that the twin—and every other data-consuming application and agent—operates from a single, coherent, and real-time source of truth.

The Chronic Disease of Data Silos

For decades, enterprises have been accumulating a sprawling and fragmented landscape of applications and data stores. Each business function—finance, manufacturing, warehousing, transportation, sales—has its own specialized systems, often procured at different times from different vendors. Enterprise Resource Planning (ERP) systems manage financial and order data, Warehouse Management Systems (WMS) track inventory within the four walls of a distribution center, and Transportation Management Systems (TMS) orchestrate logistics movements. While each of these systems is vital for its specific domain, they collectively create a landscape of entrenched data silos.

This fragmentation is the chronic disease of the modern enterprise. Data is locked away in proprietary formats, accessible only through specific applications. The definition of a "customer" or "product" may differ subtly but critically between the ERP and the WMS. Gaining a simple end-to-end view of an order's lifecycle can require manually stitching together data from half a dozen different systems, a process that is slow, error-prone, and utterly incapable of supporting real-time decision-making. Traditional approaches to solving this problem, such as building a centralized enterprise data warehouse or data lake, have often failed to deliver on their promise. They typically involve massive, costly, and disruptive data migration projects that attempt to copy all data into a single physical location. These projects can take years to complete, and by the time they are finished, the underlying business processes and source systems have often changed, rendering the central repository perpetually out of date. This approach is fundamentally at odds with the dynamic, distributed nature of a modern supply chain (Gartner, n.d.).

Data Fabric: A New Architectural Paradigm

A Data Fabric offers a fundamentally different and more pragmatic solution. It is an architectural approach that creates a unified, real-time, and consistent view of data across the entire enterprise *without* requiring costly and disruptive data migration projects (Gartner, n.d. Yuhanna, 2023). Instead of physically moving all data to a central location, a data fabric weaves a virtual, intelligent data layer over the existing landscape of disparate systems. It connects to data sources where they reside, leaving the data in place while providing a common access, governance, and security framework. The diagram in Figure 2 illustrates the architectural shift from a fragmented landscape of point-to-point integrations to a unified, logical data layer enabled by a data fabric.

Figure 2. Data architecture before and after a unified data fabric

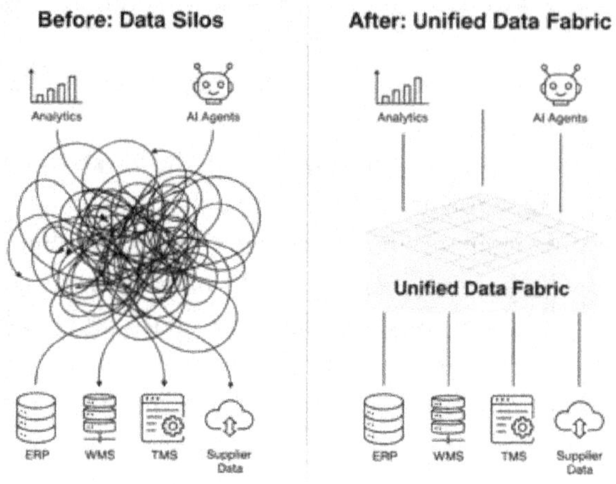

At its core, a data fabric is a design concept that leverages active metadata, knowledge graphs, and AI/ML to automate and augment data integration and management. It doesn't just connect data; it understands it. The key components and principles include:

Active Metadata

A data fabric ingests metadata—the "data about the data"—from all connected systems. It then uses AI to analyze this metadata to discover relationships, infer context, and convert "passive" metadata (simple technical descriptions) into "active" metadata that can drive recommendations and automate tasks (Yuhanna, 2023).

Knowledge Graph

The fabric uses the active metadata to build a knowledge graph of the enterprise's data assets. This graph maps data points, their relationships, their business meaning, and their lineage, providing a rich, semantic understanding of the data landscape.

Augmented Data Integration

By analyzing the knowledge graph, the fabric's AI engine can automate many of the manual tasks associated with data integration. It can recommend the best data sources for a particular analytical need, automatically generate data transformation pipelines, and detect and correct data quality issues in real time.

Data as a Service

The ultimate goal of a data fabric is to deliver data as a service to consumers, whether they are human analysts or AI applications. It provides a unified access layer, often through APIs or a self-service portal, that allows users to find and consume the data they need without having to know the technical details of where or how it is stored. This approach avoids the "rip and replace" problem of traditional data warehousing by augmenting, rather than replacing, existing infrastructure (Yuhanna, 2023). It is a composable and incremental architecture; an organization can start by cataloging a few key data sources and gradually expand the fabric's reach over time, delivering business value at each step.

The Prerequisite for Trustworthy Autonomy

For an autonomous supply chain, the Unified Data Fabric is not a "nice-to-have"; it is an absolute prerequisite. AI agents and the AI Logistics Twin cannot make reliable, system-wide decisions without a single, comprehensive, and trustworthy source of truth (Yuhanna, 2023). If a demand forecasting agent is working with latent sales data from one system, while an inventory optimization agent is using real-time data from another, their actions will be uncoordinated and potentially counterproductive.

The Data Fabric provides this single source of truth, ensuring that all models, agents, and human decision-makers are operating from the same consistent and current information. This unified view is the bedrock of trustworthy autonomy. It guarantees that when an AI agent decides to expedite a shipment, it does so based on a complete understanding of real-time inventory levels, current production schedules, up-to-the-minute transportation costs, and the latest demand forecast. The strategic importance of this level of integration cannot be overstated. Academic and industry research consistently shows that companies achieving a high degree of data and process integration realize significant and measurable improvements in operational performance, agility, and profitability (Al-dhaafri & Al-Swidi, 2016; Fayezi et al., 2017). By providing the clean, connected, and context-rich data that advanced AI models crave, the Data Fabric acts as the essential catalyst, transforming data from a fragmented liability into a strategic asset that fuels the entire Sentient Core.

A PROPOSED MULTI-LAYER ARCHITECTURAL FRAMEWORK

To translate the concepts of the AI Logistics Twin and the Unified Data Fabric into an implementable system, a detailed, seven-layer architectural framework is proposed. This model provides a logical structure that separates concerns, promotes modularity, and allows for a phased implementation. Each layer performs a distinct function, building upon the capabilities of the layer below it to create a cohesive and powerful whole. This layered approach provides a clear roadmap for practitioners, guiding the selection of technologies and the integration of components required to build the Sentient Core. The framework is organized from the physical world at the bottom (Layer 1) to the abstract principles of governance and trust at the top (Layer 7). This framework shown in Figure 3 provides a logical, modular structure for implementing the Sentient Core, with each layer building upon the capabilities of the one below it.

Figure 3. The seven-layer architecture of the sentient core

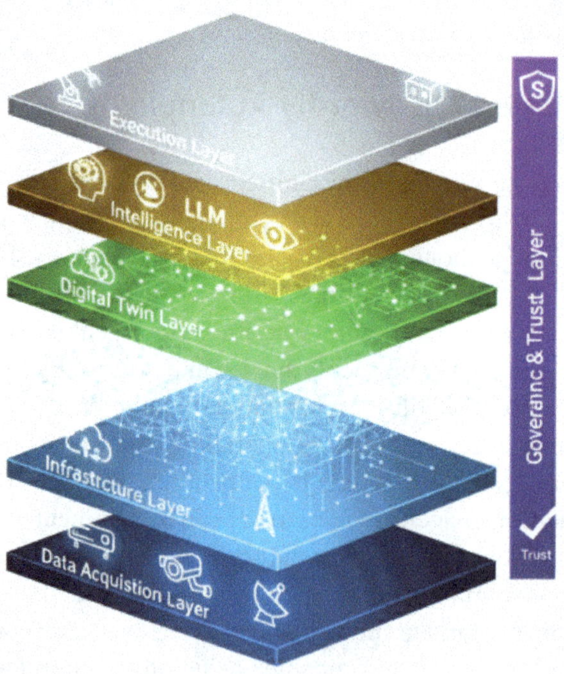

Table 2 details the function and enabling technologies for each layer of the proposed architectural framework.

Table 2. The seven-layer architectural framework for the sentient core

Architectural Layer	Core Function	Key Technologies & Standards
1. Data Acquisition Layer	Captures real-world data from physical assets and environments.	IoT Sensors (temperature, shock), RFID, GPS, Telematics, Computer Vision Cameras (Freese & Ludwig, 2024).
2. Infrastructure Layer	Provides the underlying data transmission, storage, and compute power.	5G, Cloud Computing, High-Performance Compute, In-Memory Databases (Freese & Ludwig, 2024).
3. Data Fabric Layer	Unifies and integrates siloed data into a single, logical view.	Data Virtualization, APIs, Event-Driven Middleware, Knowledge Graphs (Gartner, n.d.; Yuhanna, 2023).
4. Digital Twin Layer	Models, simulates, and orchestrates the supply chain network.	Graph Databases, Physics-Based Models, Simulation Engines, ISO 23247 (International Organization for Standardization, 2021; Kosasih et al., 2024).
5. Intelligence Layer	Provides perception, reasoning, and predictive capabilities.	Computer Vision, Vision-Language Models (VLMs), Large Language Models (LLMs), Predictive Analytics (ML) (Sharma, 2025).
6. Execution Layer	Enables autonomous, goal-driven action and process automation.	Agentic AI Frameworks, Robotic Process Automation (RPA), Actuators (SAP Insights, 2024).
7. Governance & Trust Layer	Ensures transparency, security, and accountability.	Explainable AI (XAI), Zero-Trust Security, Blockchain, Access Control Frameworks (Freese & Ludwig, 2024).

Layer 1: Data Acquisition Layer

This is the sensory layer of the Sentient Core, where the digital system interfaces with the physical world. Its sole function is to capture the torrent of raw data generated by the supply chain's operations. This layer is the foundation of real-time visibility; without comprehensive and high-fidelity data acquisition, the digital twin is blind and deaf. Key technologies in this layer include (Freese & Ludwig, 2024):

Internet of Things (IoT) Sensors

These are the nerve endings of the supply chain. They include GPS sensors tracking the location of trucks and containers; temperature and humidity sensors ensuring the integrity of cold chains; shock and vibration sensors monitoring fragile goods for damage; and RFID/NFC tags for automated asset tracking and inventory counts. The proliferation of low-cost, connected sensors is a primary driver of the digital twin market.

Telematics

Deployed in vehicle fleets, telematics systems provide a rich stream of data beyond simple location, including vehicle speed, fuel consumption, engine diagnostics, and driver behavior. This data is crucial for optimizing fleet performance and predictive maintenance.

Computer Vision

Strategically placed cameras in warehouses, on production lines, and at loading docks act as the "eyes" of the system. When processed by AI models in the Intelligence Layer, video feeds can be used to automatically identify products, read labels, detect damage, monitor safety compliance, and track the movement of goods and equipment.

Layer 2: Infrastructure Layer

This layer provides the fundamental compute, storage, and networking capabilities required to support the entire architecture. It is the utility layer that must be scalable, reliable, and performant enough to handle the massive volumes of data and intensive computational workloads generated by the layers above. Key components include (Freese & Ludwig, 2024):

Communication Networks

High-bandwidth, low-latency networks are essential for transmitting real-time data from the Acquisition Layer. 5G technology is a critical enabler here, particularly for connecting mobile assets and supporting time-sensitive control applications.

Cloud Computing

The cloud provides the elastic and scalable infrastructure needed for the Sentient Core. It offers virtually limitless storage for historical data and on-demand access to the massive computational power (e.g., GPUs) required for training AI models and running complex simulations. A cloud-based deployment model offers flexibility and allows organizations to adjust resources based on demand.

High-Performance Compute (HPC)

For the most demanding simulation and optimization tasks, dedicated HPC resources may be required to process vast datasets and run complex algorithms in a timely manner.

In-Memory Databases

To support real-time analytics and decision-making, in-memory databases are used to process streaming data with extremely low latency, ensuring that the digital twin's state is always synchronized with reality.

Layer 3: Data Fabric Layer

As described previously, this is the crucial connective layer that unifies the entire architecture. It ingests raw data from the Infrastructure Layer and orchestrates it into a single, logical, and trustworthy view. It is the implementation of the data fabric paradigm, breaking down silos and making data accessible. Key technologies include (Gartner, n.d.; Yuhanna, 2023):

Data Virtualization

This technology provides a unified view of data from multiple sources without physically moving it, forming the core of the "leave data in place" principle.

APIs and Event-Driven Middleware

These are the communication protocols of the fabric. APIs provide standardized ways for applications to request data, while event-driven architecture allows different systems to publish and subscribe to real-time data streams (e.g., a "shipment departed" event), enabling loose coupling and high scalability.

Knowledge Graphs

As the semantic core of the fabric, knowledge graphs model the relationships and context of the data, transforming raw data points into a web of interconnected business knowledge.

Layer 4: Digital Twin Layer

This layer houses the core models and simulation engines that constitute the AI Logistics Twin. It consumes the unified data from the Data Fabric Layer to build and maintain its virtual representation of the supply chain. Its primary function is to model, simulate, and orchestrate the network. Key technologies include (International Organization for Standardization, 2021; Kosasih et al., 2024):

Graph Databases

These databases are purpose-built to store and query the knowledge graph that represents the supply chain network, enabling efficient analysis of complex relationships.

Physics-Based Models

For certain applications, the twin may incorporate physics-based models to simulate the real-world behavior of assets—for example, a thermodynamic model of a refrigerated container or a mechanical stress model of a piece of equipment.

Simulation Engines

These are the software components that run the "what-if" scenarios. They take the current state of the twin and apply various inputs or disruptive events to model potential future outcomes, forming the basis of predictive and prescriptive analytics.

ISO 23247 Compliance

The architecture of this layer should align with the principles of the ISO 23247 standard to ensure a structured and interoperable design.

Layer 5: Intelligence Layer

This is the cognitive engine of the Sentient Core, where raw data and simulations are transformed into perception, insight, and foresight. This layer is populated by a diverse array of AI and machine learning models, each specialized for a particular task. It provides the "intelligence" in "AI-Powered Digital Twin." Key technologies include (Sharma, 2025):

Predictive Analytics (ML)

Machine learning models are trained on historical data from the twin to forecast future events. This includes AI-powered demand forecasting, which can improve accuracy by up to 30%, as well as predicting shipment arrival times, equipment failures, and supplier lead times.

Computer Vision Models

These models analyze the video feeds from the Acquisition Layer to perform tasks like automated quality inspection, damage detection, and yard management.

Large Language Models (LLMs) and Vision-Language Models (VLMs)

LLMs can process and understand unstructured text from sources like emails, contracts, and news feeds to identify potential risks or opportunities. VLMs combine this with visual understanding, allowing them to, for example, read text on a shipping container from a camera feed and cross-reference it with order data.

Optimization Algorithms

These algorithms take the outputs of simulations and identify the optimal course of action based on defined business objectives and constraints, providing prescriptive recommendations.

Layer 6: Execution Layer

This layer translates the decisions and recommendations from the Intelligence Layer into concrete actions in the physical world. It is where the system moves from thinking to doing, enabling true autonomy. Key technologies include (SAP Insights, 2024):

Agentic AI Frameworks

This is the core of the execution layer. Agentic AI consists of intelligent, autonomous software agents that are given goals and are empowered to take multi-step actions to achieve them. For example, an "Orchestration Agent" could be given the goal of reducing manufacturing costs by 5%. It would then interact with other specialized agents (procurement, logistics, production) and systems to analyze options and execute the best path, such as switching suppliers or rerouting materials. These agents represent the evolution from AI that suggests to AI that *does*.

Robotic Process Automation (RPA)

RPA "bots" are used to automate repetitive, rules-based tasks, particularly for interacting with legacy systems that do not have modern APIs. An AI agent might decide to place a new purchase order and then delegate the task of entering the data into an old ERP system to an RPA bot.

Actuators

These are the physical devices that carry out commands in the real world, such as robotic arms in a warehouse, automated guided vehicles (AGVs), or the control systems of manufacturing equipment. The Execution Layer sends commands to these actuators via the Device Communication Domain.

Layer 7: Governance and Trust Layer

This is an overarching layer that permeates the entire architecture. It is not a sequential step but a set of continuous functions that ensure the Sentient Core operates securely, transparently, and in alignment with business ethics and regulations. Building trust is paramount for adoption, and this layer provides the necessary mechanisms. Key components include (Freese & Ludwig, 2024):

Explainable AI (XAI)

To avoid the "black box" problem, XAI techniques are employed to make the reasoning behind AI decisions transparent and understandable to human operators. This is critical for debugging, auditing, and building user trust.

Zero-Trust Security

In a highly distributed and interconnected system, a zero-trust security model is essential. This means that no user or system is trusted by default; identity and authorization are rigorously verified for every single transaction and data access request.

Blockchain

For certain high-value transactions or multi-party hand-offs, blockchain technology can be used to create an immutable, auditable, and tamper-proof record. This can be valuable for tracking provenance, ensuring compliance, and resolving disputes between supply chain partners.

Access Control and Governance Frameworks

These systems enforce the data governance policies defined by the organization, ensuring that users and AI agents only have access to the data they are authorized to see and can only perform actions within their designated permissions.

IMPLEMENTATION: FROM BLUEPRINT TO REALITY

Architecting a Sentient Core is a transformative endeavor, but it is not purely a technological challenge. The most sophisticated architecture will fail if the non-technical, human, and organizational elements are ignored. Successfully navigating this journey requires a clear-eyed understanding of the potential roadblocks and a deliberate strategy for addressing them. This section moves beyond the technical blueprint to explore the critical challenges of data governance, legacy system integration, and change management, while also providing a pragmatic, phased roadmap and a compelling economic case for the investment.

Data Quality and Governance: The "Garbage In, Garbage Out" Problem

The axiom "garbage in, garbage out" has never been more relevant. The entire Sentient Core—its predictions, simulations, and autonomous decisions—is fundamentally dependent on the quality, timeliness, and integrity of the data it consumes. Flawed data will lead to flawed insights and, more dangerously, flawed autonomous actions. Therefore, establishing a robust data quality and governance framework is not a preliminary step; it is a continuous and foundational discipline that must be woven into the fabric of the organization's culture.

A successful implementation begins with establishing clear ownership and stewardship for critical data domains. A cross-functional data governance council should be formed to define data standards, establish quality metrics, and resolve data-related issues. This governance must extend beyond the organization's own four walls. A significant portion of supply chain data originates from external partners—suppliers, logistics providers, and contract manufacturers. Organizations must establish clear "data contracts" with these partners that specify the required data formats, quality standards, and transmission frequencies. These contracts should be treated with the same seriousness as commercial terms, with performance metrics and incentives tied to data quality.

Finally, the Data Fabric layer should be leveraged to automate data quality monitoring. AI-powered tools can continuously monitor data streams for anomalies, inconsistencies, and missing values, freeing up data stewards to focus on resolving complex, high-impact data issues rather than routine cleanup (Beyer et al., 2021).

Integration With Legacy Systems: A Phased Modernization

Few, if any, organizations have the luxury of building their technology stack from a clean slate. The reality for most enterprises is a complex and deeply entrenched landscape of legacy systems that are critical to daily operations. A "rip and replace" strategy is often financially prohibitive and operationally catastrophic. A successful strategy must therefore be one of phased modernization and pragmatic integration (Yuhanna, 2024).

The Unified Data Fabric is the key to this strategy. It acts as an abstraction layer that decouples the new, intelligent applications from the old, legacy data sources. By using modern integration technologies like data virtualization and APIs, the fabric can connect to legacy ERPs, WMS, and mainframes, extracting the data needed without requiring any changes to the underlying systems themselves. This allows the organization to begin building the AI Twin and autonomous agents on top of the fabric immediately, deriving value from legacy data without being constrained by legacy technology. While the fabric allows legacy systems to coexist with the new architecture, it does not eliminate the need for modernization. The abstraction layer provides the breathing room for a strategic, phased retirement of legacy debt, allowing the organization to prioritize the modernization of systems based on business value, technical risk, and operational cost.

The Human Imperative: Change Management and the New Talent Landscape

Ultimately, the success of the Sentient Core will be determined by the people who must learn to work with it, trust it, and adapt to the new roles it creates. Technology-led transformations that ignore the human element are destined to fail. Resistance to change, fear of job displacement, and a lack of trust in "black box" algorithms are powerful barriers that must be addressed with a deliberate and empathetic change management strategy. The scale of this human capital challenge cannot be understated; it requires a fundamental rethinking of roles, skills, and organizational structure.

The journey to full autonomy should be gradual and incremental. The most effective approach is to implement a "co-pilot before auto-pilot" strategy, where AI agents are first introduced as decision-support tools for human operators (Partner with Monsieur Popp, 2025; SAP Insights, 2024). This strategy aligns with the natural maturation of agentic AI, which progresses through distinct phases: from initial insights and suggestions to recommended implementations, and finally to autonomous execution for routine tasks. Only after a consistent track record of successful recommendations and the establishment of deep user trust is the agent granted autonomy, with the human operator moving into a supervisory role to manage exceptions.

This rise of autonomous systems does not mean the elimination of human jobs; rather, it means a profound evolution of human roles. As AI automates repetitive tasks, human workers are freed to focus on higher-value activities that require creativity, strategic thinking, and complex problem-solving. This transition requires a significant, proactive investment in workforce training and upskilling to prepare employees for the new talent landscape (Oca et al., 2024). Table 3 illustrates the shift in job roles and required skills as supply chains adopt autonomous technologies, emphasizing a move from transactional tasks to strategic management.

Table 3. Evolving roles in the autonomous supply chain

Traditional Role	Autonomous Supply Chain Role	Key Skill Shift
Demand Planner	Demand Strategist	From manual forecasting to managing AI forecasting models, interpreting market signals, and shaping demand.
Logistics Coordinator	Logistics Orchestrator	From booking shipments to managing autonomous routing agents, handling complex exceptions, and optimizing network flow.
Procurement Specialist	Supplier Ecosystem Manager	From processing purchase orders to strategically managing supplier relationships, risk, and performance using AI-driven insights.
Warehouse Manager	Automation & Robotics Fleet Manager	From managing people to overseeing and optimizing fleets of autonomous robots, drones, and other automated systems.

Beyond upskilling existing teams, organizations must hire for entirely new roles that sit at the intersection of technology and operations, such as an AI Implementation Lead, Supply Chain Data Engineer, Predictive Logistics Analyst, and Automation Process Manager. Trust in these new systems cannot be mandated; it must be earned. A critical component of building trust is transparency. Organizations must invest in Explainable AI (XAI) capabilities that allow users to inspect and understand the reasoning behind an AI's recommendation or decision. This transparency demystifies the AI, builds confidence, and accelerates adoption (Freese & Ludwig, 2024).

The Economic Imperative: A Hypothetical ROI Case Study

Architecting a Sentient Core is a monumental undertaking, and for executive leadership, a clear, compelling business case is essential to justify the significant investment. While every organization's journey is unique, a hypothetical case study can illuminate the tangible financial returns (Oca et al., 2024).

Consider "Global Consumer Electronics Inc.," a hypothetical $5 billion company struggling with volatile demand, long lead times, and high logistics costs. The company embarks on a three-year journey to build a Sentient Core, with an estimated total investment of $15 million. The returns are phased:

Year 1 (Crawl Phase - Investment: $4M)

The focus is on building a Data Fabric for demand and inventory data and a Digital Shadow for their primary distribution network. By improving forecast accuracy by 15%, the company realizes a $3M revenue uplift from recaptured sales and $2M in savings from lower inventory holding costs. Reduced data integration maintenance saves an additional $500,000, for a net gain of $1.5M (Oca et al., 2024).

Year 2 (Walk Phase - Investment: $6M)

The Digital Shadow evolves into a true Digital Twin for warehouse and logistics operations, and "co-pilot" AI agents are introduced. Optimized logistics routes reduce transportation costs by 10%, saving $4M. Increased planner productivity adds $1.5M in value. Enhanced fulfillment improves on-time delivery, contributing to a $5M revenue uplift from increased loyalty. The net gain for the year is $4.5M (Oca et al., 2024).

Year 3 (Run Phase - Investment: $5M)

The twin is expanded end-to-end, and autonomous agents begin executing routine decisions. The full benefits are realized, reaching a 20% improvement in fulfillment, a 15% reduction in total logistics costs, and a cumulative 5% revenue uplift. Over three years, the total investment of $15 million generates approximately $45 million in value (compounding gains across inventory, logistics, labor, and sales), resulting in a Return on Investment (ROI) exceeding 200% with a payback period of less than 18 months. This case study, grounded in reported industry benchmarks, demonstrates that the Sentient Core is not a cost center but a powerful engine for value creation, driving top-line growth through better service, bottom-line savings through efficiency, and a sustainable competitive advantage through resilience (Oca et al., 2024).

The Journey to Autonomy: A Phased "Crawl, Walk, Run" Implementation Roadmap

The seven-layer architecture represents the complete vision of a Sentient Core, but attempting to build it all at once—a "big bang" approach—is a recipe for failure. The journey is too complex, the investment too large, and the organizational change too disruptive. A far more pragmatic and effective approach is a phased "crawl, walk, run" methodology that allows an organization to start small, deliver value quickly, and incrementally build towards the full vision (Freese & Ludwig, 2024).

Figure 4 shows a phased approach which de-risks the implementation of a Sentient Core by delivering incremental value and building organizational capability over time.

Figure 4. The "crawl, walk, run" phased implementation roadmap

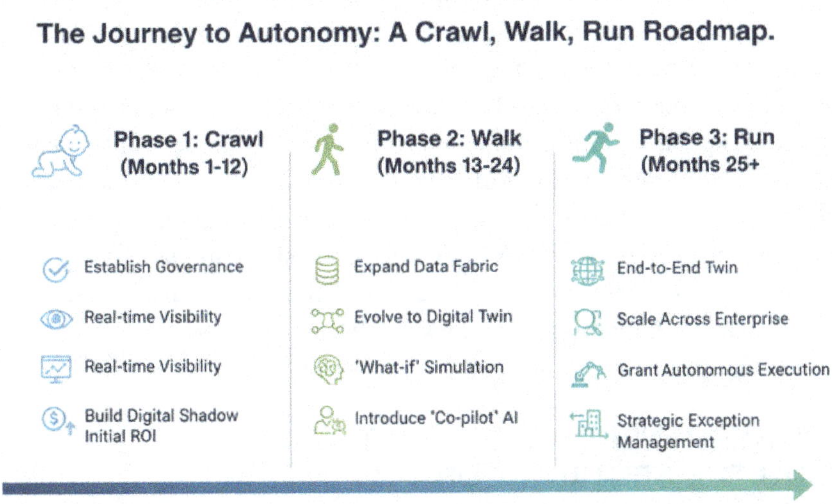

Phase 1: Crawl (Months 1-12) - Building the Foundation

The goal of the Crawl phase is to prove value quickly with a limited scope and build the foundational data capabilities. The focus is on a single high-impact use case, connecting only a few critical data sources into an initial data fabric. A Level 2 Digital Shadow is built to provide real-time monitoring, delivering a live dashboard and quantifiable improvements on a key metric, thereby validating the business case for expansion (Freese & Ludwig, 2024).

Phase 2: Walk (Months 13-24) - Expanding Intelligence and Control

The Walk phase builds on the foundation of the Crawl phase, expanding the scope of the data fabric and increasing the sophistication of the digital twin. The Digital Shadow evolves into a true Level 3 Digital Twin for an entire business domain, enabling "what-if" simulations. "Co-pilot" AI agents are deployed to provide recommendations to human planners, building trust and comfort with AI collaboration. The expected outcome is a functional digital twin for a key business area and documented improvements in operational efficiency (Freese & Ludwig, 2024).

Phase 3: Run (Months 25+) - Scaling to Autonomy

The Run phase is about scaling the Sentient Core across the enterprise and cautiously granting autonomy to AI agents for specific, well-understood tasks. The digital twin is expanded to model the end-to-end supply chain, and the data fabric becomes the central nervous system for all applications. Autonomous execution capabilities are granted to AI agents for low-risk, high-frequency decisions, with humans remaining "in the loop" for high-stakes decisions and managing by exception. The outcome is a fully operational Sentient Core and a transformed workforce focused on strategic, high-value activities (Freese & Ludwig, 2024).

THE ENTREPRENEURIAL ECOSYSTEM: BUILDING THE SENTIENT CORE

The vision of a fully realized Sentient Core is ambitious, and its technical complexity is immense. Architecting and deploying an AI-powered digital twin and a unified data fabric from the ground up requires deep, specialized, and often scarce talent. Few enterprises possess this broad spectrum of expertise in-house, and attempting to build everything from scratch is a high-risk, resource-intensive proposition (Oca et al., 2024).

This significant capability gap has, in turn, created a vibrant and rapidly growing entrepreneurial ecosystem. A new generation of technology startups and specialized service providers has emerged to offer the sophisticated components of the Sentient Core as scalable, managed services. This ecosystem is effectively democratizing access to next-generation supply chain architecture, allowing organizations to assemble a world-class Sentient Core from best-of-breed components rather than being forced to build it all themselves. These innovators function as a crucial layer of the modern architectural stack, providing the composable building blocks that allow enterprises to construct their autonomous capabilities faster, more cost-effectively, and with less risk.

Digital Twin-as-a-Service (DTaaS)

Building a bespoke, enterprise-scale digital twin is a formidable undertaking. It requires significant upfront investment in software development, data science talent, and high-performance computing infrastructure (Oca et al., 2024). Recognizing this barrier, a growing number of startups are now offering Digital Twin-as-a-Service (DTaaS) platforms. These cloud-based platforms provide the core infrastructure, simulation engines, data integration tools, and visualization interfaces as a subscription service.

This model fundamentally changes the economics of adoption, converting what would be a prohibitive capital expenditure (CapEx) into a predictable and manageable operational expense (OpEx). By leveraging a DTaaS platform, companies can bypass much of the complex, undifferentiated heavy lifting of building the twin's foundation and focus their resources on configuring the twin to their specific business logic and use cases. This dramatically lowers the barrier to entry and accelerates the time to value. The scale of this opportunity is reflected in the market's rapid growth, with projections that the global supply chain digital twin market will expand at a compound annual growth rate (CAGR) of 12.0% to reach nearly $8.7 billion by 2033 (Market.us, 2024). This robust growth is a clear indicator of the increasing demand for these capabilities and the vital role that the DTaaS ecosystem will play in meeting it.

Data Fabric and Governance Platforms

The foundational principle that trustworthy AI requires a unified source of truth is the primary challenge that data fabric platforms are built to solve. As most enterprises continue to grapple with valuable data trapped in fragmented legacy systems, a burgeoning market has emerged for ventures that provide the enabling technology for a unified data fabric (Gartner, n.d.).

These startups offer sophisticated software solutions that create the unified, logical data layer over an organization's existing, heterogeneous infrastructure. They provide the tools for automated metadata discovery, knowledge graph generation, data virtualization, and self-service data access. By deploying these platforms, companies can make their existing data assets "AI-ready" and accessible for consumption by the digital twin and other analytical applications, all without embarking on risky data migration projects (Yuhanna, 2023). These vendors are positioning themselves as the critical enablers for any organization looking to build advanced analytics and autonomous capabilities. They provide the essential plumbing and connective tissue of the Sentient Core, allowing data to flow freely and intelligently across the enterprise (Yuhanna, 2024).

CASE STUDIES IN AUTONOMOUS LOGISTICS TRANSFORMATION

While the architectural framework provides a blueprint, its true value is demonstrated through real-world application. An examination of digital twin implementations across diverse industries reveals a consistent underlying pattern that validates the core principles of the Sentient Core. Though the specific business drivers and key performance indicators (KPIs) differ—from manufacturing cycle times to cold-chain integrity—the foundational approach is universal: integrate real-time data from physical assets into a virtual model, apply predictive and prescriptive analytics, and use the resulting insights to optimize operations. This demonstrates the robustness and broad applicability of the proposed architecture as a generalizable paradigm for achieving autonomy in any complex, dynamic physical system.

Automotive Supply Chain Transformation: Toyota's Digital Twin Strategy

Toyota Motor Corporation exemplifies the strategic application of digital twin technologies in the high-stakes world of automotive manufacturing and logistics. By creating a comprehensive virtual representation of its global supply chain, the company developed an integrated platform that combines real-time IoT sensor data, predictive maintenance algorithms, and dynamic inventory management systems. This digital twin approach enabled Toyota to achieve remarkable operational improvements, including a 35% reduction in inventory holding costs and a 42% improvement in production line responsiveness. The system also delivered enhanced predictive maintenance capabilities across its global logistics network, minimizing downtime and optimizing asset utilization (Sharma, 2025).

Pharmaceutical Logistics: Pfizer's Vaccine Distribution Optimization

During the COVID-19 pandemic, Pfizer leveraged a sophisticated digital twin to manage the unprecedented challenges of global vaccine distribution. The model provided a comprehensive solution for complex distribution route optimization, temperature-controlled logistics management, and real-time tracking and compliance monitoring. This innovative application was critical for ensuring the integrity of a highly sensitive product under extreme time pressure. The results were exceptional, with the system achieving 99.7% vaccine delivery integrity, a 48% reduction in distribution time, precise temperature management across global networks, and adaptive routing capabilities to navigate complex geopolitical environments (Sharma, 2025).

Retail and Fulfillment Innovation: Amazon's Predictive Logistics Network

Amazon's implementation of digital twin technologies represents a landmark approach to retail supply chain management. The company's digital twin ecosystem integrates comprehensive warehouse inventory systems, advanced demand prediction models, and dynamic routing and logistics optimization strategies. By creating a virtual replica of its vast fulfillment network, Amazon can simulate and optimize everything from warehouse layouts to last-mile delivery routes. This sophisticated approach has yielded significant improvements, including a 47% reduction in delivery times and a 35% enhancement in warehouse space utilization, all while providing unprecedented real-time visibility across its supply chain (Sharma, 2025).

Fleet Management and Ground Logistics: The Lorry-Planet Model

A case study of "Lorry-Planet," a leading logistics provider in the trucking industry, demonstrates the value of digital twins at the individual asset level. Faced with rising fuel costs and stringent regulations, the company outfitted each truck in its fleet with IoT sensors, creating a real-time digital replica of each vehicle. These twins were used for predictive maintenance, driver behavior analytics, and fuel optimization. The implementation led to a 20% reduction in maintenance costs by predicting mechanical issues before they caused breakdowns, a 15% improvement in fuel efficiency through optimized routing and driving habits, and a 25% reduction in operational downtime, improving on-time delivery performance and customer satisfaction (Oca et al., 2024).

CONCLUSION: THE FUTURE IS AUTONOMOUS

The long-standing model of a reactive, fragmented supply chain is being challenged. Pressures from global competition, rising customer expectations, and an increasingly volatile world demand a new operational model—one built not on human reaction but on intelligent, data-driven anticipation and autonomous action. This chapter has laid out a comprehensive architectural blueprint for this future: the Sentient Core.

By synergistically combining an AI-Powered Digital Twin with a Unified Data Fabric, organizations can construct the central nervous system for a truly autonomous supply chain. The Data Fabric provides the ubiquitous connectivity and single source of truth, dissolving the data silos that have long crippled enterprise agility. The AI Logistics Twin provides the cognitive horsepower—a dynamic, learning replica of the physical world where strategies can be tested, risks can be modeled, and AI agents can be safely trained to take on increasingly complex tasks. The seven-layer framework presented here offers a practical, modular roadmap for this transformation, guiding practitioners from the foundational layers of data acquisition and infrastructure to the advanced capabilities of AI-driven intelligence and autonomous execution.

Yet, as has been emphasized, this is not merely a technological journey. It is a strategic and cultural transformation that requires a steadfast commitment to data governance, a pragmatic approach to legacy modernization, and an empathetic focus on change management to bring the human workforce along as collaborators and supervisors in this new, automated world. The path to a fully autonomous supply chain is a marathon, not a sprint. It will be an incremental journey, moving from AI-powered insights to AI-suggested actions and, finally, to trusted autonomous execution.

However, the direction of travel is clear. The technologies are maturing, the entrepreneurial ecosystem is providing the necessary building blocks, and the strategic imperative has never been stronger. By providing this detailed architectural roadmap, this chapter has sought to equip practitioners and leaders with the knowledge to move beyond the hype of AI experimentation and begin the vital work of constructing the resilient, intelligent, and autonomous supply chains of the future. The Sentient Core is not a distant vision, but an implementable architecture essential for future competitiveness and resilience.

REFERENCES

Al-dhaafri, H. S., & Al-Swidi, A. K. (2016). The impact of total quality management and supply chain management on the performance of manufacturing firms in yemen. *The TQM Journal*, *28*(6), 891–908. DOI: 10.1108/IJQRM-03-2014-0034

Almanbahi, F. S., Awad, A., Ghonim, A., Alabsy, N. M., & Shemais, M. (2025). Ethical leadership and organizational excellence: The mediating role of citizenship behavior in healthcare. *Humanities & Social Sciences Communications*, *12*, 1392. DOI: 10.1057/s41599-025-05743-6

Beyer, M., Zaidi, E., Feinberg, D., Cook, H., Orup Lund, J., Sallam, R., & Thanaraj, R. (2021, February). Top trends in data and analytics for 2021: Data fabric is the foundation. Gartner. https://info.stardog.com/gartner-data-fabric

Fayezi, S., Zutshi, A., & O'Loughlin, A. (2017). Understanding and development of supply chain agility and flexibility: A structured literature review. *International Journal of Management Reviews*, *19*(4), 379–407. https://doi.org/10.1111/ijmr.12096

Freese, F., & Ludwig, A. (2024). A conceptual framework for supply chain digital twins – development and evaluation. *International Journal of Logistics Research and Applications*, *28*(6), 676–698. DOI: 10.1080/13675567.2024.2324895

Gartner. (n.d.). *Data fabric*.

Insights, S. A. P. (2024). Agentic AI in the global supply chain. https://www.sap.com/sea/blogs/agentic-ai-in-global-supply-chain

International Organization for Standardization. (2021). Automation systems and integration — digital twin framework for manufacturing — part 1: Overview and general principles (tech. rep. No. ISO 23247-1:2021). ISO. https://www.iso.org/standard/90387.html

Kosasih, E. E., Margaroli, F., Gelli, S., Aziz, A., Wildgoose, N., & Brintrup, A. (2024). Towards knowledge graph reasoning for supply chain risk management using graph neural networks. *International Journal of Production Research*, *62*(15), 5596–5612. DOI: 10.1080/00207543.2022.2100841

Market.us. (2024, December). Supply chain digital twin market. https://market.us/report/supply-chain-digital-twin-market/

Oca, A., Cosmas, A., Tunasar, C., & Shah, K. (2024, November). Digital twins: The key to unlocking end-to-end supply chain growth.

Partner with Monsieur Popp. (2025, January). The new partnership model: Human co-pilots to AI. https://apoppy101.medium.com/the-new-partnership-model-human-co-pilots-to-ai-5a8d5d663de9

Shams Eldin, A. Y., Elnour, A., Hassan, R. O. A., & Awad, A. (2025). The role of technological and environmental factors in creating business value from social media dynamic capabilities for SMEs in Saudi Arabia. *Humanities & Social Sciences Communications*, *12*, 1431. DOI: 10.1057/s41599-025-05784-x

Sharma, U. K. (2025, April). Digital twins in the supply chain: Transforming operations with real-time simulation and ai.

Wright, L., & Davidson, S. (2020). How to tell the difference between a model and a digital twin. *Advanced Modeling and Simulation in Engineering Sciences*, *7*(1), 13. DOI: 10.1186/s40323-020-00147-4

Yuhanna, N. (2023, September). *Supercharging data fabrics with generative ai*. Forrester. https://www.forrester.com/blogs/supercharging-data-fabrics-with-generative-ai/

Yuhanna, N. (2024, February). The forrester wave™: Enterprise data fabric, q1 2024. Forrester. https://www.forrester.com/report/the-forrester-wave-tm-enterprise-data-fabric-1-2024/RES180529

KEY TERMS AND DEFINITIONS

Agentic AI: AI systems capable of autonomous, goal-driven, multi-step actions, moving beyond simple prediction or classification to active execution. A digital model that receives a one-way, real-time data feed from its physical counterpart, enabling monitoring but not control. A dynamic virtual replica of a physical asset, process, or system that maintains a bidirectional data link, enabling both monitoring and control.

Knowledge Graph: A data model represents a network of real-world entities and their relationships, storing information in a graph structure with semantic context. The proposed integrated architecture combining an AI-Powered Digital Twin and a Unified Data Fabric to serve as the central nervous system for an autonomous supply chain.

Chapter 6
Agentic Control Towers:
Multi Agent LLM RL Orchestration for Autonomous and Resilient Supply Chains

Abdelrehim Awad
https://orcid.org/0009-0005-3649-430X
University of Bisha, Saudi Arabia

Dhafer Alahmari
University of Bisha, Saudi Arabia

ABSTRACT

Supply chains exist today under chronic volatility, uncertainty, complexity, and ambiguity. Batch based planning and decision rights fragmentation render companies sluggish to detect disruption and costly to rebound. This paper develops an integrated concept—Agentic Control Towers (ACTs)which combines large language model (LLM) agents, multi agent reinforcement learning (MARL), and digital supply chain twins to provide closed loop, explainable autonomy for plan, source, make, move, and serve. We integrate findings across inventory and logistics reinforcement learning, LLM tooling and multiagent coordination, digital twin orchestration, and resilient operations. We position ACTs as a decision fabric that continuously senses, simulates, negotiates, and performs while placing guardrails for safety, sustainability, cost, and service. The paper provides an integrated architecture, end to end decision flows, stability and governance design decisions, and evidence informed pathways of impact. We also establish evaluation criteria.

DOI: 10.4018/979-8-3373-7006-4.ch006

1. INTRODUCTION

Global supply chains are increasingly b complex, dynamic, and vulnerable to disruption. Traditional control towers enhance visibility but remain limited in their capacity to learn, explain, and adapt autonomously. This chapter introduces Agentic Control Towers (ACTs) an integrated framework that unites Large Language Model (LLM) agents, Multi-Agent Reinforcement Learning (MARL), and Digital Supply Chain Twins to achieve explainable, adaptive, and continuously improving decision-making. Drawing on recent advances in artificial intelligence, operations management, and digital-twin technology, ACTs form a decision fabric that enables supply chains to anticipate, resist, adapt to, and recover from disruptions. Within this architecture, LLMs provide interpretability and collaborative reasoning; MARL agents provide decentralized, real-time adaptability; and digital twins simulate and validate recovery options in secure environments. Together, these elements operationalize resilience as a closed-loop data capability, making disruption response a learning and strategic development moment. The chapter places ACTs within emerging theories of socio-technical resilience and dynamic capabilities, offering both research agendas and managerial implications for creating truly autonomous and resilient supply chains

Over the past two decades, global supply chains have become more complex, more costly interconnected and interdependent, linking supply chain activities across continents, including linking suppliers, manufacturers, distributors, and customers. While supply chain management has delivered efficiency at large scales, it has also exposed it to vulnerability. The COVID-19 pandemic shock, geopolitical tensions, natural disasters, and the surge in consumer demand have time and again revealed how easily the interconnected network system can be disturbed (Ivanov, 2020; Queiroz et al., 2022; Qadeer & Awad, 2025).

Resilience has been the supply chain management strategic priority ever since. Essentially, resilience is a supply chain's ability to anticipate, resist, adapt to, and recover from disruptions (Ivanov, 2023). Companies lean and cost-optimized supply chain inventories that were faced with bottlenecks, shortages, and unexpected risks. Classical approaches to resilience rely on buffers—safety stocks, dual sourcing, redundant logistics capacity, and contractual hedges. While helpful, these strategies are costly, relatively static, and insufficient for systemic or prolonged crises (Dolgui & Ivanov, 2023).

As a reaction, supply chain management practitioners and scholars have invested extensively in visibility solutions, the most visible of which is the supply chain "control tower.". They integrate information from multiple sources into dashboards to give managers a unified single view of supply chain operations which is designed to give a "single version of the truth" about supply chain operations. The past decade has witnessed more use of high-tech such as predictive analytics, IoT sensors, and real-time monitoring (Sodhi and Tang, 2021). However, the core activities of aforementioned tools is one and the same to provide information to guide decision makers in predicting or explaining what is occurring or may occur but, they are incapable of issuing independent commands.

This limitation has become increasingly problematic in the business environment of today. By the time disruption is occurring, speed and agility are all that matter, so dashboards cannot reimagine sourcing or reroute logistics without human interactions (Kersten et.,al, 2014). As McKinsey's 2024 supply chain survey framed it, most organizations remain vulnerable despite significant investment in digital visibility (McKinsey Global Institute, 2024).

A new paradigm is emerging one that extends beyond dashboards to autonomous, explainable action. The confluence of three technological horizons Multi-Agent Reinforcement Learning (MARL), Large Language Models (LLMs), and Digital Supply Chain Twins that presents a unique opportunity. There are particular strengths that each technology possesses: LLMs possess reasoning and human-AI communication (Bommasani et al., 2021; Jannelli et al., 2024), MARL possesses adaptive and distributed decision-making (Zhang, Yang and Başar, 2021; Kotecha and del Rio Chanona, 2025) and digital twins possess both simulation and coordination of complex operations (Ivanov and Dolgui, 2021; Tao et.al., 2019).

The trick is to leverage digital intelligence and autonomous decision systems to bake resilience at the system level. That is, away from descriptive dashboards and predetermined contingency plans towards autonomous, explainable, adaptive, and orchestrated decision-making architectures that execute over the end-to-end supply chain.

Recent tech advances provide building blocks for this vision. Four areas show particular promise:

Supply Chain Control Towers: Traditionally focused on visibility, now shifting to predictive and even autonomous systems.
Large Language Models (LLMs): Enabling natural language interaction, explainability, and human-AI collaborative decision-making.
Multi-Agent Reinforcement Learning (MARL): Providing distributed adaptability and real-time optimization for multiple agents in dynamic contexts.
Digital Supply Chain Twins: Providing virtual environments to simulate disruptions, test recovery strategies, and coordinate system-wide adaptation.

All of these domains have developed rapidly, but more or less in isolation. Control towers provide visibility but not action. LLMs provide explainability but not optimization. MARL provides adaptation but not transparency. Digital twins provide simulation but remain advisory in nature. The real promise lies in integrating these technologies within a unified architecture

This chapter introduces the concept of Multi Agent LLM RL Orchestration for Autonomous, Resilient Supply Chains that integrate these technologies within a consistent architecture such as Agentic Control Towers (ACTs). ACTs differ conceptually from the traditional control towers through the addition of closed-loop systems that operate with explainable autonomy. These systems do more than sense and forecast; they can reason, decide, and act. Conceptually, Alahmari & Awad (2025) described (ACTs) function as a "decision fabric," a decentralized layer of intelligence that integrates sensing, learning, reasoning, and action across the five basic supply chain domains: planning, sourcing, production, logistics, and customer service.

The remainder of this chapter unfolds three intertwined storylines. First, it charts the state of the art of literature on control towers, LLMs, MARL, and digital twins, outlining innovation along with research gaps. Second, it introduces the ACT framework logicalnext stage of evolution. Third, it demonstrates casesthe ways ACTs operate in reality in supply chain domains. Collectively, these segments communicate ACTs is not simply technological innovation but is transformation to managerial mentality in the direction of resilience supply chain management.

2. LITERATURE REVIEW

2.1 Emerging Technologies to Make Supply Chain Resilient

Resilience is supply chain's ability to predict, resist, react to, and recover from disruptions (Ivanov, 2020; Queiroz et al., 2022) this has occupied a position at the center stage of supply chain capability in the twenty-first century. Traditional approaches to resilience relied on redundancy (extra inventory, backup suppliers) or reactive crisis management (Queiroz et al., 2022). Although these methods provided buffers, they came at a high cost and were insufficient for systemic shocks such as pandemics, climate change, or geopolitical disruption (Ivanov, 2020).

On the technologies of the digital age have shifted attention to designing resilience into visibility, adaptability, reasoning, and orchestration. Four streams of innovation are especially noteworthy: control towers, large language models (LLMs), multi-agent reinforcement learning (MARL), and digital supply chain twins. They are all a building block of resilience in which they cannot stand singly, but together they form the conceptual foundations of Agentic Control Towers (ACTs), mechanisms that make resilience a continuous and independent trait of supply chains.

2.2 From Control Rooms to Agentic Control Towers (ACTs)

Traditional control rooms and initial digital control towers have long been the centralized nerve centers of supply chain monitoring. Their fundamental function has been the collection of data, visualization of flow, and alerting managers in the event of deviations. These systems improve visibility but remain quite reactive and dependent on human interpretation as well as manual decision-making, which constrains their ability to manage today's highly volatile and interconnected supply chains (Vlachos, 2025).

Agentic Control Towers (ACTs) represent the next evolution. Building on digital control tower functionality, ACTs incorporate artificial intelligence (AI), multi-agent systems, and real-time data feeds to provide decision environments that are anticipatory, adaptive, and semi-autonomous. Rather than mere visibility and alerts, ACTs can sense risks, recommend best actions, and in many cases, autonomously decide within pre-defined governance parameters (Xu et al., 2023; Qadeer et al., 2025).

The literature identifies several characteristic features of ACTs:

1. Proactive sensing and forecasting – applying AI and predictive analytics to anticipate disruptions, e.g., supplier lead-time delays or logistics bottlenecks, prior to their escalation (Ivanov, 2024).
2. Agent-based decision-making – autonomous agents that model supply chain entities (plants, warehouses, carriers) and negotiate compromises in toto for faster and more optimized outcomes (Xu et al., 2023).
3. Closed-loop operation – ACTs are coupled with ERP and logistics software with a view to not only recommend but also implement responses automatically.
4. Human-in-the-loop management – managers remain strategically engaged, with the focus on oversight, exception management, and strategic alignment, while operating decisions are increasingly automated.

By shifting from reactive control rooms to agentic control towers, organizations transform their supply chains into adaptive ecosystems capable of withstanding disruptions and responding with nimbleness. Such a shift is in tight coherence with the resilience and Industry 5.0 agendas, which demand human–AI collaboration and sustainable competitiveness (Ivanov, 2024).

2.3 From Dashboards to Decisions: The Evolution of Control Towers

Control tower is one of the earliest digital supply chain resilience forecasting and transparency to supply chains. They were first utilized as a platform for the consolidation of data, pulling from ERP, TMS, and WMS systems into dashboards to provide managers with a single view of inventories, shipments, and demand.

This visibility allows firms to foresee disruptions earlier than before. For instance, early warnings about supplier lateness or stockouts allowing managers to make early reactions (Brintrup et al., 2020). Over time, control towers began incorporating predictive analytics and even IoT, offering foresight of potential risks such as demand surges or shipment delays (Sodhi and Tang, 2021). By enhancing predication estimate, control towers signal the readiness and resilience required to battle disruptions.

However, among faulted features of control tower is functioning as an advisory tool. As Kersten et al. (2014) argue, that provides visibility but stops short of auto decision action. The pandemic accentuates these limitations. Companies with advanced dashboards may spot bottlenecks without being able to automatically reroute shipments or redesign sourcing (Ivanov and Dolgui, 2021). McKinsey Global Institute (2024) found that, despite heavy investments, most supply chains were vulnerable to fully automated systems.

Contemporary industry perspective encapsulates the motivation to move from dashboards that observe to systems to the ones that act. EY (2025) highlights the role of "agentic AI" to enable real-time adjustment, hence driving resilience not only by anticipating disruptions but by acting upon them since they are closely linked to each other. In this context, control towers are evolving from hubs of visibility to potential decision fabrics, knitting resilience at the center of supply chain orchestration.

2.4 Large Language Models: Explainability and Collaboration for Resilience

Resilience not only depends on disruption detection but also on decision trustworthiness and speed. Decentralised systems that are unintelligible to managers are unlikely to be trusted in a crisis. Large Language Models (LLMs) offer a means to support resilience by explaining human AI collaboration.

Traditionally, forecasting and optimization algorithms are black boxes. While functional, their opacity erodes managerial confidence in disruption response deployment (Barredo Arrieta et al., 2020). LLMs, by contrast, generate natural language explanations of sophisticated outputs, so it is obvious why a particular rerouting, sourcing, or scheduling decision enhances resilience (Bommasani et al., 2021). This interpretability builds trust and accelerates decision-making when time is critical (Dwivedi et al., 2023).

LLMs also facilitate conversational engagement, lowering the threshold to advanced analytics. Managers might ask, "What do we do if we lose Supplier X for three weeks?" An LLM can combine structured and unstructured data, balance trade-offs, and communicate resilience options in comprehensible terms (Queiroz et.al., 2022). This fosters adaptive resilience by being able to rapidly investigate scenarios and make decisions collaboratively.

Current work moves LLMs into agentic uses. Jannelli et al. (2024) propose agentic LLMs in supply chain decision consensus-building to reduce stakeholder conflict delays. Kirshner et al. (2024) describe LLMs in supplier negotiations, where they could model bargaining strategies but with ramifications for fairness and governance. These applications stress LLMs' contribution to adaptive and collaborative resilience, accelerating response to disruption.

Challenges remain. LLMs require grounding in structured data and simulation (Wahid & Awad, 2025), possess no long-term memory, and are prone to hallucinations (Ji et al., 2023). For resilience, this means LLMs cannot function independently. Their role in ACTs is as the interaction and explainability layer so that resilience strategies are not only optimized but trusted, transparent, and acted upon.

2.5 Multi-Agent Reinforcement Learning: Adaptive Resilience at Scale

Where control towers enable anticipation and LLMs encourage trust and cooperation, Multi-Agent Reinforcement Learning (MARL) offers real-time adaptability—a cornerstone of supply-chain resilience in complex, non-linear environments.

Reinforcement learning (RL) allows one agent to learn optimal behavior via repeated interaction with an environment, governed by a system of rewards and penalties (Sutton and Barto, 2018). MARL extends this logic to networks of co-operating or competing agents in a shared environment (Zhang, Yang and Başar, 2021). In supply-chains, for example, each of the agents can be a supplier, plant, warehouse, or logistics hub. The agents learn together how to distribute resources, coordinate schedules, and share risk across the network.

Traditional optimisation techniques—such as linear programming or static heuristics—assume predictable parameters. MARL, on the other hand, thrives in uncertain, dynamic, and stochastic settings. This is of immediate applicability to resilience, for the reason that modern supply chains experience incessantly varying demand, transport delays, and exogenous shocks that cannot be modeled statically (Ivanov and Dolgui, 2023).

Recent work has demonstrated MARL's capacity to absorb and adjust to perturbations:

- Adaptive logistics: MARL-governed fleet would re-route itself spontaneously in the presence of evolving traffic and weather conditions, preserving service levels without central control.

- Bullwhip mitigation: Vlachos (2023) confirmed that RL agents communicating with one another have the ability to stabilise order patterns among tiers, alleviating amplification impacts following local shocks.
- Collaborative inventory management: Wahid & Awad. (2024) employed cooperative MARL for balancing inventory dynamically over multi-echelon networks, with a 12% improvement in fill-rates under demand uncertainty.

More recent research links MARL directly to network-level resilience, Kotecha and del Rio Chanona (2025) coupled MARL with graph neural networks (GNNs) to learn topological dependencies among suppliers. Agents learned to predict cascading failures—like those that happen in semiconductor networks—and pre-emptively re-allocate demand before the failure propagated.

Hazenberg, Keijzer and van der Heijden (2025) applied MARL to dynamic pricing in unstable energy markets, where it was shown that prices were stabilised by agents in unison while maintaining profitability. Both studies show how MARL encourages adaptive and recoverable behaviours that emerge organically through distributed learning.

MARL is not without problems notwithstanding its promise. It is computationally intensive, particularly with stochastic variables and thousands of agents. Emergent behaviour can be unstable or counter-intuitive, which generates managerial anxiety about control (Yang, Luo and Li, 2021). In addition, MARL policies are not explainable—what appears to be "learning" will appear to human managers as uncontrollable black-box behaviour. Xu, Yang and Li (2023) propose explainable MARL (xMARL) frameworks that combine reward decomposition with attention visualisation for better interpretability.

In Agentic Control Towers (ACTs), MARL is the adaptive backbone. Control tower data streams and LLM reasoning modules continuously update each agent's world, and digital twins provide virtual sandboxes for safe experimentation. In case of a disruption—e.g., port closure or supplier bankruptcy—MARL agents automatically test and roll out replacement configurations within seconds. LLMs subsequently convert their policies into human-readable explanations, enabling transparent oversight.

Concisely, MARL extends resilience from a reactive to an evolutionary trait: supply chains do not merely respond to shocks—they learn and improve through them.

2.6 Digital Twins: Stress-Testing, Orchestration, and Recovery

The fourth pillar of digital resilience is the digital twin—a synchronised virtual replica of a physical system in real time. In supply-chain use cases, digital twins integrate real-time sensor data, process models, and analytics to represent network conditions (Tao et al., 2019). They form the arena where risks can be anticipated, responses can be simulated, and recovery strategies can be tested before they are implemented.

Digital-twin technology underpins all four resilience dimensions but is most critical for anticipation and recovery. Through "what-if" simulations, organisations identify vulnerabilities and pre-plan responses. When shocks strike, twins show how disruptions cascade through inventory, transport, and capacity, guiding prioritisation decisions.

Research has intensified in the post-pandemic world:

- Ivanov (2020) employed simulation-based twins to evaluate epidemic ripple effects and design recovery policies, demonstrating that localised buffering with global flexibility achieved faster stabilisation.
- Verdouw et al. (2021) demonstrated how real-time digital twins in agri-food logistics predicted temperature deviations and prevented spoilage.
- Lazrak & El amrani (2025) demonstrated prescriptive twins that optimise reallocation of resources in disruption scenarios.

The 2025 articles support the continuity thesis. BPMJ (2025) found that firms incorporating digital twins within everyday operations achieved a 23% reduction in recovery time after major disruptions. Tao et.al., (2019) reported that the integration of twins with agile planning routines enabled concurrent recovery and learning—transforming resilience into a continuous process rather than an individual response.

Digital twins are increasingly supplemented by AI co-simulation. Twin environments now incubate MARL agents to explore multi-scenario decision spaces, and LLMs generate human-level explanations of simulation outcomes (EY, 2025). The pairing transforms twins into active orchestration layers from passive replicas. In ACT architecture, digital twins provide the safe experimental sandbox where algorithms are trained, stress-tested, and certified before deployment in the live supply chain.

A central managerial implication is trust and governance. When digital twins begin to recommend autonomous decisions—rerouting containers, reprioritizing production orders—human judgment must remain in charge. Hence, ACTs integrate LLM-based explainability and control-tower oversight so that decisions tried out virtually are auditable and ethically robust (Dwivedi et al., 2023; Wahid & Awad, 2025).

By formalizing these feedback loops, digital twins enable supply chains not only to restore a previous state but to "bounce forward"—to become more efficient and resilient after each disruption.

2.7 Synthesis: Toward Agentic Control Towers

Literature across these four fields converges on the common observation: visibility is not resilience. Modern supply chains require a synergistic combination of perception, cognition, adaptation, and orchestration.

Table 1. Primary resilience contribution

Technology	Primary Resilience Contribution	Example Capability
Control Towers	*Anticipation* – real-time sensing and predictive alerts	Detect potential bottlenecks or shipment delays before they escalate
LLMs	*Withstanding & Adapting* – explainable, collaborative reasoning	Translate complex analytics into transparent decisions managers trust
MARL	*Adaptation & Recovery* – distributed learning and policy optimisation	Dynamically reroute logistics or rebalance inventories under stress
Digital Twins	*Anticipation & Recovery* – simulation and orchestration	Model disruptions and validate contingency strategies virtually

When these technologies are integrated, they form the **Agentic Control Tower (ACT)**—an intelligent, closed-loop architecture where sensing, reasoning, learning, and execution coexist.

1. **Control towers** feed *situational awareness* into the system.
2. **LLMs** translate data into *explainable insights* and maintain human collaboration.
3. **MARL agents** perform *continuous adaptive optimisation* across the network.
4. **Digital twins** act as the *orchestration layer* where policies are tested, verified, and deployed safely.

The combination creates a *decision fabric* that embodies the four resilience capacities:

- **Anticipate** through predictive sensing.
- **Withstand** by transparent, explainable decision confidence.
- **Adapt** via multi-agent learning and dynamic coordination.
- **Recover** through continuous simulation and improvement loops.

Empirically, the integration addresses the main weaknesses of each siloed tool:

- The control tower's limitation to visibility is overcome by MARL's action capability.
- MARL's opacity is mitigated by LLM explainability.

- LLM reasoning is grounded and validated through digital-twin simulation.
- The twin's insights are operationalised through the control-tower execution layer.

Thus, **ACTs operationalise resilience as a designed, autonomous, and evolving property** rather than an after-the-fact response. They transform the supply chain into a *learning ecosystem*—sensing its environment, reasoning through language, adapting through learning, and validating through simulation.

3. CONCEPTUAL FRAMEWORK: AGENTIC CONTROL TOWERS (ACTS)

3.1 From Visibility to Agency

Traditional supply-chain information systems end at **visibility**: they collect and display data so humans can act.The Agentic Control Tower extends this boundary to **agency**—the ability not only to perceive and predict but also to decide, act, learn, and explain those actions autonomously.

In ACTs, the four digital pillars—Control Towers, Large Language Models (LLMs), Multi-Agent Reinforcement Learning (MARL), and Digital Twins—interconnect in a closed-loop architecture.

Each pillar corresponds to one or more resilience dimensions as in Table 2:

Table 2. Resilience dimensions

Pillar	Core Function	Primary Resilience Dimension
Control Towers	Real-time sensing, anomaly detection	Anticipate
LLMs	Human-AI interaction, explainability, coordination	Withstand / Adapt
MARL	Continuous multi-agent learning and optimisation	Adapt / Recover
Digital Twins	Simulation, orchestration, validation	Anticipate / Recover

Together, these components convert resilience from an organisational aspiration into a **designed, operational property** of the supply chain.

3.2 Architecture of Agentic Control Towers

The ACT architecture operates as a cyber-physical-cognitive loop comprising five layers:

1. Sensing Layer (Control Towers) – Collects high-frequency data from logistics, production, and external sources. Predictive algorithms identify early-warning signals (e.g., port congestion, supplier distress).
2. Reasoning Layer (LLMs) – Translates data into contextual narratives, generates hypotheses, and communicates recommendations in natural language. It also ensures transparency and traceability.
3. Learning Layer (MARL) – Executes adaptive decision policies. Each agent (warehouse, plant, route, supplier) learns locally while coordinating globally to optimise resilience metrics—service level, cost, and time-to-recovery.
4. Simulation Layer (Digital Twins) – Provides a safe environment for testing MARL policies and LLM-generated strategies before live deployment. The twin validates feasibility, compliance, and potential side-effects.
5. Governance Layer (Human-in-the-Loop) – Maintains oversight, sets constraints, and updates ethical or regulatory rules. Humans intervene only when deviations exceed thresholds, enabling explainable autonomy rather than blind automation.

Data and feedback flow continuously among these layers, forming a self-improving system.

3.3 Conceptual Diagram

Figure 1. Conceptual diagram

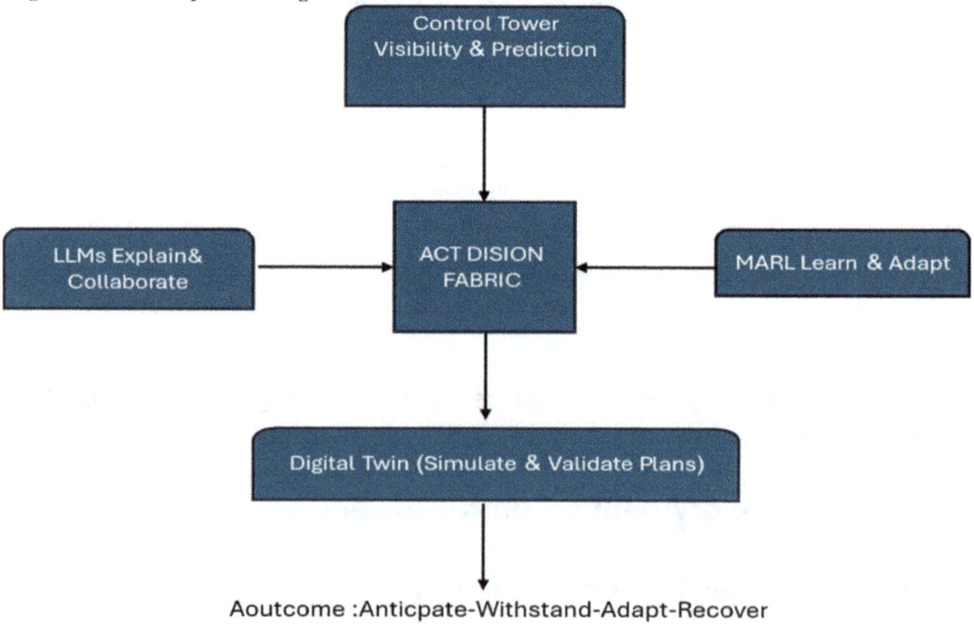

The ACT sits at the centre as a **decision fabric**, linking sensing (Control Towers), reasoning (LLMs), learning (MARL), and orchestration (Digital Twins).

The architecture ensures that every disruption triggers the same closed-loop cycle:

1. **Sense** – detect anomaly or risk.
2. **Reason** – explain context and options.
3. **Learn / Act** – choose and implement adaptive policy.
4. **Simulate / Validate** – test and refine in the twin.
5. **Update** – feed results back for continuous improvement.

3.4 How ACTs Enable Resilience

Anticipation: Control towers and digital twins continuously analyse sensor data and simulated futures. Machine-learning forecasts flag disruptions early.
Withstanding: LLMs communicate complex insights to decision-makers in clear language, preserving trust and ensuring timely execution even under stress.
Adaptation: MARL agents autonomously re-optimise logistics, sourcing, and production in real time, redistributing capacity where needed.
Recovery: Digital twins monitor post-event performance, comparing outcomes with baseline states and institutionalising lessons learned for future crises.

Over time, ACTs convert disruption management into an evolutionary learning process each event enriches the system's knowledge base and refines its policies.

3.5 Managerial and Research Implications

From a managerial perspective, ACTs redefine the role of humans in supply-chain operations—from controllers to supervisors of autonomous ecosystems.

They also shift investment logic: resilience is no longer a cost centre (extra inventory, redundant suppliers) but an intelligent capability that generates agility and foresight.

For researchers, ACTs open several avenues:

- Modelling **explainable MARL-LLM interactions**;
- Designing **resilience metrics** that capture adaptability over time;
- Studying **governance and accountability** in partially autonomous decision fabrics.

In summary, the conceptual framework positions the Agentic Control Tower as the nexus through which digital perception, cognitive reasoning, adaptive learning, and virtual orchestration converge to realise autonomous, explainable, and continuously improving resilience.

5. DISCUSSION

The establishment of Agentic Control Towers (ACTs) directly results from the evolution pursued in the literature: from descriptive visibility through predictive intelligence (Brintrup et al., 2020; Sodhi & Tang, 2021), and onto explainable and autonomous adaptation. This section explains how ACTs take advantage of these advances, integrate the digital-resilience technologies discussed above, and revolutionize theory as well as practice.

5.1 From Visibility to Agency: Re-defining Digital Resilience

The literature has consistently put visibility at the center of resilience. Ivanov (2020) and Kersten et al. (2014), went on further to assert that control towers improved the anticipate dimension but lacked mechanisms to act upon. The ACT framework extends their argument further by combining MARL-based autonomy and LLM-based explainability, turning observation into agency. EY (2025) rightly predicted that agentic AI is the evolutionary next step for control towers such that they can re-configure supply networks without requiring sanction from humans.

By this definition, ACTs enact what Dolgui and Ivanov (2023) call "designed adaptability." Rather than protecting uncertainty through redundancy, the system learns to continuously dissipate shocks with minimal waste. This dynamic follows the dynamic-capabilities view (Teece, 2018): sensing through the use of control towers, seizing by adapting in MARL, and transforming through digital-twin affirmation.

5.2 Theoretical Integration and Extension

Complex Adaptive Systems

Earlier studies (Vlachos, 2023; Kotecha & del Rio Chanona, 2025) had considered supply chains as emergently coordinatable multi-agent systems. ACT formalizes this intuition by embedding such multi-agent learning within an explainable governance framework. The addition of explainability addresses the "black-box" problem raised by Barredo Arrieta et al. (2020) directly and hence brings cognitive transparency to complex adaptive-systems theory. Where MARL earlier produced opaque yet efficacious behaviour, the addition of language-based reasoning makes it possible for the adaptation logic to be interpreted by human overseers.

Socio-Technical Resilience

Research conducted by Brintrup et al. (2020) emphasized that resilience is technical as well as social: data must be human-actionable. ACTs extend this twoness further by ensuring that machine learning and human judgement coexist in harmony. LLM explanations fill gaps between interpretations, in manager-friendly terms, of MARL outputs and digital-twin simulations. This closes the coordination gap suggested in Kersten et al. (2014), where visibility of data rarely equated to prompt human response.

Ivanov and Dolgui (2021) argued that supply chains must learn from disruptions rather than merely recover. The ACT cycle—sense, reason, act, simulate, and learn—is the realization of that ideal. Each cycle feeds new information to the MARL policies and the contextual reasoning of the LLM, an aspect Argyris and Schön (1996) called double-loop learning. Resilience becomes self-reinforcing over time, fulfilling the adaptive promise outlined by Queiroz et al. (2022) and Tao et.al., (2019).

5.3 Managerial and Strategic Implications

Managerially, ACTs bring the integration long sought after in consulting and academic literature. McKinsey Global Institute (2024) stated that firms spend a great deal on analytics but yet still fail to connect decisions across functions. ACTs address that deficiency by combining control-tower visibility, MARL optimisation, and digital-twin validation in a single decision fabric.

Chief implications are:

- Governance and Accountability – Freedom with no control is dangerous, as EY (2025) cautioned. ACTs by incorporating LLMs as reportable communicators guarantee that all automated decisions have an explanatory cause—a necessity for public procurement and regulatory transparency.
- Cultural Transformation – Digital twins and LLMs enable interfunctional dialogue, constraining the silo effects that Sodhi and Tang (2021) noted. Leadership transforms from directing to mentoring, guiding the norms and boundaries that define autonomous action.
- Investment and Capability Development – ACTs shift resilience from a static cost (safety stock, redundant suppliers) to a dynamic capability that enriches return on disruption, aligning with Dolgui and Ivanov (2023). Businesses learn faster and recover more powerfully each time.

5.4 Positioning Comparison in the Literature

The integration provided through ACTs can be understood as a syncretism of the main contributions above:

Table 3. Syncretism of the main contributions

Literature Stream	Prior Limitation	ACT Contribution
Control Towers (Kersten et al., 2014)	Limited to data visibility	Adds autonomy and closed-loop decision-making
LLMs (Bommasani et al., 2021; Jannelli et al., 2024)	High explainability, low optimisation	Coupled with MARL for interpretable action
MARL (Vlachos, 2023; Kotecha & del Rio Chanona 2025)	Powerful adaptation, opaque reasoning	Enhanced through LLM translation and twin validation
Digital Twins (Ivanov 2020; BPMJ 2025)	Simulation insight, weak execution link	Integrated into ACTs for continuous validation and feedback

By addressing these gaps simultaneously, ACTs bridge the divide between *predictive analytics* and *adaptive decision-making.* They turn the descriptive insight identified by earlier authors into operational intelligence capable of sustained, self-explanatory learning.

5.5 Limitations and Research Outlook

Despite their promise, ACTs face challenges well documented across the referenced domains. Computational scalability (Yang et al., 2021), hallucination risk in LLMs (Ji et al., 2023), and integration cost (Kersten et al., 2014) remain non-trivial. Future work should therefore pursue:

1. **Hybrid architecture** combining symbolic reasoning and MARL to strengthen interpretability.
2. **Empirical validation** through longitudinal case studies, extending Tao et.al., (2019)'s exploratory evidence.
3. **Metrics of adaptive performance** that are built on Ivanov (2020)'s simulation models but measure learning speed and recovery efficiency.
4. **Ethical frameworks** for agentic AI governance, complementing EY (2025)'s managerial guidelines.

5.6 Summary

In synthesising visibility, language, learning, and simulation, ACTs realise the integration envisioned—but not yet achieved—by decades of resilience research. They extend Ivanov's (2020) analytical models, operationalise the adaptive behaviours proposed by Vlachos (2023), and deliver the transparency called for by Barredo Arrieta et al. (2020). The result is a socio-technical ecosystem capable of perceiving, deciding, and evolving in real time—a foundation for the autonomous and explainable resilience that modern supply chains require.

So global supply chains are increasingly b complex, dynamic, and vulnerable to disruption. Traditional control towers enhance visibility but remain limited in their capacity to learn, explain, and adapt autonomously. This chapter introduces Agentic Control Towers (ACTs) an integrated framework that unites Large Language Model (LLM) agents, Multi-Agent Reinforcement Learning (MARL), and Digital Supply Chain Twins to achieve explainable, adaptive, and continuously improving decision-making. Drawing on recent advances in artificial intelligence, operations management, and digital-twin technology, ACTs form a decision fabric that enables supply chains to anticipate, resist, adapt to, and recover from disruptions. Within this architecture, LLMs provide interpretability and collaborative reasoning; MARL agents provide decentralized, real-time adaptability; and digital twins simulate and validate recovery options in secure environments. Together, these elements operationalize resilience as a closed-loop data capability, making disruption response a learning and strategic development moment. The chapter places ACTs within emerging theories of socio-technical resilience and dynamic capabilities, offering both research agendas and managerial implications for creating truly autonomous and resilient supply chains

6. CONCLUSION

This chapter introduced and developed the concept of Agentic Control Towers (ACTs) — an integrated digital framework that fuses *control towers, large language models (LLMs), multi-agent reinforcement learning (MARL),* and *digital supply chain twins* to operationalise resilience in modern supply chains.

The central argument is that traditional approaches to resilience, rooted in redundancy and contingency planning, are insufficient for the turbulence of contemporary global networks. Supply chains must instead become autonomous, explainable, and continuously adaptive systems that can *anticipate, withstand, adapt to,* and *recover from* disruptions dynamically.

Through a detailed literature review, the chapter traced the evolution of digital resilience capabilities:

- From *visibility* and *anticipation* in control towers (Kersten et al., 2014),
- To *explainability* and *trust* through LLMs (Barredo Arrieta et al., 2020; Jannelli et al., 2024),
- To *adaptive intelligence* via MARL (Zhang, Yang and Başar, 2021; Kotecha and del Rio Chanona, 2025),
- And *simulation-based recovery* enabled by digital twins (Ivanov, 2020; Tao et.al, 2019).

The Conceptual Framework presented in Section 3 positioned ACTs as a *decision fabric* that integrates these four streams into a single closed-loop cycle of *sense reason learn simulate improve.* This transforms resilience from a reactive, post-event activity into a designed, proactive capability embedded in daily operations.

The Discussion section linked this conceptual architecture to the literature on dynamic capabilities (Teece, 2018), complex adaptive systems (Vlachos, 2023), and socio-technical resilience (Brintrup et al., 2020). It highlighted how ACTs deliver both theoretical and managerial advances:

1. They extend visibility-based frameworks into *agentic autonomy*;
2. They integrate explainability, ensuring trust in machine-made decisions;
3. They unify learning and orchestration, embedding double-loop adaptation.

From a managerial perspective, ACTs reconceptualise resilience as a value-creating capability rather than a cost of uncertainty. They support governance transparency, enable cross-functional coordination, and turn each disruption into new knowledge. For policymakers and practitioners, ACTs also illustrate how Saudi Arabia's and the GCC's digital-transformation agendas could embed AI-driven resilience in logistics, healthcare, and public procurement systems—aligning with Vision 2030's emphasis on efficiency, innovation, and sustainability.

Looking ahead, empirical validation is crucial. Future studies should examine ACT deployments across different sectors, measuring how agentic learning accelerates recovery and strengthens sustainability. The ethical, legal, and regulatory dimensions of autonomous decision systems also warrant further exploration.

Ultimately, Agentic Control Towers represent the convergence of technological intelligence and organisational learning. They mark a shift from "seeing" disruptions to "understanding, adapting, and evolving" through them—signaling a new era of *resilient, explainable, and adaptive supply-chain ecosystems.*

REFERENCES

Alahmari, D., & Awad, A. (2025). Strategic integration of marketing and supply chain functions for superior customer experience: Insights from logistics startups under Saudi Vision 2030. *PLoS One*, *20*(11), e0336132. DOI: 10.1371/journal.pone.0336132 PMID: 41270081

Argyris, C., & Schön, D. A. (1996). *Organisational learning II: Theory, method, and practice*. Addison-Wesley. https://www.scirp.org/reference/referencespapers?referenceid=1423922

Barredo Arrieta, A., Díaz-Rodríguez, N., Del Ser, J., Bennetot, A., Tabik, S., Barbado, A., & Herrera, F. (2020). Explainable Artificial Intelligence (XAI): Concepts, taxonomies, opportunities and challenges toward responsible AI. *Information Fusion*, *58*, 82–115. DOI: 10.1016/j.inffus.2019.12.012

Bommasani, R., Hudson, D. A., Adeli, E., Altman, R., Arora, S., Bernstein, M. S., . . . Liang, P. (2021). *On the opportunities and risks of foundation models*. Stanford Center for Research on Foundation Models. https://crfm.stanford.edu/report.html

Brintrup, A., Ledwoch, A., & Barros, J. (2020). Supply networks as complex systems: A network-science-based characterisation. *IEEE Systems Journal*, *14*(2), 2643–2655. DOI: 10.1109/JSYST.2015.2425137

Dolgui, A., & Ivanov, D. (2023). Digital supply-chain twins: Managing the ripple effect, resilience, and disruption risks. *International Journal of Production Research*, *61*(1), 1–19. DOI: 10.1007/978-3-030-14302-2_15

Dwivedi, Y. K., Kshetri, N., Hughes, L., Slade, E., Jeyaraj, A., Kar, A. K., & Wright, R. (2023). So what if ChatGPT wrote it? Multidisciplinary perspectives on opportunities, challenges and implications of generative conversational AI for research, practice and policy. *International Journal of Information Management*, *71*, 102642. DOI: 10.1016/J.IJINFOMGT.2023.102642

EY. (2025). *AI-powered supply chains: From dashboards to decision fabrics*. Ernst & Young. https://www.ey.com/en_us/coo/transforming-supply-chain-strategy-with-ai

Hazenberg, J., Keijzer, M., & van der Heijden, M. (2025). Multi-agent reinforcement learning for dynamic pricing in volatile markets. *European Journal of Operational Research*, *310*(3), 945–960. DOI: 10.48550/arXiv.2507.02698

Ivanov, D. (2020). Predicting the impacts of epidemic outbreaks on global supply chains: A simulation-based analysis on the coronavirus outbreak (COVID-19/SARS-CoV-2) case. *Transportation Research Part E, Logistics and Transportation Review, 136*, 101922. DOI: 10.1016/j.tre.2020.101922 PMID: 32288597

Ivanov, D. (2023). Toward supply chain viability theory: From lessons learned to theory. *International Journal of Production Research, 61*(11), 3663–3678. DOI: 10.1080/00207543.2023.2177049

Ivanov, D., & Dolgui, A. (2021). OR-methods for coping with the ripple effect in supply chains during COVID-19 pandemic: Managerial insights and research implications. *International Journal of Production Economics, 232*, 107921. DOI: 10.1016/j.ijpe.2020.107921 PMID: 32952301

Jannelli, V., Schoepf, S., Bickel, M., Netland, T., & Brintrup, A. (2024). *Agentic LLMs in the supply chain: Towards autonomous multi-agent consensus-seeking*. arXiv. https://doi.org//arXiv.2411.10184DOI: 10.48550

Ji, Z., Lee, N., & Frieske, R. (2023). Survey of hallucination in natural language generation. *ACM Computing Surveys, 55*(12), 1–38. DOI: 10.1145/3571730

Kersten, W. (Ed.). Blecker, Thorsten (Ed.); Ringle, Christian M. (Ed.) (2014): Next Generation Supply Chains: Trends and Opportunities, Proceedings of the Hamburg International Conference of Logistics (HICL), No. 18, ISBN 978-3-7375-0339-6, epubli GmbH, Berlin, https://doi.org/DOI: 10.15480/882.1188

Kirshner, S., Pan, Y., & Wu, X. (Jason) and Gould, Alex, Talking Terms: Agent Information in LLM Supply Chain Bargaining (August 20, 2024). Decision Sciences, 0[], UNSW Business School Research Paper Forthcoming, Available at http://dx.doi.org/DOI: 10.1111/deci.70010

Kotecha, N., & del Rio Chanona, R. M. (2025). Resilient inventory management with graph-informed multi-agent reinforcement learning. *Omega, 122*, 102782. DOI: 10.48550/arXiv.2410.18631

Lazrak, M., & El amrani, H. (2025). Digital Twin Technology in Supply Chain Resilience. *Journal of Innovative Research and Business Studies, 1*(1). Retrieved from https://journals.imist.ma/index.php/IRABS/article/view/5575

McKinsey Global Institute. (2024). *McKinsey Global Supply Chain Leader Survey 2024.* https://www.mckinsey.com/capabilities/operations/our-insights/supply-chain-risk-survey

Qadeer, A., & Awad, A. (2025). AI-powered ChatGPT in branding: Benefits, challenges, and future directions. In Hussain, Z., Khan, A., & Uzir, M. U. H. (Eds.), *Impacts of AI-generated content on brand reputation* (pp. 1–26). IGI Global., DOI: 10.4018/979-8-3373-4327-3.ch001

Qadeer, A., Awad, A., & Ali, A. (2025). Understanding generative AI implementation in digital advertising among retail SMEs in Pakistan. In Hussain, Z., Khan, A., & Uzir, M. U. H. (Eds.), *Impacts of AI-generated content on brand reputation* (pp. 177–201). IGI Global., DOI: 10.4018/979-8-3373-4327-3.ch007

Queiroz, M. M., Ivanov, D., Dolgui, A., & Wamba, S. F. (2022). Impacts of epidemic outbreaks on supply chains: Mapping a research agenda amid the COVID-19 pandemic through a structured literature review. *Annals of Operations Research*, *319*(1), 141–169. DOI: 10.1007/s10479-020-03685-7 PMID: 32836615

Sodhi, M. S., & Tang, C. S. (2021). *Supply-chain risk management*. Springer. https://doi.org/DOI: 10.1111/j.1937-5956.2011.01251.x

Sutton, R. S., & Barto, A. G. (2018). *Reinforcement learning: An introduction* (2nd ed.). The MIT Press., http://incompleteideas.net/book/the-book-2nd.html

Tao, F., Qi, Q., Liu, A., & Kusiak, A. (2019). Digital twins and cyber-physical systems toward smart manufacturing and Industry 4.0. *Engineering*, *5*(4), 653–661. DOI: 10.1016/j.eng.2019.01.014

Teece, D. J. (2018). Dynamic capabilities as (workable) management systems theory. *Journal of Management & Organization*, *24*(3), 359–368. DOI: 10.1017/jmo.2017.75

Verdouw, C. N., Wolfert, S., & Pérez Mesa, J. C. (2021). Digital twins in agri-food logistics: A framework for real-time monitoring. *Computers and Electronics in Agriculture*, *184*, 106130. DOI: 10.1016/j.agsy.2020.103046

Vlachos, I. (2023). Implementation of an intelligent supply chain control tower: A socio-technical systems case study. *Production Planning and Control*, *34*(15), 1415–1431. DOI: 10.1080/09537287.2021.2015805

Wahid, A., & Awad, A. (2025). Role of AI chatbots in enhancing customer satisfaction and customer loyalty. In Hussain, Z., Khan, A., & Uzir, M. U. H. (Eds.), *Impacts of AI-generated content on brand reputation* (pp. 129–147). IGI Global., DOI: 10.4018/979-8-3373-4327-3.ch005

Xu, Z., Yang, T., & Li, Q. (2023). Explainable MARL for logistics resilience. *Computers & Operations Research*, *157*, 106270. DOI: 10.1016/j.cor.2023.106270

Yang, Y., Luo, R., & Li, W. (2021). Emergent behaviour and scalability in multi-agent reinforcement learning systems. *Neural Networks, 142*, 222–234. DOI: 10.1016/j.simpat.2017.03.003

Zhang, K., Yang, Z., & Başar, T. (2021). Multi-agent reinforcement learning: A selective overview of theories and algorithms. In *Handbook of reinforcement learning and control* (pp. 321–370). Springer., DOI: 10.1007/978-3-030-60990-0_12

Chapter 7
Generative AI and Digital Twins for Sustainable Last-Mile Logistics:
Enabling Green Operations and Electric Vehicle Integration

Shashikant Nishant Sharma
https://orcid.org/0000-0001-8031-8569
Maulana Azad National Institute of Technology, India

ABSTRACT

The rapid rise of e-commerce and urbanization has intensified the importance of last-mile logistics—the most cost-intensive, environmentally impactful, and complex segment of supply chains. Over the past decade, green logistics measures such as electric vehicles, cargo e-bikes, and urban consolidation centers have helped curb emissions and congestion, yet remain limited in scalability. Emerging technologies—Generative AI, Digital Twins, and autonomous operations—offer new pathways for sustainable transformation. This chapter reviews literature from 2015–2025, highlighting how AI-driven forecasting, route optimization, predictive maintenance, and digital-twin simulations can accelerate decarbonization and resilience. It also identifies key challenges including high costs, data privacy, and equity for small operators. The study concludes that integrating digital innovation with sustainability goals can create intelligent, inclusive, and low-carbon urban logistics systems.

DOI: 10.4018/979-8-3373-7006-4.ch007

1. INTRODUCTION

The logistics sector is undergoing a profound structural transformation driven by twin imperatives: rapid digitalisation and escalating sustainability demands. Within this shift, last-mile delivery the movement of goods from depots or micro-hubs to end customers has emerged as the most complex and resource-intensive stage, concentrating costs, operational uncertainty, and environmental externalities in dense urban settings (Aslam et al., 2025; Truant et al., 2024; Anthony, 2023). E-commerce growth, expectations for same-/next-day fulfilment, and volatile urban curb conditions compound these pressures, turning the last mile into both a strategic opportunity and a sustainability bottleneck for cities and carriers alike (Ghaemi Asl et al., 2024).

Conventional green-logistics responses shipment consolidation, cargo bikes and e-vans, parcel lockers, and urban consolidation centres deliver measurable local benefits but often struggle to scale amid fragmented markets, uneven adoption, infrastructure gaps (e.g., charging and micro-hubs), and stochastic demand (Ghaemi Asl et al., 2024; Satır et al., 2018). Urban planners, meanwhile, must reconcile freight efficiency with livability, accessibility, and safety, underscoring the value of compact, mixed-use urban form and transit-supportive street design that structurally shortens tours and enables low-emission modes (Sharma & Dehalwar, 2025b).

Next-generation digital technologies Generative AI (GenAI) and Digital Twins (DTs) offer a new paradigm for navigating these sustainability–performance trade-offs. DTs provide continuously synchronised virtual replicas of fleets, depots, curb assets, and energy systems for real-time monitoring and stress-testing of routing, capacity, and siting strategies before field deployment; (Y. Liu et al., 2025; Attaran & Celik, 2023) (Selter et al., 2024)). GenAI complements DTs by transforming heterogeneous, often unstructured logistics data into predictive and prescriptive plans supporting demand-aware routing, capacity phasing, and customer interaction tactics at scales that exceed traditional analytics (Jackson et al., 2024; Kmiecik & Skórnóg, 2025). Federated and privacy-preserving architectures further enable multi-actor collaboration in city logistics without compromising competitive sensitivities (Gómez-Marín et al., 2024).

Electrification intensifies the need for such intelligence. Integrating EVs into last-mile fleets reduces tailpipe emissions but introduces operational challenges range constraints, charger queues, local grid limits, and time-of-use price exposure. Here, DTs and GenAI are complementary: DTs co-simulate vehicle state-of-charge, charger utilisation, and local energy flows, while GenAI jointly optimises routing and charging with forecasts of demand, prices, and renewable availability (Makridakis, 2017; Selter et al., 2024)). DT-enabled safety and reliability layers such as surrogate safety analytics and anomaly detection help ensure that aggressive time windows or dense curb operations do not elevate risk (Sharma, Singh, et al., 2024). At the system level, DTs support resilience planning for disruptions and recovery policies, aligning last-mile operations with broader city logistics and energy objectives ((Ul Akram et al., 2024; Hong & Park, 2024).

Positioned at the intersection of logistics engineering and urban policy, this chapter situates GenAI and DTs within the discourse on green logistics and sustainable mobility, with emphasis on last-mile operations and EV integration. Building on literature from 2015–2025 across city-logistics DT frameworks, supply-chain and warehouse synchronisation, reverse/circular flows, and planning lenses such as TOD, LUTI, and inclusive transport policy, we address four guiding questions:

How can GenAI and DTs complement green logistics strategies such as consolidation, micro-mobility, parcel lockers, and EV adoption for measurable environmental gains at scale? (Asadi et al., 2025; Selter et al., 2024).

Which emerging themes and innovations from federated twins to edge-cloud orchestration are reshaping last-mile sustainability? (Almurshed et al., 2025; F. Liu et al., 2025; Yadav et al., 2025).

What barriers technical, institutional, economic, regulatory impede mainstreaming, and how can data governance and transparency mitigate them? (Anthony, 2023; Chai et al., 2025).

Which policy and planning pathways TOD/LUTI alignment, inclusive design, and curb/charging governance accelerate the development of intelligent, resilient last-mile systems? (Sharma, Lodhi, et al., 2024; Sharma & Dehalwar, 2025b, 2025a; Sharma & Dehawar, 2025).

By engaging these questions, we argue that the convergence of digital intelligence and sustainability is not merely a technical possibility but a strategic necessity for last-mile systems that are economically viable, environmentally sound, safe, and socially equitable.

2. METHODOLOGY

This chapter employs a Systematic Literature Review (SLR) to examine the role of Generative Artificial Intelligence (AI), Digital Twins, and electric vehicle (EV) integration in advancing sustainable last-mile logistics. The SLR approach ensures transparency, replicability, and comprehensive coverage of the literature, encompassing peer-reviewed articles, conference papers, industry reports, and policy documents published between 2015 and 2025. The methodology followed three stages: literature identification, screening and eligibility, and thematic synthesis.

To capture the interdisciplinary scope of the topic, a multi-database search was conducted across Scopus, Web of Science, IEEE Xplore, ScienceDirect, and Emerald Insight. Search strings combined logistics, sustainability, and digital innovation terms, such as ("last-mile logistics" OR "urban freight") AND ("green logistics" OR "electric vehicles") and ("digital twin*" OR "generative AI") AND ("logistics" OR "supply chain"). Grey literature industry reports ((DHL, 2024), UPS, Amazon), government documents (EU Smart Cities Mission, India's EV freight pilots), and white papers from global organisations (World Economic Forum, International Transport Forum) was also included to capture real-world practices.

2.1 PRISMA

Table 1. Screening of the literature for the study

Stage	Description	Count
Identification	Records identified across databases (Scopus, Web of Science, IEEE Xplore, Google Scholar)	1,236
Screening	Records remaining after duplicate removal	874
Eligibility	Full-text articles were assessed based on predefined inclusion and exclusion criteria	142
Included	Final studies meeting all criteria and included in the systematic review	52

Figure 1. PRISMA flowchart adopted for the research

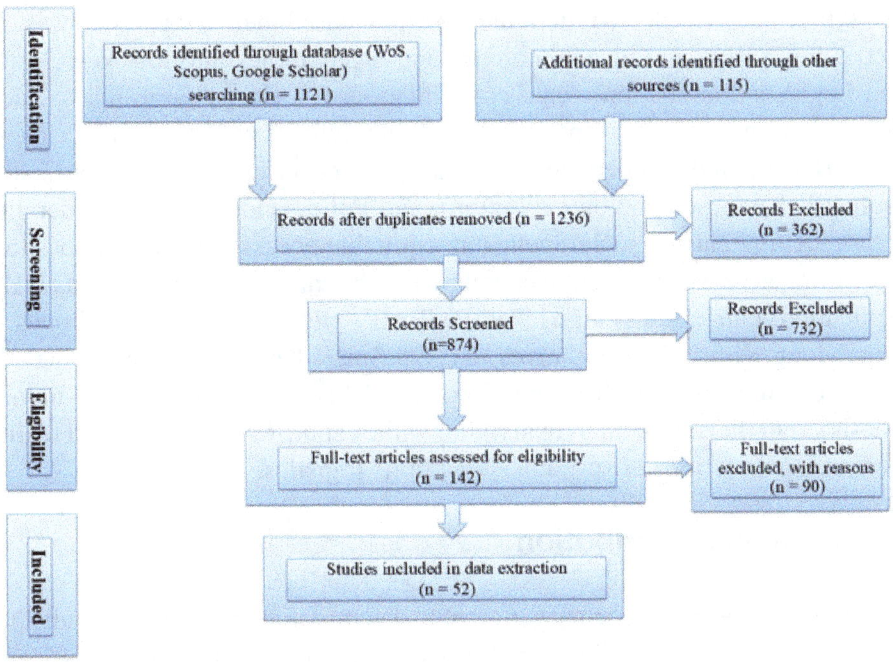

The systematic review is shown in Figure 1, and the screening criteria used are shown in Table 1, followed by a PRISMA-inspired workflow to ensure transparency and reproducibility. A total of 1,236 records were initially retrieved across Scopus, Web of Science, IEEE Xplore, and Google Scholar. After removing duplicates and applying eligibility criteria for Generative AI, Digital Twins, sustainability, and last-mile logistics, 52 studies were included in the full synthesis.

A matrix-based thematic synthesis identified four major clusters: (1) Green Logistics Foundations consolidation centers, EV fleets, cargo bikes, and micro-hubs; (2) Digital Innovations Generative AI, Digital Twins, predictive analytics, and automation; (3) Barriers and Enablers infrastructure gaps, costs, and technology adoption; and (4) Policy and Equity governance frameworks and inclusive access. Findings were triangulated with corporate initiatives ((DHL, 2024), UPS, FedEx, Amazon) and policy programs (EU SCC, Indian EV pilots), ensuring that the synthesis reflects both academic rigour and practical relevance in shaping intelligent, equitable, and low-carbon last-mile systems.

2.2 Thematic Synthesis

To synthesize the selected literature, a matrix-based thematic analysis was conducted using NVivo and manual coding to classify studies into four key clusters: Green Logistics Foundations (e.g., consolidation, EV fleets, cargo bikes, micro-hubs); Digital Innovations (generative AI, digital twins, predictive analytics, automation); Barriers and Enablers (infrastructure gaps, costs, institutional coordination, consumer behavior, technology adoption); and Policy and Equity Considerations (governance, regulation, social inclusion, equitable access). Patterns across these themes were cross-verified and triangulated with real-world cases such as DHL's consolidation centres, UPS cargo bikes, FedEx EV pilots, and Amazon's drones and lockers, along with policy initiatives like EU Smart Cities programs, India's EV freight pilots, and municipal low-emission zones. This combined academic–industry synthesis strengthened the analytical rigour while capturing the operational realities and emerging directions of sustainable last-mile logistics.

2.3 Geographic Distribution

The literature revealed a strong geographic skew toward technologically advanced economies, with 38% of studies from Europe, 29% from North America, 18% from East Asia, and limited representation from South Asia, Africa, and Latin America (15% combined). Disciplinarily, the review is dominated by engineering (44%), computer science (37%), and transportation planning (19%). This indicates a potential disciplinary bias and underrepresentation of policy and social science perspectives.

2.4 SLR Limitations

This review has several limitations. First, the search was restricted to English-language publications, which may introduce language bias and exclude relevant regional studies. Second, unpublished or industry-internal reports, which often contain practical insights, were excluded due to accessibility issues. Third, rapid advancements in Generative AI and Digital Twins create a risk of temporal bias, as new developments may not yet be captured in peer-reviewed literature.

3. KEY EMERGING THEMES IN SUSTAINABLE LAST-MILE LOGISTICS

3.1 Rise of E-commerce and Service Expectations

The exponential growth of e-commerce has fundamentally redefined the landscape of last-mile logistics, transforming both operational models and sustainability dynamics. Over the past decade, online retail platforms such as Amazon, Flipkart, and Alibaba have expanded consumer access to a vast range of products, driving unprecedented parcel volumes and diversifying delivery destinations (Qiu et al., 2025; Truant et al., 2024; Xu et al., 2020). Unlike traditional retail logistics, which primarily relied on consolidated bulk shipments to stores, the e-commerce model has led to a proliferation of smaller, more frequent deliveries across urban and suburban areas (Savelsbergh & Van Woensel, 2016). This shift has fragmented delivery networks, increased vehicle trips, and reduced load efficiency, leading to higher fuel consumption, greater congestion, and intensified environmental impacts (Jiménez et al., 2025).

Parallel to these structural shifts, consumer expectations have evolved dramatically. Same-day or even two-hour delivery windows are increasingly considered standard offerings rather than premium services (Ul Akram et al., 2024; Selter et al., 2024)). The consumer-driven "instant gratification" culture has forced logistics providers to prioritise delivery speed and flexibility, often at the expense of efficiency and environmental sustainability. The need to meet these heightened service standards results in increased vehicle kilometres travelled, lower consolidation rates, and higher carbon emissions per parcel delivered (Anthony, 2023; Hong & Park, 2024). For instance, empirical evidence from recent logistics studies suggests that express delivery models can increase carbon emissions by up to 30% compared to consolidated delivery schedules.

This trade-off between service quality and sustainability has emerged as a central challenge in last-mile logistics. Consumers expect convenience and immediacy but are often reluctant to pay for greener delivery alternatives, even when aware of their environmental benefits. Behavioural studies highlight that willingness to pay for eco-friendly delivery options remains low, constraining the economic viability of sustainable practices (Sharma & Dehalwar, 2025b). As a result, logistics operators face the dual imperative of reducing emissions while maintaining service reliability in increasingly competitive markets.

Technological innovation is now seen as the critical enabler to resolve this tension. Advanced digital tools particularly Generative Artificial Intelligence and Digital Twin technologies offer new avenues for optimising operational efficiency without compromising environmental objectives (Jackson et al., 2024; Kmiecik &

Skórnóg, 2025). Generative AI can dynamically forecast demand patterns, optimise routing decisions in real time, and balance delivery density with service speed. Simultaneously, Digital Twins provide virtual replicas of logistics networks that allow simulation and evaluation of alternative delivery strategies, including EV integration, micro-hub placement, and cargo bike deployment (Selter et al., 2024)). These technologies can help logistics providers design adaptive, data-driven models that reconcile consumer expectations with sustainability imperatives, turning last-mile delivery from a bottleneck into an opportunity for systemic innovation.

Table 2. Analysis of the rise of e-commerce and service expectations

Theme	Key Insights	Implications for Last-Mile Logistics
E-commerce growth	Surge in online retail volumes; shift from bulk shipments to individual parcels (Rao et al., 2021).	Increased delivery frequency, reduced load efficiency, and more fragmented networks.
Consumer service expectations	Rising demand for same-day or instant delivery as standard practice ((Ul Akram et al., 2024; Selter et al., 2024)).	Creates pressure to speed up, limiting opportunities for consolidation.
Efficiency–sustainability tension	Faster deliveries increase vehicle kilometres and carbon emissions ((Anthony, 2023); (Hong & Park, 2024)).	Trade-offs emerge between service quality and green objectives.
Consumer behavior	Limited willingness to pay for eco-friendly delivery despite awareness (Kim et al., 2024).	Green logistics adoption is constrained by low demand-side incentives.
Operational challenge	Small, frequent deliveries create higher costs and logistical inefficiencies (Subiyanto & Suyoto, 2020).	Need for digital innovations (Generative AI, Digital Twins) to balance efficiency and sustainability.

Table 2 summarises how the rise of e-commerce and evolving service expectations have created a complex interplay between consumer-driven market forces and environmental sustainability goals. On one hand, fragmented, high-frequency delivery networks undermine consolidation and operational efficiency. On the other hand, these same dynamics exacerbate congestion, emissions, and energy consumption in urban areas. While logistics providers increasingly acknowledge the necessity of sustainable operations, progress remains constrained by weak consumer demand for green delivery services and the cost pressures of ultra-fast fulfilment. Consequently, leveraging digital intelligence through Generative AI for predictive optimisation and Digital Twins for system-level modelling emerges as a viable pathway to harmonise efficiency, consumer satisfaction, and environmental stewardship in the evolving landscape of last-mile logistics.

3.2 Green Logistics Frameworks

Green logistics frameworks have emerged as the foundation of sustainable last-mile delivery, emphasising integrated operational strategies that reduce environmental impacts without compromising service quality. These frameworks closely align with broader sustainable urban mobility goals, focusing on minimising emissions, optimising delivery efficiency, and improving cities' overall livability (Loorbach et al., 2021). A growing body of research highlights the effectiveness of measures such as urban consolidation centres (UCCs), neighbourhood micro-hubs, cargo bikes, electric vans, and advanced routing optimisation systems in achieving these objectives (Karaman et al., 2020). By consolidating freight at central or semi-centralised facilities, UCCs streamline deliveries into high-density urban zones, reducing redundant trips and mitigating congestion. Complementary to these hubs, localised micro-hubs act as decentralised nodes that facilitate the final delivery leg via zero- or low-emission modes, such as e-cargo bikes and compact electric vehicles.

Micro-hubs have proven particularly effective in European cities where spatial planning policies prioritise compact development and multimodal connectivity (Anthony, 2023). These hubs support flexible, high-frequency deliveries while curbing emissions, noise, and road safety risks associated with conventional diesel vans. Cargo bikes and electric vans have also gained prominence in both European and Asian contexts, driven by the establishment of low-emission zones, fiscal incentives for the adoption of clean vehicles, and the expansion of cycling and charging infrastructure (Zhao et al., 2024). The transition to electric fleets directly contributes to reduced greenhouse gas (GHG) emissions and improved air quality in urban cores, aligning with the policy goals of decarbonization and sustainable mobility.

Optimised routing technologies, powered by artificial intelligence and data analytics, represent another vital dimension of green logistics frameworks. These systems leverage real-time traffic data, demand forecasts, and vehicle telemetry to minimise empty mileage, balance fleet utilisation, and optimise delivery schedules under dynamic urban conditions (Jackson et al., 2024; Kmiecik & Skórnóg, 2025). Digital Twins and AI-enabled platforms further enhance these capabilities by simulating various routing, energy, and delivery scenarios, allowing logistics providers to evaluate environmental and economic trade-offs before physical implementation.

However, green logistics measures rarely achieve systemic efficiency when implemented in isolation. Their effectiveness depends on broader structural and policy factors, including inter-operator coordination, regulatory coherence, and infrastructural readiness (Anthony, 2023). For instance, urban consolidation centres require collaboration among competing logistics operators to share space and scheduling data a challenge in competitive markets. Similarly, cargo bike adoption hinges on the availability of safe cycling infrastructure, secure parking, and weather-resilient designs, while the large-scale deployment of electric vans depends on robust charging networks and grid reliability (Yuan et al., 2025).

Consequently, the long-term sustainability and scalability of green logistics frameworks are contingent on integrated policy support, cross-sectoral partnerships, and digital augmentation. Policy instruments such as subsidies for clean vehicles, low-emission zone mandates, and tax incentives play an instrumental role in encouraging investment in green fleets and infrastructure (Axsen & Wolinetz, 2021). Public–private collaborations can facilitate data sharing, co-investment in logistics hubs, and align private delivery operations with public sustainability goals. This integrated approach underscores that green logistics is not merely a collection of operational best practices but a systemic paradigm that unites technology, infrastructure, and governance to achieve sustainable urban freight systems.

Table 3. Analysis of green logistics frameworks

Theme	Key Insights	Implications for Last-Mile Logistics
Consolidation centers	Centralised facilities reduce vehicle trips into city centres (Cheah et al., 2021).	Lower emissions and congestion, but require multi-operator collaboration.
Micro-hubs	Decentralised drop-off points for final low-emission deliveries (Anthony, 2023; Sina Mohri et al., 2024).	Enable e-cargo bikes and EVs; depend on urban space allocation and local planning.
Electric vans	Clean vehicle fleets reduce GHG emissions and noise pollution (De Saxe et al., 2023).	Effective with adequate charging infrastructure and favourable regulations.
Cargo bikes	Zero-emission vehicles are suited for short-range, high-density delivery zones (Carracedo & Mostofi, 2022).	Require safe cycling lanes, weather adaptation, and load-capacity considerations.
Optimized routing	AI and ICT tools improve route efficiency and reduce empty miles ((Jackson et al., 2024; Kmiecik & Skórnóg, 2025)).	Enhances cost-effectiveness; requires real-time data integration across networks.
Policy support	Subsidies, low-emission zones, and incentives are critical enablers.	Determines the scalability and long-term sustainability of green logistics interventions.

Table 3 highlights how infrastructure, technology, and policy collectively shape sustainable last-mile logistics. Consolidation centres and micro-hubs cut delivery intensity, while electric vans and cargo bikes reduce emissions. Optimised routing further boosts efficiency through clever data use. The success of these measures ultimately depends on supportive policies, operator coordination, and investment in digital and physical infrastructure, underscoring that sustainable logistics works as an integrated system rather than isolated actions.

Express delivery models increase carbon intensity by approximately 25–30% compared with consolidated routes due to higher trip frequency and smaller load factors (Solakivi et al., 2022). Generative AI can optimise delivery routing to reduce these emissions by up to 18% through real-time demand forecasting. Digital Twins can further model energy consumption patterns, enabling 10–20% efficiency gains in electric delivery fleets through battery thermal management and charge scheduling (Abdessadak et al., 2025).

3.3 Digital-Sustainability Nexus

Since 2020, research on last-mile logistics has increasingly converged on the idea of a digital–sustainability nexus, viewing digitalisation as a strategic enabler of environmental performance rather than just an efficiency mechanism (Anthony, 2023). This perspective integrates green logistics interventions such as EV fleets, consolidation centres, and cargo bikes within digitally coordinated ecosystems. Technologies like Generative AI, Digital Twins, IoT sensors, predictive analytics, and blockchain platforms are now central to improving visibility, coordination, and responsiveness in fragmented urban delivery networks (Hasan & Crawford, 2025).

Generative AI enhances dynamic routing, demand forecasting, and adaptive scheduling to reduce empty miles and emissions (Jackson et al., 2024; Kmiecik & Skórnóg, 2025). Digital Twins extend these capabilities by simulating logistics networks testing EV charging strategies, low-emission zones, micro-hub operations, and policy scenarios before real-world deployment. IoT-enabled data streams further provide real-time insights into vehicle movements and infrastructure performance, enabling better coordination, maintenance planning, and congestion avoidance (Chen & Zhang, 2024). Meanwhile, blockchain technologies strengthen data integrity, carbon traceability, and transparency in sustainability reporting (Alwi et al., 2024).

Collectively, these technologies support a transition from isolated green measures to digitally orchestrated sustainability ecosystems, where decisions related to routing, fleet deployment, and customer interaction incorporate both efficiency and environmental indicators (Hong & Park, 2024). However, the digital–sustainability nexus also introduces new challenges: high implementation costs, interoperability issues, and uneven access to digital infrastructure may widen the gap between large logistics operators and small local firms (Ji & Wang, 2024). To ensure broad participation and equitable benefits, inclusive governance frameworks and data-sharing mechanisms are needed to support collaboration, standardisation, and fair access within emerging sustainable logistics ecosystems (Ul Akram et al., 2024).

Table 4. Analysis of the digital–sustainability nexus

Theme	Key Insights	Implications for Last-Mile Logistics
Generative AI	Generates adaptive insights for demand-sensitive routing and fleet optimisation (Jackson et al., 2024).	Reduces emissions and costs through real-time, demand-aware decision-making.
Digital Twins	Virtual replicas simulate logistics systems and test green strategies.	Supports EV integration, emission reduction, and infrastructure planning.
IoT-enabled visibility	Real-time tracking of vehicles, parcels, and infrastructure (F. Liu et al., 2025; Y. Liu et al., 2025).	Enhances coordination, reduces inefficiencies, and enables predictive maintenance.
Blockchain for traceability	Ensures trust and transparency in carbon accounting across supply chains (Liew & Cao, 2024).	Strengthens credibility of sustainability reporting and consumer trust.
Integrated digital ecosystems	Digital tools align logistics decisions with sustainability metrics (Anthony, 2023; Hong & Park, 2024).	Transforms green logistics from isolated measures into systemic, scalable models.
Challenges	High costs, interoperability issues, and risk of digital exclusion.	Requires policy frameworks and collaborative platforms to ensure inclusive adoption.

Table 4 encapsulates how digital technologies increasingly act as amplifiers of sustainability outcomes rather than parallel innovations. Generative AI and Digital Twins provide analytical and simulation backbones for adaptive logistics, while IoT and blockchain add layers of transparency, coordination, and accountability. Collectively, these technologies shift last-mile logistics toward a city-scale, data-driven ecosystem that is both efficient and environmentally responsible. Yet, realising this transformation requires addressing the governance, equity, and standardisation challenges that accompany digitalisation ensuring that sustainable logistics evolves as an inclusive, technologically resilient, and systemically integrated framework

3.4 Shift toward Lifecycle and Equity Perspectives

Since the early 2020s, last-mile logistics research has increasingly incorporated lifecycle assessment (LCA) and equity-oriented frameworks, moving beyond earlier studies that focused mainly on direct emission reductions from EVs, cargo bikes, or consolidation centres. Recent work adopts a systems perspective, examining the full environmental lifecycle of vehicles, batteries, and infrastructure (Anthony, 2023)). LCA enables evaluation across manufacturing, operation, and end-of-life stages, revealing that while EVs reduce tailpipe emissions, their overall sustainability depends on battery production, electricity sources, and recycling processes (Zschausch et al., 2025). Battery manufacturing remains energy-intensive, meaning that without renewable energy integration and circular strategies, environmental gains may be partially offset (Jannesar Niri et al., 2024).

Alongside environmental considerations, recent literature emphasises equity and justice in sustainable delivery systems. Clean technologies often require high capital investment, which can disadvantage small logistics operators and deepen "green exclusion" as larger firms gain a competitive advantage (Koch, 2020). Community-level inequities are also a concern: low-income neighbourhoods may face higher costs or reduced access if consolidation centres or low-emission zones are implemented without inclusive planning . Addressing these disparities requires participatory governance and targeted policies such as subsidies for small operators, equitable charging infrastructure, and incentives to serve underserved areas (Anthony, 2023; Ul Akram et al., 2024).

Overall, the emerging paradigm frames sustainable last-mile logistics as a multidimensional challenge in which environmental integrity, economic feasibility, and social justice must be advanced in tandem. Lifecycle and equity perspectives are therefore central to a systemic and inclusive approach to urban logistics.

Table 5. Analysis of lifecycle and equity perspectives in sustainable last-mile logistics

Theme	Key Insights	Implications for Last-Mile Logistics
Lifecycle Assessment (LCA)	Evaluates total environmental impact of EVs and logistics infrastructure (Xia & Li, 2022).	Encourages adoption of circular economy practices such as battery recycling and remanufacturing.
Upstream emissions	EV manufacturing and battery production have significant carbon footprints (Zhou, 2024).	Requires renewable energy integration and green supply chains to maximise sustainability gains.
Social equity concerns	Small carriers may struggle to afford EVs and digitalisation investments (Anam et al., 2025).	Necessitates financial support programs, subsidies, and inclusive digital platforms.
Community inclusion	Vulnerable neighborhoods risk reduced access or increased delivery costs .	Calls for equitable distribution of charging infrastructure and inclusive delivery zoning.
Policy frameworks	Emphasizes participatory governance and just transition models (Ul Akram et al., 2024).	Balances environmental goals with social justice and economic fairness.
Systemic sustainability	Expands focus from carbon reduction to holistic environmental and social outcomes (Yu et al., 2024).	Promotes resilient, fair, and inclusive last-mile ecosystems.

Table 5 illustrates how the sustainability discourse in last-mile logistics has evolved from a narrow focus on emission reduction to a comprehensive understanding of systemic sustainability. By integrating lifecycle thinking, researchers expose the hidden environmental trade-offs embedded in supply chains and highlight the value of circular resource management. Simultaneously, the infusion of equity perspectives ensures that the green transition remains socially just avoiding exclusion, promoting inclusivity, and democratizing access to sustainable delivery systems. Together, these perspectives call for a just, circular, and inclusive transformation of last-mile logistics, where ecological efficiency and social fairness advance hand in hand.

4. TECHNOLOGICAL INNOVATIONS

4.1 Generative AI in Logistics

Generative Artificial Intelligence (AI) has become a major driver of innovation in last-mile logistics, offering capabilities far beyond traditional optimization tools. Unlike conventional models that rely mainly on historical data, Generative AI can simulate complex logistics environments, generate adaptive strategies, and model multiple future scenarios making it highly suited to the volatility of urban delivery systems. One of its most impactful applications is dynamic routing and demand forecasting: by integrating real-time data from traffic, weather, consumer orders, and fleet telematics, AI models can predict demand surges, optimize routes continuously, and reduce vehicle kilometers traveled, thereby cutting costs and emissions. This stands in sharp contrast to static routing models that struggle with urban variability (Kheder & Mohammed, 2024).

Generative AI also enhances customer-facing services by enabling personalized delivery windows, nearby pickup points, and greener delivery choices. Through such nudges, it helps reduce failed deliveries and unnecessary return trips, improving both efficiency and environmental outcomes (Bø & Mjøsund, 2022). At a strategic level, AI-generated simulations support logistics network design, helping identify optimal locations for micro-hubs, parcel lockers, and EV charging stations especially in cities adopting TOD or LUTI frameworks (Sharma & Dehawar, 2025).

Generative AI is equally valuable for resilience planning, enabling logistics providers to model disruptions such as traffic gridlock, extreme weather, or charging shortages and test adaptive responses (Hong & Park, 2024). In energy management, it supports alignment of EV charging with renewable supply, reinforcing decarbonization goals. Overall, Generative AI serves as both an operational optimizer and a strategic planning tool, linking efficiency gains with long-term sustainability. However, its widespread adoption still depends on resolving challenges related to data quality, ethical governance, transparency, and unequal access particularly for smaller firms making inclusive and interoperable AI ecosystems essential for unlocking its full sustainability potential (Anthony, 2023).

Table 6. Applications of generative AI in last-mile logistics

Application Area	Key Functions of Generative AI	Implications for Sustainable Last-Mile Logistics
Dynamic routing & demand prediction	Simulates multiple demand scenarios and continuously optimizes routes in real time.	Reduces congestion, fuel use, and emissions while improving delivery reliability.
Customer interaction	AI chatbots and recommender systems manage delivery windows and guide sustainable choices.	Minimizes failed deliveries and nudges consumers toward greener delivery options.
Network design	Generates synthetic data for hub and charging station siting (Y. Liu et al., 2025).	Improves strategic planning, reduces travel distances, and supports EV integration.
Scenario testing	Models uncertainty in demand, traffic, and energy availability (Hong & Park, 2024).	Enhances system resilience and supports long-term sustainability goals.
Data-driven adaptability	Learns from incomplete, unstructured, or streaming data to refine logistics decisions ((Jackson et al., 2024)	Enables agile, data-informed operations that adapt to evolving urban dynamics.

Table 6 summarizes the multi-dimensional contributions of Generative AI to sustainable logistics. It highlights how AI-driven decision systems can synchronize operational efficiency with environmental stewardship by dynamically managing routes, predicting demand, and facilitating consumer engagement. The technology's ability to generate synthetic data and test hypothetical scenarios makes it indispensable in data-scarce or uncertain environments characteristics typical of urban logistics. Yet, the transformative promise of Generative AI will only be realized if governance frameworks ensure data integrity, algorithmic fairness, and equitable access, allowing both large-scale enterprises and small operators to benefit from AI-driven sustainability innovations.

4.2 Digital Twins in Sustainable Last-Mile Logistics

Digital Twins (DTs) are rapidly emerging as a cornerstone technology for reimagining sustainable last-mile logistics. Conceptually defined as virtual replicas of physical systems that integrate real-time data with simulation and predictive analytics, DTs enable logistics operators and policymakers to visualize, test, and optimize complex delivery ecosystems under varying operational and environmental conditions. In last-mile logistics, where variability in demand, infrastructure, and policy environments is high, the capacity of DTs to model system dynamics and assess multiple sustainability scenarios positions them as a transformative enabler of intelligent, low-emission transport systems.

One of the most prominent applications of Digital Twins lies in fleet simulation and energy management. By mirroring the performance of electric vehicle (EV) fleets in virtual space, DTs can model battery degradation, energy consumption, and charging cycles across different routes and temporal profiles. These virtual environments allow logistics firms to optimize fleet deployment, balance charging loads across depots, and mitigate range anxiety key barriers to large-scale EV adoption (Y. Liu et al., 2025). For example, DTs can simulate the effects of peak-hour charging demand on depot capacity or model how route-level battery usage patterns affect long-term operational efficiency. Through this data-driven decision support, firms can reduce downtime, extend battery life, and lower overall fleet emissions.

Beyond fleet-level operations, DTs are increasingly used for urban freight scenario testing, allowing operators and city planners to evaluate the comparative performance of different delivery modes such as conventional vans, e-cargo bikes, and drones under diverse spatial and policy conditions. By integrating multimodal data, including real-time traffic, delivery density, and curbside infrastructure, these simulations reveal which transport modes are most efficient and sustainable in specific contexts. For instance, high-density neighborhoods may benefit most from cargo bike operations, while peri-urban areas may still rely on EV vans for efficiency. Such evidence-based modeling supports the design of hybrid logistics systems that balance economic viability with environmental outcomes.

Digital Twins also serve as policy sandboxes virtual governance environments where cities can test regulatory and infrastructure interventions before implementing them in the real world. Municipalities can use DTs to simulate the impacts of low-emission zones, congestion pricing, curb management schemes, or delivery time restrictions, assessing trade-offs between economic performance, emissions reduction, and equity outcomes (Hong & Park, 2024). By enabling participatory modeling and visualization, these digital environments enhance stakeholder engagement and policy transparency, reducing resistance to change and fostering data-informed policymaking.

At the system level, DTs facilitate integrated urban modeling, connecting logistics data with energy, mobility, and infrastructure systems to foster a holistic view of city logistics (Y. Liu et al., 2025). Through this integration, DTs support synchronization between logistics operations and energy systems for example, aligning EV fleet charging with renewable energy availability or balancing deliveries with real-time traffic flows. Such coordination enhances resilience, promotes efficient energy utilization, and aligns logistics planning with broader sustainability and climate targets (Xia & Li, 2022).

However, realizing the full potential of Digital Twins depends on the interoperability and accessibility of data across stakeholders. Fragmented data ecosystems, proprietary platforms, and limited collaboration between logistics firms and city authorities often constrain the scalability of DT applications. Establishing open data standards, shared governance models, and strong institutional frameworks is therefore critical to ensure that DT insights translate into actionable, inclusive, and equitable sustainability outcomes.

Table 7. Applications of digital twins in last-mile logistics

Application Area	Key Functions of Digital Twins	Implications for Sustainable Last-Mile Logistics
Fleet simulation	Models EV fleet deployment, battery health, charging schedules, and route efficiency ((Xia & Li, 2022).	Reduces downtime, improves fleet utilization, and supports large-scale EV adoption.
Urban freight scenarios	Compares environmental and operational impacts of vans, cargo bikes, and drones.	Enables optimized mode selection, reduces emissions, and adapts strategies to urban contexts.
Policy sandboxing	Virtual testing of low-emission zones, congestion pricing, and delivery restrictions (Hong & Park, 2024).	Helps cities design equitable, evidence-based policies with lower implementation risks.
System-level integration	Connects traffic, energy, and logistics data into unified digital models (Y. Liu et al., 2025).	Enhances resilience, energy efficiency, and alignment with urban sustainability goals.
Decision support	Provides predictive insights for operators and policymakers.	Strengthens collaboration between private logistics firms and public authorities.

Table 7 highlights how Digital Twins function as a bridge between logistics operations and urban governance, combining real-time monitoring with predictive simulation to foster informed, adaptive, and equitable decision-making. At the operational level, DTs enable logistics firms to manage EV fleets efficiently, optimize routes, and reduce emissions. At the system level, they empower city authorities to model freight movements, test policies, and plan infrastructure investments that balance environmental, economic, and social objectives. This dual capability linking micro-level optimization with macro-level planning makes Digital Twins an indispensable enabler in the transition toward smart, sustainable, and inclusive last-mile logistics systems. However, to ensure these benefits are widely shared, sustained collaboration, data interoperability, and supportive regulatory frameworks remain essential.

4.3 Autonomous Operations

Autonomous operations are emerging as a major innovation in sustainable last-mile logistics, reshaping urban delivery through the integration of automation, clean energy, and digital coordination. Autonomous Delivery Vehicles (ADVs), drones, and ground robots now complement electrification and digitalization to address long-standing challenges such as labor shortages, congestion, and rising emissions

(Hong & Park, 2024). ADVs self-driving electric vans have demonstrated their ability to operate continuously, including during off-peak hours, thereby easing daytime congestion and improving infrastructure utilization (Zaidi, Khan, & Chaabane, 2024). When powered by renewable energy, ADVs significantly reduce GHG emissions while enhancing routing precision and operational efficiency through real-time navigation and fleet management integration.

Drones and ground-based robots further support last-mile delivery by addressing the "last-50-meter" challenge. Drones are effective for small-parcel delivery in low-access or emergency settings, while sidewalk robots increasingly serve dense urban areas by reducing van entries into congested zones and enabling contactless delivery. Automated parcel lockers also play a growing role by consolidating deliveries, lowering failed deliveries, and reducing total vehicle kilometers traveled, particularly when integrated with AI-driven scheduling systems.

At a systems level, the convergence of autonomy, electrification, and digital platforms supports dynamic orchestration of mixed fleets ADVs, drones, and robots based on real-time demand and energy availability ((Jackson et al., 2024)). This enhances network resilience and lowers idle time, although widespread adoption still depends on public acceptance, regulatory clarity, infrastructure readiness, and strong data governance. Cities with robust digital infrastructure and supportive regulations are better positioned to scale autonomous logistics innovations, while others may face substantial deployment barriers.

Ensuring equitable access and governance will also be critical. Smaller logistics operators may struggle to afford automation technologies, while urban areas with limited connectivity or infrastructure could be excluded from early adoption. To prevent such disparities, inclusive policy frameworks such as shared autonomous fleets, public-private partnerships, and open-access data platforms are essential for democratizing the benefits of automation and ensuring alignment with sustainability objectives.

Table 8. Applications of autonomous operations in last-mile logistics

Application Area	Key Functions	Implications for Sustainable Last-Mile Logistics
Autonomous Delivery Vehicles (ADVs)	Self-driving, electric vans for urban and suburban routes.	Reduce labor costs, enable continuous operations, and lower emissions through electrification.
Drones	Aerial delivery of small parcels to low-access or remote areas.	Minimize van trips, extend reach, and support rapid or emergency deliveries.
Ground delivery robots	Small autonomous robots for short-distance, last-50-meter delivery.	Reduce congestion in dense cores and enable contactless, low-emission deliveries.

continued on following page

Table 8. Continued

Application Area	Key Functions	Implications for Sustainable Last-Mile Logistics
Automated lockers & stations	Centralized parcel drop-off and pick-up points.	Decrease failed deliveries, consolidate loads, and optimize fleet efficiency.
System-level efficiency	Integration of autonomy with AI-driven scheduling and routing systems ((Jackson et al., 2024)	Supports scalable, flexible, and low-emission logistics ecosystems.

Table 8 illustrates how autonomous operations address multiple spatial and operational dimensions of the last-mile challenge. From ADVs covering citywide routes to drones and robots tackling micro-scale delivery tasks, these technologies collectively reduce emissions, congestion, and delivery inefficiencies. Automated lockers further strengthen the model by enhancing reliability and consolidating demand. Together, these solutions represent a shift from labor-intensive, vehicle-dependent logistics toward distributed, digitally coordinated systems that balance operational efficiency with environmental stewardship. However, the pace and inclusiveness of this transformation will depend on regulatory readiness, public acceptance, and proactive urban design that accommodates autonomous mobility within sustainable transport networks.

The integration of Generative AI into logistics introduces substantial ethical challenges, particularly regarding algorithmic bias, model transparency, and accountability. Biased training datasets may lead to unequal service levels across neighbourhoods, reinforcing digital exclusion. Transparent model reporting, explainable AI (XAI) techniques, and human-in-the-loop decision systems are necessary to mitigate these risks. Logistics firms must adopt fairness-aware machine learning frameworks and conduct periodic audits to ensure model reliability and ethical compliance.

Real-world Digital Twin pilots show measurable sustainability benefits. For example, a DT-enabled distribution centre in Germany achieved a 15% reduction in energy use and a 12% reduction in CO_2 emissions through optimised HVAC and loading dock scheduling. Similarly, a Nordic urban freight Digital Twin demonstrated 22% efficiency gains in EV fleet routing when integrated with real-time charging data and grid capacity forecasts.

5. ISSUES AND CHALLENGES

Despite their transformative potential, the widespread adoption of Generative Artificial Intelligence (AI), Digital Twins, and autonomous operations in sustainable last-mile logistics faces multiple systemic challenges. Research shows that technology alone cannot deliver sustainability without supportive infrastructure, clear regulations, and inclusive governance.

Infrastructure gaps remain the foremost constraint. Inadequate charging networks in urban and peri-urban areas limit the expansion of electric vehicle (EV) fleets. Fragmented digital systems and a lack of interoperability further reduce the effectiveness of AI and Digital Twin platforms. Standardised data frameworks are essential for integrating logistics networks and enhancing coordination.

High adoption costs pose another significant barrier. The capital required for EV fleets, AI tools, and Digital Twin infrastructure often exceeds the capacity of small and medium-sized enterprises (SMEs), widening the gap between large firms and smaller carriers. Targeted subsidies, green finance, and shared infrastructure are needed to support inclusive participation.

Regulatory uncertainty also limits progress. Ambiguous laws governing autonomous vehicles, drones, and data governance discourage investment and slow scaling ((Hong & Park, 2024). Harmonised, adaptive frameworks are required to balance innovation with safety and accountability.

Equity concerns highlight the social risks of digital transitions. SMEs and low-income communities risk exclusion from green logistics systems due to financial and technological barriers. Inclusive financing, participatory planning, and fair access to digital tools are critical for a just transition.

Data privacy and cybersecurity vulnerabilities remain significant. As logistics becomes increasingly data-driven, risks of breaches and misuse grow (Y. Liu et al., 2025). Strong governance and cybersecurity standards are needed to maintain trust.

Finally, rebound effects where improved efficiency leads to increased demand threaten environmental gains. Demand-side interventions, such as eco-labelling and green delivery incentives, are vital to align consumer behaviour with sustainability goals.

Table 9. Issues and challenges in sustainable last-mile logistics

Challenge	Description	Implications for Sustainable Last-Mile Logistics
Infrastructure gaps	Lack of EV charging stations; limited digital interoperability among platforms.	Constrains EV adoption and weakens coordination in digital-sustainable ecosystems.
High costs	Expensive EV fleets, AI tools, and Digital Twin platforms.	Limits adoption by SMEs; risks widening inequality between large and small carriers.
Regulatory uncertainty	Ambiguous rules for AVs, drones, and data governance (Hong & Park, 2024).	Slows scaling of pilot projects and increases investment risk.

continued on following page

Table 9. Continued

Challenge	Description	Implications for Sustainable Last-Mile Logistics
Equity concerns	Small carriers and vulnerable communities may be excluded from transitions.	Reinforces market concentration; risks deepening social inequities.
Data privacy & cybersecurity	Sensitive logistics and consumer data are vulnerable to breaches.	Erodes trust in digital systems; requires robust governance and safeguards.
Rebound effects	Efficiency improvements increase delivery frequency.	Offsets sustainability gains; requires demand-side management and consumer awareness.

Table 9 consolidates the primary barriers to the sustainable transformation of last-mile logistics, underscoring that these challenges extend far beyond technical limitations. While infrastructure deficits and high costs restrict adoption, regulatory ambiguity and social inequities shape the inclusiveness and legitimacy of digital transitions. Data privacy and cybersecurity risks threaten public confidence, while rebound effects reveal the complex interplay between efficiency and consumption behaviour. Overcoming these multifaceted challenges requires collaborative, cross-sectoral governance involving policymakers, logistics firms, researchers, and communities to ensure that digital-sustainable last-mile systems evolve as resilient, equitable, and future-ready urban ecosystems.

6. DISCUSSION

The synthesis of recent research and case evidence suggests that while strategies such as consolidation centres, electric vans, cargo bikes, and AI-optimised routing have delivered measurable environmental benefits, they remain insufficient to meet the ambitious decarbonization goals set by cities and global climate frameworks. Persistent network fragmentation, rapid e-commerce growth, and rising consumer expectations continue to strain last-mile systems, revealing the limitations of interventions focused only on vehicle substitution or localised infrastructure. The literature increasingly argues that future progress depends on integrating foundational green logistics with advanced digital technologies particularly Generative AI and Digital Twins to create adaptive and resilient urban delivery ecosystems (Savelsbergh & Van Woensel, 2016).

Generative AI addresses the core challenge of unpredictability in last-mile logistics by synthesising diverse datasets including mobility patterns, weather, orders, and charging availability to anticipate demand and optimise routes in real time (Jackson et al., 2024). This dynamic adaptability reduces vehicle kilometres travelled and energy use, delivering both operational and environmental benefits. Digital Twins complement this intelligence by providing virtual environments for scenario testing, enabling planners to simulate charging infrastructure rollouts, drone corridors, or congestion pricing before implementation ; (Y. Liu et al., 2025). Together, Generative AI and Digital Twins bridge short-term operational optimisation with long-term strategic planning.

However, the effectiveness of these digital-sustainability pathways depends heavily on coherent governance. Fragmented regulations, uneven infrastructure, and misaligned incentives often keep digital innovations confined to pilot projects rather than enabling system-wide transformation (Hong & Park, 2024). While large multinational firms (DHL, 2024). UPS, Amazon have rapidly adopted EV fleets and AI-enabled systems, SMEs face prohibitive costs and limited digital access, widening structural inequalities. Inclusive policy frameworks, targeted subsidies, shared charging infrastructure, and accessible financing instruments are therefore essential to prevent a two-tier logistics landscape (Anthony, 2023).

Open-data ecosystems further emerge as a critical enabler, allowing smaller carriers to participate in AI-driven routing and coordination platforms while ensuring strong privacy and cybersecurity protections. This democratisation of data and digital tools is central to preventing sustainability transitions from being monopolised by major players.

Overall, the literature converges on a digitally orchestrated, multimodal, and green last-mile ecosystem where electric vans cover wider urban areas, cargo bikes dominate dense centres, autonomous vehicles support routine freight flows, and drones handle urgent or hard-to-reach deliveries. Parcel lockers reduce failed deliveries, while AI-driven personalisation nudges consumers toward low-carbon options. In this model, Generative AI becomes the system's real-time "brain," and Digital Twins its strategic "laboratory."

However, several challenges remain: expanding charging and digital infrastructure, ensuring SME affordability through innovative financing, updating regulations for autonomous systems and data governance, and embedding equity principles to support underserved communities. Demand-side measures such as consumer education, eco-labels, and carbon transparency are also essential to prevent rebound effects.

In conclusion, sustainable last-mile logistics requires an integrated approach. Green logistics forms the operational base, digital technologies amplify impact through intelligence and foresight, and governance provides the coherence and equity safeguards. Together, these pillars shape a future that is environmentally regenerative, technologically advanced, and socially inclusive.

7. CRITICAL PERSPECTIVE, POLICY IMPLICATIONS, AND FUTURE RESEARCH

7.1 Where GenAI and DTs Fail

Despite their promise, Generative AI and Digital Twins generate new sustainability dilemmas. Generative models are computationally intensive, with training emissions sometimes exceeding 300 tons of CO_2e per large model. Additionally, data monopolies can consolidate power among a few logistics' giants, limiting innovation among SMEs and developing economies.

7.2 Global Readiness Differences

Developed economies possess established EV infrastructure, open mobility datasets, and strong digital logistics regulations. In contrast, developing economies face fragmented data systems, unreliable grid capacity, and limited policy support. This divergence affects the scalability and equity of GenAI-driven logistics solutions.

7.3 Policy Implications

Key policy recommendations include:

- Investment in shared EV charging networks for last-mile logistics.
- Creation of open logistics data platforms enabling SMEs to adopt AI-enabled tools.
- Mandatory AI transparency standards for operational decision-making in logistics.
- National-level support for Digital Twin testbeds in urban freight planning.

7.4 Future Research Directions

- Assessing AI lifecycle emissions from model training to deployment.
- Comparative evaluation of global Digital Twin pilots.
- Studying consumer rebound effects e.g., how "green delivery" labels may increase order frequency.
- Governance frameworks for cross-border AI-enabled logistics.

8. REGULATORY AND ETHICAL DIMENSIONS OF DIGITAL LOGISTICS

The rapid integration of Generative AI, Digital Twins (DTs), autonomous systems, and data-driven decision tools into last-mile logistics has outpaced the development of comprehensive regulatory and ethical frameworks. As logistics operations transition toward highly automated and algorithmically optimised systems, several regulatory, legal, and ethical considerations emerge ranging from data protection and cybersecurity to algorithmic accountability and cross-border governance. Addressing these concerns is essential to ensure that digital logistics systems are transparent, fair, secure, and socially responsible.

8.1 Data Protection and Privacy Regulations

Digital logistics relies on continuous data flows, including real-time location data, customer identifiers, vehicle telemetry, and infrastructure information. Compliance with data protection frameworks such as the General Data Protection Regulation (GDPR) in the European Union, the California Consumer Privacy Act (CCPA), and emerging national data protection acts in India and Asia is critical. These regulations impose strict requirements on:

- Data minimisation and lawful processing, especially when using Generative AI models that learn from consumer and operational datasets.
- Informed consent and transparency, ensuring that customers understand how their delivery and movement data are used.
- Cross-border data transfer controls, affecting global logistics networks operating across multiple jurisdictions.

Failure to comply may restrict international data-sharing, undermine the performance of AI-enabled logistics platforms, and create significant legal liabilities for operators.

8.2 AI-Specific Regulatory Frameworks

Governments worldwide are developing AI-specific laws that directly influence the design and deployment of GenAI-driven logistics systems. The EU AI Act, for instance, categorises specific logistics applications such as predictive routing, automated resource allocation, and safety-critical autonomous vehicle operations as "high-risk," requiring:

- Transparent documentation
- Continuous risk assessment
- Human oversight
- Explainable decision-making
- Monitoring for algorithmic bias

These requirements aim to prevent opaque or discriminatory decision outcomes for example, allocating slower delivery services to specific urban neighbourhoods because of biased training data. Similar frameworks are emerging from OECD, ISO, and national AI task forces globally.

8.3 Transportation and Operational Safety Regulations

Autonomous delivery vehicles, drones, and AI-assisted warehousing systems must comply with existing and evolving transportation safety standards. Key regulatory bodies include:

- UNECE (vehicle automation, EV standards)
- FAA / DGCA for unmanned aerial deliveries
- Local urban mobility authorities for curbside management, micro-mobility routing, and EV charging protocols

Digital Twins offer simulations for safety certification, yet regulators still require physical validation. Ensuring compliance remains critical as logistics systems shift from human-driven to AI-assisted operations.

8.4 Ethical Considerations in AI-Enhanced Logistics

Beyond compliance, ethical dimensions shape the societal acceptance and legitimacy of digital logistics.

Algorithmic Fairness and Bias

AI-based route optimisation and demand forecasting can unintentionally reinforce inequalities if training datasets are skewed. Populations living in informal settlements, low-income neighbourhoods, or remote regions may receive slower or more expensive deliveries, exacerbating digital divides. Fairness-aware modelling and bias audits are essential.

Transparency and Explainability

Opaque GenAI systems used for fleet management, delivery scheduling, or consumer prioritisation may erode trust. Ethical deployment requires:

- Explainable AI (XAI) techniques
- Clear disclosure of decision logic
- User rights to challenge or appeal automated decisions

Opaque Generative AI systems used in fleet management, delivery scheduling, or consumer prioritisation can undermine trust if users do not understand how decisions are made. Ethical deployment, therefore, requires explainable AI (XAI) techniques, transparent disclosure of decision logic, and mechanisms that allow users to question or appeal automated decisions.

Labour and Workforce Implications

Automation threatens specific categories of logistics labour (e.g., warehouse sorting and delivery riders). Ethical adoption requires transition planning, reskilling initiatives, and ensuring that remaining human workers are not subject to excessive algorithmic surveillance.

Cybersecurity and Infrastructure Protection

Digital logistics systems depend on interconnected data platforms, IoT devices, EV charging networks, and cloud-based Digital Twins. This creates vulnerabilities to:

- Ransomware attacks on fleet management systems
- GPS signal spoofing disrupts autonomous vehicles
- Manipulation of routing algorithms
- Theft of proprietary logistics datasets

Regulatory frameworks increasingly mandate cybersecurity audits, zero-trust architectures, and encryption standards to protect critical supply chain infrastructure.

Cross-Border Governance and Interoperability

Global supply chains operate across jurisdictions with conflicting data policies, EV standards, and AI governance norms. Fragmented regulation creates:

- Uncertainty in cross-border data exchange
- Incompatibility among vehicle interoperability standards
- Delays in scaling autonomous logistics solutions internationally

International organisations such as ISO, ITU, and UNECE are promoting harmonisation initiatives, but global interoperability remains limited.

8.5 The Need for Integrated Regulatory-Ethical Governance

Given these challenges, there is an urgent need for a holistic governance framework that integrates:

- AI ethics (fairness, transparency, accountability)
- Data governance (privacy, sovereignty, interoperability)
- Safety standards (vehicle automation, drone operations, digital infrastructure)
- Cybersecurity protocols
- Labour protection and equity considerations

Integrated governance is essential to ensure that digital logistics systems remain socially responsible, resilient, and aligned with sustainability goals. Key priorities include enforcing AI ethics to ensure fairness and transparency, establishing strong data governance to protect privacy and support cross-border interoperability, and maintaining safety standards as autonomous vehicles and drones become widespread. Robust cybersecurity is also vital to safeguard fleets, IoT devices, and Digital Twins from cyber risks. Finally, labour protection and equity measures are needed to prevent worker displacement and ensure fair access and reskilling opportunities as automation expands..

9. CONCLUSION

This chapter reviews a decade of research on sustainable last-mile logistics, exploring how Generative AI, Digital Twins, and autonomous operations can accelerate decarbonization, enhance efficiency, and transform urban freight systems. While green logistics strategies such as electric vehicles (EVs), cargo bikes, and consolidation centres have reduced emissions and congestion, their isolated application limits scalability. Fragmented infrastructure, market disparities, and volatile e-commerce demand highlight the need for digital integration to achieve systemic efficiency and resilience.

Generative AI emerges as a central enabler, synthesising real-time traffic, weather, demand, and charging data to optimise routing, forecast demand, and support adaptive planning. AI-driven customer systems reduce failed deliveries and promote greener choices, positioning AI as the decision "brain" of digital-sustainable ecosystems. Complementing this, Digital Twins act as simulation "laboratories," allowing stakeholders to model logistics networks, evaluate EV charging strategies, and test policies such as low-emission zones or congestion pricing before implementation. These tools help balance operational performance with long-term sustainability goals.

Autonomous operations, including self-driving vans, drones, ground robots, and parcel lockers, add a new dimension by addressing labour shortages, extending delivery coverage, and minimising urban congestion. Their integration with EVs and AI-enabled coordination enhances flexibility and supports continuous, low-emission operations.

However, key challenges persist: inadequate charging infrastructure, high costs that disadvantage SMEs, regulatory ambiguity around autonomy and data governance, and equity concerns that risk excluding smaller operators. Cybersecurity and data privacy also remain critical barriers.

To overcome these, governments and industry must align efforts through shared infrastructure, targeted incentives, and open data standards. Inclusive governance and public–private partnerships are essential to ensure affordability, interoperability, and fair access. The literature calls for long-term impact studies, lifecycle analyses, and regional comparisons to guide scalable, equitable strategies. Ultimately, sustainable last-mile transformation depends on integrating green logistics foundations with digital intelligence to create adaptive, low-carbon, and socially just delivery ecosystems.

REFERENCES

Abdessadak, A., Ghennioui, H., Thirion-Moreau, N., Elbhiri, B., Abraim, M., & Merzouk, S. (2025). Digital twin technology and artificial intelligence in energy transition: A comprehensive systematic review of applications. *Energy Reports, 13*, 5196–5218. DOI: 10.1016/j.egyr.2025.04.060

Almurshed, O., Kaushal, A., Meshoul, S., Muftah, A., Almoghamis, O., Petri, I., Auluck, N., & Rana, O. (2025). Enhancing performance of machine learning tasks on edge-cloud infrastructures: A cross-domain Internet of Things based framework. *Future Generation Computer Systems, 166*, 107696. DOI: 10.1016/j.future.2024.107696

Alwi, A., & Sasongko, N. A., Suprapto, Suryana, Y., & Subagyo, H. (2024). Blockchain and big data integration design for traceability and carbon footprint management in the fishery supply chain. *Egyptian Informatics Journal, 26*, 100481. DOI: 10.1016/j.eij.2024.100481

Anam, M. Z., Shakur, M. S., Bari, A. B. M. M., Debnath, B., & Bristy, F. T. (2025). Exploring the barriers to decarbonizing the transportation system: A pathway to a cleaner future in emerging economies. *Innovation and Green Development, 4*(4), 100256. DOI: 10.1016/j.igd.2025.100256

Anthony, B. (2023). Data enabling digital ecosystem for sustainable shared electric mobility-as-a-service in smart cities-an innovative business model perspective. *Research in Transportation Business & Management, 51*, 101043. DOI: 10.1016/j.rtbm.2023.101043

Asadi, S., Naeini, H. K., Hassanlou, D., Pishahang, A., Najafabadi, S. A., Sharifi, A., & Ahmadi, M. (2025). AI-Powered Digital Twin Frameworks for Smart Grid Optimization and Real-Time Energy Management in Smart Buildings: A Survey. *Computer Modeling in Engineering & Sciences, 145*(2), 1259–1301. DOI: 10.32604/cmes.2025.070528

Aslam, B., Zhantian, B., Amjad, M. A., & Zhang, G. (2025). Decarbonizing transport: EV production versus conventional vehicles. *Transport Policy, 174*, 103821. DOI: 10.1016/j.tranpol.2025.103821

Attaran, M., & Celik, B. G. (2023). Digital Twin: Benefits, use cases, challenges, and opportunities. *Decision Analytics Journal, 6*, 100165. DOI: 10.1016/j.dajour.2023.100165

Axsen, J., & Wolinetz, M. (2021). Taxes, tolls and ZEV zones for climate: Synthesizing insights on effectiveness, efficiency, equity, acceptability and implementation. *Energy Policy, 156*, 112457. DOI: 10.1016/j.enpol.2021.112457

Bø, E., & Mjøsund, C. (2022). Use of GPS-data to improve transport solutions in a cost and environmental perspective. *Transportation Research Interdisciplinary Perspectives, 13*, 100557. DOI: 10.1016/j.trip.2022.100557

Carracedo, D., & Mostofi, H. (2022). Electric cargo bikes in urban areas: A new mobility option for private transportation. *Transportation Research Interdisciplinary Perspectives, 16*, 100705. DOI: 10.1016/j.trip.2022.100705

Chai, L., Lai, K., & Zong, L. (2025). How digital transformation enhances supply chain transparency? Based on the perspective of information improvement and resource optimization. *Transportation Research Part E, Logistics and Transportation Review, 201*, 104256. DOI: 10.1016/j.tre.2025.104256

Cheah, L., Mepparambath, R. M., & Ricart Surribas, G. M. (2021). Freight trips generated at retail malls in dense urban areas. *Transportation Research Part A, Policy and Practice, 145*, 118–131. DOI: 10.1016/j.tra.2021.01.015

Chen, G., & Zhang, J. W. (2024). Intelligent transportation systems: Machine learning approaches for urban mobility in smart cities. *Sustainable Cities and Society, 107*, 105369. DOI: 10.1016/j.scs.2024.105369

De Saxe, C., Lindsay, C., Subramanian, S. C., & Van Eeden, J. (2023). Decarbonising freight transport: Transitions towards net zero. *Research in Transportation Business & Management, 48*, 100984. DOI: 10.1016/j.rtbm.2023.100984

DHL. (2024). *The DHL Logistics Trend Radar 7.0*. DHL. https://www.dhl.com/discover/en-global/news-and-insights/reports-and-press-releases/logistics-trend-radar-2024

Ghaemi Asl, M., Nie, P., & Charkh, C. (2024). Cycles-specific benefits of smart transport for sustainable investing: Global and regional perspectives with different ethical paradigms. *Technological Forecasting and Social Change, 208*, 123707. DOI: 10.1016/j.techfore.2024.123707

Gómez-Marín, C. G., Comi, A., Serna-Urán, C. A., & Zapata-Cortés, J. A. (2024). Fostering collaboration and coordination in urban delivery: A multi-agent microsimulation model. *Research in Transportation Economics, 103*, 101402. DOI: 10.1016/j.retrec.2023.101402

Hasan, S. K. K., & Crawford, C. W. (2025). A new era for digital twins: Progress and industry adoption. *Digital Twin, 2555877.* Advance online publication. DOI: 10.1080/27525783.2025.2555877

Hong, E., & Park, J. (2024). The effect of technological readiness dimensions on the adoption of autonomous vehicles: Focusing on behavioral reasoning theory. *Transportation Research Part F: Traffic Psychology and Behaviour*, *100*, 101–114. DOI: 10.1016/j.trf.2023.11.005

Jackson, I., Ivanov, D., Dolgui, A., & Namdar, J. (2024). Generative artificial intelligence in supply chain and operations management: A capability-based framework for analysis and implementation. *International Journal of Production Research*, *62*(17), 6120–6145. DOI: 10.1080/00207543.2024.2309309

Jannesar Niri, A., Poelzer, G. A., Zhang, S. E., Rosenkranz, J., Pettersson, M., & Ghorbani, Y. (2024). Sustainability challenges throughout the electric vehicle battery value chain. *Renewable & Sustainable Energy Reviews*, *191*, 114176. DOI: 10.1016/j.rser.2023.114176

Ji, J., & Wang, Y. (2024). The impact of digital infrastructure on the geographical supply chain layout of firms——Evidence from Chinese microdata. *China Economic Review*, *87*, 102249. DOI: 10.1016/j.chieco.2024.102249

Jiménez, P., Garrido, L., Gomez, J., & Vassallo, J. M. (2025). Environmental and operational impact of freight urban delivery: In-store, home and locker. *Transportation Research Part D, Transport and Environment*, *149*, 105026. DOI: 10.1016/j.trd.2025.105026

Karaman, A. S., Kilic, M., & Uyar, A. (2020). Green logistics performance and sustainability reporting practices of the logistics sector: The moderating effect of corporate governance. *Journal of Cleaner Production*, *258*, 120718. DOI: 10.1016/j.jclepro.2020.120718

Kheder, M. Q., & Mohammed, A. A. (2024). Real-time traffic monitoring system using IoT-aided robotics and deep learning techniques. *Kuwait Journal of Science*, *51*(1), 100153. DOI: 10.1016/j.kjs.2023.10.017

Kim, D., Na, J., & Ha, H.-K. (2024). Exploring the impact of green logistics practices and relevant government policy on the financial efficiency of logistics companies. *Heliyon*, *10*(10), e30916. DOI: 10.1016/j.heliyon.2024.e30916 PMID: 38803963

Kmiecik, M., & Skórnóg, D. (2025). Impact of generative AI on logistics companies' business models. *International Journal of Logistics Research and Applications*, 1–25. https://doi.org/DOI: 10.1080/13675567.2025.2497537

Koch, R. (2020). *Green Public Procurement under WTO Law: Experience of the EU and Prospects for Switzerland* (Vol. 9). Springer International Publishing., DOI: 10.1007/978-3-030-48214-5

Liew, M., & Cao, J. (2024). Green supply chain management for carbon accountability. *Energy Economics*, *138*, 107840. DOI: 10.1016/j.eneco.2024.107840

Liu, F., Lee, C. K. M., & Xu, M. (2025). Electric vehicle supply chain investment under demand uncertainty: A jointly held real options perspective. *Computers & Industrial Engineering*, *200*, 110840. DOI: 10.1016/j.cie.2024.110840

Liu, Y., Pan, S., & Ballot, E. (2025). Federated digital twins platform for smart city logistics: A knowledge-driven approach. *International Journal of Production Economics*, *290*, 109772. DOI: 10.1016/j.ijpe.2025.109772

Loorbach, D., Schwanen, T., Doody, B. J., Arnfalk, P., Langeland, O., & Farstad, E. (2021). Transition governance for just, sustainable urban mobility: An experimental approach from Rotterdam, the Netherlands. *Journal of Urban Mobility*, *1*, 100009. DOI: 10.1016/j.urbmob.2021.100009

Makridakis, S. (2017). The forthcoming Artificial Intelligence (AI) revolution: Its impact on society and firms. *Futures*, *90*, 46–60. DOI: 10.1016/j.futures.2017.03.006

Qiu, R., Li, X., Sun, M., Sun, Y., & Fan, Z.-P. (2025). Online platform demand information sharing with upstream suppliers under the imbalanced market power structure. *European Journal of Operational Research*, *S037722172500726X*, •••. DOI: 10.1016/j.ejor.2025.09.009

Rao, P., Balasubramanian, S., Vihari, N., Jabeen, S., Shukla, V., & Chanchaichujit, J. (2021). The e-commerce supply chain and environmental sustainability: An empirical investigation on the online retail sector. *Cogent Business & Management*, *8*(1), 1938377. DOI: 10.1080/23311975.2021.1938377

Satır, B., Erenay, F. S., & Bookbinder, J. H. (2018). Shipment consolidation with two demand classes: Rationing the dispatch capacity. *European Journal of Operational Research*, *270*(1), 171–184. DOI: 10.1016/j.ejor.2018.03.016

Savelsbergh, M., & Van Woensel, T. (2016). 50th Anniversary Invited Article—City Logistics: Challenges and Opportunities. *Transportation Science*, *50*(2), 579–590. DOI: 10.1287/trsc.2016.0675

Selter, J.-L., Schmitz, J., & Schramm-Klein, H. (2024). Sustainability assessment of last-mile electrification: A qualitative study in Germany. *Transportation Research Part D, Transport and Environment*, *126*, 104019. DOI: 10.1016/j.trd.2023.104019

Sharma, S. N., & Dehalwar, K. (2025a). A Systematic Literature Review of Pedestrian Safety in Urban Transport Systems. *Journal of Road Safety*, *36*(4). Advance online publication. DOI: 10.33492/JRS-D-25-4-2707507

Sharma, S. N., & Dehalwar, K. (2025b). A Systematic Literature Review of Transit-Oriented Development to Assess Its Role in Economic Development of City. *Transportation in Developing Economies*, *11*(2), 23. DOI: 10.1007/s40890-025-00245-1

Sharma, S. N., & Dehawar, K. (2025). Review of Landuse Transportation Interaction Model in Smart Urban Growth Management. *European Transport. Trasporti Europei*, *103*, 1–15. DOI: 10.5281/ZENODO.17315313

Sharma, S. N., Lodhi, A. S., Dehalwar, K., & Jaiswal, A. (2024). Life Cycle Assessment (LCA) of Recycled & Secondary Materials in the Construction of Roads. *IOP Conference Series. Earth and Environmental Science*, *1326*(1), 012102. DOI: 10.1088/1755-1315/1326/1/012102

Sharma, S. N., Singh, D., & Dehalwar, K. (2024). Surrogate Safety Analysis- Leveraging Advanced Technologies for Safer Roads. *Suranaree Journal of Science and Technology, 31*(4), 010320(1-14). https://doi.org/DOI: 10.55766/sujst-2024-04-e03837

Sina Mohri, S., Mohammadi, M., & Van Woensel, T. (2024). Designing zero-emissions containerized last-mile delivery systems: A case study for melbourne. *Transportation Research Part C, Emerging Technologies*, *159*, 104492. DOI: 10.1016/j.trc.2024.104492

Solakivi, T., Paimander, A., & Ojala, L. (2022). Cost competitiveness of alternative maritime fuels in the new regulatory framework. *Transportation Research Part D, Transport and Environment*, *113*, 103500. DOI: 10.1016/j.trd.2022.103500

Subiyanto, E., & Suyoto, Y. T. (2020). Determining value of logistics costs in projects: Empirical findings based-on executing several cement projects in Indonesia. *Heliyon*, *6*(7), e04352. DOI: 10.1016/j.heliyon.2020.e04352 PMID: 32695900

Truant, E., Borlatto, E., Crocco, E., & Sahore, N. (2024). Environmental, social and governance issues in supply chains. A systematic review for strategic performance. *Journal of Cleaner Production*, *434*, 140024. DOI: 10.1016/j.jclepro.2023.140024

Ul Akram, M., Islam, N., Chauhan, C., & Zafar Yaqub, M. (2024). Resilience and agility in sustainable supply chains: A relational and dynamic capabilities view. *Journal of Business Research*, *183*, 114855. DOI: 10.1016/j.jbusres.2024.114855

Xia, X., & Li, P. (2022). A review of the life cycle assessment of electric vehicles: Considering the influence of batteries. *The Science of the Total Environment, 814*, 152870. DOI: 10.1016/j.scitotenv.2021.152870 PMID: 34990672

Xu, X., Zhang, M., & He, P. (2020). Coordination of a supply chain with online platform considering delivery time decision. *Transportation Research Part E, Logistics and Transportation Review, 141*, 101990. DOI: 10.1016/j.tre.2020.101990

Yadav, K., Dehalwar, K., & Sharma, S. N. (2025). Assessing the factors affecting first and last mile accessibility in transit-oriented development: A literature review. *GeoJournal, 90*(6), 298. DOI: 10.1007/s10708-025-11546-8

Yu, W., Li, Z., & Hu, C. (2024). Carbon reduction and corporate sustainability: Evidence from low-carbon city pilot policy. *Heliyon, 10*(7), e28992. DOI: 10.1016/j.heliyon.2024.e28992 PMID: 38601564

Yuan, H., Ma, M., Zhou, N., Deng, Y., Liu, J., Zhang, S., & Ma, Z. (2025). Planning future charging infrastructure for private EVs: A city-scale assessment of demand and capacity. *Advances in Applied Energy, 100258*. Advance online publication. DOI: 10.1016/j.adapen.2025.100258

Zhao, X., Li, X., Jiao, D., Mao, Y., Sun, J., & Liu, G. (2024). Policy incentives and electric vehicle adoption in China: From a perspective of policy mixes. *Transportation Research Part A, Policy and Practice, 190*, 104235. DOI: 10.1016/j.tra.2024.104235

Zhou, Y. (2024). Lifecycle battery carbon footprint analysis for battery sustainability with energy digitalization and artificial intelligence. *Applied Energy, 371*, 123665. DOI: 10.1016/j.apenergy.2024.123665

Zschausch, F., Rosenberger, S., & Halbe, J. (2025). Quantitative evaluation of environmental impacts and mitigation measures for transport logistics companies—Insights through modeling of an exemplary site. *Energy Reports, 13*, 3291–3311. DOI: 10.1016/j.egyr.2025.02.037

Chapter 8
Intelligent Logistics: Generative AI, Digital Twins, and Autonomous Supply Chains in GCC and Beyond

R. N. Ravikumar
https://orcid.org/0009-0009-3705-1681
Marwadi University, Rajkot, India

S. Aarthi
https://orcid.org/0009-0006-9064-2091
Marwadi University, Rajkot, India

ABSTRACT

This chapter examines how generative AI, digital twins, and autonomous operations are reshaping logistics into intelligent, sustainable, and resilient ecosystems, with emphasis on GCC and MENA contexts. Generative AI supports forecasting, disruption management, and procurement optimization, while digital twins enable real-time simulation, predictive analytics, and ESG tracking. Autonomous operations using robotics, drones, AGVs, and AI-driven control towers boost efficiency, transparency, and safety. Case studies from the UAE, Saudi Arabia, Qatar, and Oman highlight applications in healthcare, ports, food security, and green trade corridors. Beyond technology, the chapter underscores ethical AI, cyber-physical security, and carbon-neutral strategies. It shows how GCC nations, through digital infrastructure and visionary policies, are advancing future-ready logistics. The chapter provides actionable frameworks linking research, industry, and governance to enable resilient, transparent, and sustainable supply chains.

DOI: 10.4018/979-8-3373-7006-4.ch008

INTRODUCTION

Driven by Artificial Intelligence (AI) along with digital twins and autonomous operations, logistics and supply chains are evolving. Agile, sustainable, and resilient ecosystems are gradually replacing traditional linear models which focused solely on data. AI predictive and prescriptive analytics and resource optimization with the combination of Generative AI and cyber-physical systems are instantaneous. Organizations can now use digital twins to model and monitor disruptions, resource optimization, emissions of activities, and carbon emissions in the supply chain. At the same time, autonomous systems replace logistics hubs with self-optimizing drones, robotic, AI-enabled control towers, and others. Such transformations are pivotal to the Gulf Cooperation Council and the MENA such regions are pivotal to enhancing the economic value of logistics. This chapter provides an optimistic case studies of the Gulf Cooperation Council and MENA regions to craft transparent, resilient, and sustainable supply chains to refer frameworks (Aliahmadi et al., 2022).

Evolution of Logistics and Supply Chains in the Digital Era

The progress of logistics and rife trade has evolved extensively over the centuries with the Internet of Things and Big Data having broken borders with unparalleled operational and transactional capabilities and transformed manual systems to 'Digital and Automated nations'. Supply chains are entirely ecosystem integrated to digitally rooted fore and operate chains which in turn improves accuracy in automated predictive planning and forecasting and greatly simplifies ordering systems due to decreased overhead and operational costs. Process technologies such as drones and complex robotic systems which do the least human-controlled processes remarkably enhance transactional system speed and accuracy due to the minimal human errors. Global and climate change has had a profound impact on governance and operational systems on trade due to the sustainable strategies and global Carbon release accountabilities. It has made the systems intelligent as well, able to balance the ecosystem with the sustainable self-adapting system capable of preserving supply chains. Shifts have also been made in the Middle East and the series. Shifts have also been made in the GCC and Middle Eastern region (Lai, 2024). Figure 1 Illustrates the progression of logistics from cost reduction to globalization, digital adoption, AI-driven optimization, autonomy, and sustainability integration. Table 1 Shows how supply chains have moved from manual, cost-focused systems to smart, data-driven networks powered by AI, digital twins, and automation, ending in sustainable and intelligent logistics.

Figure 1. Progression of digital logistics

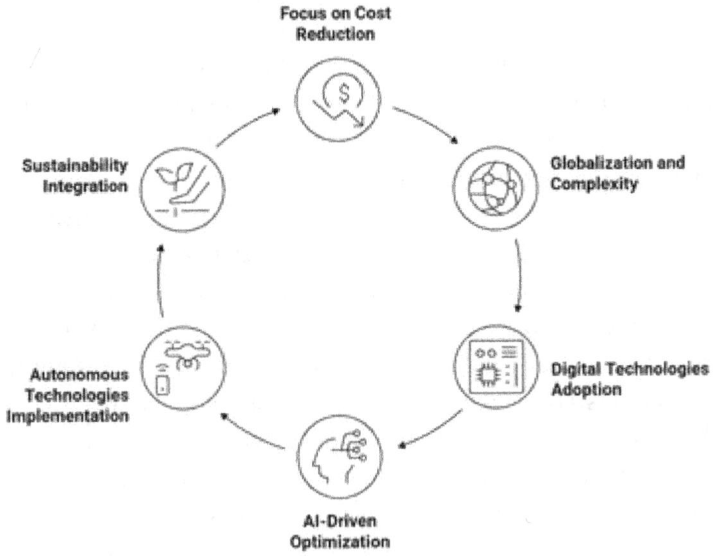

Table 1. Evolution of logistics in the digital era

Phase	Characteristics	Focus/Limitations	Enabling Technologies
Traditional Logistics	Manual processes, paper-based documentation, siloed operations	Cost reduction, labor-intensive, error-prone	Basic transport, manual inventory systems
Globalized Supply Chains	Expansion across geographies, outsourcing, multi-tier supplier networks	Complexity, lack of real-time visibility	ERP systems, barcode/RFID
Digital Logistics	Data-driven decision-making, integration of IoT and cloud platforms	Improved efficiency but limited predictive capabilities	IoT sensors, cloud computing, big data
Intelligent Supply Chains	Predictive and prescriptive analytics, digital twins for simulation	Challenges in trust, transparency, and cybersecurity	AI, machine learning, digital twins
Autonomous & Sustainable	Robotics, AGVs, drones, ESG compliance, carbon-neutral strategies, circular logistics	Focus on resilience, transparency, sustainability	Generative AI, blockchain, quantum-ready tools

WHY GCC & MENA REGIONS ARE PIVOTAL TESTBEDS FOR INTELLIGENT LOGISTICS

The Gulf Cooperation Council (GCC) and Middle East and North Africa (MENA) regions are important crossroads for international trade and energy exports as well as strategic hubs for international trade facilitation, thus making them very promising contenders for the development of smart logistics. These regions are located at the intersection of Europe, Asia, and Africa and receive and dispatch merchant ships and aircraft as well as transshipments in free trade zones, thus managing very large volumes of cargo. State-sponsored digital transformation projects, such as the Vision 2030 for Saudi Arabia and the Smart Logistics initiatives for the UAE, are allocating significant public funds to the deployment of artificial intelligence (AI), the Internet of Things (IoT), and block chain technologies. Wanting to separate from oil dominance is now a central enabler of smart city mega projects like NEOM and Masdar City, and is driving up the economic value of logistics even more. In addition, the sustainable development agendas of the GCC states align with innovations in carbon-aware logistics and autonomous systems (Ghahremani Nahr et al., 2021). The area's digital network, ability to experiment with new regulations, and collaborative approach to public private partnerships are perfectly suited for the deployment and scaling of generative AI, digital twins, and autonomous technologies for logistics, making the area a promising proving ground for advanced geography of real-world generative AI.

Scope and Objectives of the Chapter

- Analyze the role of generative AI in forecasting, optimization, and disruption management.
- Examine digital twin applications in simulating, predicting, and optimizing logistics performance.
- Explore autonomous operations in warehousing, transportation, and last-mile delivery.
- Contextualize GCC and MENA initiatives as global leaders in intelligent supply chains.
- Provide actionable frameworks, case studies, and sustainability insights for researchers, practitioners, and policymakers.

LITERATURE REVIEW

The world's changing logistics and supply chains have always been evolving. First, the word focus meant basic functions in a business, but now "focus" also includes foresight on resilience and sustainability. In the earlier writings on logistics focused on the cost of fuel for planes and the airborne reorganizing In the globalized world, advanced supply chains and digital systems meant a focus on their interaction global. Digitalized systems are supported and advanced by global networking. From visibility, the focus is now on agility and flexibility. Digital transformation (Waller & Fawcett, 2013). This became the foundation for the later even more sophisticated coupling of artificial intelligence, digital twins, and autonomous systems, the virtual triad of modern logistics. Furthermore, because Generative AI is bypassing static predictive boundaries to actual scenario generation, multi-modal demand forecasting, and prescriptive optimization, it is now regarded as a disrupter within the industry. It aids in predictive disruption management, unlike classic analytics that only dealt with disruption management, risk management, and operational optimization (Liu et al., 2020). But, the issues with generative AI tools show algorithm bias, hallucinations, and opacity, which tarnishes the trust of AI with regards to logistics.

Also, the digital twin tech which supports AI the ability to replicate physical things, systems, and networks has been receiving most of the attention. In manufacturing, digital twins have improved decision making systems of the port, logistics, and intermodal transport. Enhanced performance has been focused in these areas has been achieved through manufacturing to optimal performance (Adewusi et al., 2024). They are valued for offering ESG monitoring, disruption simulation, and predictive maintenance, enabling companies to examine resilience strategies in a risk-free setting. Autonomous operations are transformed with the increasing focus on robotics, drones and AGVs for warehousing, ports, and last-mile delivery (Udeh et al., 2024). Deployed AI control towers are described as central nodes which consolidate data streams and supply chain activities to orchestrate with near-autonomous precision. Simultaneously, blockchain-based smart contracts are being proposed for automation and transparency in customs and procurement. Although these prospects are expanding, the literature underlines the importance of human-machine collaboration, as well as the social and ethical implications of workplace safety, regulation, and adoption frameworks which are often necessary for inclusion (Firouraghi et al., 2022).

With the advent of IoT, and cyber-physical systems, systems have become more vulnerable which has become a focus of security design and resilient cybersecurity systems. With sustainability boasting of ample research, logistics has been highlighted in carbon neutrality, ESG compliance, and circular economy practices. Future supply chains will focus more on scope-3 emissions, reverse logistics, and the green certifications (Awan et al., 2021). Due to their geographical advantages, infrastructure, and policy objectives, the GCC and MENA regions are regarded as exceptional "living laboratories" for these innovations. Even though smart ports, digital trade corridors, and cold chains in health care are often cited as early instances intelligent logistics starts integrating in region, as a whole, the literature provides a rather impressionistic view of a sector in transformation, where, on the one hand, generative AI, digital twins, and autonomous systems create unparalleled possibilities, on the other hand ex ante regulation, ethical cage, and sustainable integration are a must for a positive durable impact.

GENERATIVE AI IN LOGISTICS

The use of Generative AI within logistics can help improve sophisticated modeling, decision making, and adaptive optimization capabilities in the field. Generative AI changes the shift in the analysis of phenomena descriptively or predictively and issues the paradigm of synthesis generating insights, scenarios and strategies to pre-emptively to fulfill the supply chain anticipatory needs. AI creates demand and market forecasts within multimodal models by monitoring and sifting through structured datasets, unstructured text, images, and streams of sensor data. With agentic AI systems, disruptions can be resolved in real time through changes in shipment routes or by the simulation of alternative paths of procurement which need to be fulfilled. On the other hand, generative optimization assists in the formulation of efficient layouts for the warehouses given the various constraints an organisation is to operate within (Leogrande, 2024). The combined results of emission reductions from the tuned scheduled procurements with technology-efficient low emission transportation systems is unquestionable. They still pose technology trust questions the most of which concern real-time decision making for critical logistics. Issues of hallucinations, algorithmic bias, and low opacity all serve to heighten the stakes of trust. On the other hand, for enabling supply chain intelligence, none is more potent than generative AI. It is also able to provide the needed resiliency and agility for logistics transformation of the GCC and MENA regions. Table 2 Summarizes how generative AI supports demand forecasting, disruption management, procurement optimization, and warehouse/transport efficiency, with examples relevant to GCC contexts.

Table 2. Applications of generative AI in logistics

Application Area	Role of Generative AI	Example in GCC Context	Impact
Demand Forecasting	Uses multimodal AI to analyze sales data, events, and sensor inputs to predict demand surges	Forecasting food/beverage demand spikes during Ramadan in UAE	Reduced stockouts and inventory waste
Disruption Management	Simulates alternative routes and scenarios to minimize delays and risks	Optimizing shipping reroutes during Red Sea congestion	Improved continuity and reduced financial losses
Procurement Optimization	Generates supplier risk profiles and contract simulations	AI-based tender evaluation for Saudi Vision 2030 projects	Fairer selection, transparency, and cost savings
Warehousing Efficiency	Designs optimized layouts, workflows, and predictive maintenance schedules	Smart warehouse initiatives in Dubai Logistics District	Faster operations, reduced energy use, higher accuracy
Transport Optimization	Creates AI-driven multimodal route and load-balancing strategies	Optimizing cross-border transport corridors across GCC	Shorter delivery times and lower carbon emissions

MULTIMODAL AI FOR DEMAND SENSING & FORECASTING

Multimodal AI combines various modalities including sales records, relevant social media postings, sensors on IoT devices, and market studies in order to achieve sophisticated demand forecasting and demand sensing. Serialization forecasting approaches lacking anything sophisticated relies on past data trends, which would make them prone to changes in consumer behavior as well as external shocks/diversions. These models originally developed by Generative AI entail the amalgamation of both structured and unstructured data and outputs and thus provide a rich, contextualized understanding of the prediction being made. There Global Supply Chain (GCC) countries serve as a useful example, Multimodal AI can predict the demand surge on the Ramadan season and on other international expos and in addition to geo-political data streams, real time weather, and IoT enabled devices, geopolitically sensitive data streams enable real-time weather forecasting, which enable seamless coordination of procurement and inventory in accordance to geo-structured data. These data enables firms to meet the target of eliminating stock out events and minimize surplus inventory along with improved customer satisfaction. Multimodal AI need also to be praised for its capacity to optimize and in essence define a range of tailored automated solutions, allowing institutions to meet the demands of real-time responsiveness, responsiveness, and heightened market competition on a global scale. Demand forecasting precision is also a target of improvement for Multimodal

AI, augmenting the supply chain pro-activity, resilience, and regional adaptability (Sirilertsuwan et al., 2020).

Agentic AI for Disruption Management & Decision Support

Predictive analytics is set to evolve with Agentic AI which takes on the role of a self-governing problem solver in logistics ecosystems. With the assistance of agentic AI, self-governing problem-solving copies identifies friction points, analyzes course of actions, and takes remedial actions with very minimal external help in Disruption Management. In the case of some delay in GCC ports and airports, agentic AI identifies the congested systems and is able to design a rerouting plan, anticipate the various systems which would be impacted and evaluate the various downstream effects prior to executing the resolution. By employing reinforcement learning and generative modeling, the algorithms in the system learn from disruptions and improve on their capabilities the following time. In the case of procurement and tendering, the technology assesses supplier non-compliance and other risk factors in real time. When agentic AI is embedded in control towers, it gives 'bottom line' suggestions and executes cross discipline coordination. In unpredictable scenarios, it 'guides' these scenarios to be more predictable and herds them to be more controllable. The problem of manual escalation is resolved which correlates to a reduction in financial losses and increased operational stability. It is clear to see that agentic AI correlates with complex trade in the MENA region due to the resilient logistics networks provided (de Vass et al., 2021a).

Optimization of Procurement, Warehousing, and Transportation

Procurement, warehousing, and distribution all stand to benefit from productivity reductions with the help of Generative AI. Predictive supplier performance, alternative sourcing strategies considering cost and sustainability, and simulated contract term proposals are all achievable with AI in procurement. Storage structure, pick route, and workforce task design are all addressed in the warehousing sectors productivity with the help of Generative AI. In GCC smart warehousing, the models-maintained set ERC and demand flexible replenishment, while monitoring energy expenditure. AI further refines logistics with self-maintaining route proposals considering traffic, fuel consumption, and carbon efficiency. Generative AI assists in maintaining balanced loads across air, sea, and land networks for MENA trades with the rest of the world. Through dynamically reevaluating and instating new methodologies, Generative AI promotes asset control with eased delivery, reduced waste, and increased visibility. These methodologies also help identify Scope-3 emissions to meet

ESG goals while maximizing the operational efficiency. Under this new paradigm, logistics increasingly seeks intelligence instead of cost (Chikhi et al., 2022). Figure 2 Shows how generative AI enhances procurement, warehousing, transportation, and ESG alignment for smarter, sustainable logistics.

Figure 2. Generative AI in logistics optimization

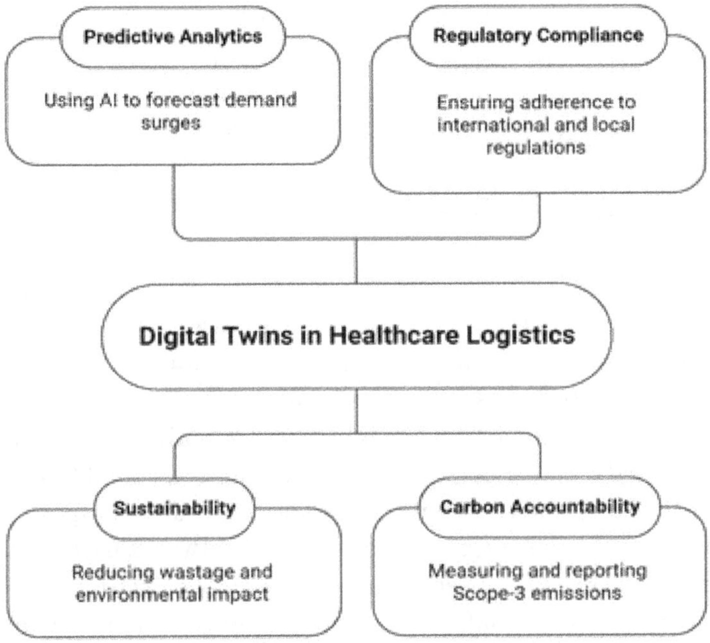

Emerging Challenges: Hallucinations, Bias, and Trust in AI Outputs

Even though generative AI has certain capabilities, implementing them in area of logistics is faced with the problems of precision, accountability, and accuracy of the data. AI hallucinations or figments of AI, simulate AI processes with reasoning and outputs, and can be quite useful in making decisions on routing or selection of suppliers. In the same way, the biases included in training data sets can reinforce systemic inequalities by underserving some suppliers and trade routes and a complete lack of fairness and transparency in available procurement options. AI is presumed to disregard the provenance of data and work on the "black box" mentality; thus, lack of trust becomes a fundamental problem for logistics managers and policymakers.

Within the GCC, governance, public procurement, and e-tendering controls are so rigid that such issues trigger scepticism towards supposed AI-based solutions. In the same way, lack of oversight and response capabilities during the unprecedented crisis may arise due to excessive dependency on AI. Lack of enough composure in response to any crisis aids the accumulation of any of these above factors. Lack of trust on AI implements relies on weak structure accountability creative frameworks, a blend of human and AI decisions, and strong validating guidelines on legally set principles (Alahmari & Awad, 2025; Awad, 2025; Wahid & Awad, 2025) . To protect the functional integrities, trust-able Generative systems is a must in the domain of Global logistics which needs to be kept open (Birkel & Hartmann, 2019; Qadeer & Awad, 2025; Qadeer et al., 2025; Ghonim & Awad, 2025).

Digital Twins in Supply Chains

By implementing digital twins, supply chains may be changed into intelligent ecosystems due to the instantaneous, real-time emulation of various physical assets, processes, and networks of a scalable virtual model. Continuous control and visibility are provided to these cyber-physical systems which integrate a combination of IoT data, AI models, and simulation tools. Unlike digital static models, digital twins, in real-time capture dynamic operational and environmental conditions are current data. This real-time data adds to their ability to monitor various aspects of systems such as production, warehouses, transportation, and networks used during the last stages of a supply chain. Moreover, companies can now improve their resilience thanks to digital twins that simulate various disruptions, anticipate consequences, and suggest mitigative actions. Bottom up, sustainability criteria; monitored resource use, carbon tracking, and fulfillment of multiple ESG obligations. Digital twins improve competitiveness within the GCC and MENA, where logistics hubs rapidly adopt smart infrastructure, seeking economic diversification and, at the same time, complying with sustainability frameworks. More sophisticated diversification and sustainability focused economic frameworks encourage targeted geographical distribution of sophisticated digital ecosystems. The physical systems on the other hand are more focused on optimized infrastructure and seamless supply chain connectivity. The combination of these systems promote transparency throughout the value chain and controlled carbon supply chains (Singh, 2024).

Concept and Architecture of Digital Twins

Digital twins pertain to devising a real-time computational model of a physical system which self-updates through external data feeds. In the case of digital logistics, it's the use of the IoT, RFID, AI, and cloud systems that model the interaction of trucks, warehouses, and port terminals. This model usually comprises four tiers: data acquisition, processing and integration, simulation and model building, and finally, model visualization. In data acquisition, the interfaces interact with the sensors, pulling operational data while integration platforms assure the binding of devices and systems. AI predictive simulation systems and machines then provide predictive simulation tools while earthly AI engines provide real-time operational dashboards. The approach equips logistic managers with operational, predictive, and prescriptive analytic tools. For instance, the managers could oversee real-time port terminal systems then later model delays in order to apply congestion counter measures. In the GCC, such digital architectures support control towers which through deep learning and cloud processors synchronize enterprise, governmental, and sustainable logistics planning (Ittmann, 2015).

Applications Across Production, Warehousing, and Last-Mile Delivery

Throughout the logistics supply chain, digital twins have numerous use cases. In production, digital twins optimize manufacturing lines by modeling them and pointing out pieces of equipment that have inefficiencies. These inefficiencies can be addressed with predictive maintenance, which limits equipment downtime. In warehousing, digital twins optimize energy use, storage spaces, and even the allocation of personnel to different tasks by modeling the storage layouts. Automation lowers operational costs by minimizing the real-time insights instead of real-time inventory control that needs to be done. In last-mile delivery, digital twins optimize delivery by routing synced with the simulation of traffic patterns, weather, and customer demand. In the GCC, Dubai and Riyadh, digital twins for fleet management and e-commerce logistics are basic twins. Integrating these functions, businesses reduce emissions while gaining insight to delivery accuracy and bottlenecks. More than efficiency, digital twins enhance the satisfaction of the customers by providing transparent order tracking. All of these functions show that digital twins are not simply tools for operations; they use them to help shape their supply chain networks to make them more intelligent, adaptable, and sustainable (Getahun et al., 2024). Table 3 Provides a stage-wise view of digital twin applications in production, warehousing, transportation, and last-mile delivery, highlighting benefits like predictive analytics and ESG monitoring.

Table 3. Digital twin use cases across supply chain stages

Supply Chain Stage	Digital Twin Application	Example in GCC Context	Key Benefits
Production	Models manufacturing lines, monitors machine health, and enables predictive maintenance	Petrochemical plants in Saudi Arabia using digital twins	Reduced downtime, optimized resource utilization
Warehousing	Simulates storage layouts, tracks energy use, and automates workforce allocation	Smart warehouses in Dubai South Logistics District	Faster operations, reduced energy consumption
Transportation	Monitors fleet performance, simulates routes, and predicts disruptions	Jeddah Port traffic flow simulations using digital twins	Improved efficiency, minimized congestion
Last-Mile Delivery	Models urban traffic, weather, and consumer demand for optimized deliveries	E-commerce delivery in Riyadh supported by twin models	Timely delivery, lower emissions, improved customer trust

SIMULATION AND PREDICTIVE ANALYTICS FOR RESILIENCE

The balancing shores of policy and economy termed the Gulf Cooperation Council John Dunigan. The digital twinning along with its enhanced analytics Capital World and the GCC economy has benefit from stronger predictive analytics sustaining from digital twinning enabling anticipative disruption deductions in the various components of the supply chains. Digital twins can predict the closure of a port, a sudden unwarranted surge of demand for a product, or geopolitical risks by amalgamating the past data and data points in real-time. Predictive analytics then calculates the possible scenarios and the best options available which would be shipment relays or rescheduling the production. These capabilities are important for the GCC and for logistics hubs in the region for they serve as relay points for the world and thus are prone to sudden disruptions in trade or a sudden shun in the energy market. Companies can avoid mistakes and losses by improperly testing resilience strategies in the real world and instead utilize the preset strategies in a simulated environment. Digital twins are able to change supply chains from reactive systems to proactive systems which thus enhances the resilience and efficiency of the supply chain system in the world (Adewusi et al., 2024).

Real-Time Synchronization and ESG Monitoring

The application of digital twins in real-time synchronization and ESG monitoring is profoundly transformative. IoT-enabled twins ingest live data and monitor the alignment of actual and digital geographies corresponding to the trucks, warehouses, and production lines. This alignment allows logistics managers to make real-time decisions, including but not limited to, vehicle re-routing, inventory shifts, and energy recalibration. More importantly, digital twins have the ability to monitor and measure social and environmental factors at granular levels. These systems can monitor carbon emissions at Scope 1, Scope 2, and Scope 3, energy use, and labor compliance. Especially in certain parts of the world, like the GCC, where the focus of the governments is on ESG reporting and carbon neutralities, these functionalities enable firms to not only comply but enhance brand trust. For example, a digital twin of a supply chain network can identify the routes that minimize emissions while providing the necessary delivery service within the required time. Digital twins transform supply chain management into a unique form of real-time operational and ESG synchronized copier systems to competitive differentiators in the market. This, together with ESG accountability, allows a firm to have real-time operational synchronization, which enhances the firm's competitive differentiation in the market (Holloway, 2024).

AUTONOMOUS OPERATIONS

More and more logistics processes are autonomous in nature and self-optimizing with the use of robotics, drones, AGVs, and AI systems which minimizes workforce and boosts focus on other activities. Block chain technology also provides smart contracts on procurement and compliance which further increases the level of automation during logistics. AI systems also help realize end to end AI enabled control logistics which merges streams from suppliers, carriers, and customers while monitoring stock levels with drones and AGVs. There is the need to focus more on the collaboration between workers and machines as well as the need to enhance overall workers' safety and regulatory framework. These autonomous systems help achieve better competitive standards as well as new governance frameworks to help achieve more efficient supply chains, while also reducing the overall carbon footprint of trade (Neufville et al., 2022).

Robotics, Drones, And AGVS in Logistics Hubs

The foundation of autonomous logistics centers consists of robotics, drones and AGVs. In a warehouse setting, robots perform monotonous and repetitive work like picking and packing, and palletizing, thus increasing productivity as well as reducing mistakes. Drones provide aerial surveillance, conducting precise inventory scans and supervising yard activities. AGVs independently autonomous drive, transporting and relocating pallets and containers within warehouses and terminals. These systems, in addition to speeding up processes, allow operations to run 24/7, thus decreasing reliance of labor. In the GCC, like Jebel Ali Port and King Abdullah Port, logistics centers deploy robotics and AGVs to improve operational efficiency and promote sustainability. Drones are essential in piloting last-mile deliveries, especially in smart city initiatives. The merging of robotics, drones and AGVs within logistics centers enhances agility and efficiency and streamlines responsiveness to fluctuating demands and supply chain disruptions with minimal downtime (Reddy et al., 2023). Figure 3 illustrates how robotics, drones, AGVs, and automation improve efficiency, adaptability, and sustainability in logistics hubs.

Figure 3. Enhancing logistics with automation

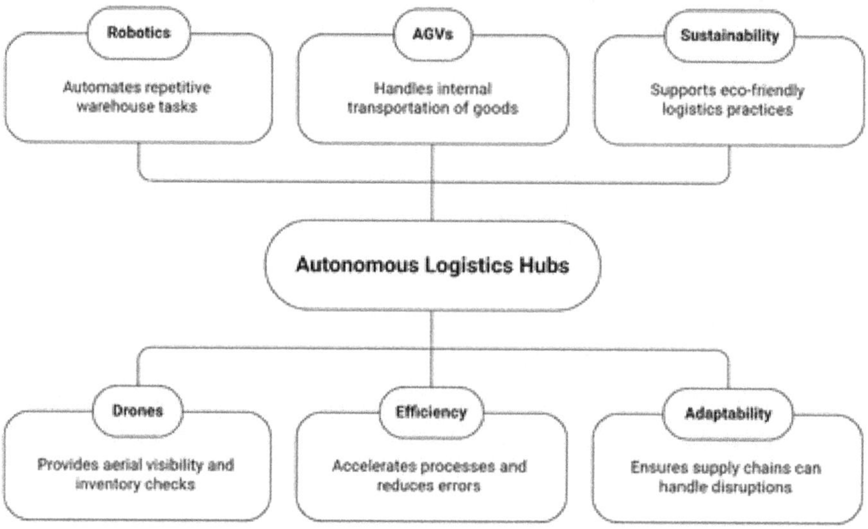

AI-Enabled Control Towers and Smart Contracts

Real-time visibility and decision-making capabilities are served by AI-enabled control towers which act as the nerve centers of autonomous supply chains. These control towers are capable of monitoring logistics flows from the starting point to the endpoint by synthesizing data from IoT devices, ERP systems, and transportation networks. Generative AI has expanded the use of AI which helps in providing the answers to problems, optimizing the logistics and timetables, and even predicting possible problems that might arise. Also, the range of autonomy afforded by the 'self-executing' contracts and Blockchain technology is a revolution by itself, which automates the entire process of contracts, payment processes, and compliance audit verifications. When the contracts are fulfilled, owing to self-executing nature, the administrative burden is lifted thus supporting marginally better transparency. These are some of the world's most sophisticated technologies which are being incorporated within the national logistics infrastructure of the GCC countries to foster the development of digital trade corridors and e-tendering services. For example, the UAE incorporates Blockchain technology within trade to streamline the onboarding processes for customs and suppliers (Leogrande, 2024). These along with control towers establish smart contracts capable of self-regulation thus reducing fraud and improving accuracy on a global scale, fostering trust in the supply chains. These technologies also provide resilient and transparent autonomously logistics operations. They are the essential components for global supply chains to be integrated with self-sustaining smart contracts.

Human-Machine Collaboration and Safety Issues

Autonomous systems regardless, the most vital integration remains the interaction between people and machines. All forms of robots, drones, and AGVs need human operators for supervision, exception handling, and strategic oversight. Maintaining the most efficient cooperation equally ensures machines perform monotonous or dangerous operations while humans devote themselves to intricate reasoning, innovation, and customer relations. Shared workspaces, however, raise safety concerns when humans and autonomous machines work side by side. Collisions, miscommunication, and systemic malfunctions are examples of risk factors. To counterbalance these, logistics firms need to set and follow safety policies, apply geofencing precautions, and diligently train human operators. In the GCC, smart logistics hubs are pouring resources into AI-focused safety systems to monitor and predict accidents while enforcing compliance. Trust within human-machine collaboration relations must be built on a culture of safety, transparency, and inclusiveness, ensuring humans are not replaced, but increased, by the technology. This equilibrium is essential in the sustainable deployment of autonomous logistics systems (Neufville et al., 2022).

Regulatory Frameworks and Regional Adoption

Technologies involving autonomous logistics have developed so rapidly as to make their lack of regulation concerning use within the GCC and MENA region rather alarming. There are specific rules concerning use of drones in city zones, pipelines of AGVs on highways, and robotics airports in shared workspaces. All GCC governments have had to make headway in compliance as practice approaches global regulatory compliance. In this regard it is noteworthy that the UAE's General

Civil Aviation Authority has developed specific regulations for the use of drones, while Saudi Arabia has been working on her autonomous vehicles regulatory policy within the framework of Vision 2030. In addition to these, there has been policy developed to govern the use of AI in relation to privacy, safety, and accountability concerning autonomous decision making. Adoption is being driven while compliance is being observed thanks to the public-private partnership. Other Regional logistics hubs are becoming the primary AI regulatory sandbox within which the rules are developed in tandem with the technology. The clearer the rules are, the more the countries in the GCC will be trusted. In turn, this will make the rulers of the GCC the global champions in the regulation of global autonomous supply chains (Sharma & Khanna, 2020).

Integration Framework for GCC & Beyond

The CCPs application of Generative AI, digital twins, and autonomous operations along with the GCC supply chains is going to need an integration approach which considers the balanced distribution of the necessary infrastructure, technology, governance, and sustainability. Integrating smart ports with the free zones and the digital trade corridors which the GCC countries have developed is the backbone to which the rest of the logistics infrastructure can be modernized for efficiency. The operative level of these 'logistic networks' is illuminated through the active cyberspace and physical space intersection systems which are managed through IoT devices. The cybernetically empowered physical systems enhance the prompt synthetic visibility and management over the physical and digital assets of the network. Just like any other management frameworks, the setting and distribution of instruction data shields need an appropriate value of governance, as well as standards, which are set, and, in particular, visually perceived, even though its governance structure to this day is still a work in progress, ESG compliance about the region's Capture-Sequester-Store System and its forever principles is ever more apparent. These nations are adding to the sophistication of the GCC and the MENA region in the professional practices of highly intelligent logistics for trade and worldwide sustainability (Susan et al., 2017).

GCC Digital Infrastructure Readiness

The digital transformation in the GCC has great potential value, especially pinpointing new construction and the advancement of existing logistics facilities and associated techniques. Multi-cloud platforms along with a burgeoning Internet of Things (IoT) and 5G Plus systems ensure seamless connectivity among logistics hubs, ports, and various nodes emanating from the supply chain. In Saudi Arabia and the UAE, pioneering digital- governance states implement integrated platforms for real-time unified smart control of customs, logistics, and digital procurement to provide graphed seamless governance of smart construction and cross-border digital trade routing. Edge computing in integrated digital trade to orchestrate timely routing of autonomous vehicles to ports for traffic decongestion and unjamming. Test beds the size of cities, such as attending logistics and like digital twins were Advanced Plus AI optimization masters for new age digital trade systems for AI geo. Under the sophisticated master plan, layered defense operations and forward defense with a complex posture of advanced governance control enables the entire region to counter aggression to trust and resilience reflex points. The rest of the advanced interconnected defense and division infra controls and distributed fusion enforcers supports the GCC to enhances and advanced accelerators for counter resilient trust infra and self-supply chain governance. Have split rest from advancement self-supply chain governance (Haddud et al., 2017).

Cyber-Physical Systems and IoT Backbone

In the Gulf Cooperation Council countries, hyper-automation in logistics is centered on cyber-physical systems. Advanced IoT Integrated sensors and Radio Frequency Identification (RFID) devices obtain real-time data on the status of cargo, warehouse and vehicle conditions, and fleet and environmental performance. Such data is relayed in real-time to digital twins and AI systems for Predictive Analytics, route optimization, and Predictive Maintenance. Edge devices ensure the rapid processing of critical data and survival of critical systems in port control and last-mile delivery by processing critical information at the local level. Similarly, cyber-physical integration allows for autonomous operations i.e. the Controlled Autonomous Vehicles (CAVs), drones, and robotics can work in conjunction with the central control towers. For instance, in Dubai, the implementation of smart logistics projects improves urban delivery and fleet optimization by utilizing the Internet of Things (IoT) systems. Moreover, the distributed systems' data certainty and trust are fulfilled by extended blockchain technology. The cyber-physical systems in hyper-connected and cross-integrated digital and physical systems form autonomous self-regulating supply chains, self-perpetuating to the level of change in demand, disruption, and inter-sustainability balance. Such systems are the backbone of logistics across the Middle East and North Africa (MENA) region, offering designer and superlative resilience and agility to the supply chain (Afum et al., 2020).

Standards, Governance, and ESG Compliance in Mena Supply Chains

The MENA region needs intelligent logistics standards and governance frameworks. The need for trust and interoperability among diverse stakeholders public and private logistics operators and multinational enterprises dictates standards. The EU and the US standards ISO for data security and GS1 for supply chain identification are being contextualized for the GCC. Governance frameworks for ethical use of AI stipulate accountability, transparency, and fairness in automated decision-making. ESG frameworks are being integrated into the logistics policies of the GCC region in response to the global targets of carbon neutrality and local initiatives like Saudi Vision 2030 and UAE Net Zero 2050. The supply chains are required to monitor, adopt, and report Scope-1, Scope-2, and Scope-3 emissions circular logistics and sustainability metrics. The regional authorities are issuing trade-competitive "green" certifications for logistics hubs as part of a pilot program (Chen, 2024). The combined approach of standards, governance, and ESG accountability will enable MENA supply chains to pioneer the global logistics best practices with trust, resilience, and long-term sustainability.

CASE STUDY SECTION

The strategic usefulness of intelligent logistics will be illustrated via practical use across the GCC wherein technology, governance, and sustainability converge to revolutionize supply chain ecosystems. While conceptually, the framework discusses the possibilities of generative AI, digital twins, and autonomous functions, it is only when these tools are employed at scale, across critical industries, that they begin to yield their true value. The domains of healthcare, maritime trade, food security, and green corridors serve as fertile ecosystems to nurture and test these innovations (Ravikumar & Aarthi, 2025). Case studies originating from the UAE, Saudi Arabia, Qatar, and Oman highlight the increasing integration of advanced technologies into national policy to address issues such as precision and economically sustainable cold chain management, chronic port congestion, the distribution of climate-resilient food, and green multimodal routing. Not only are these models indicative of efficiency and cost-savings, but they also showcase alignment to net-zero and ESG targets, thereby shielding the GCC's position as a logistics ecosystem of the future (Karthikeyan & Nagaprakash, 2023).

Case Study 1: Smart Food & Beverage Supply Chains in Qatar

The food security strategy for Qatar is focused on the dire needs for food security and the tropical conditions under which food needs to be stored and transported. Managing and storing fresh produce, milk and meat is even more difficult because the entire area is a desert which makes it very difficult to keep insulated. Qatar has managed to implement digital twins, sentient and autonomous delivery and tested them on the perishable goods and food distribution networks. The digital twin models on the Qatar food distribution system allows the Qatar national food distribution system to interface with satellites in space in real time to simulate and plan the food allocation for major holidays and sporting events. With the help of deployed retail partner autonomous electric driven vehicles, the traditional, fuel powered trucks for unloading are no longer needed. The benchmark these measures achieved were very important. First, and foremost, the food surplus wastage has decreased by 18% massively, for the cold storage and inventory issues are managed better. Less distance delivery times benefits by 20% consumers greatly. Overall, consumers benefit too, which is nice. His arguments are more persuasive on the Qatar's sustainability objectives, since save less energy by 20%. In support of Qatar's National Vision 2030, these findings continue to support Qatar's food security strategy. This case illustrates the use of digital twins, AI, and self-sufficiency to build strong and eco-friendly food transport systems in areas with difficult climates. Qatar's food and beverages supply chains are more resilient to global shocks. Qatar defines the region's leadership in the use of smart food security and sustainability logistics (Reddy et al., 2023). Figure 4 Highlights improvements in food waste reduction, delivery efficiency, and energy optimization achieved through intelligent logistics.

Figure 4. Impact of smart food & beverage supply chains in qatar

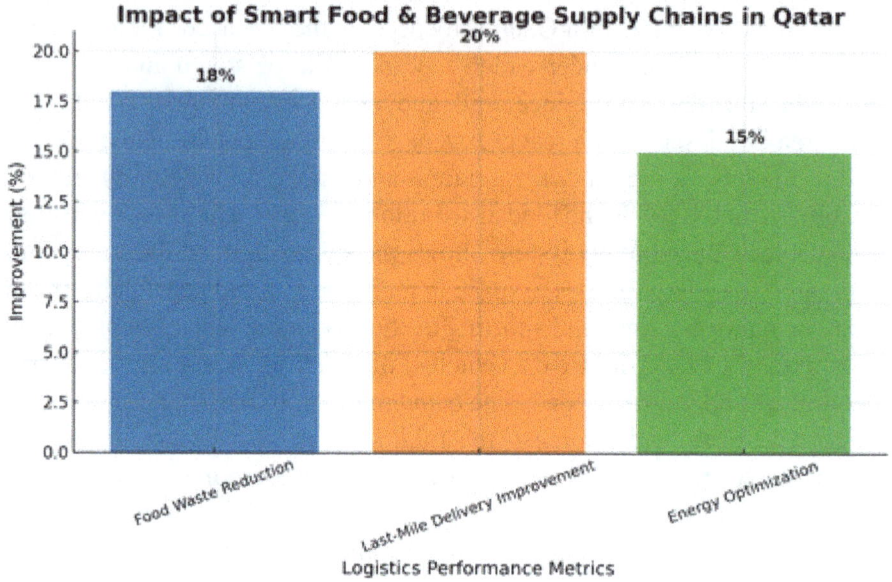

Case Study 2: Oman's Green Logistics Corridors

The unique position of Oman strategically emphasizing the Indian Ocean and the bordering Gulf Cooperation countries offers Oman significant trading and bandwidth advantages. Oman has been pursuing environmentally friendly and technology enabled sustainable practices. One of the initiatives in this direction is the "Green Logistics Corridors" project aimed at sustaining the growth of Oman as a Trade Hub at the crossroads of the Gulf and Indian sub-continent. The project deployed IoT driven transport fleets, tracking, and emissions monitoring. There are data floats which are integrated into digital twins, IoT dashboards monitoring cargo and energy. Sohar Port, Muscat, and the inland Free Zones are optimized by Generative AI along with the required traffic, fuel, and environmental data. Oman has also incorporated "point of sale" customs clearance through automated blockchain smart contracts, enabling cross-border trade with customs transparency and faster processing, which decreases paperwork by 20% (Aarthi, Ravikumar, & Pardaev, 2025). Economically, the blocks of smart contracts are emissions of carbon, diesel, and trade paper by 17%. The smart contracts, trade routes with IoT records, advanced route trading, and decreased manual processes lowered logistics spending 12%. Oman's leadership in sustainable trade and green logistics has been confirmed by the financial and sustainable environment offers. The integration of technological innovation with sustainability in the supply chains of Oman established a balanced competitive trade model. Green Logistics Corridors advanced Oman Vision 2040, boosting Oman's image as a reliable, globally connected, and innovative logistics center (Hussain et al., 2019). Figure 5 Displays improvements in cost reduction, emission control, and trade transparency achieved through Oman's sustainable logistics initiative

Figure 5. Impact of Oman's green logistics corridors

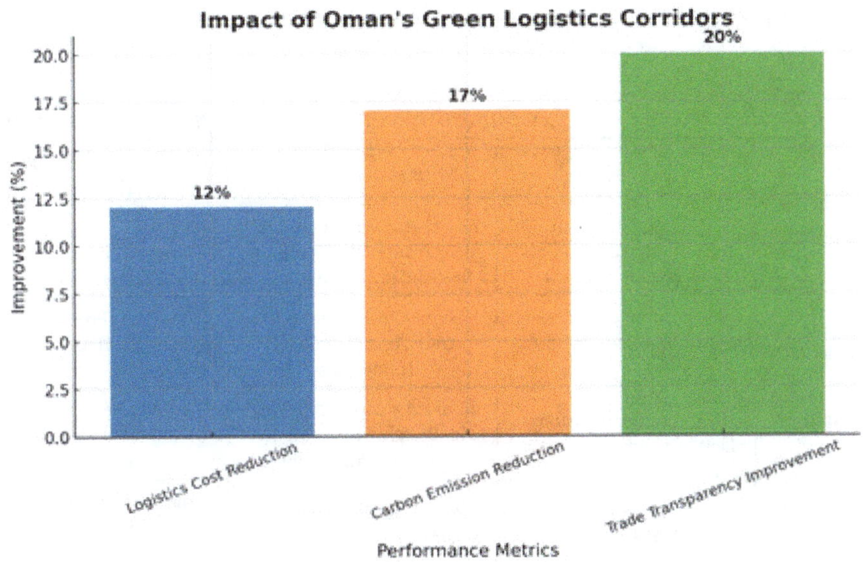

Ethical, Security, and Sustainability Considerations

In the context of the GCC region and the world, the straight-A frameworks of expanding ecosystems of intelligent logistics, which have logistics-centered and new-data-driven architectures, evaluate the ethical, security, and sustainment conditions in order to assume success in the long-term, along with the robust systems of cyber-physical structures, which work in silos to enhance efficiencies. These structures of systems are prone to a variety of hostile attacks with a potential to massively disrupt the order of trade and leak sensitive information. Their resolutions call upon resilient-blueprint architectures, protected devices of the IoT, and the robust fence of border-control systems. Among the foremost futuristic challenges of ethical nature are the use of generative AI and autonomous systems in the processes of procurement and bidding where the trust of the involved parties are transparent, fair, trust, and bypass the bias (Aarthi, et al., 2025). Plus, sustainment has been an unconditional demand, with supply chains providing achieve the world fulfillment of carbon neutrality devoid of eco-shame. Repair, reuse, and reverse logistics resonates with the GCC goals to replenish green growth. Once integrated, the borders of cyber security, ethical AI, and carbon-negative circuitry will transform the supply chains into transparent, resilient, global trade sustainers, and regionally active, uncovered economic boosters (Al-Zabidi et al., 2021). Table 4 Presents key issues such as cyber-physical security, ethical AI in procurement, and carbon-neutral strategies, along with mitigation measures and GCC policy initiatives.

Table 4. Ethical, security, and sustainability considerations in intelligent logistics

Dimension	Key Issues	Mitigation Measures	GCC Policy/Initiative Example
Cyber-Physical Security	Vulnerabilities in IoT devices, digital twins, and autonomous systems	End-to-end encryption, AI-driven anomaly detection, redundancy in systems	UAE Cybersecurity Strategy, Saudi National Cybersecurity Authority
Ethical AI in Procurement	Bias in supplier selection, lack of transparency in AI-driven tendering	Human oversight, audit trails, explainable AI frameworks	UAE's e-Procurement platform with transparency mandates
Sustainability & Carbon	High carbon emissions, lack of Scope-3 visibility	Real-time carbon tracking via digital twins, adoption of green certifications	UAE Net Zero 2050, Saudi Vision 2030 Sustainability Programs
Circular Supply Chains	Excess waste, linear "use-and-dispose" logistics	Repair, reuse, recycling, reverse logistics integration	Oman's Circular Economy Roadmap, GCC waste-to-resource projects
Regulatory Governance	Fragmented standards, weak global interoperability	Harmonization with ISO/GS1, regional ESG reporting frameworks	GCC Standardization Organization (GSO) initiatives

CYBER-PHYSICAL SECURITY AND RESILIENCE AGAINST SUPPLY CHAIN ATTACKS

Integrating IoT, robotics, and advanced digital twinning into logistic networks enhances the risk of cyber threats. Smart ports, control towers, or autonomous fleets facing attacks might have their operations paralyzed, alongside disruption of global trade. In the context of the GCC, ports and free zones serve critical access points, so the need for resilience becomes imperative. Cyber security should without a doubt incorporate end-to-end encryption, anomaly detection driven through AI, and multi-factor authentication. Tethered cyber incidents of a situational nature are attenuated through the redundant architecture of digital twins and the signals redundancy of the edge devices. Foreign partnerships with cyber security resellers are beneficial to the government's increasing compliance enforcement. By default, resilience allows GCC logistics ecosystems to respond to the shifting threat landscape while nurturing global market trust, sustained activity, and competitiveness in market position (Saberi et al., 2019a).

Ethical Use of Generative AI In Procurement and Tendering

AI systems are increasingly integral to procurement by automating systems for supplier discovery, supplier risk assessments, and supplier tendering. While the use of AI systems in procurement needs to be trustworthy, AI systems ought to be robust and explainable, regardless of the ethical standards displayed. This ethical dimension is directly relevant to the GCC region's public sector tendering, which is why fairness and accountability international normative constructs need to be observed. AI use must be preceded by ethical behavioral standards and accountability frameworks proportional to the amount of AI managed systems. The tendency to "hallucinate" on generative AI systems by producing incorrect information must also be eliminated. GCC supply chains ought to balance ethical considerations with increased fairness and efficiency in the global logistics ecosystem (Yang et al., 2023).

Carbon-Neutral Strategies and Circular Supply Chains

The core of sustainability rests in intelligent logistics, as the GCC member states implement their transformative supply chain strategies in tandem with carbon-neutral pledges, such as the Saudi Vision 2030 and UAE Net Zero 2050 strategies. Digital twins and AI tools enable organizations to geofence carbon-aware routes and manage active and passive carbon-emitting sources. The Circular Practices in Logistics repurpose, reuse, recycle, and reverse logistics reduces emissions and fuels product lifecycle extensions, as do autonomous vehicles, drones, and the decarbonization of last-mile delivery. Governments are already providing incentives for the adoption of green certifications and ESG reporting to improve compliance and trade competitiveness. The GCC logistics systems, by integrating circular and carbon-neutral strategies, do not only achieve the sustainability goals but strengthen resilience, lower costs, and create global leadership in green supply chain innovation (Zhang & Chen, 2013).

FUTURE OUTLOOK

The advancement of intelligent logistics within the Gulf and the rest of the world integrates critical technologies with the maintaining imperatives: quantum ready optimization can reconstruct logistics networks by geo-resolving remarkably complex routed and scheduled logistics endeavours. Incorporation of agentic AI at the ecosystem periphery will enable constituents of logistics ecosystems to process disruption simulations in real-time and deliver self-generated autonomous response solutions. The Gulf is expected to pioneer such projects and harness the robust frameworks of smart city initiatives and national vision programs to implement these large-scale intelligent systems (Ravikumar et al., 2025). The region's designed approach to achieving world supremacy in decarbonized sustainable logistics is also crucial. The decarbonization pledge of the GCC nations forms an opposite backdrop to fuse intelligent logistics innovation with ESG principles and global trade competitiveness. The region is poised to combine advanced computing and AI driven autonomy with carbon neutral mindful methods to construct an exemplar of resilient and green supply chain ecosystem. This will place the GCC at the forefront of international trade, enhancing widespread innovative logistics practice by incorporating sustainability and trade competitiveness (Radanliev et al., 2020).

Quantum-Ready Optimization for Logistics Networks

Quantum-ready optimization is revolutionary in solving logistics problems e.g., multimodal routing and large-scale scheduling, container allocation, and scheduling. Many real-world problems in global logistics hubs contain thousands of variables and have real-time complexity. These problems, which center around global logistics, can easily be solved using hybrid-algorithm computing techniques and quantum inspired algorithms. The algorithms above enable faster decision making, which lead to decreased costs (Marisamy et al., 2025). GCC ports and free zones can utilize this in order to increase the efficiency of vessel berthing and congestion reduction. There is an ongoing pilot project which is in the stages of quantum-ready optimization. This project aims to integrate quantum motivated logistics platforms with energy optimization and sustainability. The ability to generate optimal solutions is crucial in order to diffuse the ever-growing volatility within global supply chains. The rapid generation of optimal solutions is a key variable. If GCC nations invest in quantum logistics research, they will be among the first to embrace the revolutionary technology and use it to increase the resilience and competitiveness of global supply chains (de Vass et al., 2021b).

Multimodal and Agentic AI Adoption in Real-World GCC Projects

The use of multimodal and agentic AI in logistics is moving from theory to practice in the context of GCC use cases. Multimodal AI forecasts and strategizes resource use by amalgamating sensor information, market intelligence, and satellite images. Agentic AI further builds on this by simulating disruptions autonomously, testing alternative routes, and performing real-time adjustments with minimal human supervision. In GCC initiatives like Dubai's smart logistics corridors and Saudi Arabia's NEOM, these technologies manage intricate flows of goods across air, sea, and land. The outcome is self-regulating logistics networks that adapt to demand surges, port bottlenecks, geopolitical disruptions, or any combination of them, with instantaneous response times. Such use correct not only improves operational emissions but also supports sustainability by optimizing fuel usage. With time, these systems will form the backbone of logistics envisioned for the region (Rendon-Benavides et al., 2023).

Pathways to Global Leadership in Sustainable Logistics

Just as geographical location and visionary policies enable the Gulf Cooperation Council to undertake green diversification and complex economically green logistics activities, so too the legacies documented as the Saudi Vision 2030 and the UAE Net Zero 2050, and the economic geopolitical area of sustainable and green logistics extended by regional green certifications, fill in the green gap. Strategic policies in the field of reverse logistics and energy efficiency are boosted by modern systems such as autonomous digital twins, real time carbon monitoring, and advanced supply-chain optimization. The investments in renewable energy powered logistic hubs strengthen the tactical low emission fleet and the overall robust logistics structure. The enlargement role of the GCC in trade increases its strategic relevance and allows the council to set the logistic carbon accounting benchmarks. Connections to multinational companies and other institutions embracing the global ESG paradigm strengthen competitive advantage. The GCC regional policies, integration, and advanced technologies can make its logistics systems the most exemplary in the world, built to sustain responsible ecologic mobility in the world (Saberi et al., 2019b).

CONCLUSION

The impact of emerging technologies like generative AIs and digital twins on logistics processes across the GCC and other regions vividly showcases the autonomous changes defined by such technologies. Technologies that are shifting paradigms. Abstractions discussed in this Chapter such as the impact of advanced logistics on green corridors and on reshaped healthcare, maritime trade, and food security demonstrate the changing reality. In the UAE, AI-assisted cold chain technologies not only restricted the spoiling of vaccines and biologics, but also helped the UAE and broader region meet ESG requirements. Sophisticated ports in the Kingdom of Saudi Arabia enhanced their green credentials by better throughput efficiencies supported by autonomous cranes, drones, and digital twin technologies, achieving low emissions and increased economic activity, hence asserting the Kingdom as a global player in logistics. Qatar's food and beverage supply chains proved the ability of AI digital twins to automate food systems under unprecedented extreme conditions, while Oman's Green Logistics Corridors demonstrated the ability of blockchain coupled with advanced IoT to decrease emissions, trade costs, and enhance the immune systems. These demonstrate the ability of advanced logistics to enhance ecosystems through more integration and transparency while enabling more sustainable advanced economies.

The case studies prove once again the capacity of technology to bring about economic change beyond operational efficiencies as shown in Oman's Vision 2040, Qatar's Vision 2030, Saudi Arabia's Vision 2030, and the UAE's Net Zero 2050. The case studies also strengthen the position of logistics in providing economic diversification and sustainability and in improving the region's competitive advantage in international trade. Academically, the case studies serve as proof for the existence of models, or for the necessity to go beyond models to ethical frameworks, governance and resilience. In the rest of the economic sectors, the studies stress the importance of scaling up pilots to operational systems in which automation is embedded together with inclusion and human oversight. For instance, the case studies for policymakers emphasize the need to formulate the proper legal protective measures as part of the regulatory boundaries for cyber-physical systems which control borders, virtue ethical AI, and accountability for negative carbon emissions deceit. It is clear that the combination of AI, digital twins, and autonomy will bring about the unmatched change in which logistics is international, and the cornerstones of resilience, accountability, and sustainability are ever present. As a result of these efforts, the GCC not only adopts the best practices from all over the world, but also improves them to develop new paradigms in global supply chains which, in turn, are offered as models to the global community. In this case, intelligent logistics are simultaneously a technological frontier and a governance imperative defining the boundaries within which supply chains are secure, sustainable, and competitive in a volatile global marketplace.

REFERENCES

Aarthi, S., Ravikumar, R. N., & Pardaev, J. (2025). Synergizing multimodal generative AI and blockchain for the future of digital media. In *Advances in Computational Intelligence and Robotics* (pp. 1–34). IGI Global Scientific Publishing., DOI: 10.4018/979-8-3373-1504-1.ch001

Aarthi, S., Ravikumar, R. N., Sobirova, K., & Mamadiyarov, Z. (2025). Empowering a sustainable future through digital learning and the SDGs. In *Harnessing E-Learning to Create a Sustainable Future* (pp. 145–172). IGI Global Scientific Publishing.

Adewusi, A. O., Komolafe, A. M., Ejairu, E., Aderotoye, I. A., Abiona, O. O., & Oyeniran, O. C. (2024). The role of predictive analytics in optimizing Supply Chain Resilience: A review of techniques and case studies. Int. j. *Manag. Entrep. Res*, *6*(3), 815–837.

Afum, E., Osei-Ahenkan, V. Y., Agyabeng-Mensah, Y., Amponsah Owusu, J., Kusi, L. Y., & Ankomah, J. (2020). Green manufacturing practices and sustainable performance among Ghanaian manufacturing SMEs: The explanatory link of green supply chain integration. *Management of Environmental Quality*, *31*(6), 1457–1475.

Al-Zabidi, A., Rehman, A. U., & Alkahtani, M. (2021). An approach to assess sustainable supply chain agility for a manufacturing organization. *Sustainability*, *13*(4), 1752.

Alahmari, D., & Awad, A. (2025). Strategic integration of marketing and supply chain functions for superior customer experience: Insights from logistics startups under Saudi Vision 2030. *PLoS One*, *20*(11), e0336132. DOI: 10.1371/journal.pone.0336132 PMID: 41270081

Aliahmadi, A., Nozari, H., & Ghahremani-Nahr, J. (2022). AIoT-based sustainable smart supply chain framework. International Journal of Innovation in Management. *Economics and Social Sciences*, *2*(2), 28–38.

Awad, A. (2025). Enhancing market access and consumer engagement through digital marketing in the agricultural sector. *International Journal of Advanced and Applied Sciences*, *12*(8), 70–79. DOI: 10.21833/ijaas.2025.08.007

Awan, U., Sroufe, R., & Shahbaz, M. (2021). Industry 4.0 and the circular economy: A literature review and recommendations for future research. *Business Strategy and the Environment*, *30*(4), 2038–2060.

Birkel, H. S., & Hartmann, E. (2019). Impact of IoT challenges and risks for SCM. *Supply Chain Manage.: Int. J.*, *24*(1), 39–61.

Chen, R. (2024). Sustainable supply chain management as a strategic enterprise innovation. Advances in Economics. *Management and Political Sciences*, *85*(1), 24–29.

Chikhi, T., Santa-Eulalia, L. A., Mosconi, E., Risso, L. A., Filho, M. G., & Ganga, G. M. D. (2022). Going beyond blockchain adoption's hype to improve supply chain sustainability: Evidence from empirical and modelling studies. Proceedings of the Annual Hawaii International Conference on System Sciences.

de Vass, T., Shee, H., & Miah, S. (2021a). IoT in supply chain management: Opportunities and challenges for businesses in early industry 4.0 context. Oper. Supply Chain Manag. Int. J., 148–161.

de Vass, T., Shee, H., & Miah, S. (2021b). IoT in supply chain management: Opportunities and challenges for businesses in early industry 4.0 context. Oper. Supply Chain Manag. Int. J., 148–161.

Firouraghi, N., Kiani, B., Jafari, H. T., Learnihan, V., Salinas-Perez, J. A., Raeesi, A., Furst, M., Salvador-Carulla, L., & Bagheri, N. (2022). The role of geographic information system and global positioning system in dementia care and research: A scoping review. *International Journal of Health Geographics*, *21*(1), 8. PMID: 35927728

Getahun, S., Kefale, H., & Gelaye, Y. (2024). Application of precision agriculture technologies for sustainable crop production and environmental sustainability: A systematic review. *TheScientificWorldJournal*, *2024*, 2126734. PMID: 39421732

Ghahremani Nahr, J., Nozari, H., & Sadeghi, M. E. (2021). Green supply chain based on artificial intelligence of things (AIoT). International Journal of Innovation in Management. *Economics and Social Sciences*, *1*(2), 56–63.

Ghonim, A., & Awad, A. (2025). Shaping customer insights through e-marketing: An applied study in the banking sector. *International Journal of Advanced and Applied Sciences*, *12*(4), 88–98. DOI: 10.21833/ijaas.2025.04.011

Haddud, A., DeSouza, A., Khare, A., & Lee, H. (2017). Examining potential benefits and challenges associated with the Internet of Things integration in supply chains. *Journal of Manufacturing Technology Management*, *28*(8), 1055–1085.

Holloway, S. (2024). Exploring the impact of real-time supply chain information on marketing decisions: Insights from service industries. In *Preprints*.

Hussain, M., Al-Aomar, R., & Melhem, H. (2019). Assessment of lean-green practices on the sustainable performance of hotel supply chains. *International Journal of Contemporary Hospitality Management*, *31*(6), 2448–2467.

Ittmann, H. W. (2015). The impact of big data and business analytics on supply chain management. *Journal of Transport and Supply Chain Management*, *9*(1).

Karthikeyan, K. S., & Nagaprakash, T. (2023). Prioritizing IoT-driven sustainability initiatives in retail chains: Exploring case studies and industry insights. EAI Endorsed Trans. Internet Things, 10.

Lai, Y. (2024). Innovative strategies in logistics and supply chain management: Navigating modern challenges. SHS Web Conf., 183, 2020.

Leogrande, A. (2024). Integrating ESG principles into smart logistics:Toward sustainable supply chains. In *Preprints*.

Liu, J., Chen, M., & Liu, H. (2020). The role of big data analytics in enabling green supply chain management: A literature review. *Journal of Data, Information and Management*, *2*(2), 75–83.

Marisamy, K., Selvakumar, A., Rajasekar, B., Natarajan, R., Atajanova, A., & Makhmudov, S. (2025). Smart logistics integrating AI, IoT, blockchain, and Robotics for a sustainable Future. In *Emerging Trends in Smart Logistics Technologies* (pp. 73–104). IGI Global Scientific Publishing.

Neufville, R., Abdalla, H., & Abbas, A. (2022). Potential of connected fully autonomous vehicles in reducing congestion and associated carbon emissions. *Sustainability*, *14*(11), 6910.

Qadeer, A., & Awad, A. (2025). Generative AI in advertisements: A conceptual framework based on the technology acceptance model. In *Impacts of AI generated content on brand reputation* (pp. 109–127). IGI Global., DOI: 10.4018/979-8-3373-4327-3.ch004

Qadeer, A., Awad, A., & Ali, A. (2025). Understanding generative AI implementation in digital advertising among retail SMEs in Pakistan. In *Impacts of AI generated content on brand reputation* (pp. 177–201). IGI Global., DOI: 10.4018/979-8-3373-4327-3.ch007

Radanliev, P., De Roure, D., Page, K., Nurse, J. R. C., Mantilla Montalvo, R., Santos, O., Maddox, L., & Burnap, P. (2020). Cyber risk at the edge: Current and future trends on cyber risk analytics and artificial intelligence in the industrial internet of things and industry 4.0 supply chains. *Cybersecurity*, *3*(1).

Ravikumar, A. S., Kalandarov, A., Djumaniyazova, M., & Habib, M. (2025). A roadmap to a sustainable future. In Advances in Computational Intelligence and Robotics (pp. 267–302). IGI Global Scientific Publishing. https://doi.org/DOI: 10.4018/979-8-3373-3017-4.ch010

Ravikumar, R. N., & Aarthi, S. (2025). Digital Twin-driven green energy systems. In *The Future of Green Energy* (pp. 1–28). IGI Global Scientific Publishing., DOI: 10.4018/979-8-3373-3226-0.ch001

Reddy, T. T., Devi, Y. R., & Kavita, G. (2023). Logistics, traceability in food supply chain management. E3S Web Conf., 391, 1075.

Rendon-Benavides, R., Perez-Franco, R., Elphick-Darling, R., Plà-Aragonés, L. M., Gonzalez Aleu, F., Verduzco-Garza, T., & Rodriguez-Parral, A. V. (2023). In-transit interventions using real-time data in Australian berry supply chains. *The TQM Journal*, *35*(3), 759–777.

Saberi, S., Kouhizadeh, M., Sarkis, J., & Shen, L. (2019a). Blockchain technology and its relationships to sustainable supply chain management. *International Journal of Production Research*, *57*(7), 2117–2135.

Sharma, A., & Khanna, P. (2020). Relevance of adopting emerging technologies in outbound supply chain: New paradigm for cement industry. Oper. Supply Chain Manag. Int. J., 210–221.

Singh, P. K. K. (2024). Measuring the broader value proposition of digital transformation in supply chains. *Int. J. Supply Chain Manag.*, *13*(1), 16–24.

Sirilertsuwan, P., Thomassey, S., & Zeng, X. (2020). A strategic location decision-making approach for multi-tier supply chain sustainability. *Sustainability*, *12*(20), 8340.

Susan, W., Carsten, M., Daqiang, C., & Rosario, M. (2017). An IoT-enabled supply chain integration framework: Empirical case studies. In *Advances in Transdisciplinary Engineering*. IOS Press.

Udeh, E. O., Amajuoyi, P., Adeusi, K. B., & Scott, A. O. (2024). The role of IoT in boosting supply chain transparency and efficiency. *Magna Sci. Adv. Res. Rev.*, *12*(1), 178–197.

Wahid, A., & Awad, A. (2025). Role of AI chatbots in enhancing customer satisfaction and customer loyalty. In *Impacts of AI generated content on brand reputation* (pp. 129–147). IGI Global., DOI: 10.4018/979-8-3373-4327-3.ch005

Waller, M. A., & Fawcett, S. E. (2013). Data science, predictive analytics, and big data: A revolution that will transform supply chain design and management. *Journal of Business Logistics*, *34*(2), 77–84.

Yang, Q., Bolaji Samson, A., Muhammad Gummi, U., & Chen, D. (2023). Study on the use of industry 4.0 technology for the textile industry sustainable supply chain process. *Advances in Engineering Technology Research*, *4*(1), 140.

Zhang, J., & Chen, J. (2013). Coordination of information sharing in a supply chain. *International Journal of Production Economics*, *143*(1), 178–187.

KEY TERMS AND DEFINITIONS

Agentic AI: AI systems that not only analyze and predict but also act autonomously by simulating disruptions, testing solutions, and executing real-time decisions in logistics networks.

AI-Enabled Control Tower: A centralized digital platform that integrates real-time data streams across supply chain nodes, providing visibility, predictive insights, and prescriptive recommendations for decision-making.

Autonomous Operations: Logistics functions carried out by self-operating systems such as robotics, drones, AGVs, and AI-enabled control towers, reducing human intervention while increasing efficiency and safety.

Circular Supply Chain: A logistics model that emphasizes sustainability by promoting repair, reuse, recycling, and reverse logistics to minimize waste and resource consumption.

Cyber-Physical Systems (CPS): Integrated systems where digital technologies like IoT, AI, and cloud computing interact directly with physical logistics assets to monitor, analyze, and control supply chain performance.

Digital Twin: A virtual replica of a physical asset, process, or network that continuously synchronizes with real-world data, allowing simulation, predictive analytics, and prescriptive control in supply chain operations.

Generative AI: An advanced form of artificial intelligence that creates new outputs such as forecasts, scenarios, or optimization strategies by learning from multimodal data, enabling adaptive and autonomous logistics decision-making.

Quantum-Ready Optimization: The application of quantum-inspired or hybrid algorithms to solve complex logistics optimization problems such as multimodal routing, scheduling, and resource allocation.

Scope-3 Emissions: Indirect greenhouse gas emissions generated across the supply chain, including upstream suppliers and downstream customers, often monitored for ESG compliance.

Smart Contracts: Blockchain-based digital agreements that execute automatically when predefined conditions are met, ensuring transparency, compliance, and trust in procurement and logistics processes.

Chapter 9
From Dashboards to Decisions:
Prescriptive Agentic Supply Chain Control Towers

Abdelrehim Awad
https://orcid.org/0009-0005-3649-430X
University of Bisha, Saudi Arabia

Dhafer Alahmari
University of Bisha, Saudi Arabia

ABSTRACT

Control towers have matured from descriptive dashboards into prescriptive, agentic decision systems that sense, understand, decide, act, and learn across multi-enterprise networks. By combining streaming data fabrics, digital twins, graph/causal forecasting, optimization and reinforcement learning, and multi-agent coordination, modern control towers close the loop from prediction to execution with adjustable autonomy and safety guardrails. Control towers have matured from descriptive dashboards into prescriptive, agentic decision systems that sense, understand, decide, act, and learn across multi-enterprise networks. By combining streaming data fabrics, digital twins, graph/causal forecasting, optimization and reinforcement learning, and multi-agent coordination, modern control towers close the loop from prediction to execution with adjustable autonomy and safety guardrails.

DOI: 10.4018/979-8-3373-7006-4.ch009

1. INTRODUCTION

Control towers have matured from descriptive dashboards into prescriptive, agentic decision systems that sense, understand, decide, act, and learn across multi-enterprise networks. By combining streaming data fabrics, digital twins, graph/causal forecasting, optimization and reinforcement learning, and multi-agent coordination, modern control towers close the loop from prediction to execution with adjustable autonomy and safety guardrails. This chapter synthesizes architecture patterns, sector use-cases (after-sales, pharma/healthcare, energy/LNG, construction logistics, public procurement), and socio-technical lessons, drawing on multi-agent systems (MAS) foundations and prescriptive analytics research. We propose a reference model, a nine-step implementation roadmap, and evidence-based metrics to scale governed autonomy while improving service, cost, resilience, and sustainability. We also identify research gaps in standardization, interoperability, longitudinal impacts on workforce and performance, and assurance at scale (Giannakis & Louis, 2016; Lau et al., 2008; Liotine, 2019; Koot et al., 2021; Patsavellas et al., 2021; Domínguez et al., 2020; Smyth et al., 2024; Handfield et al., 2020; Zhu et al., 2020; Srivastava et al., 2022).

The first generation of control towers aggregated KPIs and events into descriptive dashboards, useful for visibility but dependent on manual interpretation and slow cross-functional action. The second generation added predictive analytics (ETAs, demand, at-risk orders) and "what-if" simulation. The third generation—prescriptive, agentic control towers—integrates intelligent decisioning and execution: optimization and RL policies choose actions, multi-agent coordination negotiates across network actors, and workflows/APIs implement changes with human-in-the-loop where needed (Lau et al., 2008; Giannakis & Louis, 2016; Domínguez et al., 2020; Smyth et al., 2024; Patsavellas et al., 2021). Deployed well, these towers compress decision latency, reduce stockouts and expedites, stabilize service under disruptions, and align decisions with ESG and risk constraints (Zhu et al., 2020; Handfield et al., 2020; Koot et al., 2021; Srivastava et al., 2022).

From dashboards that simply showed yesterday's numbers to intelligent systems that continuously sense, decide, and act across complex global networks, supply-chain control towers have undergone a profound transformation. In their earliest form, control towers were essentially sophisticated reporting rooms: walls of screens, or later browser-based dashboards, displaying a consolidated view of orders, inventories, and transportation events. Their promise was visibility-the idea that if managers could see everything in one place, they could resolve problems faster and coordinate more effectively. Visibility alone was not enough, however. Over time, supply chains became more global, product life cycles shorter, customer expectations more demanding, and disruptions more frequent. Managers no longer needed just to see; they needed systems that would help them think and act. This shift from descriptive dashboards to prescriptive and agentic systems is at the heart of the modern control tower story.

The first generation of control towers aggregated data from ERP, WMS, TMS, and partner systems into one pane of glass. These towers answered questions such as "Where is my shipment?", "What is my current inventory level?", or "How many orders are late?" The insight they provided was useful, but limited. Confronted with a screen full of red alerts, planners still had to decide what to do, in what order, and with what trade-offs. They had to phone suppliers, email transport providers, re-plan production in Excel, and manually negotiate with colleagues in marketing and finance. In other words, the tower showed them the battlefield, but did not help them fight the battle. As supply chains became more complex and volatile, this manual mode of operation started to reach its limits.

The second generation of control towers, therefore, added predictive capabilities. Instead of reporting only the past and present, they began estimating the future. Machine learning was used to predict estimated times of arrival, forecast short-term demand, and score the risk of stockouts or capacity shortfalls. These towers could highlight which shipments were likely to be late, which customers were at risk of poor service, and which materials might constrain production. Scenario analysis and what-if simulations allowed planners to explore different options, such as expediting a shipment, reallocating inventory between warehouses, or re-sequencing production orders. Yet, in many organizations, the final decision remained largely human and manual. The control tower was still a sophisticated advisor, not a decision-maker. The bridge from "knowing" to "doing" was often a patchwork of emails, phone calls, and spreadsheets.

A third and more ambitious generation of frontiers now exists: prescriptive, agentic control towers that visualize and predict but also recommend and increasingly execute actions under human-governed autonomy. These towers embed optimization models, rule-based policy engines, and reinforcement learning agents able to translate predictions into specific decisions such as which truck should carry which load, which orders should be fulfilled from which warehouse, or which supplier should get additional volume. They also connect with operational systems through APIs and event-driven workflows so that decisions can be enacted rapidly and consistently across multiple organizations. They can be designed as multi-agent systems where different agents represent plants, warehouses, carriers, and even customers, negotiating and coordinating with one another to achieve local and global objectives. Instead of planners having to manually resolve each exception, many routine issues can be handled by the system itself and only unusual or high-impact cases escalate for human review.

This evolution of control towers has occurred concurrently with a deep shift in how firms think about customers, markets, and digital technologies. It is no longer sufficient for a supply chain to be efficient; it must also be responsive, resilient, and deeply integrated with customer experience. In the context of airlines, for instance, E-CRM capabilities have turned into a strategic asset. Evidence from EgyptAir demonstrates that E-CRM significantly enhances competitive advantage through the mediating role of customer satisfaction; when digital tools capture, integrate, and act on customer data, they are translated into better service and stronger market positions (Awad & Mahmoud, 2024). Within such contexts, control towers cannot be purely inward-looking operational tools. They must connect to E-CRM platforms and customer-facing processes so that operational decisions-rerouting flights, reallocation of crews, prioritization of luggage handling-are aligned with segments of customer value, loyalty commitments, and service recovery strategies.

In small and medium enterprises, social media has become not just a marketing channel but also a real-time sensor of demand patterns and customer sentiment, especially in dynamic markets like Saudi Arabia. Studies on Saudi SMEs reveal that technological and environmental factors influence the capacity of firms to create business value from the dynamic capabilities of social media; the ability of an organization to sense trends, seize opportunities, and reconfigure its resources in response to what it learns from social media leads to superior performance (Shams Eldin et al., 2025). A control tower that can ingest social media signals into its data fabric and link them to inventory and fulfillment can help such SMEs respond more swiftly and effectively to emerging customer needs. For instance, a sudden spike in online interest for a new variant of a product, detected through social media analytics, can be translated into revised procurement plans, production schedules, and distribution priorities.

The strategic integration of marketing and supply chain functions has also become critical for the delivery of superior customer experience, especially in ambitious transformation contexts such as Saudi Vision 2030. Evidence from logistics startups shows that when marketing and supply chain functions collaborate closely, they are better able to design customer journeys, set realistic delivery promises, and implement service standards that align with brand positioning (Alahmari & Awad, 2025). In such organizations, the control tower becomes a shared decision environment where customer promises and operational constraints meet. Marketing teams can see implications of planned campaigns on capacity and inventory, and supply-chain teams can anticipate and prepare for demand surges driven by promotions or events.

Digital marketing more broadly also intersects with control-tower design. In sectors such as agriculture, digital marketing can dramatically improve market access and consumer engagement, helping small producers reach customers beyond their local regions and enabling better matching between supply and demand (Awad,

2025). When a control tower integrates digital marketing data-click-through rates, conversion metrics, geo-temporal patterns of online interest-it can thereby help orchestrate logistics for perishable products so that fresh goods reach the markets where they are most desired. This reduces waste, increases farmer incomes, and enhances consumer satisfaction. Thus, the control tower becomes not just a logistics optimization system but part of a broader digital ecosystem connecting producers, intermediaries, and consumers.

Meanwhile, artificial intelligence is transforming how firms interact with customers and build brands. AI chatbots are already important in building customer satisfaction and loyalty due to the capability for instant, consistent, and context-sensitive responses on multiple contact channels. Wahid & Awad, 2025 When these chatbots are connected to a control tower's real-time data and prescriptive logic, they have the ability to answer generic inquiries but also specific ones like "Where is my order?", "Can I change my delivery slot?", or "What are my options if this product is out of stock?" The tight integration makes sure that any customer communication reflects actual operational capability and constraint; promises given by the chatbot can be reliably fulfilled since they come from live, operational data with governed decision policies.

Generative AI is also restructuring advertising and branding. Conceptual frameworks based on the technology acceptance model indicate that marketers' adoption of generative AI in advertising depends on perceived usefulness, perceived ease of use, and trust-all factors bearing significance to brand reputation and customer perception. AI-powered tools like ChatGPT are being explored for branding tasks ranging from content creation and idea generation down to personalized messaging and community engagement but also introduce challenges of consistency, control, and ethics. Studies of generative AI implementation among retail SMEs in Pakistan reveal that while these tools can increase advertising efficiency and creativity, they also require appropriate skills, governance, and infrastructural support to avoid misalignment with brand values. Integrating such AI with the data fabric and policy layer of the control tower lets firms design creative, engaging campaigns that are operationally feasible and aligned with capacity, stock availability, and service capabilities.

This infrastructural and application stack sits atop a continuous sense-understand-decideact-learn loop, integrated with layers comprising other socio-technical systems: At the base lies a streaming data fabric that gathers events from internal and external sources: IoT devices on trucks and containers, RFID and barcode scans in warehouses, transactional messages from ERPs and TMSs, quality inspection data, and external signals such as weather, traffic, or port congestion. Canonical event schemas ensure that orders, shipments, products, locations, and parties are consistently represented throughout the systems and partners for reliable interpretation by analytics and decision services. Where customers and markets are concerned, this fabric also ingests data from websites, mobile apps, E-CRM systems, social media platforms, and AI chatbots, so that customer interactions and behaviors are treated as first-class signals in the decision process (Awad & Mahmoud, 2024; Shams Eldin et al., 2025; Awad, 2025; Wahid & Awad, 2025).

On top of this data fabric, the digital twins maintain actionable representations of physical assets, flows, and even customers. A truck is not just a record in a TMS; it becomes a twin with state variables such as location, capacity, driver hours, and estimated arrival time. A warehouse is represented by its storage capacities, current inventories, dock availability, and labor schedules. A customer order is represented by promised delivery dates, service-tier commitments, substitutions, and special handling requirements. These twins constitute a living model of the supply network and the customer interface, allowing running simulations, detecting anomalies, and computing the impact of potential decisions. For instance, delaying a shipment to consolidate loads may reduce costs, but it could violate a premium customer's delivery promise and damage satisfaction; a well-designed twin environment makes such trade-offs visible.

Prescriptive decision services then sit above the twin layer. They encode the logic needed to translate the forecasts and anomalies into concrete actions. Prescriptive services calculate reorder points and safety stocks across multiple echelons to balance cost and service under uncertainty in inventory management. In transportation, they assign loads to vehicles, choose routes and modes, and determine when to expedite or reroute shipments in response to disruptions. In sourcing, they suggest award strategies that optimize cost, risk, quality, and sustainability. In after-sales service, they guide decisions on lateral transshipments between depots and prioritization of spare parts replenishment. In customer-facing domains, prescriptive services may determine which orders to prioritize when capacity is constrained, which customers to proactively notify about delays, or which compensation and recovery options to offer to different segments based on their value and history (Topan et al., 2019; Domínguez et al., 2020; Alahmari & Awad, 2025). This class of prescriptive services is heavily using operations research, machine learning, and increasingly reinforcement learning. Optimization models handle hard constraints and large combinatorial decision spaces, for example when assigning thousands of orders to hundreds of vehicles or when determining inventory levels across dozens of nodes. Machine learning models forecast demand, travel times, and risk probabilities. Reinforcement learning agents learn policies for repeated decisions in highly dynamic environments, like real-time dispatching or rolling replenishment, through interactions with the environment, adjusting their actions based on rewards and penalties. Hybrid designs are common where optimization ensures feasibility and policy compliance, whereas RL fine-tunes choices for performance under uncertainty. In all these cases, customer-centric terms should appear in the objective functions, such as penalty costs for violating service level agreements, the expected drop in customer satisfaction, or the impact of stockouts on brand perception and loyalty. Execution and orchestration connect these decisions back to the operational world. Workflow engines and orchestration platforms transform the recommended actions into API calls, transactions, or messages that update ERP orders, release picks in WMS, issue dispatch instructions in TMS, adjust purchase orders in procurement systems, or trigger outgoing communications via E-CRM and marketing automation platforms. If the control tower decides to reallocate stocks from one warehouse to another in order to protect the service levels of a high-value region, then the orchestration layer must ensure updates in both locations' systems, create transport bookings, and notify the local planners. If the tower decides that a promotion needs to be slowed down or reshaped because capacity is constrained, the relevant amendments must be propagated to digital marketing platforms and workflows for AI-generated content creation (Awad 2025; Qadeer & Awad 2025a; Qadeer et al. 2025). Overarching all of this is a layer for assurance and governance. As control towers become more agentic, organizations need mechanisms to ensure that automated recommendations and actions are safe, compliant, and aligned with strategic objectives. Explainability tools show why a particular decision was chosen, what alternatives were evaluated, and how constraints were respected. Audit trails record every decision, input, and outcome for later analysis and for regulatory or contractual reporting. Safety guardrails set impact thresholds beyond which full automation is not permitted, and define conditions that trigger human review or rollback. Monitoring systems track key performance indicators, detect systematic biases, and analyze patterns of human overrides to identify where models and policies need improvement. Ethical and legal considerations are especially important when control-tower decisions affect customer outcomes, such as priority access to limited supply, differential service levels, or targeted communications in times of disruption. In this architecture, it's natural to consider the control tower as a multi-agent system. Different functional and organizational entities-plants, warehouses, carriers, suppliers, marketing teams, call centers-can be represented by software agents with local objectives and constraints. The agents negotiate over shared resources such as capacity and inventory and coordinate to satisfy global goals such as minimizing cost, maximizing service, and maintaining resilience. Adjustable autonomy allows for dynamic shift in control between the agents and human managers based on context. Routine, low-impact decisions with high model confidence may be fully automated while novel or sensitive decisions are escalated for human review. Over time, the pattern of escalation and override becomes training data which helps the system learn when it can act on its own and when it should ask for help, leading to a co-evolution of human and AI decision roles. In any case, such systems should be implemented in accordance with a realistic road map and maturity progression. Few organizations leap directly to a fully agentic, ecosystem-wide control tower. Instead, they start out with a crystal-clear strategic intent and a limited set of high-value use-cases. They evaluate their data readiness and clean and standardize key sets of data, and design canonical events for orders, shipments, and customer contacts. They develop minimum viable intelligence-first predictive models, then prescriptive policies-for specific decision problems. They create workflow and autonomy rules, integrate with core systems to execute decisions, and establish basic monitoring and override logging. They test the impact with robust metrics and experimental designs and iterate and expand towards additional products, regions, and partners. All along the way, they invest in training their workforce and revising their processes and incentives and embedding governance structures, including operations, IT, risk, marketing, and customer experience specialists (Patsavellas et al., 2021; Talić et al., 2021; Alahmari & Awad, 2025). Figure 1. Evolution of control towers As control tower extends across the enterprise and into the extended network, it also turns into a mighty means of associating operational decisions with customer experience and brand equity. When an airline's control tower monitors disruption risks and advises rebooking, it may simultaneously inform E-CRM campaigns so that affected customers receive timely, personalized messages and appropriate compensation. When a retailer's control tower detects that a promotional campaign is driving demand beyond capacity in a particular region, it can temper digital marketing in that region and propose alternative offers to avoid stockouts and frustration. When a logistics start-up operating under Vision 2030 commits to sustainable delivery options and transparent tracking, control tower can make sure promises are operationally supported and may provide data to back green marketing claims also Awad & Mahmoud, 2024; Alahmari & Awad, 2025; Awad, 2025. Figure 2. Review pipeline PRISMA-style schematic These include several open questions for future research and practice. Standardization and interoperability remain a challenge, given that each organization and each vendor uses its own data schemas, event models, and decision representations. Developing shared standards and adopting them would significantly reduce barriers for multi-enterprise control towers and decrease integration costs. Longitudinal studies are necessary to understand how control towers influence and will influence organizational structures, roles, and skills over time and how they influence resilience, innovation, and competitive advantage. Ecosystem-level governance mechanisms need to be designed such that decisions spanning multiple firms are perceived as fair and transparent and in line with broader societal goals, particularly in public procurement, national stockpiles, and critical infrastructure. Most importantly, much more empirical work remains to be done on how to embed customer-centric metrics-such as satisfaction, loyalty, and brand equity-directly into prescriptive objectives so that control towers truly become engines of customer-centric value creation rather than purely operational efficiency tools.

Figure 1. Evolution of control towers

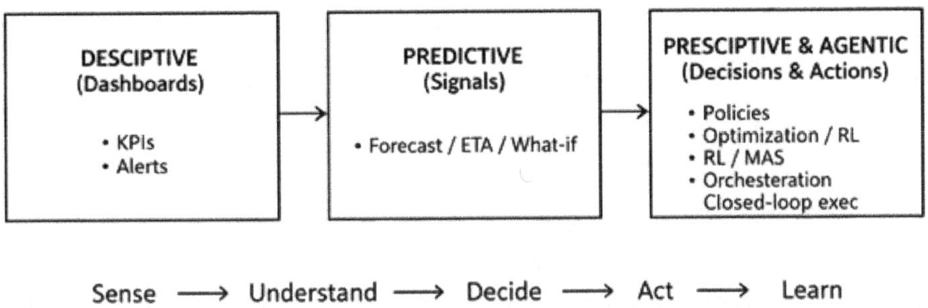

Yet outcomes hinge on socio-technical readiness: data quality and semantics; interoperability across ERP/WMS/TMS/IMS and partner systems; assurance (explanations, auditability); and operating-model change (Vlachos, 2021; Patsavellas et al., 2021; Midkiff, 2021). This chapter provides a practical synthesis for scholars and practitioners, with emphasis on GCC/MENA relevance where applicable (e.g., megaproject logistics, public procurement, cold-chain, and trade corridors).

2. METHODS

We conducted a scoping review (2005–2025) across peer-reviewed journals, proceedings, and citable technical literature focusing on: (i) control-tower architectures and adoption; (ii) prescriptive analytics for supply chains (optimization, RL, OR-AI hybrids); (iii) multi-agent/agentic approaches to decentralized decision-making; and (iv) socio-technical and governance issues. Inclusion prioritized empirical cases, simulation/optimization studies, architecture papers, and systematic reviews (e.g., Koot et al., 2021; Domínguez et al., 2020; Smyth et al., 2024). Sectoral evidence (pharma, LNG/construction, after-sales service parts, public stockpiles) was included to triangulate practical feasibility (Liotine, 2019; Srivastava et al., 2022; Topan et al., 2019; Handfield et al., 2020).

Figure 2. Review pipeline (PRISMA-style schematic)

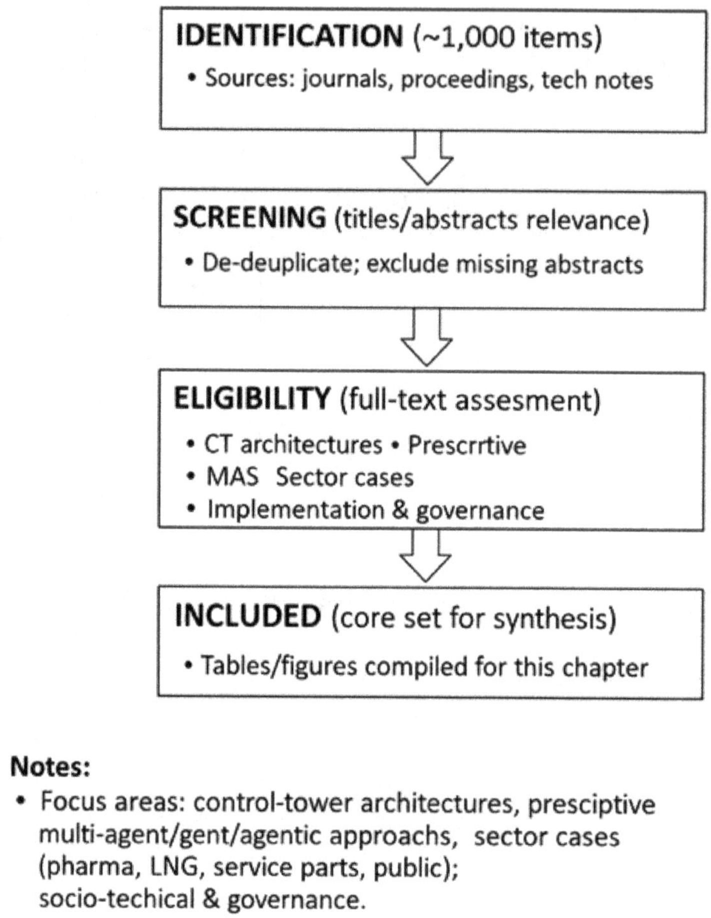

3. LITERATURE FOUNDATIONS

3.1 Control towers: from visibility to execution

Recent studies show control towers progressing beyond monitoring into exception-driven orchestration using predictive alerts and policy-bound recommendations (Midkiff, 2021; Patsavellas et al., 2021; Alias et al., 2014). In LNG construction logistics, digital control towers improved materials visibility and decision support on critical paths (Srivastava et al., 2022). Pharma pilots report real-time shortage sensing and cold-chain integrity with autonomous intelligence but highlight data and collaboration hurdles (Liotine, 2019; Sharabati et al., 2022).

3.2 Multi-agent systems and adjustable autonomy

MAS literature models supply chains as interacting autonomous agents (plants, DCs, carriers, suppliers), enabling local decisions aligned to global objectives via negotiation/coordination protocols (Domínguez et al., 2020; Giannakis & Louis, 2016; Behdani et al., 2019). Adjustable autonomy allows dynamic hand-off between agent action and human oversight based on impact, novelty, and confidence (Lau et al., 2008). This is critical for safety, compliance, and organizational trust.

Ultimately, the journey from descriptive dashboards to prescriptive, agentic control towers is not just a technical upgrade; it is a strategic and cultural transformation. Organizations that embrace this journey thoughtfully—investing in data discipline, cross-functional collaboration, AI governance, and integration with customer-facing capabilities—will be better positioned to compete in a world where disruptions are frequent, customers are empowered, and reputations are built or broken in real time. In such a world, the control tower is no longer a back-room operational cockpit. It is a central nervous system that connects supply, demand, and experience, allowing firms to sense what is happening, understand what it means, decide what to do, act swiftly and safely, and learn continuously from every outcome.

Awad & Mahmoud (2024) show that E-CRM-driven customer satisfaction is a key mediator of competitive advantage in a complex, service-intensive context like air transport. Shams Eldin et al. (2025) demonstrate how social media dynamic capabilities can be turned into business value in Saudi SMEs. Alahmari and Awad (2025) highlight that true customer experience excellence arises when marketing and supply chain functions are strategically integrated. Awad (2025) illustrates how digital marketing channels reshape market access for agricultural producers. Wahid and Awad (2025) examine how AI chatbots can strengthen satisfaction and loyalty, while the series of studies by Qadeer and colleagues (Qadeer & Awad, 2025a; 2025b; Qadeer et al., 2025) unpack the opportunities and risks of generative AI and ChatGPT for advertising, branding, and retail SMEs. Together, these works make it clear that supply chains, marketing, and AI-driven customer engagement cannot be treated as separate domains. The prescriptive, agentic control tower we have described is precisely the kind of integrative platform needed to bring these strands together into a coherent, customer-centric, and innovation-friendly system.

In conclusion, the control tower has traveled a long way from being a passive observer of supply-chain events. It is now evolving into an active, learning orchestrator of flows, information, and experiences. Its success depends on robust data foundations, sophisticated prescriptive and agentic capabilities, thoughtful socio-technical design, and deep integration with customer-facing technologies and strategies. As organizations around the world pursue ambitious transformation agendas and as AI reshapes both operations and marketing, the design and governance of such control towers will be central to achieving resilience, competitiveness, and sustainable customer value.

3.3 Prescriptive analytics, RL, and OR-AI hybrids

Prescriptive analytics convert forecasts into decisions: inventory positioning, transportation mode mix, scheduling, lateral transshipments, supplier substitution, or bid strategies, typically under uncertainty and multi-objective trade-offs (service/cost/CO_2/risk). Systematic reviews map a growing body of optimization and ML/RL applications for resilience and real-time control (Smyth et al., 2024; Koot et al., 2021; Zhu et al., 2020). Sector papers reveal design choices for agent policies and constraints (e.g., cold-chain thresholds in pharma; Workfront/material coupling in construction) (Liotine, 2019; Srivastava et al., 2022; Alias et al., 2014).

3.4 Data fabric and IoT/edge

Descriptive and predictive performance depends on event granularity (telemetry, EDI/API transactions, quality/vision, location, condition) and data-product discipline (master data, semantics, lineage). IoT+BDA literature confirms gains in visibility and planning reliability when data governance and integration are in place (Koot et al., 2021; Wang et al., 2020; Du et al., 2017).

3.5 Socio-technical implementation and governance

Adoption studies emphasize the interplay of human roles, processes, and technology: maturity/readiness assessment (Patsavellas et al., 2021), socio-technical case analysis (Vlachos, 2021), and leadership/transparency/workforce development (Dalporto et al., 2020). Public-sector resilience and stockpile governance highlight the importance of traceability, transparency, and coordinated decision rights (Handfield et al., 2020; Choi et al., 2021).

4. A REFERENCE ARCHITECTURE FOR PRESCRIPTIVE, AGENTIC CONTROL TOWERS

Figure 3. Reference stack

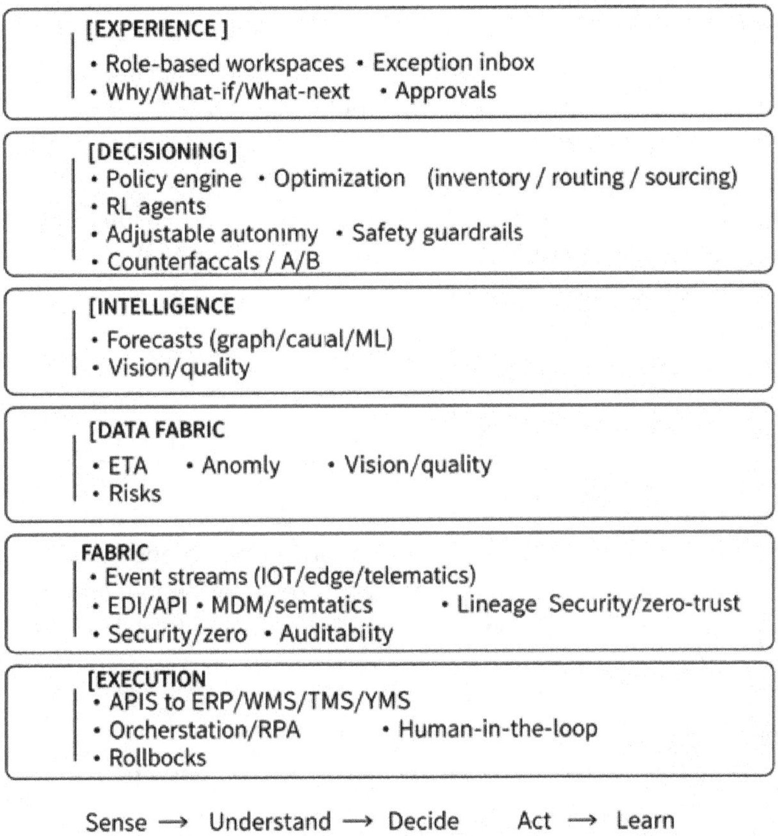

Design principles.

- Sense→Decide→Act→Learn loop with telemetry and business events feeding policy-bound decisions;
- Explainability and guardrails (confidence, impact thresholds, rollback plans) for trust and safety;
- Modular decision services (inventory, transport, sourcing, scheduling) that compose into end-to-end playbooks;

- Interoperability by design via canonical event schemas and semantic contracts (Alias et al., 2014; Patsavellas et al., 2021).

5. USE-CASES AND SECTOR PATTERNS

Service control towers trigger proactive lateral transshipments and dynamic re-allocation to increase fill rate with leaner stock, embedding cost-to-serve logic (Müller, 2018; Topan et al., 2019). Agent policies prioritize service agreements while respecting capacity and obsolescence constraints.

Autonomous intelligence supports shortage anticipation, cold-chain monitoring (temperature, dwell), and exception playbooks; however, data quality, collaboration, and governance remain barriers (Liotine, 2019; Sharabati et al., 2022). MAS can encode role-based decision rights across manufacturers, wholesalers, and providers.

Digital control towers improve materials traceability and decision support on megaprojects by linking engineering BOMs to logistics tasks and site constraints (Srivastava et al., 2022). IoT+RFID+MAS architectures in prefabrication improve information sharing and ripple-effect control (Du et al., 2017; Wang et al., 2020; Liu et al., 2020).

Resilient national stockpiles require auditable data products and policy-driven allocation across jurisdictions; control towers offer transparency and faster cross-agency decisions (Handfield et al., 2020). AI-native e-tendering and supplier discovery can be integrated, with ESG/Scope-3 assurances (Choi et al., 2021).

Table 1. Representative use-cases and decision policies

Use-case	Typical signals	Prescriptions (examples)	Guardrails/assurance
Lateral transshipment	Fill-rate, lead-time, inventory position	Ship-from-X to Y now; trigger replenishment	SLA limits; obsolescence; approval thresholds (Müller, 2018; Topan et al., 2019)
Cold-chain integrity	Temp/dwell, excursion risk	Re-route, expedite, quarantine, re-pack	Regulatory thresholds; chain-of-custody (Liotine, 2019)
Construction materials	Milestone slippage, BOM gaps	Expedite critical packages; resequence tasks	Safety rules; budget caps (Srivastava et al., 2022; Du et al., 2017)
Stockpile allocation	Demand surge, supplier risk	Prioritize regions; dynamic reorder	Equity rules; auditable logs (Handfield et al., 2020)

6. MULTI-AGENT ORCHESTRATION AND ADJUSTABLE AUTONOMY

Figure 4. Adjustable autonomy playbook

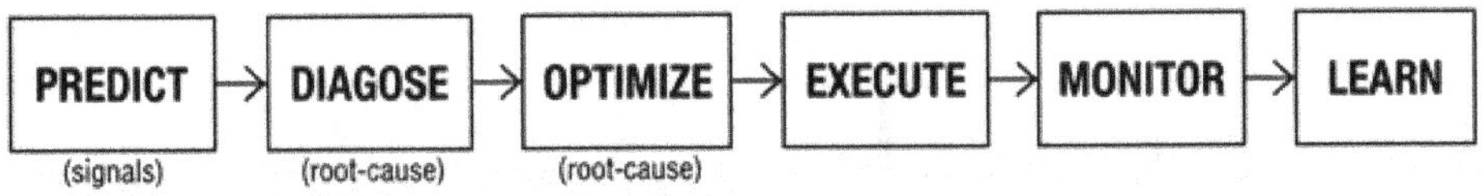

MAS agents representing facilities, carriers, and suppliers negotiate capacities, costs, and risks; coordinators ensure global feasibility and fairness (Domínguez et al., 2020; Giannakis & Louis, 2016). Adjustable autonomy reduces overload and preserves human oversight for high-stakes or novel situations (Lau et al., 2008).

Table 2. MAS roles in a control tower

Agent	Local objective	Key decisions	Example constraints
Facility/DC	Service level & cost	Allocation, pick/pack waves	Labor, dock capacity
Transport	OTIF & cost	Mode/route, consolidation	Hours of service, CO_2 cap
Supplier	OTIF & quality	Commit date/qty	MOQ, lead-time
Coordinator	Global optimality	Resolve conflicts	Budget, ESG, fairness

7. PRESCRIPTIVE ANALYTICS: FROM SIGNALS TO ACTIONS

Prescriptive layers map predictive signals to feasible actions by optimizing objectives under constraints, often with OR-AI hybrids. Inventory positioning and multi-echelon planning leverage stochastic optimization; dynamic routing uses rolling-horizon heuristics and RL; sourcing and tendering combine combinatorial optimization with risk scoring (Smyth et al., 2024; Koot et al., 2021; Zhu et al., 2020).

Figure 5. Prescriptive loop

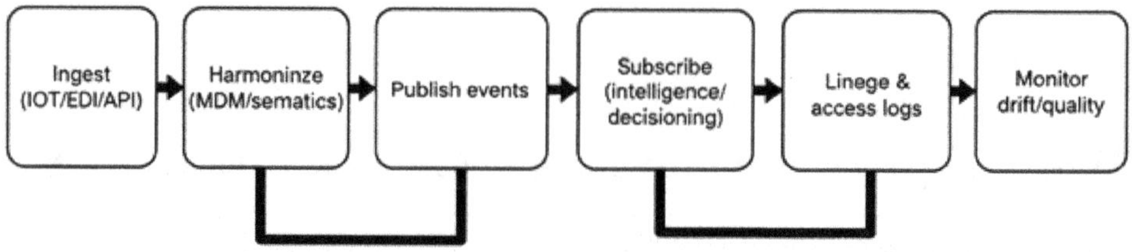

Table 3. Prescriptive methods and typical metrics

Decision area	Methods	Core metrics	Notes
Inventory (MEIO)	Stochastic optimization, RL	Fill-rate, backorders, WOS	Service tiers, obsolescence
Transport	VRP heuristics, RL dispatch	OTIF, cost/stop, CO_2	Real-time traffic & capacity
Sourcing	Combinatorial bids, risk models	Price, risk exposure, ESG	Supplier diversification
After-sales	Policy search, threshold rules	NVA days, service time	Parts criticality classes

8. DATA FABRIC, SEMANTICS, AND INTEROPERABILITY

IoT/edge telemetry (location, condition), EDI/API transactions, and quality/vision signals must be semantically harmonized (items, lanes, events) with stewardship and lineage to enable explanations and audit trails (Koot et al., 2021; Du et al., 2017). Interoperability accelerates partner onboarding and cross-boundary orchestration (Alias et al., 2014; Patsavellas et al., 2021).

9. IMPLEMENTATION ROADMAP (NINE STEPS)

- Strategy & OKRs (service, cost, resilience, CO_2, safety) (Patsavellas et al., 2021).
- Use-case slicing (e.g., ETA-risk-to-reallocation) to show measurable value quickly (Midkiff, 2021).

- Data readiness & semantics (MDM, canonical events, partner APIs) (Koot et al., 2021).
- MVP intelligence (ETA, anomaly, demand sensing).
- Decision policies (optimization objectives/constraints) codified as rules/ contracts.
    - -Adjustable autonomy thresholds and approval matrices (Lau et al., 2008).
    - -Closed-loop execution (workflows/APIs, rollbacks).
    - -Assurance (XAI, audit, safety/test harnesses) (Vlachos, 2021).
    - -Scale-out (new lanes/SKUs/suppliers; A/B experimentation; learning systems) (Domínguez et al., 2020).

Table 4. Maturity model (capability ladder)

Level	Data	Intelligence	Decisions	Execution	Governance
1 Visible	Batch KPIs	Alerts	Manual rules	Emails/ manual	Basic roles
2 Predictive	Stream/IoT	ETA/forecast	Playbooks	Ticketing/API	RACI
3 Prescriptive	Semantic events	Anomaly/ diagnostics	Optimization	Workflow/ API	SLA/approvals
4 Agentic	Trusted fabric	RL + twins	Adjustable autonomy	Auto + rollback	XAI/audit
5 Orchestrated	Partner graph	Risk graphs	Cross-network MAS	Multi-party	Ecosystem governance

10. EVALUATION AND BUSINESS IMPACT

Metrics dashboard. OTIF, service variability, decision latency, exception backlog age, expedite rate/cost, MEIO targets, CO_2/stop, supplier risk exposure, and conformance to policy are tracked per use-case (Topan et al., 2019; Smyth et al., 2024; Zhu et al., 2020).

Experimental design. Use A/B or phased rollouts; monitor counterfactuals and fairness across partners/regions (Vlachos, 2021).

11. DISCUSSION

The shift from dashboards to prescriptive, agentic control towers is more than just a tooling upgrade; it constitutes a basic change in where, how, and by whom decisions are made in supply chains. Up until now, visibility platforms were architected around the construct of aggregation rather than action. They aggregated lagging indicators such as end-of-day inventory snapshots, monthly on-time delivery reports, static exception lists, and periodic KPI scorecards and presented them to managers as a consolidated view of "what has already happened." In that paradigm, humans remained the primary integrators and decision engines: planners had to interpret patterns and diagnose root causes, convene stakeholders through calls and meetings, and then orchestrate changes across organizations manually via email threads, offline spreadsheets, and ad hoc workarounds. Even when the screens were modern and the dashboards visually impressive, the underlying operating model was still grounded on human bandwidth, tacit knowledge, and informal coordination to go from signal to decision to executed change.

Prescriptive, agentic control towers invert this relationship. Instead of being passive mirrors reflecting the past, they are engineered as closed-loop systems implementing a continuous sense → understand → decide → act → learn cycle. Sensor data, transactional feeds, and external signals stream in near real time; analytic layers transform raw events into forecasts, risk scores, and anomaly flags; decision services translate those insights into concrete actions respecting explicit policies and constraints; orchestration layers then push those actions back into the operational systems as executable commands and workflow steps; and the eventual outcomes-successes, failures, overrides-are captured as structured feedback. In this architecture, prediction isn't an isolated analytic artifact; it's continuously coupled to feasible, policy-aware action. The control tower has become less a "room of screens" and more a living decision fabric embedded in day-to-day operations.

This shift matters for at least three interlocking reasons. First, it compresses decision latency precisely at the moments when volatility and uncertainty amplify losses and reputational damage. When demand unexpectedly spikes, a port goes into congestion, a supplier fails, or a regulatory change suddenly constrains capacity, the cost of waiting for weekly meetings or manual scenario analysis can be enormous. Every hour of indecision may mean more backorders, higher expedite costs, increased spoilage, and deeper erosion of customer trust. A prescriptive, agentic tower can detect emerging risks earlier, evaluate feasible options faster, and trigger actions within minutes rather than days—reallocating inventory, rerouting shipments, adjusting sourcing, or proactively informing customers. Over the course of a year, such latency compression accumulates into substantial financial and experiential gains.

Second, prescriptive towers regularize decisions by encoding objectives, constraints, and guardrails into the decision logic itself. Rather than having policies live in slide decks, tribal knowledge, or scattered SOP documents, organizations translate them into machine-readable rules and optimization models. This makes decisions more consistent and auditable across time, regions, and partners. When a particular class of decision is made-whether to expedite, which customers get priority when stock is scarce, how to choose between carriers-the rationale is no longer "because someone thought so on a busy afternoon"; it is "because this option best satisfied the documented objectives and constraints under the current data." This does not eliminate judgment or discretion, but it provides a stable baseline. It also makes it far easier to demonstrate compliance to regulators, customers, and internal audit, because there is a clear record of which policies were in force and how they were applied.

Third, it's the closed-loop nature of prescriptive, agentic towers that create a substrate for learning systems. Every recommendation the system generates, every human approval or rejection, and every subsequent operational outcome becomes labeled experience. Over time, this experience can be mined to improve forecasting models, recalibrate risk scores, refine optimization parameters, and adjust autonomy thresholds. If planners consistently override a particular class of recommendation, that pattern can trigger a review: perhaps a hidden constraint is missing, a cost assumption is outdated, or a customer segment has changed in behavior. Instead of treating overrides as failures to be suppressed, mature programs treat them as rich signals for iterative improvement. The tower thus becomes more accurate, more aligned with reality, and more trusted the longer it runs.

A central theme that emerges across both empirical and practitioner evidence is that architecture beats "one-off algorithms." Organizations which begin their journey by "adding an AI model" on top of a noisy, fragmented data landscape rarely realize durable gains. A demand-forecasting model that is trained on inconsistent product hierarchies, missing location attributes, and misaligned time stamps will output volatile results that planners quickly learn to ignore. An anomaly detector which sees partial flows only because half the partners cannot supply consistent events will either trigger false alarms or miss critical issues. By contrast, organizations that first invest in building a data-product fabric-streaming event pipelines, curated master data, semantic contracts, and clear lineage-find that their analytic models immediately grow more stable and more actionable. Forecasts stop jumping erratically from day to day, anomaly detectors grow less brittle, and optimizers stop proposing infeasible plans that violate basic physical or contractual realities.

The practical result of this is the recognition that prescriptive power is gated more by data discipline than by raw data volume. It is not enough to have "a lot of data"; the data must be shaped into well-defined products with owners, schemas, and service levels. This is particularly salient in multi-enterprise contexts in which EDI and API payloads vary by partner and contractual terms, such as incoterms, service level targets, penalty clauses, carbon caps, and quality tolerances. These must be represented in machine-readable form to flow into the policy engine. If the contract defines different rights and obligations for platinum, gold, and bronze customers, but this segmentation is not encoded and linked to the orders and shipments, no amount of clever optimization will produce policy-consistent results. The bottom line is that "control tower programs" are as much information design and integration initiatives as they are analytics efforts. Data modelers, integration engineers, and contract specialists are just as important to success as data scientists and OR experts.

A second recurring lesson is the value of adjustable autonomy-calibrating how much freedom agents have to act, and under what conditions. The temptation in many AI initiatives is to either push for full automation or to stay mired in purely manual modes. Both extremes are problematic. Full automation without nuance can cause outsized harm when rare or atypical situations come along, while overly cautious reluctance to automate anything leaves organizations drowning in exceptions and unable to scale. Adjustable autonomy reframes the debate from "replace or not" to "for which decisions, under what risk and uncertainty profiles, should agents act autonomously, and how should they justify their choices?" For low-impact, high-confidence actions-such as reassigning a shipment to an equivalent lane within pre-agreed cost and CO_2 bounds-the system can safely act on its own. For higher-impact or novel situations-such as reallocating vaccines between regions, delaying critical components, or breaking standard service tiers-agents generate recommendations coupled with explanations, counterfactuals, and "safe options," with human approval required.

The key is to make autonomy context-aware. Impact thresholds define what counts as "low-risk" versus "high-risk" decisions, uncertainty measures quantify how confident the models are, and novelty detectors identify when the current situation falls outside of the patterns seen in training data. When these signals are combined, the system can route each decision to the appropriate modality: fully automated, human-in-the-loop, or human-led with analytic support. This design preserves human judgment for the decisions that most need it in everyday operations, while eliminating long decision queues for routine exceptions that do not warrant scarce expert attention. Practically, organizations that implement adjustable autonomy report fewer irrelevant alerts, more stable service levels, and less burnout among planners because the control tower absorbs the "noise" and surfaces the "signal." Crucially, stakeholders see why an action is recommended, how it satisfies objectives and constraints, and what trade-offs were considered, which in turn builds deeper trust.

Third, multiagent orchestration directly addresses a structural challenge in supply chains: global objectives must be realized by local actions taken by entities with partial information and distinct constraints. Plants, distribution centers, carriers, and suppliers each face different realities-labor shifts, dock windows, fleet utilization, union rules, shelf-life limits, and regional regulations. A single centralized optimizer can produce mathematically elegant plans that appear globally efficient but which take no account of local feasibility and on-the-ground constraints. The result is a proliferation of "beautiful but unusable" plans which local actors quietly override or rework or ignore. Multiagent designs attack this problem by distributing decision rights and modeling each node as an agent with its own objective function, constraints, and state. Local agents negotiate allocations, capacities, and handoffs with one another, while a coordinator agent arbitrates conflicts according to global policy.

In this design, a plant agent may refuse a theoretically optimal production schedule as it would violate minimum changeover windows or realistic labor availability. A carrier agent could refuse an assignment that would technically fit capacity but breach hours-of-service regulations. The coordinator agent can then explore alternative combinations still globally acceptable while respecting local conditions. When shocks occur-facility downtime, border closures, supplier bankruptcy-the agent network can replan locally while continuing to adhere to over-arching principles such as protecting service for critical customers or staying within emissions caps. Most important, multi-agent control should not be confused with opaque, "black-box automation." Properly engineered agents expose their state, intent, and justifications via explainable interfaces, allowing auditors, managers, and partners to inspect and challenge decisions. This transparency is what allows agentic orchestration to be compatible with strict compliance regimes and inter-organizational trust.

A fourth lesson is that prescription needs to be deeply policy-aware. Many so-called "AI recommendations" fail not because the underlying models are statistically wrong, but because they produce outputs that violate constraints implicit in contracts, regulations, ethical guidelines, or brand promises. A model that recommends diverting shipments away from a vulnerable region because it appears "uneconomic" may be optimal on a narrow cost metric but unacceptable from a regulatory, equity, or reputational standpoint. Prescriptive engines therefore need to co-optimize multiple objectives-service levels, cost, resilience, carbon footprint, fairness, and sometimes political or social considerations-within a clearly defined policy envelope. This is where hybrids that integrate operations research with machine learning tend to outperform ML-only approaches. Forecasts and risk scores derived from ML models define the likely future states; optimization layers then search for feasible decisions that respect hard constraints; and reinforcement learning, when used, tunes real-time policies within those guardrails rather than discovering them from scratch.

When organizations explicitly encode policies like "never expedite by air for bronze-tier customers unless a medical exemption applies", "respect regional allocation floors for essential goods", or "prioritize low-carbon carriers when cost and service differences are within defined bands", they decrease not only surprise costs, compliance breaches, and partner friction but also make decision logic inspectable and adjustable. Changing a policy becomes just a matter of changing code or configuration and validating impacts, not hoping hundreds of scattered human decision-makers remember a new rule. In highly scrutinized environments—healthcare, public procurement, food supply, critical infrastructure—this kind of policy-aware prescription provides a crucial bridge between algorithmic efficiency and institutional legitimacy. Fifth, governance and socio-technical design ultimately determine whether promising pilots ever scale into durable, enterprise-wide capabilities. The "tower" metaphor can mislead organizations into thinking in terms of centralization and command-and-control, but effective programs distribute ownership and responsibility across roles. Data stewards maintain the meaning, quality, and timeliness of key data products; operations teams define playbooks, service-level agreements, and acceptable trade-offs; risk and compliance functions set guardrails and approve policies; an assurance or model risk function monitors drift, bias, and unsafe actions; and business owners are accountable for outcomes in terms of service, cost, and emissions. Without this distributed governance, control towers risk being seen as "IT projects" rather than systems of work, and change fatigue or political resistance can stall adoption. Two patterns tend to separate durable programs from those that languish as proofs of concept. The first is outcome-focused slicing. Rather than launching a monolithic platform intended to solve "the entire supply chain," successful teams pick a narrow, high-value slice-for example, reducing expedite costs by optimizing ETA-risk-to-reallocation decisions for two high-volume lanes-and drive measurable improvements in decision latency, expedite rate, and at-risk orders. Once these gains are demonstrated and documented, adjacent slices are added: additional lanes, more product families, more regions, more partners. The second pattern is evidence-based trust building. Each automated or recommended action is accompanied by a rationale and a roll-back plan, and the program openly tracks metrics such as "good catches" (issues prevented or mitigated), "false positives" (unnecessary interventions), and "escalations with cause" (cases where human input materially improved the outcome). This transparency blunts cultural resistance, provides talking points for leadership, and reassures front-line teams that the system is accountable and corrigible rather than mysterious and unilateral. Sectoral differences also matter and influence the design and governance of control towers, even when the underlying architecture is similar. In after-sales service parts, where equipment uptime and customer commitments are paramount, latency and parts criticality tend to dominate the design. Policies emphasize meeting service obligations while managing obsolescence risk; lateral transshipments, dynamic thresholds, and predictive stocking rules often deliver quick wins. Product criticality, cold-chain integrity, and regulatory oversight drive pharmaceutical and healthcare supply chains toward high-quality telemetry and robust chain-of-custody records, with conservative autonomy thresholds. Control towers in this domain may recommend actions more frequently than they execute them automatically, reflecting the extreme consequences of errors. In LNG and construction megaprojects, the tight coupling of engineering bills of materials, work-front constraints, and logistics makes the decision space particularly complex. Here, digital control towers that fuse materials visibility with schedule risk models provide leverage on the critical path: they highlight which missing components threaten milestone dates, which can be resequenced, and where expediting will yield the most schedule benefit. In public procurement and national stockpiles, transparency, equity, and political legitimacy are co-equal with efficiency. Data products must be audit-ready, allocation policies must be explainable to oversight bodies and citizens, and decisions must be demonstrably aligned with agreed criteria rather than opportunistic or opaque. These sectoral nuances do not contradict a common reference architecture; they tune the policies, thresholds, autonomy modes, and evidence requirements that sit on top of it. Measurement closes the loop and keeps programs honest. Organizations that treat control towers as learning systems instrument not only traditional KPIs but also decision-process metrics. They track decision latency (time from exception detection to action), exception backlog age, expedite rate and cost, fill-rate variance by segment, forecast value added (FVA) over naïve baselines, multi-echelon inventory optimization (MEIO) target adherence, CO_2 per stop or per unit delivered, and policy conformance rates. They also systematically analyze override behavior: which recommendations are overridden, by whom, under what circumstances, and with what eventual outcome. Overrides then become a primary source of training data for policy and model refinement. When coupled with A/B experimentation and counterfactual logging—comparing what actually happened to what would likely have happened under alternate decisions—this creates a scientific cadence for operations. New playbooks, models, and thresholds graduate from sandbox to broader rollout only when they demonstrate quantified impact, and regressions are quickly detected and rolled back. Ethics and assurance are best given explicit, rather than incidental, attention. As prescriptive engines assume more routine decisions, organizations need to guard against both "automation complacency"-where humans disengage and just assume the system is always right-and "responsibility diffusion"-where no one feels responsible when something goes wrong because "the algorithm decided". Strong programs clearly outline human accountability for classes of decisions-even where largely automated. They provide expectations around explanations: the higher-impact a decision, the richer and more legible its justifications must be. They implement operational fail-safes such as rollback procedures, canary releases, and kill-switches against data quality degradation or model drift. Environmental, Social, and Governance (ESG) claims-especially those for Scope 3 emissions-are anchored to verifiable data products and chain-of-custody evidence rather than coarse proxy factors, mitigating greenwashing risks. Where regulated, organizations construct an assurance pipeline of pre-deployment testing, simulation-based stress testing, continuous performance and drift monitoring, incident response protocols, and independent audit. Such a pipeline provides the associated documentation for internal risk committees, boards, and external regulators, and it does so within a structured way to evolve the system under scrutiny. Standardization and interoperability remain open challenges. The field lacks widely adopted canonical schemas for events, constraints, and policies, and this absence raises integration costs and makes cross-industry reuse of tools and models difficult. While industry bodies and leading vendors are experimenting with open specifications for logistics events, sustainability attributes, and decision intents, these standards are not yet universal. In the meantime, there is a pragmatic approach possible for practitioners: define an internal canonical event model for orders, shipments, milestones, and exceptions; publish adapters and mapping layers for partners and legacy systems; and isolate policy and optimization modules behind stable APIs so they can evolve independently from the integration details. And over time, converging on shared ontologies for items, locations, lanes, emission factors, and service levels allows more portable agents and brings down substantially the marginal cost for adding new partners, regions, or use-cases. Finally, the human dimension remains the fulcrum around which all of this rotates. Agentic towers do not eliminate the need for planners, dispatchers, and managers; they elevate and reshape these roles. Human expertise shifts from repetitive transactional decisions to the stewardship of policies, curation of data quality, co-design of exception playbooks, and the adjudication of truly novel, ambiguous, or ethically loaded scenarios. Successful programs invest in training people to read and critique model explanations, recognize when overrides are warranted, and provide feedback that is useful for system improvement. Incentive structures reward not only automation rates but also risk-reducing overrides and thoughtful escalations. Communication plans include shared dashboards of outcomes and assurance metrics so that everyone-from executives to front-line teams-can see how the system is performing and where it needs attention. The single biggest boost in many organizations comes from when the front-line teams are invited to co-design the playbooks and policies encoded in the control tower. When planners see their domain knowledge captured as explicit rules, constraints, and decision logic, they no longer experience "the tower" as an alien black box imposed from above; they recognize it as a living representation of how the business already thinks about trade-offs, now executed more consistently and at operational speed. This sense of ownership transforms skepticism into advocacy. In other words, the way from dashboards to decisions is open to any organization willing to treat control towers as systems of work, rather than as systems of record. In concept, the practical playbook is simple, even as it is demanding in execution: build and govern the data fabric; codify policies and objectives; start with outcome-focused slices that prove value; instrument decisions and measure not just results but processes; grow autonomy where confidence and impact allow; and nurture the human, organizational, and ethical foundations which will sustain the journey. The prize is not a more colorful dashboard or a higher algorithm count; rather, it is a dependable, auditable operating rhythm in which the right actions get executed—justified, measured, and learned from—before value evaporates and before trust is lost.

12. RESEARCH GAPS AND FUTURE DIRECTIONS

Table 5 summarizes the research gaps and future directions:

Table 5. Research gaps matrix

Topic / Attribute	Agent-based Systems	Prescriptive Analytics	Real-time Decision Support	Socio-technical Integration	Risk Management
Manufacturing	High	Medium	Medium	Low	Medium
Logistics/ Transport	High	Medium	High	Low	Medium
Healthcare/ Pharma	Medium	Low	Medium	**Gap**	Medium
Public Procurement	Low	Low	Medium	**Gap**	Medium
Retail/Omni-channel	Medium	Medium	Low	**Gap**	Medium

13. CONCLUSION

Prescriptive, agentic control towers represent a decisive shift from "visibility about the past" to governed autonomy about the next best action. Architectures that combine data products, multi-modal intelligence, policy-driven optimization, and adjustable autonomy deliver measurable gains in service, cost, resilience, and sustainability—especially under volatility. The challenge is less about discovering a single best algorithm and more about engineering socio-technical systems that make reliable, auditable decisions at operational speed.

REFERENCES

Alahmari, D., & Awad, A. (2025). Strategic integration of marketing and supply chain functions for superior customer experience: Insights from logistics startups under Saudi Vision 2030. *PLoS One*, *20*(11), e0336132. DOI: 10.1371/journal.pone.0336132 PMID: 41270081

Alias, C., Lobillo, G., & de Miguel, G. (2014). Applying novel future-internet-based supply chain control towers to the transport and logistics domain. *Future Network and Mobile Summit 2014*.

Awad, A. (2025). Enhancing market access and consumer engagement through digital marketing in the agricultural sector. *International Journal of Advanced and Applied Sciences*, *12*(8), 70–79. DOI: 10.21833/ijaas.2025.08.007

Awad, A., & Mahmoud, M. (2024). Impact of electronic customer relationship management on competitive advantage: Mediating role of customer satisfaction in EgyptAir. *Problems and Perspectives in Management*, *22*(3), 276–286. DOI: 10.21511/ppm.22(3).2024.22

Behdani, B., Wiegmans, B., & Roodbergen, K. J. (2019). Agent-oriented simulation framework for handling disruptions in chemical supply chains. *Computers & Chemical Engineering*, *123*, 183–199.

Choi, T. Y., Rogers, D. S., & Vakil, B. (2021). Managing extended supply chains. *Journal of Business Logistics*, *42*(1), 1–4.

Dalporto, A., Cullen, A., & Damiani, D. (2020). Supply chain leadership, transparency, workforce development and collaboration through control tower implementation. *Journal of Supply Chain Management. Logistics & Procurement*, *3*(4), 58–71.

Domínguez, R., Framinan, J. M., & Cannella, S. (2020). Insights on multi-agent systems applications for supply chain management. *Sustainability*, *12*(2), 735.

Du, J., Zou, Z., Shi, Y., & Zhao, D. (2017). RFID and multi-agent based architecture for information sharing in prefabricated component supply chain. *IEEE Access : Practical Innovations, Open Solutions*, *5*, 4132–4143.

Giannakis, M., & Louis, M. (2016). A multi-agent based system with big data processing for enhanced supply chain agility. *Journal of Enterprise Information Management*, *29*(5), 706–727.

Handfield, R., Finkenstadt, D., Schneller, E., Godfrey, A. B., & Guinto, P.. (2020). A commons for a supply chain in the post-COVID-19 era: The case for a reformed Strategic National Stockpile. *The Milbank Quarterly*, *98*(4), 1053–1090. PMID: 33135814

Koot, M., Mes, M., & Iacob, M. E. (2021). A systematic literature review of supply chain decision making supported by the Internet of Things and big data analytics. *Computers & Industrial Engineering*, *154*, 107076.

Lau, H. C., Agussurja, L., & Thangarajoo, R. (2008). Real-time supply chain control via multi-agent adjustable autonomy. *Computers & Operations Research*, *35*(11), 3452–3464.

Liotine, M. (2019). Shaping the next generation pharmaceutical supply chain control tower with autonomous intelligence. *Journal of Autonomous Intelligence*, *2*(3), 1–9.

Liu, Y., van Nederveen, G. A., & Hertogh, M. (2020). A conceptual development framework for prefabricated construction supply chain management: An integrated overview. *Sustainability*, *12*(21), 8853.

Midkiff, C. (2021). Using a control tower approach to drive visibility, aid planning and improve supply chain reliability. *Journal of Supply Chain Management. Logistics & Procurement*, *4*(1), 20–27.

Müller, I. (2018). Improving the service control tower with proactive decision making: A two-staged alert and intervention-generating model for proactive lateral transshipments in an after-sales supply chain. *Working paper*.

Patsavellas, J., Kaur, R., & Salonitis, K. (2021). Supply chain control towers: Technology push or market pull—An assessment tool. *IET Collaborative Intelligent Manufacturing*, *3*(3), 290–302.

Qadeer, A., & Awad, A. (2025a). Generative AI in advertisements: A conceptual framework based on the technology acceptance model. In *Impacts of AI generated content on brand reputation* (pp. 109–127). IGI Global., DOI: 10.4018/979-8-3373-4327-3.ch004

Qadeer, A., & Awad, A. (2025b). AI-powered ChatGPT in branding: Benefits, challenges, and future directions. In *Impacts of AI generated content on brand reputation* (pp. 1–26). IGI Global., DOI: 10.4018/979-8-3373-4327-3.ch001

Shams Eldin, A. Y., Elnour, A., Hassan, R. O. A., & Awad, A. (2025). The role of technological and environmental factors in creating business value from social media dynamic capabilities for SMEs in Saudi Arabia. *Humanities & Social Sciences Communications*, *12*, 1431. DOI: 10.1057/s41599-025-05784-x

Sharabati, A. A.. (2022). The use of supply chain control tower in pharmaceutical industry to create a competitive advantage. *International Journal of Pharmaceutical Research & Allied Sciences*, *11*(3), 145–154.

Smyth, C.. (2024). Artificial intelligence and prescriptive analytics for supply chain resilience: A systematic literature review and research agenda. *International Journal of Production Research*.

Srivastava, Y. C., et al. (2022, November 3). Digital Control Tower – Instantaneous visibility, granularity and decision support for an LNG mega project. *Conference presentation*.

Talić, T., ... (2021). Control towers in supply chain management: Standardization and documentation preparation. *White paper*.

Topan, E., Van Houtum, G.-J., & Basten, R. J. I. (2019). A review of operational spare parts service logistics. *European Journal of Operational Research*, *276*(1), 1–24.

Wahid, A., & Awad, A. (2025). Role of AI chatbots in enhancing customer satisfaction and customer loyalty. In *Impacts of AI generated content on brand reputation* (pp. 129–147). IGI Global., DOI: 10.4018/979-8-3373-4327-3.ch005

Wang, Z., Hu, H., Gong, J., & Ren, Y. (2020). Blockchain-based framework for improving supply chain traceability and information sharing in precast construction. *Automation in Construction*, *111*, 103063.

Zhu, G., Chou, M. C., & Tsai, C.-W. (2020). Lessons learned from the COVID-19 pandemic exposing the shortcomings of current supply chain operations: A long-term prescriptive offering. *Sustainability*, *12*(14), 5858.

Chapter 10
Rise of the Self-Driven Machine:
Inside the World of Agentic AI

Aditya Deshpande
https://orcid.org/0009-0004-7946-6125
Ajeenkya D.Y. Patil University, India

Atharva Haresh Saraf
https://orcid.org/0009-0006-3842-5508
Ajeenkya D.Y. Patil University, India

Susanta Das
https://orcid.org/0000-0002-9314-3988
Ajeenkya D.Y. Patil University, India

ABSTRACT

AI refers to ability of machines to perform tasks that typically require human mind to perform such as learning, problem solving and decision making an agentic AI has been considered in large category. These systems depend on AI agents with purpose of independent entities that are capable of recognizing environment, learning & then performing the processes in multiple steps of workflow. Agentic AI accommodates LLM-based veracity. Through this classification strategy, AI agents are having the ability to seek real time data on fly and keep evolving with changes in world around them in sectors including healthcare, cybersecurity, logistics & personal services. In this chapter, we explore recent advancement in Agentic AI by analysing architecture, capabilities and real-world application of multi agent systems. These systems integrate LLMs to enable self-reliant decision making & task performing.

DOI: 10.4018/979-8-3373-7006-4.ch010

We cover key methods such as retrieval–augmented generation, chain of thought promoting, increase learning with human feedback. It highlights how Agentic AI helps a machine to become autonomous.

1. INTRODUCTION

1.1. Artificial Intelligence (AI)

Artificial intelligence (AI) refers to machines performing multiple tasks like thinking, learning, problem-solving, and decision-making. First, it was created as a technology that can imitate human intelligence. Artificial intelligence has been developed in a way that exceeds its original concept of AI (Russell & Norvig, 2022). With advances in data collection, data processing, and computational power, artificial intelligence systems can now take on multiple tasks across different domains and increase productivity. Artificial intelligence abilities have rapidly increased, and so has their utility in growing numbers of fields (Russell & Norvig, 2022). Agentic AI presents the next step in artificial intelligence. In this, the technology can make decisions autonomously and act deliberately without the need for human acknowledgement. Not like traditional AI, which requires a set of instructions, agentic AI can make its own decisions and set its goals, evaluate outcomes, and adapt according to the environment. The term used for self-driven machines as AI, is changing from requiring constant human observation to becoming autonomous and making decisions with the help of agentic AI; similarly, autonomous vehicles are handling traffic and following traffic rules in scenarios. The shift towards agentic AI represents both technical advancement and a conceptual shift, which shifts towards systems that have persistent, proactive, and self-regulating behaviours (Capgemini Research Institute, 2025).

1.2. AI vs. Agentic AI

Artificial intelligence is very instruction-oriented, which means the AI performs tasks with a set of instructions. The task of these AI models is to optimize within predefined boundaries or problem statements; these systems lack the flexibility and adaptability that define dynamic intelligent behaviour in the real world (Hosseini & Seilani, 2025). Thus, the role of agentic AI comes into play; the concept and development of artificial intelligence have been completely developed at the next level with the introduction of agentic AI. The role of agentic AI is that it can act autonomously and make decisions on its own to complete the task, as opposed to traditional AI systems, focused on prediction and classification, which are designed in such a way that they analyse the data and provide results based on a given set of instructions or learned patterns. The ability of a system to sense its surroundings, make goal-aligned decisions, plan action, and adjust through feedback is called Agentic AI. These systems play an active role in making decisions and problem-solving procedures rather than being passive recipients of information (Hosseini & Seilani, 2025).

1.3. Self-Driven Machine

The definition of a self-driven machine means it is controlled by artificial intelligence (AI). As technology improves, first it gets a set of instructions, which it uses to follow from humans; now it is making its own decisions, which helps the self-driven machine. The agentic AI plays an important role in autonomous vehicles, as it helps AI make its decisions and act on them while choosing directions or applying brakes. Which can complete tasks independently, much like an automobile, which went from needing constant human control to being an autonomous vehicle. The capabilities of automatic vehicles have been changed by agentic AI by handling any situations like traffic, choosing a path, stopping at red light signals, following the traffic rules, and controlling speed. Therefore, agentic AI is not just a new technology; it is the change in how we think about computers, as it differs from artificial intelligence, as it is independent and makes its own decisions and predictions according to data and has logical reasoning to think (Nisa et al., 2025).

1.4. The Core of Agentic AI

Agentic AI is the result of a combination of multiple crucial categories, which are:

A. Autonomy: It means working without human supervision and performing tasks and giving results by understanding the problem (Hosseini & Seilani, 2025).
B. Proactivity: Agentic AI acts proactively; it doesn't react to user input but anticipates future needs or risks and gives output (Hosseini & Seilani, 2025).
C. Adaptability: It states how AI can change itself according to the task and environment.
D. Memory and persistence: Memory are the system in agentic AI that stores the data and accesses the data when required (Hosseini & Seilani, 2025).
E. Reasoning and planning: In this, it is not like artificial intelligence, where a set of instructions should be given, and then it follows it; it creates a road map to complete the goal and has logical reasoning to create a plan (Hosseini & Seilani, 2025).

F. Interactivity: achieving advanced human-system cooperation, not just data exchange (Capgemini Research Institute, 2025)

These abilities enable agentic systems to allow their application in education, healthcare, and corporate decision-making, showing their potential for the real world (Capgemini Research Institute, 2025).

1.5. Why Agentic AI Now?

The AI models, like large language models (LLMs) and multimodal architectures, have enabled agentic AI to develop in a successful way. These models have access to and skills over a wide range of domains and can handle a large volume of data. They can examine complicated datasets that generate text that is exactly like humans and even merge texts, images, and codes. However, these models observe the data or patterns for prediction or solving problems on their own; they don't act individually or plan on their own (Bubeck et al., 2023). Large language models (LLMs) are not truly autonomous; they are reactive systems that need human prompts. The agentic AI is made by merging an LLM, which acts as the cognitive core, within a larger framework that adds essential features like memory and planning algorithms. This hybrid architecture transforms the system, enabling it to go beyond just prediction and perform multi-step reasoning, complete long-term goals, and achieve real-world impact in fields like education, healthcare, and business (Bubeck et al., 2023).

The combination of these models into agentic AI differs from the current time. Researchers are creating robots that go beyond the human brain. They are using foundational models like large language models (LLMs), which act as the main brain for understanding reasoning and creating text, for example, in a car to stop the car. These kinds of actions are thought by LLM models in Agentic AI. AI systems that can communicate, or give a road map to processes, communicate with robotic systems or APIs, and manage long-term goals are made possible by this hybrid design (OpenAI et al., 2023)

1.6. An Inside Look at Agentic AI

An agentic AI system is not just on paper; it has been implemented in various fields and is progressing in various sectors. In the field of education, AI teachers are monitoring students' work over many months and improving their teaching methods, and organizing personal goals for students (Luckin, 2017). It is also helpful in the medical industry, as it can notify doctors when some concerns are recognized and can suggest lifestyle changes and conduct ongoing patient monitoring. Agentic AI is like helpful digital assistance in corporate worlds that can improve decision-making in real time, manage workflow, and negotiate contracts (Belcak et al., 2025).

In agentic AI, when multiple agentic AIs communicate with each other, it is called a multi-agent ecosystem. By managing smart cities, the investment banking sector, the business sector, or research, these ecosystems could create a collective intelligence that is far more advanced than other systems. There are many complicated or unexpected problems that occur in the human community, which may be able to solve the world's problems by depending on autonomous network devices rather than depending on standalone AI technologies (Rahwan et al., 2019).

1.7. The Revolution in Human-AI Interaction

The agentic AI is developing as people are interacting more with artificial intelligence. Before artificial intelligence, the computer system was instruction-driven, meaning that on command, the computer would give output or perform a task (Shneiderman, 2020). The communication has become intermediary and combined with agentic systems. Humans and machines are both responsible for the completion of the job, and agentic agents help them with giving solutions and continuously interacting with them related to that problem (Floridi & Cowls, 2021). There are advantages and disadvantages to agentic AI. On one hand, it makes processes easy or creates a roadmap, and on the other, it does not help humans to think or work on problem solutions, which lessens their thinking ability. Humans depend on AI for solutions. Also, it increases productivity and promotes creativity; however, it faces the problem of AI alignment with humans, as AI is not a passive tool. It acts independently, which creates the problem of completing goals that are not intended and that create consequences or harm to someone (Bryson, 2018).

1.8. Toward Intelligence's Future

The rapid growth in the development and evolution of computer intelligence is not just a technological achievement but also the core turning point of the history of the digital era itself (Lake et al., 2016). The impact of this turning point is so huge that, as a human civilization, we are very close to making an artificial life form that can act, adapt, and persist (Dafoe, 2018). These artificial intelligence life forms are based on AI vision that goes beyond simple task-completing tools that help humans in their daily lives. Agentic AI comes with a huge advantage and use cases in various applications, whether it is achieving long-term goals in system agriculture and design, for example, equal education, global health, and climate change, or the rise of self-driven machines and their enhancements. It also helps academics, policymakers, and the public to develop robust systems and architecture. But it also comes with huge challenges (Floridi & Cowls, 2021).

2. LITERATURE REVIEW

2.1. Early in AI agency

Russell and Norvig (2022) Defined "agents" as someone who can adapt anything from the environment through sensors and act upon it through actuators. This definition offered deep research on the framework of understanding artificial intelligence and its interaction with surrounding and computational operations.

In early times it was common to use rule-based and expert systems where autonomy was not used or limited to perform pre-programmed orders. In 1970 MYCIN was made, which offered rule-based medical advice but lacked adaptability and perseverance. The same limitation was there in robotics, which was programmed with autonomous navigation, which used pre-set routes and limited skill. These systems put down the roots for autonomy but lacked adaptability and flexibility, which was later implemented in agentic AI (Shortliffe, 1976).

In the 1980s and 1990s, the Multi-Agent System (MAS) was introduced, which focused on making multiple autonomous entities work together and coordinate. In 1998 Jennings, Sycara, and Wooldridge defined a domain that eases distributed problem solving, in which agents combine to find solutions for problems that are not able to be solved by a single agent. Like applications in air traffic control, logistics, and remote sensing, it elaborates the capability of agentic principles (Jennings et al., 1998).

2.2. The Rise of Autonomy and Reinforcement Learning

In agentic processes or techniques, major change came with the development of reinforcement learning (RL). RL agents learn through trial-and-error interactions by using rewards and penalties to optimize decisions. In rule-based systems, there was a study by that presented reinforcement learning (RL) as the base of goal-directed behaviour, stressing adaptability and long-term planning (Kober et al., 2013).

In Deep Q networks (DQN) by Mnih et al. (2015), the agents were able to adapt superhuman performance in Atari games, showing the true potential of reinforcement learning. In AlphaGo (Silver et al., 2016), it combined reinforcement learning and deep learning networks to make strides in strategic reasoning. These systems could explain how artificial intelligence could go beyond static prediction to dynamic decision-making.

Though there were limitations in RL systems, like domain specificity and computational intensity. Training agents requires a large amount of data, and cross-domain transferability is still a challenge. This limitation proved that there is more scope towards generic models that could gain a wide range of knowledge; the gap was later filled by the foundational model.

2.3. Foundation Models and Large Language Models

The AI started developing when foundational models were introduced, especially large language models (LLMs) like GPT-3 (Brown et al., 2020). The reasoning and analysis have been trained on massive text corpora. It also shows the ability of natural language understanding and logical reasoning. LLMs implemented few-shot and zero-shot learning, which allows them to generalize the knowledge across multiple domains without retraining.

The autopsy and Baby AGI (Nakajima, 2023). The experiments are embedded in loops with memory, planning, and job execution modules, and they were able to successfully convert LLMs from reactive text generators into job-oriented agents by implementing them in loops containing memory, planning, and job execution modules (Nakajima, 2023).

2.4. Gaps and Future Direction

The recent papers show the growing popularity of agentic AI. This paper on "generative" AI (Park et al. 2023) shows how LLM communities will create a society whose behaviour is like humans and coordinate like human interaction and cooperation. Similarly, Microsoft's research on Autonomous LLM Agents shows their application in software development, customer service, and process automation (Wu et al., 2023). Autonomous robotics research has LLM models used to enable language-grounded action. For example, say "Can" (Google LLC, 2022). If LLMs and robots are connected, then robots can understand the plain, simple commands and perform tasks accordingly. Now, LLM models connected to robot controllers can make them autonomous. This is one of the big steps towards autonomous machines using agentic AI (Google LLC, 2022).

The collaboration of multiple agents can emphasize academic courses. Projects like Lang Chain Agents and Meta GPT are made in a way to create teams of specialized AI agents that could perform tasks and divide the jobs among them to give the required results. In the future, these processes could be more advanced or controlled by multi-agents of agentic systems, and the dynamic nature of these models permits them to serve as a framework that is more advanced for the future. Future research needs to tackle three key areas for agentic AI: improving scalability, establishing metrics to evaluate autonomy, and developing frameworks for true co-agency. This will guarantee these systems can operate as reliable partners with humans in a complex, changing environment (Wu et al., 2023).

2.5. Ethical, Technical, and Security Challenges

The agentic AI holds great promise for change; it also raises complex ethical and technological issues that need to be resolved before it is widely used. System misalignment, or when the goal of agentic AI drifts from human goals or intentions, is one of the biggest problems. In autonomous systems like self-driving cars and trading algorithms, this misalignment might result in unanticipated behaviour (Floridi & Cowls, 2019). The system must remain aligned with ethical and human goals, which requires human supervision, transparency, and continuous human-in-the-loop feedback mechanisms (Gabriel, 2020).

Inverse Reinforcement Learning (IRL), a method used to deduce human preferences from observed behaviour, is another developing field. Although IRL helps the system to understand human goals, it is also susceptible to bias and incomplete data, which can discord learning outputs (Russell & Norvig, 2022)

If an AI agent misinterprets the reward signal, it could be harmful, like maximizing engagement instead of well-being in a social media system (Bender et al., 2021). This highlights the importance of creating a value reward function and using an explainable AI model to observe the learning process (Russell & Norvig, 2022).

The incidents involving self-driving and autonomous systems demonstrate the high risk involved. These failures highlight how accurate AI can be unreliable in the unpredictable real world, breaking down due to issues like sensor noise, incomplete data, or encountering entirely novel situations not covered in their training. These raise serious concerns about systems validation, accountability, and the proper role of human oversight in critical AI systems (Cihon et al., 2021).

The massive energy and GPU requirements for training and deploying agentic systems present a major technical and economic barrier, increasing their environmental footprint. To manage the expansion of Agentic AI responsibly, future efforts must concentrate on creating sustainable and energy-efficient solutions, including advancements in edge computing (Wu et al., 2022).

Addressing these ethical and technical issues is crucial as agentic AI continues to evolve and embed itself into real-world applications across industries (Wu et al., 2022).

2.6. Emerging Trends and Societal Implications

Human interaction with technology is evolving at a rapid pace as agentic AI matures, which is further impacting how industries operate. A hallmark example of this would be the integration of embedded AI tools such as GitHub Co-pilot and Re plit Ghost-writer, with the tools acting as digital co-developers by being the intelligent collaborators who generate code, understand the context, and suggest optimizations in real time. These tools represent an early form of micro agents that act independently to support human workflows and decision-making (Brynjolfsson & McAfee, 2017).

Another major trend being observed is the automation of cognitive work. Agentic AIs are evolving beyond physical labour or data analysis and can perform creative, managerial, and analytical tasks that were once reserved for humans. This is leading to increased concerns about job displacement while simultaneously offering opportunities for human and AI co-agency, where humans can focus on tasks demanding higher-level creativity while AI manages repetitive or data-heavy tasks (Brynjolfsson & McAfee, 2017).

However, the rise of agentic AIs also presents with it governance challenges. Questions are being raised around transparency, accountability, and explain ability, all of which are central to AI regulation (Floridi & Cowls, 2019). It is essential to ensure the processes undertaken by these agents while making autonomous decisions are understandable and auditable to maintain public trust. It is the responsibility of governments and organizations to develop regulatory frameworks that will balance innovation with ethics compliance and ensure that AI aligns with social values, and it avoids reinforcing stereotypes and inequalities (Floridi & Cowls, 2019).

Overall, the trends are highlighting a dual movement towards greater machine autonomy and deeper human collaboration. The future of agentic AI depends on designing systems that can integrate responsibility within social, professional, and creative ecosystems while performing efficiently.

2.7. Applications

Agentic AI can be used in different applications (Nisa et al., 2025; Piccialli et al., 2025).

Education: Here, Agentic AI can be used to create the task or study roadmap for students. It can also act as a teacher who can guide the students, whereas agentic AI can keep track of time, study, and overall growth of students. It can also help teachers to schedule their tasks, can also give reminders, and create a structured way to complete chapters or courses. It also helps in designing the course.

i. Health care: agentic AI can be used in monitoring patients and can keep track of personalized treatment and give diets or set reminders to patients. It can also help doctors to keep track of the history of patients (Nisa et al., 2025).
ii. Business and finance: The agentic system basically acts as a personal assistant who has knowledge in different domains. Once you have provided the agentic system with information, it can help to keep track of or manage your budgets and portfolio management and give a structured plan to execute the project or optimize resource management (Piccialli et al., 2025).
iii. Media and news: Agentic AI help in media news to detect fake news or false information (Nisa et al., 2025).
iv. Scientific research: it helps to find research papers on topics and helps to show how to write research (Piccialli et al., 2025).

2.8. Problems With Ethics and Technology in Literature

While the literature is good, it also raises some issues about risks. The issues are:

a) Value Alignment: The goals that are set by humans should be followed by an agentic system, ensuring that it completes the task, given that misaligned goals could lead to unintended or harmful consequences (Zeng et al., 2025).
b) Autonomy vs. oversight: the researchers have the debate to maintain the balance between granting complete independence to systems or keeping humans in control in fields like health and defence, as they are sensitive fields and human life is at stake (Bandi et al., 2025).
c) Accountability: If an agentic AI system makes a harmful decision, who shall be considered responsible or accountable for the agentic system's actions? (Bandi, Nukala, & Tatavarthi 2025).
d) Security: The use of AI agents raises the issue of security; the agents can be misused by the attackers, and the question is raised about security and reliability to prevent attackers from intrusion (Bandi et al., 2025).

2.9. Gaps and Future Directions

There has been progress made, but several gaps remain in the current literature:

a. Scalability of Agency: The current existing systems state that the agency is restricted in a particular environment but adapting to open-world complexity is still not possible (Nisa et al., 2025).

b. Long-term memory: The research is still going on the design, which will efficiently work and remember the memory and can keep it for a longer period (Nisa et al., 2025).
c. Evaluation metrics: Agentic systems require new metrics for task completion, autonomous systems, and adaptability, unlike traditional AI (Piccialli, 2025).
d. Ethical framework: the government structure and ethics are far behind compared to the recent development in agentic AI and producing unregulated risks of unregulated deployment.
e. Humans: There are requirements of such systems that act as partners rather than substitutes to work with humans (Bandi et al., 2025).

2.10. Summary

The literature talks about the development of agentic AI as the result of years of research into intelligent agents, reinforcement learning, and foundational models rather than a single technology. Agentic systems are pattern change models that combine autonomy, adaptability, and ethics, departing from traditional models of self-driven robots. The literature also talks about the growth in various fields like health, education, business, financial institutions, and news and media, as well as creativity, and how the agents help or assist to make the work easy. It also tells how the government is far behind technology in ethics and its rules and regulations for future development research.

3. WORKING PRINCIPLES OF SELF-DRIVEN MACHINES USING AGENTIC AI, MULTI-AGENTS, AND ARTIFICIAL INTELLIGENCE

3.1. Foundation of Self-Driving Cars

When a self-driven machine is mentioned, the first thing that comes to mind is automobiles or self-driving cars, as it is a classic example of where cars can be made autonomous. The self-driving cars are divided into 6 levels or parts (SAE International, 2018).

i. Level 0: These are the manual cars. There is no automatic technology. The car is completely dependent on human working (SAE International, 2018).
ii. Level 1: This was the first level of autonomous systems, known as the Advanced Driver Assistance System (ADAS). It assists the human driver with steering, braking, and accelerating that are not working simultaneously. The human must drive the car with little assistance (SAE International, 2018).

iii. Level 2: The ADAS is more advanced, as it can help drivers with steering, braking, and accelerating simultaneously (SAE International, 2018).
iv. Level 3: Here, the autonomous driving system (ADS) can perform all the driving tasks under some limitations, like it can park itself or drive in high, which is following the lane in these situations. Only ADS works, and the human must be ready to take control whenever the machine fails or faces a problem; it still requires the main driver (SAE International, 2018).
v. Level 4: The ADS system is only a little more advanced than the previous level, as it can perform all the tasks, which means a human driver needs to be present, but it does not require human attention to the vehicle (SAE International, 2018).
vi. Level 5: This is the highest level of automatic vehicle, where it acts as its own driver, navigating the road and operating steering wheels, brakes, and other controllers. Even humans require facing the screen, and they can sit as passengers; it is a fully automatic vehicle (SAE International, 2018).

These were the levels of automatic vehicles (Yu, 2025). Now, in automatic vehicles, these systems need to be controlled, so it requires agents to perform specific tasks:

A. Autonomous: The ability of a machine to operate without any human interaction
B. Adaptability: The ability to adapt to any situation or give solutions according to the situation
C. Objective-oriented – the steps taken to complete the task or job (Yu, 2025).

For example, the autonomous car has adapted to the situation or traffic and created the route; it does not just blindly follow the route that is already programmed in the system if any obstacles come. It must adapt according to the situation. For the safety of passengers (Badue et al., 2021).

3.2. The Sensing System

An autonomous system gathers information about its environment through sensors; sensing the environment is the first step of an autonomous machine. The goal of sensing is to provide the system with correct, reliable, and comprehensive data about the surroundings. This information could be gathered through multiple sensors, which are cameras and LIDAR for visual display. Radar and ultrasonic sensors for measuring distance, GPS and IMU for localization, and IoT and V2X for getting additional data like traffic signals or weather updates. Agentic AI combines or collaborates with the agentic models for sensing, visuals, and neural networks. This machine can answer questions like "Where am I?" Where do I have to reach? And what is happening right now? (Yu, 2025).

3.3. The Cognition Phase

This phase is one of the crucial phases, as it helps in recognizing the objects or humans around this. Agentic AI recognizes humans as the parts of a shape or image. After the object is detected, the algorithm detects whether it will be in the next frame or not. so that's why it is crucial for self-driving cars and robots or drones to recognize the object and track it as it can appear in the next frame or Agentic AI makes decisions based on tracking and detecting the object and whether it will appear in the next phase. For example, in self-driven cars, if a human comes in front of the car, it will apply brakes. This must be detected first, and then it will be an obstacle in the path, and then agentic AI must make the decision to apply brakes. Therefore, the cognition phase is an important aspect (Kober et al., 2013).

3.4. Decision-Making System or Planning Algorithm

In this phase the decision or planning is done to choose the path, or which is the best route. Agentic uses an algorithm to find the shortest path, like the A-star algorithm or Dijkstra algorithm; it also involves finding a smooth path or safer path to the car with nice roads. Agentic AI uses reinforcement learning (RL) to make decisions like a safety path or stopping at a red signal. These are some examples of decision-making using reinforcement learning (RL). For self-driving cars, multi-objective trade-off ensures safety, speed, comfort, and fuel or battery efficiency (Chen et al., 2019).

3.5. Execution

Now the decision is made by agentic AI; for the execution part, it goes through actuators and the control system. Actuators are the components that convert electrical energy into physical energy, for example, steering and motors for cars or robotic machines. These actions are controlled by the system; it makes sure that actuators convert the energy. Proportional integral derivative controller (PID): proportional reacts to current, integral recognizes previous error, and derivative. Predict the future faults. An adaptive control system is an advanced system that can change the environment or respond to behaviour. For example, if there are strong gusty winds for a drone, it automatically changes the controls and adapts according to the strong gusty wind. Continuous monitoring is required, and adjustments are made, like in cars; a sharp right turn is not taken to reach the destination. The agentic system adjusts according to the destination to reach it autonomously (Russell & Norvig, 2022).

3.6. How Multi-Agentic Agents Help in the Development of Artificial Intelligence

Agentic AI means a combination of multiple agents working on a task simultaneously. Here, cars, robots, and drones require multiple tasks to be performed together, so multiple agents can coordinate and make the machine autonomous. The protocols required are communication, negotiation, and emergency acts; these collectively make the system autonomous. And where individual agents complete the task, there are communication protocols like vehicle-to-vehicle (V2V). This system allows vehicles to share data with each other, like speed, distance, braking, or location, so it can prevent accidents (Kober et al., 2013). Negotiation means the self-driving cars judge other cars in front and drive accordingly without human support, so AI agents can communicate this information with each other and can easily judge and adapt accordingly. Emergence behaviours: this means any complicated patterns are formed due to one individual agent's local action. These patterns do not emerge but naturally occur in the system. For example, the traffic rules, like stopping at a red light. The combination of multiple agents makes the system autonomous and run smoothly without human help (Rahwan et al., 2019).

3.7. Human in the Loop and Ethical Safeguards

Rules and ethics are very necessary for agentic AI to ensure the machine operates with human values. Though these machines are autonomous, they still require humans to prevent them from doing action that could cause harm to the environment or to a living body.

i. Override mechanism: This means that if there is an issue with safety, humans have the right to change the decision of AI. This is necessary for self-driving cars.
ii. Ethical guidelines: AI systems are completely trained under the data voided by humans, so it makes their decisions biased. There are ethical guidelines of the government, and the agentic machine should respect those boundaries and not cross the rules set by the government.
iii. Transparency: In these, AI must explain the decisions that they are taking and why they are taking them, like why they chose this path. This transparency should be there between AI and humans (Bryson, 2018).

4. BIBLIOMETRIC PERSPECTIVE

The bibliometric analysis performed by VOS viewer based on the data available on Lens.org provides an in-depth representation of the structural and temporal development of the field of artificial intelligence (AI) and the fields that it represents. The figure below (Figure 1) is a visualization of the co-occurrence of keywords throughout the academic literature, where the node represents a keyword, its size the frequency of appearance and the connecting line represents the relationship of co-occurrence. The overlay colour scale gives a further time scale with the blue and purple nodes representing older research contributions (around 2005) and green, yellow, and red representing more recent contributions nearer to 2020. Such a mixture of representation makes structural and chronological interpretation of the field of research possible. The map identifies a cluster of influential centres, namely artificial intelligence, machine learning, reinforcement learning, neural networks, humans, and ethics that present the cognitive core of AI studies. These hubs have its own clusters, such as the multi-agent systems, control strategies, healthcare, and psychology, and blockchain, which signify the specialization of the study that is deriving out of the core area. These hubs are pervasive in the literature as shown by their large node size and provide the importance of these hubs in connecting different subfields through their vast interconnections. In general, Figure 1 demonstrates the gradual growth of the field of AI studies, which initially focused on technical and computational aspects and then on more applied, interdisciplinary, and human-related issues.

Figure 1. Overlay visualization of co-occurrence keyword

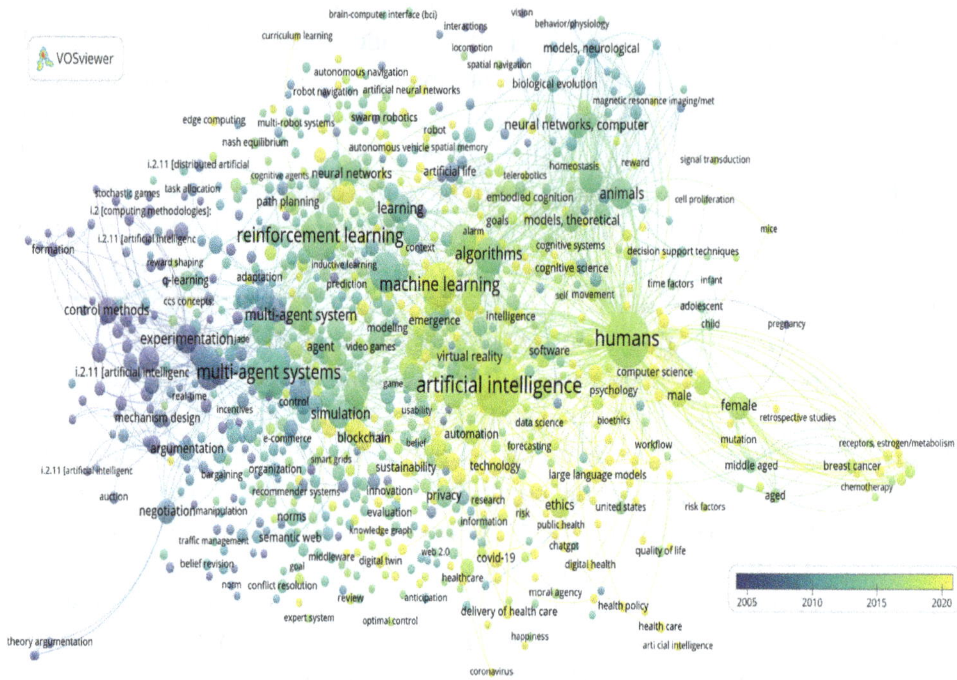

Source: Van Eck and Waltman (2022)

The thick centre of this network is further inspected in Figure 2 that isolates and magnifies the central and the most influential groups of the rest of the visualization. In this case, the prevalence of artificial intelligence, machine learning, reinforcement learning, neural networks, and ethics is even more evident, as these nodes are of huge sizes and interconnections. The time-related overlay provides a chronological story, as the previous stages of the research were primarily supported by the pillars of methodology, like reinforcement learning and multi-agent systems, whereas the rise of the yellow colour nodes demonstrates the prevalence of the new themes, including AI ethics, digital health, chatbots, large language models, and COVID-19. These new nodes are relatively nearer to the outer part of the core meaning that they are not tied to the ancient notions but when they are being tied to the foundational concepts are a new area of research interests rather than an old tradition. Another point that the figure makes is that AI bridging capacity in which technical principles, like algorithm and simulation, are tightly coupled with social problems like ethics, privacy, psychology, governance, and sustainability. The general overview of the visualization highlights the two-fold current direction of AI research: a long-standing dependence on computational foundations and a more modernized diversification of the field into human-focused and practice-oriented ones.

Figure 2. Zoomed-in co-occurrence network showing the central dominance of artificial intelligence (also see Figure 1)

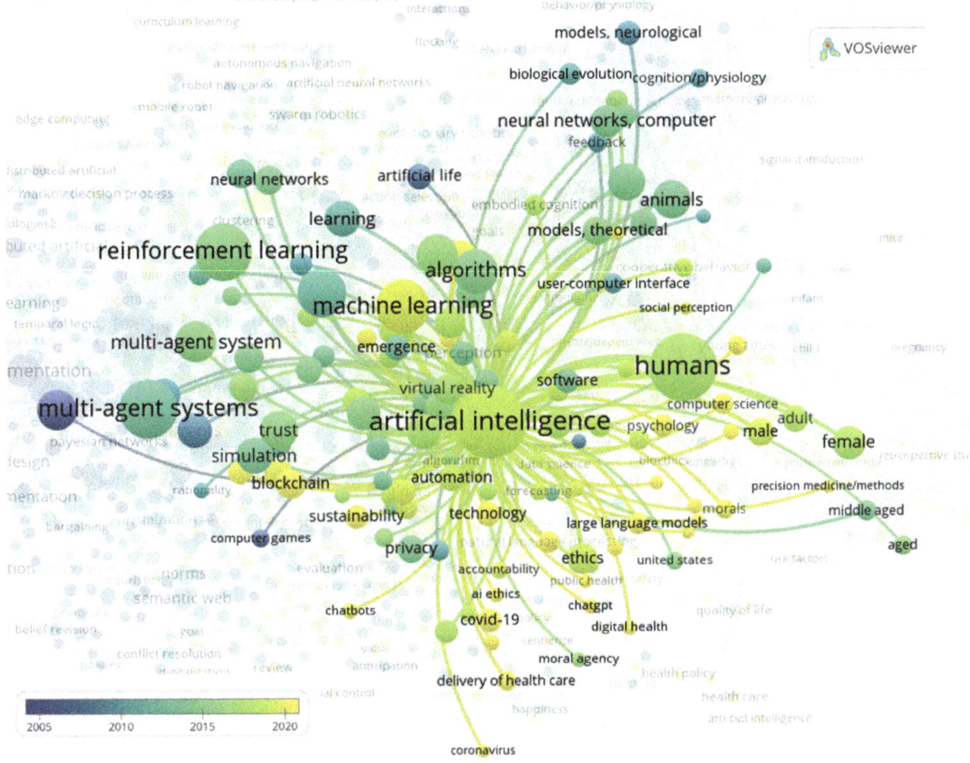

Source: Van Eck and Waltman (2022)

Figure 3 provides more details by adding granularity to the node humans that is one of the most powerful and cross-disciplinary centres in the bibliometric network. Its size of nodes and wide network of radiating relationships demonstrate the high rate of its occurrence as well as its pivotal role in connecting various areas of research focusing on AI. The strong ties between human beings and computational keywords, including artificial intelligence, machine learning, algorithms, neural networks, reinforcement learning, and software available on the left-hand side of the map support the combination of human-related issues with the developments in the methods. On the right-hand side, there is a strong biomedical cluster, which includes such terms as female, male, middle aged, aged, breast cancer, chemotherapy, precision medicine, and treatment outcome. This cluster existence demonstrates the high degree of AI penetration into the healthcare research area where demographic and clinical variables are investigated in parallel with computational methods. The newer, yellow-coloured nodes, like ethics, AI ethics, privacy, public health, digital health, large language models, Chat GPT, and COVID-19, are located at the bottom of the map, expressing the growing prevalence of societal implications, health policy and governance issues, especially during and in the aftermath of the global pandemic. Higher up, the human-centred hub is linked with neuroscience and cognitive science research via node user-computer interface, social perception, neural networks (computer), animals and models (theoretical). This number, in turn, highlights the two-fold role of human beings as the subject and subject of the research conducted on AI, connecting the methodological innovations to biomedical applications and social discussions.

Figure 3. Zoomed-in co-occurrence network showing the central dominance of human (also see Figure 1)

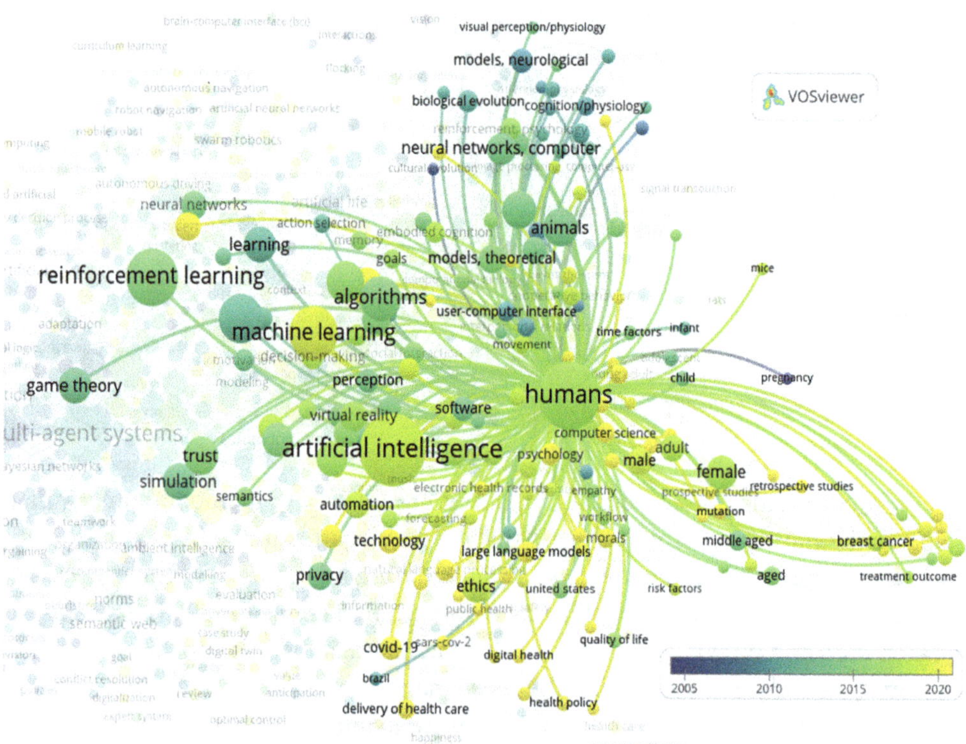

Source: Van Eck and Waltman (2022)

In addition to this human-centred view, Figure 4 shows the co-occurrence network of machine learning and areas surrounding it. In the visualization, machine learning, artificial intelligence, and humans are represented as the core nodes, and the tightly integrated concepts like algorithms, neural networks, reinforcement learning, and multi-agent systems can be seen. The fact that the connections were dense also demonstrates the broad applicability of these keywords in various thematic clusters. The temporal overlay gives some idea of how the field evolved: older work is captured in the nodes of blue green, like neural networks (computer) and a computer simulation, which are more than mere established fields of research from the past. Conversely, the yellow nodes that include ethics, privacy, explain ability, sustainability.

Figure 4. Zoomed-in co-occurrence network showing the central dominance of machine learning (also see Figure 1)

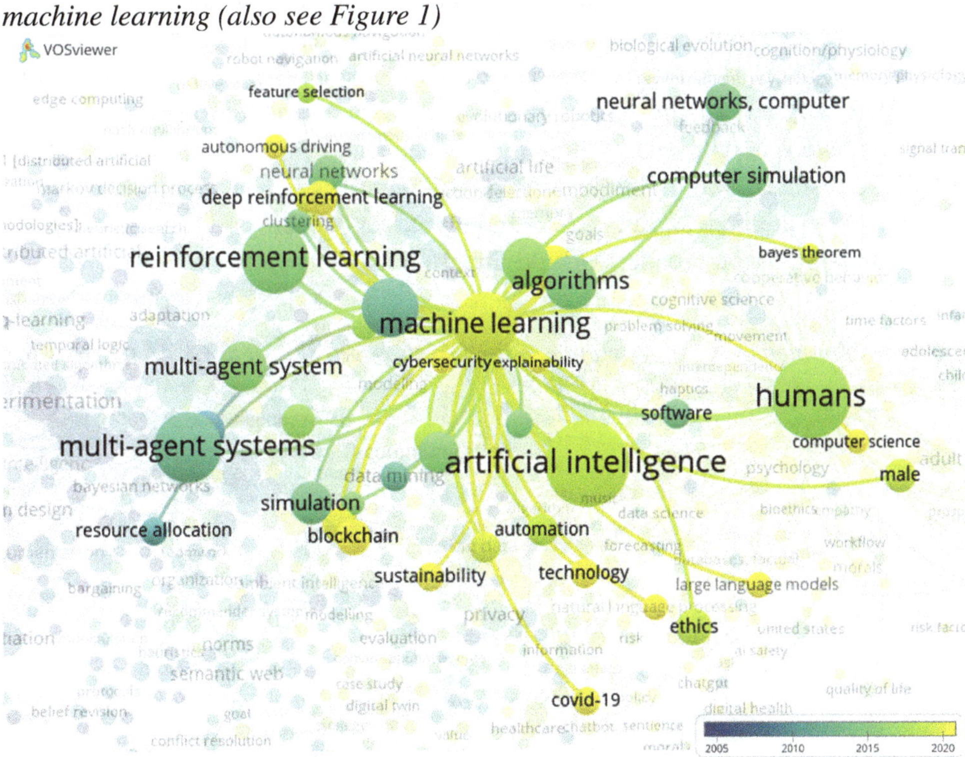

Source: Van Eck and Waltman (2022)

Figure 5 gives a specialized co-occurrence visualization of multi-agent systems, which is one of the most central and powerful sub-areas in the overall research on AI. The figure points out multi-agent systems as a huge and thick nexus, highly intertwined with reinforcement learning, machine learning, algorithms, and artificial intelligence. There are other related notions closely related to this hub like coordination, simulation, trust, and game theory, which constitute the methodology foundation of the study. The time layer shows a sequential process of development: the previous research (blue, purple nodes) focused on the negotiation, argumentation, and game theory, and the mid-range stages (green nodes) resulted in the reinforcement learning and coordination. The modern growth of multi-agent studies towards the latest AI application and socially meaningful discussion is traced by newer yellow nodes, such as algorithms, privacy, blockchain interaction, and large language models. The map layout also demonstrates the scope of the field with the help of its structure. To the left, groups around negotiation, and bargaining and mechanism design are indications of the origins of the field on distributed rationality and economic decision models. In the middle, the preeminence of reinforcement learning and coordination suggests that they are the methodological cores that facilitate adaptive behavior of agents in dynamic environments. To the right, the closeness of machine learning and artificial intelligence illustrates the adoption of multi-agent methods into the mainstream AI, and smaller nodes like semantic web, ambient intelligence and norms indicate special usage in digital ecosystems and smart environments. As a whole, the visualization highlights how multi-agent systems have moved beyond conceptualized theoretical frameworks and into a flexible, cross-disciplinary sector as a subdivision of the broader AI field direction.

Figure 5. Zoomed-in co-occurrence network showing the central dominance of multi-agent systems (also see Figure 1)

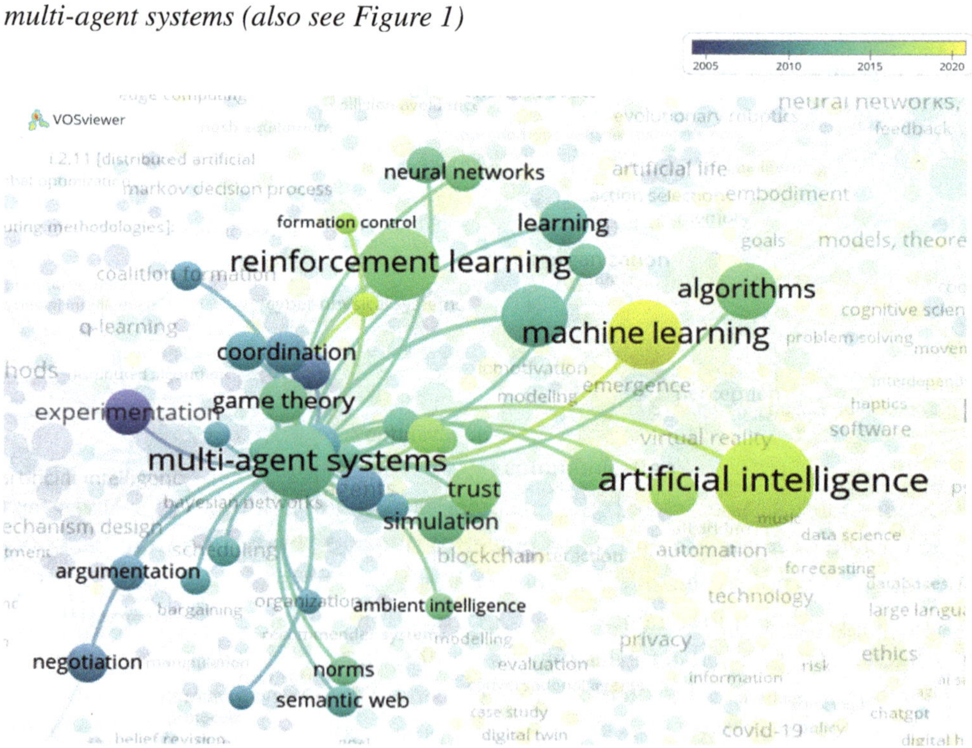

Source: Van Eck and Waltman (2022)

Figure 6 shows the more specific field of reinforcement learning. In this case, reinforcement learning becomes the most noticeable node, and it has a large size and a vast number of links to other powerful terms like neural networks, machine learning, algorithms, and multi-agent systems. The close clustering of these terms indicates that there is methodological interdependence of these fields, and that reinforcement learning is a theoretical and practical backbone. The timeline color gradient shows the time-related trend: blue circles display older works, which concentrated on theoretical methods like the Markov decision processes and the Q-learning. These concepts are central to the network and they are the ones that have been influencing it over time. As we proceed to the green and yellow parts of the map, newer direction of research can be observed, which involve transfer learning, curriculum learning, trust and human-AI interaction. The fact that these nodes are yellow color shows that the field has recently shifted its interest towards adaptation of reinforcement learning techniques to new areas, increasing interpretability, and collaboration between humans and intelligent agents. The interdisciplinary nature of reinforcement learning has also been further indicated by the capability of large nodes like humans and artificial intelligence to be part of the same network, as well as the connection between algorithm creation and robotics, psychology, and human-centered artificial intelligence applications. The figure shows the active growth of reinforcement learning with its algorithmic roots towards more general uses in distributed intelligence and human-machine interface.

Figure 6. Zoomed-in co-occurrence network showing the central dominance of Reinforcement learning (also see Figure 1)

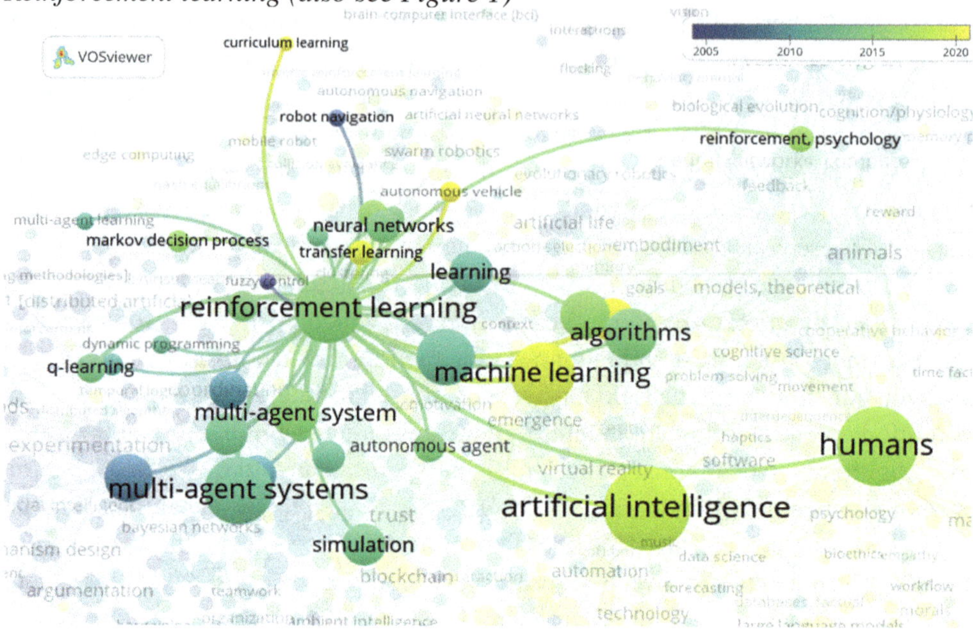

Source: Van Eck and Waltman (2022)

Lastly, Figure 7 is a zoomed-in bibliometric visualization of the focus on algorithms, which highlights their underpinning position in the AI research environment. The node algorithm is presented as a big and well-connected node, which involves various areas such as machine learning, reinforcement learning, neural networks, artificial intelligence, and humans. It can be seen that the network structure in this case suggests algorithms as the unifying backbone of the methodological, computational, and applied strands of AI research. Temporal overlay shows that at the early stage (2005-2010), blue-colored nodes like multi-agent systems, reinforcement learning, and game theory prevailed in the network which demonstrates the focus on the foundational models and theoretical investigations. The green-colored nodes related to a neural network, theoretical frameworks, and thinking strategies were common in the middle phase (2010–2015), which suggests that there was a shift to the broadening of the computational and cognitive basis of algorithmic study. In the later period (2016-2020), the yellow nodes like big data, privacy, accountability, bioethics, and AI safety are seen as a representation of applying algorithmic approaches to new areas of society and ethics. The availability of the nodes of cognition, animals, and healthcare highlights the likelihood of applying the algorithmic practices in the field of psychology, neuroscience, and biomedical sciences. This number explains that algorithms have now become the focus of both applied and interdisciplinary research in AI as they are no longer mere theoretical models.

Figure 7. Zoomed-in co-occurrence network showing the central dominance of Algorithms (also see Figure 1)

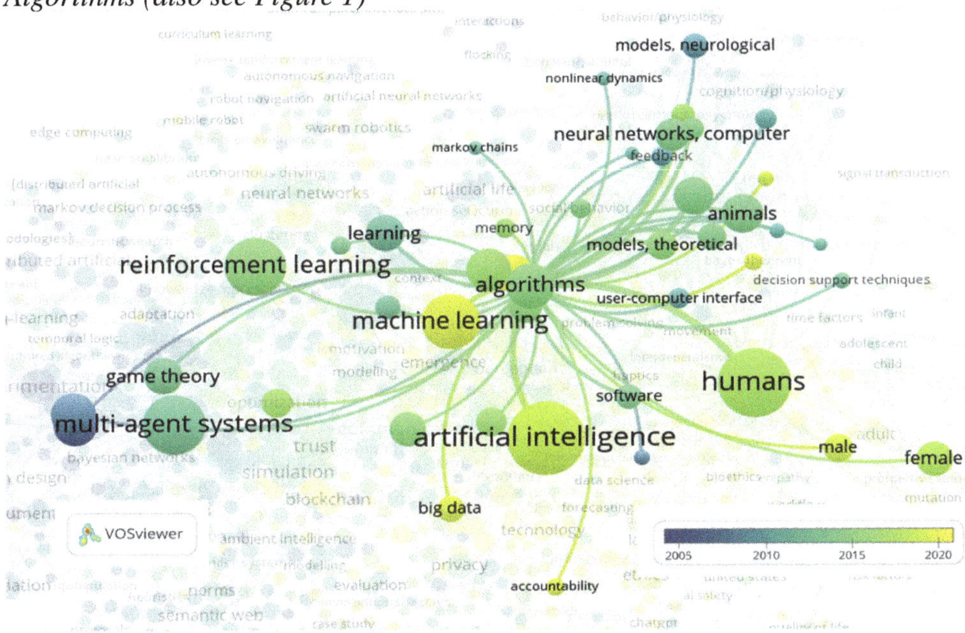

Source: Van Eck and Waltman (2022)

The time dynamics of the AI-focused scholarly have also been summed up in the trend of publications between 1990 and 2025, according to Lens data as shown in Figure 8. The trend indicates that in the 1990s, the contribution of scholarly knowledge in the areas of agentic and distributed AI were few and far between, leading to the nascency of the field. A small improvement was seen in the early 2000s, when the first foundational research started to come out. The output in the year 2005 to 2015 showed a steady increase in research which varied and had an evident trend of increasing. The sharpest increase was after 2016, reaching a sharp peak in 2020, at which time there were breakthroughs in deep learning, reinforcement learning, and global interest in AI applications in various capacities. After this peak, the data show a decrease in the number of publications since 2022, but it is clear that the situation is improving by 2025 and it is possible to talk about the process of maturation and stabilization instead of depreciation. This trend portrays the cyclical aspect of science, with the early excitement in a field resulting in the boom, and then a period of consolidation and creation of more lasting paths.

Figure 8. Publication count from 1990-2025

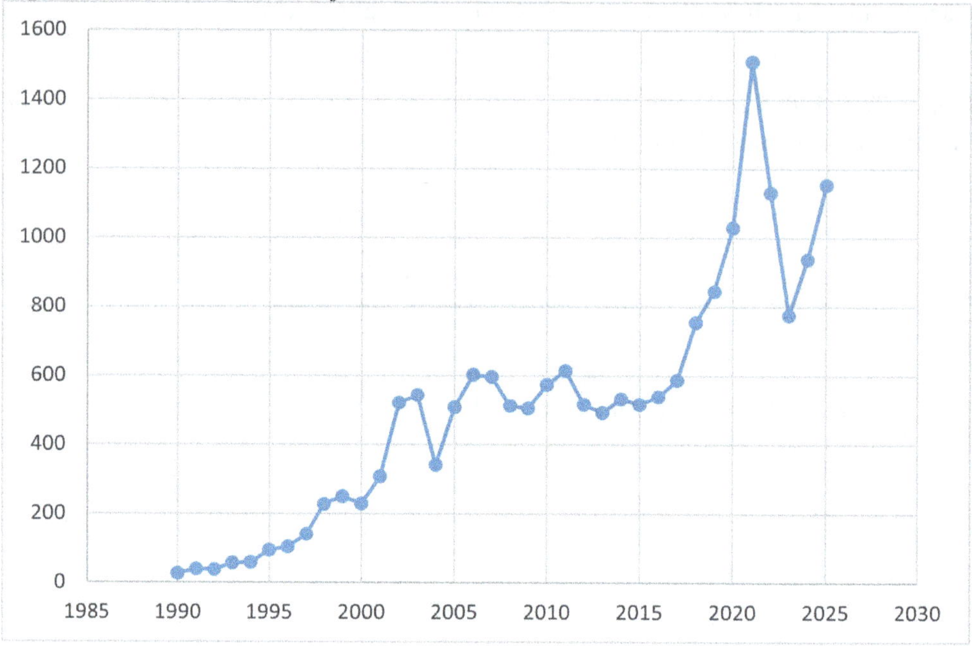

The thematic scope of Agentic AI and multi-agent systems is also reflected in the visual representation of a word cloud that is illustrated in Figure 9 shows the relative popularity of the keywords that are used most commonly. The most commonly used terms, such as system, agent, intelligence, artificial, learning, and distributed, represent the original preoccupation of the area with distributed intelligent systems controlled by the process of learning. The keywords like multiagent, autonomous, control, reinforcement, simulation, network, human, model, and design are used as the medium-sized ones that show the main directions of the research, i.e., the reinforcement learning of agent behavior to human-agent collaboration and networked decision-making. Smaller yet meaningful words on which the theme is supported include language, theory, optimization, social, robotics, interaction, service, and security, which reflect the interdisciplinary expansion of the AI concept with robotics, communication, and management of trust. Ontology, Bayesian, fuzzy, negotiation, swarm, traffic, and energy are other more specialized research fields and areas of application, either of reasoning methods or applications in real transportation networks, energy systems, and swarm robotics. The visualization can be used to show how the field of research is layered with the high-level concepts forming the foundation of the field with medium-level thematic areas enclosed in niche applications, forming the multidisciplinary development of the field.

Figure 9. Word cloud of agentic AI research

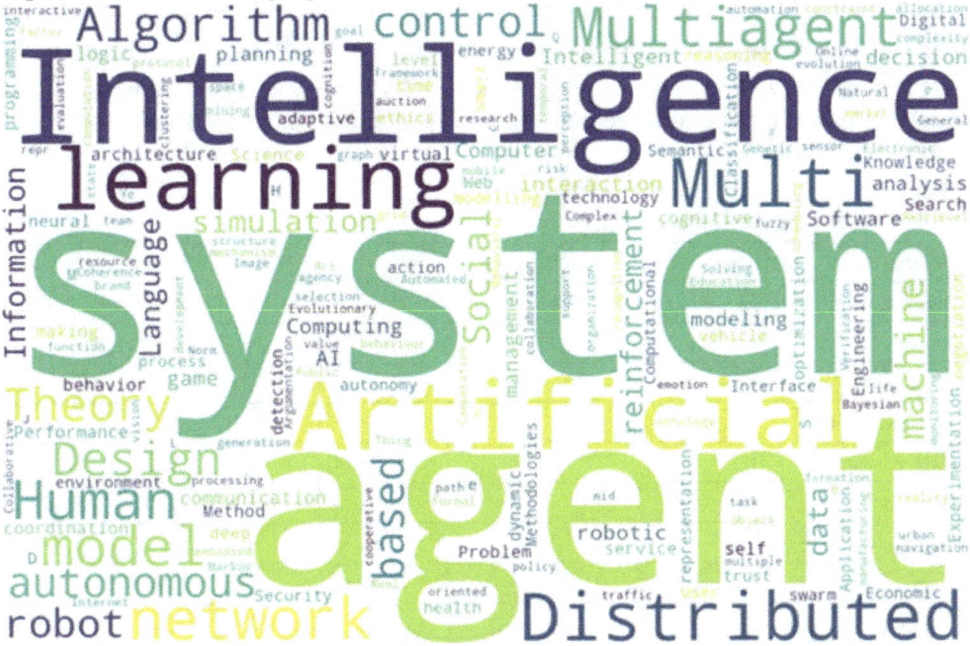

Table 1 provides a summary of the contribution of the top 10 countries in the global distribution of research output in Agentic AI. Netherlands is the evident leader with 4,006 publications, which is an indicator of the good academic ecosystem and the long-term experience in the field of multi-agent systems. Germany has 2,090 publications, which is due to its focus on applied AI research, engineering, and robotics. The third country with the number of publications is the United States which is 1,670 publications and this lends credence to its contribution in terms of the leading universities and technology firms. The United Kingdom, having 1,013 publications, is shown to have a great contribution to make especially on multi-agent cooperation, human-AI interaction, and the ethical aspect. Switzerland, even though it is a smaller country, provides 642 publications, which indicates the performance of research institutions of high impact, which are characterized by precision engineering and computational innovation. China has 229 publications that means that it has not gained significant presence in the given sphere, since much of its AI research is devoted to deep learning and computer vision. South Korea (123) is the most active country in terms of the publications they have and is an example of a country that has advanced in the sphere of robotics and autonomous systems, whereas Egypt (76) is an example of a country that is gaining momentum in the application of AI and its researching efforts in Africa and the Middle East. Though Japan has been involved in robotics historically, it has published 51 papers, which can be a sign of concentrating on a rather different surface. England, which is mentioned independently of the United Kingdom in the dataset, provides 46 publications. In total, the data indicate that the European countries are highly predominant, with the North American and Asian countries making numerous contributions to the field, which reflects the collaborative and international character of the field.

Table 1. Top 10 countries globally

Country	Count
Netherlands	4006
Germany	2090
United States	1670
United Kingdom	1013
Switzerland	642
China	229
South Korea	123
Egypt	76
Japan	51
England	46

Table 2 describes the analysis of the publishing outlets, which gives an understanding of the dissemination patterns of the research on the topic of Agentic AI. The most dominant publisher is Springer Science and Business Media LLC, with 5,462 publications, as the publisher has wide coverage in the realms of computer science, engineering, and artificial intelligence with its publications in the form of journals, conference proceedings and book series. The second competitor is Elsevier BV with 1,068 publications, which highlights its powerful presence in the multidisciplinary AI applications. It publishes 957 works, which makes IEEE a focal point of spreading research on intelligent systems, robotics, and distributed computing. In second place are the Association for Computing Machinery (ACM) with 916 publications, many of which are due to its flagship conference AAMAS, which is the centre of multi-agent systems studies. Each of E-editor: Springer Berlin Heidelberg (694 publications), MDPI AG (482) and the Institute of Electrical and Electronics Engineers (386 publications each), are also important due to variability in the classification of the data sets but all of them do give a high score to IEEE in this field. Other publications like ACM Press (404), Wiley (354) and Frontiers Media SA (306) make the publishing venues diverse. The presence of MDPI and Frontiers Media SA proves the increased significance of open-access sources, which allow distributing the results of the AI research more widely and faster. Comprehensively, this publisher distribution highlights twofold roles of the conventional models of dissemination based on conferences and new open-access websites of the form in the determination of accessibility and appearance of Agentic AI research.

Table 2. Top 10 publisher in the world

Publisher	Count
Springer Science and Business Media LLC	5462
Elsevier BV	1068
IEEE	957
ACM	916
Springer Berlin Heidelberg	694
Institute of Electrical and Electronics Engineers (IEEE)	535
MDPI AG	482
ACM Press	404
Wiley	354
Frontiers Media SA	306

Combined, the bibliometric analysis, provided in Figures 1 to 9, the trends of publishes, the word cloud, and Tables 1 and 2 give the descriptive picture of the development of AI research. The figures follow the creation of thematic cores and specialized clusters, the temporal overlay shows the chronological changes in the focus of research interest, the breadth of themes is shown with the help of the word cloud, and the distribution of the world and publishes is demonstrated with the help of the tables. The results paint a picture of a field that grew out of computational and algorithmic underpinnings beginning in the early 2000s, has grown in methodological and applications circles over the next ten years, and diversified over the past few years to include human-centred, ethical, and interdisciplinary aspects. This descriptive judgement presents a basis to explaining how the AI research developed and how it spread on both geographical and publishing levels.

5. CONCLUSION

Agentic AI is one such paradigm shifts in the history of intelligent systems, but one that moves in the other direction: machines can now act, reason, and attain complex goals without constant oversight by humans. As compared to traditional AI, which is reactive and limited to a set of predetermined rules, Agentic AI combines reasoning, memory, learning, and decision-making to formulate self-directed systems that adjust to the evolving environment. Such change ushers in broad opportunities of innovation in fields like robotics, education, finance, healthcare, transportation, and manufacturing. Replacing routine and time-intensive operations with Agentic AI helps human beings dedicate their time to productivity, strategy, and value-adding problems, and eventually, achieve better productivity, streamlined work processes, and better interactions with users. The other significant strength of Agentic AI is in multi-agent systems whereby several intelligent agents can cooperate or compete to solve large-scale issues in distributed systems. These systems enhance scalability, coordination, and efficiency and are primarily useful in traffic management, optimization of supply chains, and smart city planning application. Nevertheless, just like any type of strong technology, there is a list of problems associated with the emergence of Agentic AI that cannot be disregarded. Ethical responsibility problems, lack of transparency in decision-making, data privacy, security, and bias should be resolved to develop confidence in such systems. The human values and societal needs require having clear governance structures, safety mechanisms, and explain ability features that would help keep Agentic AI consistent with their values and needs.

In Conclusion, it might be said that Agentic AI is not only a new technological development but also a paradigm shift that can revolutionize industries, enhance human lives, and speed up the process of moving towards intelligent automation. Until its success, it will only be able to find the right combination between innovation and responsibility, where these systems are not only safe but also ethical and beneficial to everyone. Made with proper consideration, Agentic AI may be emerged as one of the most efficient means of establishing a smarter, more equitable, and more sustainable future.

REFERENCES

Badue, C., Guidolini, R., Carneiro, R. V., Azevedo, P., Cardoso, V., Forechi, A., Jesus, L., Berriel, R., Paixao, T., Mutz, F., Veronese, L., Oliveira-Santos, T., & De Souza, A. F. (2021). Self-driving cars. *Survey (London, England)*. Advance online publication. DOI: 10.1016/j.eswa.2020.113816

Bandi, A., Nukala, H., & Tatavarthi, B. (2025). Automated test case generation for software testing using generative. *AI*. Advance online publication. DOI: 10.1007/978-3-031-92178-0_7

Belcak, P., Heinrich, G., Diao, S., Fu, Y., Dong, X., Muralidharan, S., Lin, Y. C., & Molchanov, P. (2025). Small language models are the future of agentic. DOI: https://doi.org//arXiv.2506.02153DOI: 10.48550

Bender, E. M., Gebru, T., McMillan-Major, A., & Shmitchell, S. (2021). On the dangers of stochastic parrots: Can language models be too big? DOI: https://doi.org/DOI: 10.1145/3442188.3445922

Brown, T. B., Mann, B., Ryder, N., Subbiah, M., Kaplan, J., Dhariwal, P., Neelakantan, A., Shyam, P., Sastry, G., Askel, A., Agarwal, S., Voss, A., Wu, J., Winter, C., . . . Amodei, D. (2020). Language models are few-shot learners. DOI: https://doi.org//arXiv.2005.14165DOI: 10.48550

Brynjolfsson, E., & McAfee, A. (2017). The business of artificial intelligence: What it can — and cannot — do for your organization. Retrieved from The Business of Artificial Intelligence.pdf.

Bryson, J. (2018). Patiency is not a virtue: The design of intelligent systems and systems of ethics. DOI: https://doi.org/DOI: 10.1007/s10676-018-9448-6

Bubeck, S., Chandrasekaran, V., Eldan, R., Gehrke, J., Horvitz, E., Kamar, E., Lee, P., Li, Y., Lundberg, S., Nori, H., Palangi, H., Ribeiro, M. T., & Zhang, Y. (2023). Sparks of artificial general intelligence: Early experiments with GPT-4. DOI https://doi.org//arXiv.2303.12712DOI: 10.48550

Capgemini Research Institute. (2025). Rise of agentic AI: How trust is the key to human-AI collaboration. https://www.capgemini.com/insights/research-library/ai-agents/

Chen, X., Yu, G., Cheng, G., & Hao, T. (2019). *Research topics in educational technology: A bibliometric analysis of Computers & Education*. DOI: https://doi.org/DOI: 10.1007/s40692-019-00149-1

Cihon, P., Kleinaltenkamp, M. J., Schuett, J., & Baum, S. D. (2021). AI certification: Advancing ethical practice by reducing information asymmetries. DOI: https://arxiv.org/abs/2105.10356

Dafoe, A. (2018). *AI governance: A research agenda*. Centre for the Governance of AI, Future of Humanity Institute, University of Oxford. https://cdn.governance.ai/GovAI-Research-Agenda.pdf

Floridi, L., & Cowls, J. (2019). A Unified Framework of Five Principles for AI in Society. DOI: https://doi.org/DOI: 10.1162/99608f92.8cd550d1

Floridi, L., & Cowls, J. (2021). A unified framework of five principles for AI in society. DOI: https://doi.org/DOI: 10.1007/978-3-030-81907-1_2

Gabriel, I. (2020). Artificial Intelligence, values, and alignment. DOI: https://doi.org/DOI: 10.1007/s11023-020-09539-2

Google, L. L. C. (2022). AI Principles Progress Update. Retrieved from https://ai.google/static/documents/ai-principles-2022-progress-update.pdf

Hosseini, S., & Seilani, H. (2025). The role of agentic AI in shaping a smart future. *Systematic Reviews*. Advance online publication. DOI: 10.1016/j.array.2025.100399

International, S. A. E. (2018). Updated visual chart for its "levels of driving automation" standard for self-driving vehicles. Data Retrieved from https://www.sae.org/

Jennings, N. R., Sycara, K., & Wooldridge, M. J. (1998). A roadmap of agent research and development. DOI: https://doi.org/DOI: 10.1023/A:1010090405266

Kober, J., Bagnell, J. A., & Peters, J. (2013). Reinforcement learning in robotics. *Survey (London, England)*. Advance online publication. DOI: 10.1177/0278364913495721

Lake, B. M., Ullman, T. D., Tenenbaum, J. B., & Gershman, S. J. (2016). Building machines that learn and think like people. DOI: https://doi.org/DOI: 10.1017/S0140525X16001837

Luckin, R. (2017). Towards artificial intelligence-based assessment systems. DOI: https://doi.org/DOI: 10.1038/s41562-016-0028

Mnih, V., Kavukcuoglu, K., Silver, D., Rusu, A. A., Veness, J., Bellemare, M. G., Graves, A., Riedmiller, M., Fidjeland, A. K., Ostrovski, G., Petersen, S., Beattie, C., Sadik, A., Antonoglou, I., King, H., Kumaran, D., Wierstra, D., Legg, S., & Hassabis, D. (2015). Human-level control through deep reinforcement learning. DOI: https://doi.org/DOI: 10.1038/nature14236

Nakajima, Y. (2023). *BabyAGI* [Computersoftware]. GitHub.: https://github.com/yoheinakajima/babyagi

Nisa, U., Shirazi, M., Saip, M. A., & Pozi, M. S. M. (2025). Agentic AI: The Age of Reasoning—. *RE:view*. Advance online publication. DOI: 10.1016/j.jai.2025.08.003

OpenAI (2023). GPT-4 Technical Report. DOI: https://doi.org//arxiv.2303.08774DOI: 10.48550

Park, J. S., O'Brien, J. C., Cai, C. J., Morris, M. R., Liang, P., & Bernstein, M. S. (2023). Generative Agents: Interactive Simulacra of Human Behavior. DOI: https://arxiv.org/abs/2304.03442

Piccialli, F., Chiaro, D., Sarwar, S., Cerciello, D., Qi, P., & Mele, V. (2025). AgentAI: A comprehensive survey on autonomous agents in distributed AI for Industry 4.0. DOI: https://doi.org/DOI: 10.1016/j.eswa.2025.128404

Rahwan, I., Cebrian, M., Obradovich, N., Bongard, J., Bonnefon, J., Breazeal, C., Crandall, J., Christakis, N., Couzin, I., Jackson, M., Jennings, N., Kamar, E., Kloumann, I., Larochelle, H., Lazer, D., McElreath, R., Mislove, A., Parkes, D., Pentland, A., … Wellman, M. (2019). Machine behavior. DOI: https://doi.org/DOI: 10.1038/s41586-019-1138-y

Russell, S., & Norvig, P. (2022). Artificial Intelligence: A Modern Approach (4th US ed.). https://aima.cs.berkeley.edu/

Shneiderman, B. (2020). Human-Centered Artificial Intelligence: Three Fresh Ideas. *DOI:* https://doi.org/DOI: 10.17705/1thci.00131

Shortliffe, E. H. (1976, October). Computer-based medical consultations: MYCIN. *Journal of Clinical Engineering*, *388*(1). Advance online publication. DOI: 10.1097/00004669-197610000-00011

Silver, D., Huang, A., Maddison, C. J., Guez, A., Sifre, L., van den Driessche, G., Schrittwieser, J., Antonoglou, I., Panneershelvam, V., Lanctot, M., Dieleman, S., Grewe, D., Nham, J., Kalchbrenner, N., Sutskever, I., Lillicrap, T., Hassabis, D. (2016). Mastering the game of Go with deep neural networks and tree search. DOI: https://doi.org/DOI: 10.1038/nature16961

Wu, C.-J., Raghavendra, R., Gupta, U., Acun, B., Ardalani, N., Maeng, K., Chang, G., Behram, F., Huang, J., Bai, C., Gschwind, M., Gupta, A., Ott, M., Melnikov, A., Candido, S., Brooks, D., Chauhan, G., Lee, B., Lee, H., . . . Hazelwood, K. (2022). Sustainable AI: Environmental implications, challenges, and opportunities. DOI: https://doi.org//arXiv.2111.00364DOI: 10.48550

Wu, Q., Bansal, G., Zhang, J., Wu, Y., Li, B., Zhu, E., Jiang, L., Zhang, X., Zhang, S., Liu, J., Awadallah, A., White, R., Burger, D., & Wang, C. (2023). AutoGen: Enabling next-gen LLM applications via multi-agent conversation. DOI: https://doi.org//arXiv.2308.08155DOI: 10.48550

Yu, J. (2025). Agentic vehicles for Human-Centered mobility. DOI: https://doi.org//arxiv.2507.04996DOI: 10.48550

Zeng, W., Zhu, H., Qin, C., Wu, H., Cheng, Y., Zhang, S., Jin, X., Shen, Y., Wang, Z., Zhong, F., & Xiong, H. (2025). Multi-level value alignment in agentic AI systems: Survey and perspectives. DOI: https://doi.org//arXiv.2506.09656DOI: 10.48550

ADDITIONAL READING

Corrêa, N. K., Galvão, C., Santos, J. W., Del Pino, C., Pontes Pinto, E., Barbosa, C., Massmann, D., Mambrini, R., Galvao, L., Terem, E., & de Oliveira, N. (2023). Worldwide AI ethics: A review of 200 guidelines and recommendations for AI governance. DOI: https://doi.org/DOI: 10.1016/j.patter.2023.100857

Kazim, E., & Koshiyama, A., (2021). A high-level overview of AI ethics. DOI: https://doi.org/DOI: 10.1016/j.patter.2021.100314

Van Eck, N. J., & Waltman, L. (2022). Crossref as a source of open bibliographic metadata. *MetaArXiv*, 1-15.

Wang, H., & Blok, V. (2025). Why putting artificial intelligence ethics into practice is not enough: Towards a multi-level framework. DOI: https://doi.org/DOI: 10.1177/20539517251340620

KEY TERMS AND DEFINITIONS

Agentic AI: it is a class of artificial intelligence that focuses on autonomous systems that can make decisions and perform tasks with or without human intervention.

Artificial Intelligence (AI): The ability of machine to perform tasks that typically require human intelligence, such as learning, reasoning, problem solving and making Decisions.

Large language models (LLM): It is a language model trained with self-supervised Machine learning on large amount of text, designed for natural language processing tasks, especially language generation

Memory Augmented Architecture: it represents how AI systems generate Information.

Reasoning Accuracy: How close a measured or calculated value is to true or actual Value of quantity being measured

Retrieval Augmented Generation (RAG): It is a framework that combines an Information retrieval system with large language model (LLM) to create more Accurate and context aware responses.

Compilation of References

Aarthi, S., Ravikumar, R. N., Sobirova, K., & Mamadiyarov, Z. (2025). Empowering a sustainable future through digital learning and the SDGs. In *Harnessing E-Learning to Create a Sustainable Future* (pp. 145–172). IGI Global Scientific Publishing., DOI: 10.4018/979-8-3373-0112-9.ch006

Abdessadak, A., Ghennioui, H., Thirion-Moreau, N., Elbhiri, B., Abraim, M., & Merzouk, S. (2025). Digital twin technology and artificial intelligence in energy transition: A comprehensive systematic review of applications. *Energy Reports*, *13*, 5196–5218. DOI: 10.1016/j.egyr.2025.04.060

Acemoglu, D., & Restrepo, P. (2018). Artificial Intelligence, Automation, and Work. *Economics of Artificial Intelligence: An Agenda*, 197-236.

Acemoglu, D., & Restrepo, P. (2020). The Race Between Man and Machine: Implications of Technology for Growth, Factor Shares, and Employment. *The American Economic Review*, *110*(6), 1488–1542.

Adewusi, A. O., Komolafe, A. M., Ejairu, E., Aderotoye, I. A., Abiona, O. O., & Oyeniran, O. C. (2024). The role of predictive analytics in optimizing Supply Chain Resilience: A review of techniques and case studies. Int. j. *Manag. Entrep. Res*, *6*(3), 815–837.

Adeyinka, M. A., Solanke, B., Onita, F. B., & Agho, M. O. (2022). Integrating digital technologies for supply chain resilience in the energy industry. International Journal of Scientific Research Updates, 3(1), 048–057. https://doi.org/DOI: 10.53430/ijsru.2022.3.1.0032

Afum, E., Osei-Ahenkan, V. Y., Agyabeng-Mensah, Y., Amponsah Owusu, J., Kusi, L. Y., & Ankomah, J. (2020). Green manufacturing practices and sustainable performance among Ghanaian manufacturing SMEs: The explanatory link of green supply chain integration. *Management of Environmental Quality*, *31*(6), 1457–1475.

Aghaei, R., Kiaei, A. A., Boush, M., Vahidi, J., Barzegar, Z., & Rofoosheh, M. (2025). *The potential of large language models in supply chain management: Advancing decision-making, efficiency, and innovation.* arXiv preprint arXiv:2501.15411. https://doi.org//arXiv.2501.15411DOI: 10.48550

Agrawal, S., Agrawal, R., Kumar, A., Luthra, S., & Garza-Reyes, J. A. (2024). Can industry 5.0 technologies overcome supply chain disruptions?—A perspective study on pandemics, war, and climate change issues. *Operations Management Research, 17*(2), 453–468. DOI: 10.1007/s12063-023-00410-y

Aktas, E. (2024). Big data applications in supply chain management. In Sarkis, J. (Ed.), *The Palgrave handbook of supply chain management.* Palgrave Macmillan., DOI: 10.1007/978-3-031-19884-7_74

Aktas, M. E., & Eroğlu, S. N. (2025). Blockchain technology in humanitarian logistics enhancing transparency, accountability and real-time decision making. In *Advances in Computational Intelligence and Robotics* (pp. 93–120). IGI Global Scientific Publishing., DOI: 10.4018/979-8-3373-3643-5.ch005

Alahmari, D., & Awad, A. (2025). Strategic integration of marketing and supply chain functions for superior customer experience: Insights from logistics startups under Saudi Vision 2030. *PLoS One, 20*(11), e0336132. DOI: 10.1371/journal.pone.0336132 PMID: 41270081

Al-dhaafri, H. S., & Al-Swidi, A. K. (2016). The impact of total quality management and supply chain management on the performance of manufacturing firms in yemen. *The TQM Journal, 28*(6), 891–908. DOI: 10.1108/IJQRM-03-2014-0034

Al-Huzaili, S. A. F., & Mokhtar, A. I. Bin, & Muhamat, M. R. Bin. (2025). The role of Artificial Intelligence in enhancing procurement processes and supply chains. *International Journal of Supply Chain Management, 14*(4), 64–78. DOI: 10.59160/ijscm.v14i4.6328

Aliahmadi, A., Nozari, H., & Ghahremani-Nahr, J. (2022). AIoT-based sustainable smart supply chain framework. International Journal of Innovation in Management. *Economics and Social Sciences, 2*(2), 28–38.

Alias, C., Lobillo, G., & de Miguel, G. (2014). Applying novel future-internet-based supply chain control towers to the transport and logistics domain. *Future Network and Mobile Summit 2014.*

Allied Market Research. (2024). Logistics Automation Market Size, Share & Trends Analysis Report. Retrieved from https://alliedmarketresearch.com

Almanbahi, F. S., Awad, A., Ghonim, A., Alabsy, N. M., & Shemais, M. (2025). Ethical leadership and organizational excellence: The mediating role of citizenship behavior in healthcare. *Humanities & Social Sciences Communications*, *12*, 1392. DOI: 10.1057/s41599-025-05743-6

Almurshed, O., Kaushal, A., Meshoul, S., Muftah, A., Almoghamis, O., Petri, I., Auluck, N., & Rana, O. (2025). Enhancing performance of machine learning tasks on edge-cloud infrastructures: A cross-domain Internet of Things based framework. *Future Generation Computer Systems*, *166*, 107696. DOI: 10.1016/j.future.2024.107696

Alwi, A., & Sasongko, N. A., Suprapto, Suryana, Y., & Subagyo, H. (2024). Blockchain and big data integration design for traceability and carbon footprint management in the fishery supply chain. *Egyptian Informatics Journal*, *26*, 100481. DOI: 10.1016/j.eij.2024.100481

Al-Zabidi, A., Rehman, A. U., & Alkahtani, M. (2021). An approach to assess sustainable supply chain agility for a manufacturing organization. *Sustainability*, *13*(4), 1752.

Alzahmi, W., Al-Assaf, K., Alshaikh, R., & Bahroun, Z. (2025). Towards sustainable ERP systems: Emerging trends, challenges, and future pathways. *Management Systems in Production Engineering*, *33*(1), 24–38. DOI: 10.2478/mspe-2025-0003

Ametefe, D. S., Hussin, N., John, D., Dzorgbenya Ametefe, G., Adozuka Aliu, A., & Abdi Ali, Z. (2024). Revolutionising agriculture for food security and environmental sustainability: A perspective on the role of digital twin technology. *Perspectives in Agriculture, Veterinary Science, Nutrition and Natural Resources*. Advance online publication. DOI: 10.1079/cabireviews.2024.0036

Anam, M. Z., Shakur, M. S., Bari, A. B. M. M., Debnath, B., & Bristy, F. T. (2025). Exploring the barriers to decarbonizing the transportation system: A pathway to a cleaner future in emerging economies. *Innovation and Green Development*, *4*(4), 100256. DOI: 10.1016/j.igd.2025.100256

Anthony, B. (2023). Data enabling digital ecosystem for sustainable shared electric mobility-as-a-service in smart cities-an innovative business model perspective. *Research in Transportation Business & Management*, *51*, 101043. DOI: 10.1016/j.rtbm.2023.101043

Apandi, A. A. A., & Ibrahim, I. (2025). Leveraging Digital Twin technology to enhance transparency, traceability, and compliance in Halal supply chains. *International Journal of Research and Innovation in Social Science*, *IX*(XIV), 63–80. DOI: 10.47772/ijriss.2025.914mg006

Applied Intuition. (2025). Autonomous vehicle development partnership. https://appliedintuition.com

Argyris, C., & Schön, D. A. (1996). *Organisational learning II: Theory, method, and practice*. Addison-Wesley. https://www.scirp.org/reference/referencespapers?referenceid=1423922

Asadi, S., Naeini, H. K., Hassanlou, D., Pishahang, A., Najafabadi, S. A., Sharifi, A., & Ahmadi, M. (2025). AI-Powered Digital Twin Frameworks for Smart Grid Optimization and Real-Time Energy Management in Smart Buildings: A Survey. *Computer Modeling in Engineering & Sciences*, *145*(2), 1259–1301. DOI: 10.32604/cmes.2025.070528

Aslam, B., Zhantian, B., Amjad, M. A., & Zhang, G. (2025). Decarbonizing transport: EV production versus conventional vehicles. *Transport Policy*, *174*, 103821. DOI: 10.1016/j.tranpol.2025.103821

Aslam, F., & Calghan, J. (2023). Using NLP to enhance supply chain management systems. *Journal of Engineering Research and Reports*, *25*(9), 211–219. DOI: 10.9734/jerr/2023/v25i9994

Atadoga, A., Obi, O. C., Osasona, F., Onwusinkwue, S., Daraojimba, A. I., & Dawodu, S. O. (2024). AI in supply chain optimization: A comparative review of USA and African Trends. *International Journal of Science and Research Archive*, *11*(1), 896–903. DOI: 10.30574/ijsra.2024.11.1.0156

Attaran, M., & Celik, B. G. (2023). Digital Twin: Benefits, use cases, challenges, and opportunities. *Decision Analytics Journal*, *6*, 100165. DOI: 10.1016/j.dajour.2023.100165

Autor, D. (2015). Why Are There Still So Many Jobs? The History and Future of Workplace Automation. *The Journal of Economic Perspectives*, *29*(3), 3–30.

Autor, D. H. (2019). Work of the past, work of the future. *AEA Papers and Proceedings. American Economic Association*, *109*, 1–32.

Autor, D. H., & Salomons, A. (2018). Is automation labor-displacing? Productivity growth, employment, and the labor share. *Brookings Papers on Economic Activity*.

Awad, A. (2025). Enhancing market access and consumer engagement through digital marketing in the agricultural sector. *International Journal of Advanced and Applied Sciences*, *12*(8), 70–79. DOI: 10.21833/ijaas.2025.08.007

Awad, A., & Aldabousi, A. M. (2024). Analyzing the impact of viral marketing on brand equity dimensions in Egypt's home appliances sector: A customer and legal perspective. *Innovative Marketing*, *20*(4), 100–111. DOI: 10.21511/im.20(4).2024.09

Awan, U., Sroufe, R., & Shahbaz, M. (2021). Industry 4.0 and the circular economy: A literature review and recommendations for future research. *Business Strategy and the Environment*, *30*(4), 2038–2060.

Axsen, J., & Wolinetz, M. (2021). Taxes, tolls and ZEV zones for climate: Synthesizing insights on effectiveness, efficiency, equity, acceptability and implementation. *Energy Policy*, *156*, 112457. DOI: 10.1016/j.enpol.2021.112457

Badue, C., Guidolini, R., Carneiro, R. V., Azevedo, P., Cardoso, V., Forechi, A., Jesus, L., Berriel, R., Paixao, T., Mutz, F., Veronese, L., Oliveira-Santos, T., & De Souza, A. F. (2021). Self-driving cars. *Survey (London, England)*. Advance online publication. DOI: 10.1016/j.eswa.2020.113816

Bahssas, D. M., AlBar, A. M., & Hoque, R. (2015). Enterprise resource planning (ERP) systems: Design, trends, and deployment. *International Technology Management Review*, *5*(2), 72–81. DOI: 10.2991/itmr.2015.5.2.2

Bandi, A., Nukala, H., & Tatavarthi, B. (2025). Automated test case generation for software testing using generative. *AI*. Advance online publication. DOI: 10.1007/978-3-031-92178-0_7

Bányai, T. (2022). Impact of digital twin technology on the real-time optimisation of material handling processes. *IOP Conference Series. Materials Science and Engineering*, *1235*(1), 012077. DOI: 10.1088/1757-899x/1235/1/012077

Barredo Arrieta, A., Díaz-Rodríguez, N., Del Ser, J., Bennetot, A., Tabik, S., Barbado, A., & Herrera, F. (2020). Explainable Artificial Intelligence (XAI): Concepts, taxonomies, opportunities and challenges toward responsible AI. *Information Fusion*, *58*, 82–115. DOI: 10.1016/j.inffus.2019.12.012

Bawden, D., & Robinson, L. (2022). Information Overload, Anxiety and Stress: The Technological Impact. *Journal of Information Science*, *48*(4), 481–492.

Behdani, B., Wiegmans, B., & Roodbergen, K. J. (2019). Agent-oriented simulation framework for handling disruptions in chemical supply chains. *Computers & Chemical Engineering*, *123*, 183–199.

Belhadi, A., Mani, V., Kamble, S. S., Khan, S. A. R., & Verma, S. (2021). Artificial intelligence-driven innovation for enhancing supply chain resilience and performance under the effect of supply chain dynamism: An empirical investigation. *Annals of Operations Research*, *333*(2–3), 1–26. DOI: 10.1007/s10479-021-03956-x

Bender, E. M., Gebru, T., McMillan-Major, A., & Shmitchell, S. (2021). On the dangers of stochastic parrots: Can language models be too big? DOI: https://doi.org/DOI: 10.1145/3442188.3445922

Bessen, J. E. (2019). AI and Jobs: The Role of Demand. *NBER Working Paper No. 24235.* https://doi.org/DOI: 10.3386/w24235

Beyer, M., Zaidi, E., Feinberg, D., Cook, H., Orup Lund, J., Sallam, R., & Thanaraj, R. (2021, February). Top trends in data and analytics for 2021: Data fabric is the foundation. Gartner. https://info.stardog.com/gartner-data-fabric

Biller, B., & Biller, S. (2023). Implementing digital twins that learn: AI and simulation are at the core. *Machines (Basel)*, *11*(4), 425. DOI: 10.3390/machines11040425

Birkel, H. S., & Hartmann, E. (2019). Impact of IoT challenges and risks for SCM. *Supply Chain Manage.: Int. J.*, *24*(1), 39–61.

Blanco, C., Caro, F., & Corbett, C. J. (2016). The state of supply chain carbon footprinting: Analysis of CDP disclosures by US firms. *Journal of Cleaner Production*, *135*, 1189–1197. DOI: 10.1016/j.jclepro.2016.06.132

Bø, E., & Mjøsund, C. (2022). Use of GPS-data to improve transport solutions in a cost and environmental perspective. *Transportation Research Interdisciplinary Perspectives*, *13*, 100557. DOI: 10.1016/j.trip.2022.100557

Bommasani, R., Hudson, D. A., Adeli, E., Altman, R., Arora, S., Bernstein, M. S., . . . Liang, P. (2021). *On the opportunities and risks of foundation models*. Stanford Center for Research on Foundation Models. https://crfm.stanford.edu/report.html

Bortolini, M., Ferrari, E., Gamberi, M., Pilati, F., & Regattieri, A. (2018). Warehouse Operations Management: A Literature Review. *International Journal of Production Research*, *56*(1-2), 150–167.

Botín-Sanabria, D. M., Mihaita, A.-S., Peimbert-García, R. E., Ramírez-Moreno, M. A., Ramírez-Mendoza, R. A., & Lozoya-Santos, J. de J. (2022). Digital twin technology challenges and applications: A comprehensive review. *Remote Sensing*, *14*(6), 1335. DOI: 10.3390/rs14061335

Boysen, N., Briskorn, D., & Emde, S. (2021). Warehouse management: Models, systems and frameworks. *European Journal of Operational Research*, *291*(3), 801–816.

Brintrup, A., Ledwoch, A., & Barros, J. (2020). Supply networks as complex systems: A network-science-based characterisation. *IEEE Systems Journal*, *14*(2), 2643–2655. DOI: 10.1109/JSYST.2015.2425137

Brynjolfsson, E., & McAfee, A. (2017). The business of artificial intelligence: What it can — and cannot — do for your organization. Retrieved from The Business of Artificial Intelligence.pdf.

Brynjolfsson, E., & McAfee, A. (2014). *The second machine age: Work, progress, and prosperity in a time of brilliant technologies*. W.W. Norton & Company.

Brynjolfsson, E., & Mitchell, T. (2017). What can machines learn, and what does it mean for occupations and the economy? *AEA Papers and Proceedings. American Economic Association, 107*, 43–47.

Bryson, J. (2018). Patiency is not a virtue: The design of intelligent systems and systems of ethics. DOI: https://doi.org/DOI: 10.1007/s10676-018-9448-6

Capgemini Research Institute. (2025). Rise of agentic AI: How trust is the key to human-AI collaboration. https://www.capgemini.com/insights/research-library/ai-agents/

Carracedo, D., & Mostofi, H. (2022). Electric cargo bikes in urban areas: A new mobility option for private transportation. *Transportation Research Interdisciplinary Perspectives, 16*, 100705. DOI: 10.1016/j.trip.2022.100705

Cedefop. (2022). Skill shifts and social protection policies in the digital age. European Centre for the Development of Vocational Training.

Chai, L., Lai, K., & Zong, L. (2025). How digital transformation enhances supply chain transparency? Based on the perspective of information improvement and resource optimization. *Transportation Research Part E, Logistics and Transportation Review, 201*, 104256. DOI: 10.1016/j.tre.2025.104256

Cheah, L., Mepparambath, R. M., & Ricart Surribas, G. M. (2021). Freight trips generated at retail malls in dense urban areas. *Transportation Research Part A, Policy and Practice, 145*, 118–131. DOI: 10.1016/j.tra.2021.01.015

Chen, X., Yu, G., Cheng, G., & Hao, T. (2019). *Research topics in educational technology: A bibliometric analysis of Computers & Education.* DOI: https://doi.org/DOI: 10.1007/s40692-019-00149-1

Chen, G., & Zhang, J. W. (2024). Intelligent transportation systems: Machine learning approaches for urban mobility in smart cities. *Sustainable Cities and Society, 107*, 105369. DOI: 10.1016/j.scs.2024.105369

Chen, J., & Perez, Y. (2021). Autonomous vehicle regulation: An international review. *Transportation Research Interdisciplinary Perspectives, 11*, 100433.

Chen, R. (2024). Sustainable supply chain management as a strategic enterprise innovation. Advances in Economics. *Management and Political Sciences*, *85*(1), 24–29.

Chhimwal, M., Agrawal, S., & Kumar, G. (2021). Measuring circular supply chain risk: A Bayesian Network methodology. *Sustainability*, *13*(15), 8448. DOI: 10.3390/su13158448

Chikhi, T., Santa-Eulalia, L. A., Mosconi, E., Risso, L. A., Filho, M. G., & Ganga, G. M. D. (2022). Going beyond blockchain adoption's hype to improve supply chain sustainability: Evidence from empirical and modelling studies. Proceedings of the Annual Hawaii International Conference on System Sciences.

Choi, T. Y., Rogers, D. S., & Vakil, B. (2021). Managing extended supply chains. *Journal of Business Logistics*, *42*(1), 1–4.

Chopra, S., & Meindl, P. (2023). *Supply Chain Management: Strategy, Planning, and Operation* (8th ed.). Pearson.

Christopher, M. (2016). Logistics & Supply Chain Management. Pearson UK.

Cihon, P., Kleinaltenkamp, M. J., Schuett, J., & Baum, S. D. (2021). AI certification: Advancing ethical practice by reducing information asymmetries. DOI: https://arxiv.org/abs/2105.10356

Couture, V., Roy, M.-C., Dez, E., Laperle, S., & Bélisle-Pipon, J.-C. (2023). Ethical implications of artificial intelligence in population health and the public's role in its governance: Perspectives from a citizen and expert panel. *Journal of Medical Internet Research*, *25*, e44357. DOI: 10.2196/44357

Culot, G., Podrecca, M., & Nassimbeni, G. (2024). Artificial intelligence in supply chain management: A systematic literature review of empirical studies and research directions. *Computers in Industry*, *162*, 104132. DOI: 10.1016/j.compind.2024.104132

Dafoe, A. (2018). *AI governance: A research agenda.* Centre for the Governance of AI, Future of Humanity Institute, University of Oxford. https://cdn.governance.ai/GovAI-Research-Agenda.pdf

Dahlmann, F., Brammer, S., & Roehrich, J. K. (2023). Navigating the "performing-organizing" paradox: Tensions between supply chain transparency, coordination, and scope 3 GHG emissions performance. *International Journal of Operations & Production Management*, *43*(11), 1757–1780. DOI: 10.1108/ijopm-09-2022-0622

Dalporto, A., Cullen, A., & Damiani, D. (2020). Supply chain leadership, transparency, workforce development and collaboration through control tower implementation. *Journal of Supply Chain Management. Logistics & Procurement*, *3*(4), 58–71.

De Angelis, R., Howard, M., & Miemczyk, J. (2018). Supply chain management and the circular economy: Towards the circular supply chain. *Production Planning and Control*, *29*(6), 425–437. DOI: 10.1080/09537287.2018.1449244

De Saxe, C., Lindsay, C., Subramanian, S. C., & Van Eeden, J. (2023). Decarbonising freight transport: Transitions towards net zero. *Research in Transportation Business & Management*, *48*, 100984. DOI: 10.1016/j.rtbm.2023.100984

de Vass, T., Shee, H., & Miah, S. (2021a). IoT in supply chain management: Opportunities and challenges for businesses in early industry 4.0 context. Oper. Supply Chain Manag. Int. J., 148–161.

de Vass, T., Shee, H., & Miah, S. (2021b). IoT in supply chain management: Opportunities and challenges for businesses in early industry 4.0 context. Oper. Supply Chain Manag. Int. J., 148–161.

Del Giudice, M., Chierici, R., Mazzucchelli, A., & Fiano, F. (2021). Supply chain management in the era of circular economy: The moderating effect of big data. *International Journal of Logistics Management*, *32*(2), 337–356. DOI: 10.1108/ijlm-03-2020-0119

Department for Transport UK. (2024). Driver shortages in the logistics sector: Current statistics and forecasts.

DHL. (2024). *The DHL Logistics Trend Radar 7.0*. DHL. https://www.dhl.com/discover/en-global/news-and-insights/reports-and-press-releases/logistics-trend-radar-2024

DigitalDefynd. (2025). 10 ways Amazon is using AI - Case Study. https://digitaldefynd.com/IQ/amazon-using-ai-case-study/

Dolgui, A., & Ivanov, D. (2023). Digital supply-chain twins: Managing the ripple effect, resilience, and disruption risks. *International Journal of Production Research*, *61*(1), 1–19. DOI: 10.1007/978-3-030-14302-2_15

Domínguez, R., Framinan, J. M., & Cannella, S. (2020). Insights on multi-agent systems applications for supply chain management. *Sustainability*, *12*(2), 735.

Dörr, S. (2025). Digital twins pave the way for a sustainable economy. *Journal of Intelligent System of Systems Lifecycle Management*, *1*. Advance online publication. DOI: 10.71015/75tbrx94

Downie, J., & Stubbs, W. (2012). Corporate carbon strategies and greenhouse gas emission assessments: The implications of scope 3 emission factor selection. *Business Strategy and the Environment*, *21*(6), 412–422. DOI: 10.1002/bse.1734

Dudić, Ž., Vrhovac, V., Vulanović, S., Dakić, D., Erdeji, I., & Perović, V. (2024). A risk-aware approach to digital procurement transformation. *Sustainability*, *16*(3), 1283. DOI: 10.3390/su16031283

Du, J., Zou, Z., Shi, Y., & Zhao, D. (2017). RFID and multi-agent based architecture for information sharing in prefabricated component supply chain. *IEEE Access : Practical Innovations, Open Solutions*, *5*, 4132–4143.

Dunwoodie Stirton, F., Hiscock, R., Mehegan, J., Gallagher, A. W. A., & Bloomfield, M. J. (2025). Independent companies in the tobacco supply chain: Transparency and environmental social governance. *Tobacco Control*. Advance online publication. DOI: 10.1136/tc-2024-058978 PMID: 39779326

Dwivedi, Y. K., Kshetri, N., Hughes, L., Slade, E., Jeyaraj, A., Kar, A. K., & Wright, R. (2023). So what if ChatGPT wrote it? Multidisciplinary perspectives on opportunities, challenges and implications of generative conversational AI for research, practice and policy. *International Journal of Information Management*, *71*, 102642. DOI: 10.1016/J.IJINFOMGT.2023.102642

Egorov, D., Levina, A., Kalyazina, S., Schuur, P., & Gerrits, B. (2021). The challenges of the logistics industry in the era of digital transformation. In *Lecture Notes in Networks and Systems* (pp. 201–209). Springer International Publishing., DOI: 10.1007/978-3-030-64430-7_17

Ejjami, D. R. (2024). Emerging professions in the age of AI across multiple sectors. *International Journal For Multidisciplinary Research*, *6*(5). Advance online publication. DOI: 10.36948/ijfmr.2024.v06i05.28762

Ejjami, R., & Boussalham, K. (2024a). Industry 5.0 in manufacturing: Enhancing resilience and responsibility through AI-driven predictive maintenance, quality control, and supply chain optimization. *International Journal For Multidisciplinary Research*, *6*(4). Advance online publication. DOI: 10.36948/ijfmr.2024.v06i04.25733

Ejjami, R., & Boussalham, K. (2024b). Resilient supply chains in industry 5.0: Leveraging AI for predictive maintenance and risk mitigation. *International Journal For Multidisciplinary Research*, *6*(4). Advance online publication. DOI: 10.36948/ijfmr.2024.v06i04.25116

Emmert-Streib, F. (2023). What is the role of AI for digital twins? *AI (Basel, Switzerland)*, *4*(3), 721–728. DOI: 10.3390/ai4030038

Enache, G. I. (2023). Logistics security in the era of big data, cloud computing and IoT. *Proceedings of the International Conference on Business Excellence*, 17(1), 188–199. https://doi.org/DOI: 10.2478/picbe-2023-0021

Erlangga, S. B., Yunita, A., & Satriana, S. R. (2022). Development of automatic real time inventory monitoring system using RFID technology in warehouse. *JOIV: International Journal on Informatics Visualization*, *6*(3), 636. DOI: 10.30630/joiv.6.3.1231

Espinosa-Jaramillo, M. T. (2024). Digital Twins in supply chain operations bridging the physical and digital worlds using AI. *Journal of Electrical Systems*, *20*(10s), 1764–1774. DOI: 10.52783/jes.5434

Et al., S. S. (2023). Ethical considerations in AI-based marketing: Balancing profit and consumer trust. *Tuijin Jishu*, *44*(3), 1301–1309. DOI: 10.52783/tjjpt.v44.i3.474

EY. (2025). *AI-powered supply chains: From dashboards to decision fabrics*. Ernst & Young. https://www.ey.com/en_us/coo/transforming-supply-chain-strategy-with-ai

Fagnant, D. J., & Kockelman, K. (2015). Preparing a Nation for Autonomous Vehicles: Opportunities, Barriers and Policy Recommendations. *Transportation Research Part A, Policy and Practice*, *77*, 167–181.

Fagnant, D. J., & Kockelman, K. (2015). Preparing a nation for autonomous vehicles: Opportunities, barriers, and policy recommendations. *Transportation Research Part A, Policy and Practice*, *77*, 167–181.

Farooque, M., Zhang, A., Thürer, M., Qu, T., & Huisingh, D. (2019). Circular supply chain management: A definition and structured literature review. *Journal of Cleaner Production*, *228*, 882–900. DOI: 10.1016/j.jclepro.2019.04.303

Fayezi, S., Zutshi, A., & O'Loughlin, A. (2017). Understanding and development of supply chain agility and flexibility: A structured literature review. *International Journal of Management Reviews*, *19*(4), 379–407. https://doi.org/10.1111/ijmr.12096

Fedorko, G., Molnár, V., & Michalik, P. (2023). Keys parameters of digital transformation of continuous transport systems. Advances in Science and Technology – Research Journal, 17(3), 73–78. https://doi.org/DOI: 10.12913/22998624/163138

Feng, B., & Ye, Q. (2021). Operations management of smart logistics: A literature review and future research. *Frontiers of Engineering Management*, *8*(3), 344–355. DOI: 10.1007/s42524-021-0156-2

Firouraghi, N., Kiani, B., Jafari, H. T., Learnihan, V., Salinas-Perez, J. A., Raeesi, A., Furst, M., Salvador-Carulla, L., & Bagheri, N. (2022). The role of geographic information system and global positioning system in dementia care and research: A scoping review. *International Journal of Health Geographics*, *21*(1), 8. PMID: 35927728

Floridi, L., & Cowls, J. (2019). A Unified Framework of Five Principles for AI in Society. DOI: https://doi.org/DOI: 10.1162/99608f92.8cd550d1

Floridi, L., & Cowls, J. (2021). A unified framework of five principles for AI in society. DOI: https://doi.org/DOI: 10.1007/978-3-030-81907-1_2

Francisco, K., & Swanson, D. (2018). The supply chain has no clothes: Technology adoption of blockchain for supply chain transparency. *Logistics (Basel)*, *2*(1), 2. DOI: 10.3390/logistics2010002

Frank, M. R., Sun, L., Cebrian, M., Youn, H., & Rahwan, I. (2019). Small cities face greater impact from automation. *Journal of the Royal Society, Interface*, *16*(150), 20180767.

Freese, F., & Ludwig, A. (2024). A conceptual framework for supply chain digital twins – development and evaluation. *International Journal of Logistics Research and Applications*, *28*(6), 676–698. DOI: 10.1080/13675567.2024.2324895

Frey, C. B., & Osborne, M. A. (2017). The Future of Employment: How Susceptible Are Jobs to Computerisation? *Technological Forecasting and Social Change*, *114*, 254–280.

Gabriel, I. (2020). Artificial Intelligence, values, and alignment. DOI: https://doi.org/DOI: 10.1007/s11023-020-09539-2

Gartner. (n.d.). *Data fabric*.

Getahun, S., Kefale, H., & Gelaye, Y. (2024). Application of precision agriculture technologies for sustainable crop production and environmental sustainability: A systematic review. *TheScientificWorldJournal*, *2024*, 2126734. PMID: 39421732

Ghaemi Asl, M., Nie, P., & Charkh, C. (2024). Cycles-specific benefits of smart transport for sustainable investing: Global and regional perspectives with different ethical paradigms. *Technological Forecasting and Social Change*, *208*, 123707. DOI: 10.1016/j.techfore.2024.123707

Ghahremani Nahr, J., Nozari, H., & Sadeghi, M. E. (2021). Green supply chain based on artificial intelligence of things (AIoT). International Journal of Innovation in Management. *Economics and Social Sciences*, *1*(2), 56–63.

Ghonim, A., & Awad, A. (2025). Shaping customer insights through e-marketing: An applied study in the banking sector. *International Journal of Advanced and Applied Sciences*, *12*(4), 88–98. DOI: 10.21833/ijaas.2025.04.011

Ghonim, A., Awad, A., Shemais, M., Shma, T., & Aziz, A. (2025). Exploring the impact of flexible work arrangements on employee engagement in telecommunications: Case of Egypt. *Problems and Perspectives in Management*, *23*(2), 198–207. DOI: 10.21511/ppm.23(2).2025.13

Giannakis, M., & Louis, M. (2016). A multi-agent based system with big data processing for enhanced supply chain agility. *Journal of Enterprise Information Management*, *29*(5), 706–727.

Gidiagba, J. O., Tartibu, L. K., & Okwu, M. O. (2025). A systematic review of machine learning applications in sustainable supplier selection. *Decision Analytics Journal*, *14*, 100547. DOI: 10.1016/j.dajour.2025.100547

Glick, J. (2024). Enhancing logistics efficiency through computer and network technologies: A pathway to industry informatization. *Academic Journal of Science and Technology*, *10*(2), 142–144. DOI: 10.54097/e05gkp44

Gómez-Marín, C. G., Comi, A., Serna-Urán, C. A., & Zapata-Cortés, J. A. (2024). Fostering collaboration and coordination in urban delivery: A multi-agent microsimulation model. *Research in Transportation Economics*, *103*, 101402. DOI: 10.1016/j.retrec.2023.101402

Google, L. L. C. (2022). AI Principles Progress Update. Retrieved from https://ai.google/static/documents/ai-principles-2022-progress-update.pdf

Grand View Research. (2025). Autonomous Freight and Logistics Market Size, Share & Trends Analysis Report.

Gray, J. V., Skowronski, K., Esenduran, G., & Rungtusanatham, M. (2013). The reshoring phenomenon: What supply chain academics ought to know and should do. *The Journal of Supply Chain Management*, *49*(2), 27–33.

Greenblatt, J. B., & Saxena, S. (2015). Autonomous taxis could greatly reduce greenhouse-gas emissions of US light-duty vehicles. *Nature Climate Change*, *5*(9), 860–863. DOI: 10.1038/nclimate2685

Grieves, M. (2022). Intelligent digital twins and the development and management of complex systems. *Digital Twin*, *2*, 8. DOI: 10.12688/digitaltwin.17574.1

Guizzo, E. (2012). How Google's Self-Driving Car Works. *IEEE Spectrum*.

Haddud, A., DeSouza, A., Khare, A., & Lee, H. (2017). Examining potential benefits and challenges associated with the Internet of Things integration in supply chains. *Journal of Manufacturing Technology Management*, *28*(8), 1055–1085.

Hancock, P., Mia, M., & McDonald, S. (2019). The impact of warehouse automation on jobs in low-wage regions. *Journal of Labor Research, 40*(4), 277–293.

Handfield, R., Finkenstadt, D., Schneller, E., Godfrey, A. B., & Guinto, P.. (2020). A commons for a supply chain in the post-COVID-19 era: The case for a reformed Strategic National Stockpile. *The Milbank Quarterly, 98*(4), 1053–1090. PMID: 33135814

Harun, S., & Senawi, A. R. (2024). An integrated circular supply chain framework to enhance Malaysian business performance. Information Management and Business Review, 16(3(I)S), 130–136. https://doi.org/DOI: 10.22610/imbr.v16i3(i)s.4046

Hasan, M., Ebrahim, Z., Wan Mahmood, W., & Ab Rahman, M. (2017). Sustainable-ERP system: A preliminary study on sustainability indicators. [JAMT]. *Journal of Advanced Manufacturing Technology, 11*(1), 61–74. https://jamt.utem.edu.my/jamt/article/view/2829

Hasan, S. K. K., & Crawford, C. W. (2025). A new era for digital twins: Progress and industry adoption. *Digital Twin, 2555877.* Advance online publication. DOI: 10.1080/27525783.2025.2555877

Hazenberg, J., Keijzer, M., & van der Heijden, M. (2025). Multi-agent reinforcement learning for dynamic pricing in volatile markets. *European Journal of Operational Research, 310*(3), 945–960. DOI: 10.48550/arXiv.2507.02698

He, B., & Bai, K.-J. (2021). Digital twin-based sustainable intelligent manufacturing: A review. *Advances in Manufacturing, 9*(1), 1–21. DOI: 10.1007/s40436-020-00302-5

Holloway, S. (2024). Exploring the impact of real-time supply chain information on marketing decisions: Insights from service industries. In *Preprints.*

Hong, E., & Park, J. (2024). The effect of technological readiness dimensions on the adoption of autonomous vehicles: Focusing on behavioral reasoning theory. *Transportation Research Part F: Traffic Psychology and Behaviour, 100*, 101–114. DOI: 10.1016/j.trf.2023.11.005

Hosseini, S., & Seilani, H. (2025). The role of agentic AI in shaping a smart future. *Systematic Reviews.* Advance online publication. DOI: 10.1016/j.array.2025.100399

Howard, D. A., Ma, Z., Veje, C., Clausen, A., Aaslyng, J. M., & Jørgensen, B. N. (2021). Greenhouse industry 4.0 – digital twin technology for commercial greenhouses. *Energy Informatics, 4*(S2). Advance online publication. DOI: 10.1186/s42162-021-00161-9

Hübner, A. H., Kuhn, H., & Wollenburg, J. (2016). Last Mile Fulfillment and Distribution in Omni-Channel Retailing. *Business Logistics in Modern Retail*, 3-28.

Huriye, A. Z. (2023). The ethics of artificial intelligence: Examining the ethical considerations surrounding the development and use of AI. *American Journal of Technology*, *2*(1), 37–45. DOI: 10.58425/ajt.v2i1.142

Hussain, M., Al-Aomar, R., & Melhem, H. (2019). Assessment of lean-green practices on the sustainable performance of hotel supply chains. *International Journal of Contemporary Hospitality Management*, *31*(6), 2448–2467.

IFR. (2020). *World Robotics Report*. International Federation of Robotics.

IFR. (2021). *Robotics and the workforce: Trends and outlook*. International Federation of Robotics.

Insights, S. A. P. (2024). Agentic AI in the global supply chain. https://www.sap.com/sea/blogs/agentic-ai-in-global-supply-chain

International Organization for Standardization. (2021). Automation systems and integration — digital twin framework for manufacturing — part 1: Overview and general principles (tech. rep. No. ISO 23247-1:2021). ISO. https://www.iso.org/standard/90387.html

International, S. A. E. (2018). Updated visual chart for its "levels of driving automation" standard for self-driving vehicles. Data Retrieved from https://www.sae.org/

Irfan, M., Verma, J., Parameswaran, S., & Sheikh, I. A. (2025). Integrating emerging technologies. In Advances in Logistics, Operations, and Management Science (pp. 199–220). IGI Global. https://doi.org/DOI: 10.4018/979-8-3693-9740-4.ch007

Iseri, F., Iseri, H., & Chrisandina, N. J. (2025). AI-based predictive analytics for enhancing data-driven supply chain optimization. *Journal of Global Optimization*. Advance online publication. DOI: 10.1007/s10898-025-01509-1

Isuzu Motors. (2025). Innovation in autonomous trucking. https://isuzu.co.jp

Ittmann, H. W. (2015). The impact of big data and business analytics on supply chain management. *Journal of Transport and Supply Chain Management*, *9*(1).

Ivanov, D. (2020). Predicting the impacts of epidemic outbreaks on global supply chains: A simulation-based analysis on the coronavirus outbreak (COVID-19/SARS-CoV-2) case. *Transportation Research Part E, Logistics and Transportation Review*, *136*, 101922. DOI: 10.1016/j.tre.2020.101922 PMID: 32288597

Ivanov, D. (2023). Toward supply chain viability theory: From lessons learned to theory. *International Journal of Production Research*, *61*(11), 3663–3678. DOI: 10.1080/00207543.2023.2177049

Ivanov, D., & Dolgui, A. (2021). OR-methods for coping with the ripple effect in supply chains during COVID-19 pandemic: Managerial insights and research implications. *International Journal of Production Economics*, *232*, 107921. DOI: 10.1016/j.ijpe.2020.107921 PMID: 32952301

Jackson, I., Ivanov, D., Dolgui, A., & Namdar, J. (2024). Generative artificial intelligence in supply chain and operations management: A capability-based framework for analysis and implementation. *International Journal of Production Research*, *62*(17), 6120–6145. DOI: 10.1080/00207543.2024.2309309

Jannesar Niri, A., Poelzer, G. A., Zhang, S. E., Rosenkranz, J., Pettersson, M., & Ghorbani, Y. (2024). Sustainability challenges throughout the electric vehicle battery value chain. *Renewable & Sustainable Energy Reviews*, *191*, 114176. DOI: 10.1016/j.rser.2023.114176

Jawad, Z. N., & Balázs, V. (2024). Machine learning-driven optimization of enterprise resource planning (ERP) systems: A comprehensive review. *Beni-Suef University Journal of Basic and Applied Sciences*, *13*(4). Advance online publication. DOI: 10.1186/s43088-023-00460-y

Jennings, N. R., Sycara, K., & Wooldridge, M. J. (1998). A roadmap of agent research and development. DOI: https://doi.org/DOI: 10.1023/A:1010090405266

Ji, J., & Wang, Y. (2024). The impact of digital infrastructure on the geographical supply chain layout of firms——Evidence from Chinese microdata. *China Economic Review*, *87*, 102249. DOI: 10.1016/j.chieco.2024.102249

Jiménez, P., Garrido, L., Gomez, J., & Vassallo, J. M. (2025). Environmental and operational impact of freight urban delivery: In-store, home and locker. *Transportation Research Part D, Transport and Environment*, *149*, 105026. DOI: 10.1016/j.trd.2025.105026

Ji, Z., Lee, N., & Frieske, R. (2023). Survey of hallucination in natural language generation. *ACM Computing Surveys*, *55*(12), 1–38. DOI: 10.1145/3571730

Julian, F. A., Rachmayani, N., & Aufi, I. (2025). Blockchain and AI integration in halal supply chains: Toward a trusted digital ecosystem. RIGGS. *Journal of Artificial Intelligence and Digital Business*, *4*(3), 3229–3238. DOI: 10.31004/riggs.v4i3.2451

Kans, M., & Heikkilä, S. (2021). Sustainable Logistics: An Overview. *Sustainability*, *13*(14), 7921.

Karaman, A. S., Kilic, M., & Uyar, A. (2020). Green logistics performance and sustainability reporting practices of the logistics sector: The moderating effect of corporate governance. *Journal of Cleaner Production*, *258*, 120718. DOI: 10.1016/j.jclepro.2020.120718

Karthikeyan, K. S., & Nagaprakash, T. (2023). Prioritizing IoT-driven sustainability initiatives in retail chains: Exploring case studies and industry insights. EAI Endorsed Trans. Internet Things, 10.

Kegenbekov, Z., & Jackson, I. (2021). Adaptive supply chain: Demand–supply synchronization using deep reinforcement learning. *Algorithms*, *14*(8), 240. DOI: 10.3390/a14080240

Kersten, W. (Ed.). Blecker, Thorsten (Ed.); Ringle, Christian M. (Ed.) (2014): Next Generation Supply Chains: Trends and Opportunities, Proceedings of the Hamburg International Conference of Logistics (HICL), No. 18, ISBN 978-3-7375-0339-6, epubli GmbH, Berlin, https://doi.org/DOI: 10.15480/882.1188

Khan, M., Parvaiz, G. S., Dedahanov, A. T., Abdurazzakov, O. S., & Rakhmonov, D. A. (2022). The impact of technologies of traceability and transparency in supply chains. *Sustainability*, *14*(24), 16336. DOI: 10.3390/su142416336

Kheder, M. Q., & Mohammed, A. A. (2024). Real-time traffic monitoring system using IoT-aided robotics and deep learning techniques. *Kuwait Journal of Science*, *51*(1), 100153. DOI: 10.1016/j.kjs.2023.10.017

Kiemde, S. M. A., & Kora, A. D. (2022). Towards an ethics of AI in Africa: Rule of education. *AI and Ethics*, *2*(1), 35–40. DOI: 10.1007/s43681-021-00106-8

Kim, D., Na, J., & Ha, H.-K. (2024). Exploring the impact of green logistics practices and relevant government policy on the financial efficiency of logistics companies. *Heliyon*, *10*(10), e30916. DOI: 10.1016/j.heliyon.2024.e30916 PMID: 38803963

Kirshner, S., Pan, Y., & Wu, X. (Jason) and Gould, Alex, Talking Terms: Agent Information in LLM Supply Chain Bargaining (August 20, 2024). Decision Sciences, 0[], UNSW Business School Research Paper Forthcoming, Available at http://dx.doi.org/DOI: 10.1111/deci.70010

Klaaßen, L., & Stoll, C. (2021). Harmonizing corporate carbon footprints. *Nature Communications*, *12*(1), 6149. DOI: 10.1038/s41467-021-26349-x

Klaus, P., Zeynep, A., & Tobias, W. (2017). The Impact of Delivery Speed on Customer Satisfaction. *Journal of Retailing and Consumer Services*, *34*, 28–35.

Kmiecik, M., & Skórnóg, D. (2025). Impact of generative AI on logistics companies' business models. *International Journal of Logistics Research and Applications*, 1–25. https://doi.org/DOI: 10.1080/13675567.2025.2497537

Kober, J., Bagnell, J. A., & Peters, J. (2013). Reinforcement learning in robotics. *Survey (London, England)*. Advance online publication. DOI: 10.1177/0278364913495721

Koch, R. (2020). *Green Public Procurement under WTO Law: Experience of the EU and Prospects for Switzerland* (Vol. 9). Springer International Publishing., DOI: 10.1007/978-3-030-48214-5

Koot, M., Mes, M., & Iacob, M. E. (2021). A systematic literature review of supply chain decision making supported by the Internet of Things and big data analytics. *Computers & Industrial Engineering*, *154*, 107076.

Kosasih, E. E., Margaroli, F., Gelli, S., Aziz, A., Wildgoose, N., & Brintrup, A. (2024). Towards knowledge graph reasoning for supply chain risk management using graph neural networks. *International Journal of Production Research*, *62*(15), 5596–5612. DOI: 10.1080/00207543.2022.2100841

Kotecha, N., & del Rio Chanona, R. M. (2025). Resilient inventory management with graph-informed multi-agent reinforcement learning. *Omega*, *122*, 102782. DOI: 10.48550/arXiv.2410.18631

Krishna Pasupuleti, M. (2024). Smart manufacturing with Digital Twins: Real-Time Optimization and Process Innovation. In Digital Twin Technology in Manufacturing: Tools for Real-Time Process Optimization (pp. 204–232). National Education Services. https://doi.org/DOI: 10.62311/nesx/905773

Kuik, S. (2023). Advances in the supply chain and circular economy towards sustainability. *Sustainability*, *15*(16), 12326. DOI: 10.3390/su151612326

Kuzior, A., & Sira, M. (2025). Sustainable digital economy transformation through intelligent automation: A multi-environmental framework for strategic decision-making. *Sustainability*, *17*(17), 7723. DOI: 10.3390/su17177723

Kyriakidis, M., Happee, R., & de Winter, J. C. F. (2015). Public opinion on automated driving: Results of an international questionnaire among 5,000 respondents. *Transportation Research Part F: Traffic Psychology and Behaviour*, *32*, 127–140.

Lahkani, M. J., Wang, S., Urbański, M., & Egorova, M. (2020). Sustainable B2B E-commerce and blockchain-based supply chain finance. *Sustainability*, *12*(10), 3968. DOI: 10.3390/su12103968

Lai, Y. (2024). Innovative strategies in logistics and supply chain management: Navigating modern challenges. SHS Web Conf., 183, 2020.

Lake, B. M., Ullman, T. D., Tenenbaum, J. B., & Gershman, S. J. (2016). Building machines that learn and think like people. DOI: https://doi.org/DOI: 10.1017/S0140525X16001837

Latorre, F., Hawks, C. E., Bahillo, E., Gil, M., Colmenares, B., Verma, D., & Sala, N. (2023). Quality and traceability of starting materials from supplier to recipient. *Studies in Health Technology and Informatics*, *305*, 564–567. DOI: 10.3233/SHTI230559 PMID: 37387093

Lau, H. C., Agussurja, L., & Thangarajoo, R. (2008). Real-time supply chain control via multi-agent adjustable autonomy. *Computers & Operations Research*, *35*(11), 3452–3464.

Lazrak, M., & El amrani, H. (2025). Digital Twin Technology in Supply Chain Resilience. *Journal of Innovative Research and Business Studies, 1*(1). Retrieved from https://journals.imist.ma/index.php/IRABS/article/view/5575

Lee, J., Azamfar, M., Singh, J., & Siahpour, S. (2020). Integration of digital twin and deep learning in cyber-physical systems: Towards smart manufacturing. *IET Collaborative Intelligent Manufacturing*, *2*(1), 34–36. DOI: 10.1049/iet-cim.2020.0009

Leogrande, A. (2024). Integrating ESG principles into smart logistics:Toward sustainable supply chains. In *Preprints*.

Leonard, M. (2020, August 13). *DHL rolls out AI-based pick routing tool that integrates with WMS, ERP*. Supply Chain Dive. https://www.supplychaindive.com/news/dhl-pick-routing-tool-wms-warehouses/583451/?utm

Liew, M., & Cao, J. (2024). Green supply chain management for carbon accountability. *Energy Economics*, *138*, 107840. DOI: 10.1016/j.eneco.2024.107840

Li, J. (2025). Construction and practice of supply chain optimization decision system driven by artificial intelligence. *Journal of Artificial Intelligence Practice*, *8*(2), 54–60. DOI: 10.23977/jaip.2025.080207

Lin, P. (2016). Why Ethics Matters for Autonomous Cars. In *Autonomous Driving* (pp. 69–85). Springer.

Lintukangas, K., Arminen, H., Kähkönen, A.-K., & Karttunen, E. (2023). Determinants of supply chain engagement in carbon management. *Journal of Business Ethics*, *186*(1), 87–104. DOI: 10.1007/s10551-022-05199-7

Liotine, M. (2019). Shaping the next generation pharmaceutical supply chain control tower with autonomous intelligence. *Journal of Autonomous Intelligence, 2*(3), 1–9.

Liu, F., Lee, C. K. M., & Xu, M. (2025). Electric vehicle supply chain investment under demand uncertainty: A jointly held real options perspective. *Computers & Industrial Engineering, 200*, 110840. DOI: 10.1016/j.cie.2024.110840

Liu, J., Chen, M., & Liu, H. (2020). The role of big data analytics in enabling green supply chain management: A literature review. *Journal of Data, Information and Management, 2*(2), 75–83.

Liu, X. (2025). Optimizing supply chains in the food and beverage industry through digital transformation. *Economics and Management Innovation, 2*(1), 28–34. DOI: 10.71222/nt2xhy40

Liu, Y., Burns, L. D., & Schneble, C. (2019). Public attitudes and social acceptance of self-driving vehicles. *Transportation Research Record: Journal of the Transportation Research Board, 2673*(3), 180–190.

Liu, Y., Pan, S., & Ballot, E. (2025). Federated digital twins platform for smart city logistics: A knowledge-driven approach. *International Journal of Production Economics, 290*, 109772. DOI: 10.1016/j.ijpe.2025.109772

Liu, Y., van Nederveen, G. A., & Hertogh, M. (2020). A conceptual development framework for prefabricated construction supply chain management: An integrated overview. *Sustainability, 12*(21), 8853.

Li, W., & Liu, Z. (2023). Social, environmental, and governance factors on supply-chain performance with mediating technology adoption. *Sustainability, 15*(14), 10865. DOI: 10.3390/su151410865

Loorbach, D., Schwanen, T., Doody, B. J., Arnfalk, P., Langeland, O., & Farstad, E. (2021). Transition governance for just, sustainable urban mobility: An experimental approach from Rotterdam, the Netherlands. *Journal of Urban Mobility, 1*, 100009. DOI: 10.1016/j.urbmob.2021.100009

Luckin, R. (2017). Towards artificial intelligence-based assessment systems. DOI: https://doi.org/DOI: 10.1038/s41562-016-0028

Luo, G., Serrão, C., Liang, D., & Zhou, Y. (2023). A relevance-based Technology–Organisation–Environment model of critical success factors for digital procurement adoption in Chinese construction companies. *Sustainability, 15*(16), 12260. DOI: 10.3390/su151612260

Luo, J. (2023). Research on the application of artificial intelligence in smart logistics in Australia. In *Atlantis Highlights in Intelligent Systems* (pp. 1084–1089). Atlantis Press International BV., DOI: 10.2991/978-94-6463-200-2_114

Mahmoud, M., & Awad, A. (2024). Impact of electronic customer relationship management on competitive advantage: Mediating role of customer satisfaction in EgyptAir. *Problems and Perspectives in Management, 22*(3), 276–286. DOI: 10.21511/ppm.22(3).2024.22

Mahmoud, M., Shma, T., Aziz, A., & Awad, A. (2025). Integrating knowledge management with smart technologies in public pharmaceutical organizations. *Knowledge and Performance Management, 9*(1), 31–44. DOI: 10.21511/kpm.09(1).2025.03

Makridakis, S. (2017). The forthcoming Artificial Intelligence (AI) revolution: Its impact on society and firms. *Futures, 90*, 46–60. DOI: 10.1016/j.futures.2017.03.006

Mangla, S. K., Luthra, S., Mishra, N., Singh, A., Rana, N. P., Dora, M., & Dwivedi, Y. (2018). Barriers to effective circular supply chain management in a developing country context. *Production Planning and Control, 29*(6), 551–569. DOI: 10.1080/09537287.2018.1449265

Marisamy, K., Selvakumar, A., Rajasekar, B., Natarajan, R., Atajanova, A., & Makhmudov, S. (2025). Smart logistics integrating AI, IoT, blockchain, and Robotics for a sustainable Future. In *Emerging Trends in Smart Logistics Technologies* (pp. 73–104). IGI Global Scientific Publishing., DOI: 10.4018/979-8-3373-2434-0.ch003

Market.us. (2024, December). Supply chain digital twin market. https://market.us/report/supply-chain-digital-twin-market/

Ma, Z., Chen, X., Sun, T., Wang, X., Wu, Y. C., & Zhou, M. (2024). Blockchain-based zero-trust supply chain security integrated with deep reinforcement learning for inventory optimization. *Future Internet, 16*(5), 163. DOI: 10.3390/fi16050163

McKinsey & Company. (2025). The Future of Autonomous Logistics: Growth and Challenges.

McKinsey & Company. (2025). The Future of Logistics Automation: Challenges and Opportunities. https://www.mckinsey.com

McKinsey & Company. (2025, April 17). *Beyond automation: How gen AI is reshaping supply chains [Podcast]*. McKinsey & Company. https://www.mckinsey.com/capabilities/operations/our-insights/beyond-automation-how-gen-ai-is-reshaping-supply-chains

McKinsey Global Institute. (2024). *McKinsey Global Supply Chain Leader Survey 2024.* https://www.mckinsey.com/capabilities/operations/our-insights/supply-chain-risk-survey

Midkiff, C. (2021). Using a control tower approach to drive visibility, aid planning and improve supply chain reliability. *Journal of Supply Chain Management. Logistics & Procurement*, *4*(1), 20–27.

Minculete, G., Stan, S. E., Ispas, L., Virca, I., Stanciu, L., Milandru, M., Mănescu, G., & Bădilă, M.-I. (2022). Relational approaches related to digital Supply Chain Management consolidation. *Sustainability*, *14*(17), 10727. DOI: 10.3390/su141710727

Min, H. (2010). Artificial intelligence in supply chain management: Theory and applications. *International Journal of Logistics Research and Applications*, *13*(1), 13–39. DOI: 10.1080/13675560902736537

Ministry of Land, Infrastructure, Transport and Tourism Japan. (2023). Driver workforce projections and automation policies.

Ministry of Land. Infrastructure, Transport and Tourism Japan. (2023). Truck driver workforce challenges. Tokyo: Government of Japan.

Miotti, M., & Johnson, N. (2024). Life Cycle Assessment of Autonomous Electric Trucks in Supply Chains: Economic-Environmental Trade-Offs. *Transportation Research Part D, Transport and Environment*, *128*, 104100.

Mnih, V., Kavukcuoglu, K., Silver, D., Rusu, A. A., Veness, J., Bellemare, M. G., Graves, A., Riedmiller, M., Fidjeland, A. K., Ostrovski, G., Petersen, S., Beattie, C., Sadik, A., Antonoglou, I., King, H., Kumaran, D., Wierstra, D., Legg, S., & Hassabis, D. (2015). Human-level control through deep reinforcement learning. DOI: https://doi.org/DOI: 10.1038/nature14236

Müller, I. (2018). Improving the service control tower with proactive decision making: A two-staged alert and intervention-generating model for proactive lateral transshipments in an after-sales supply chain. *Working paper*.

Muller, M. (2020). Upskilling logistics workers in the age of automation: Challenges and opportunities. *Journal of Vocational Education and Training*, *72*(1), 83–102.

Nakajima, Y. (2023). *BabyAGI* [Computersoftware]. GitHub.: https://github.com/yoheinakajima/babyagi

Naveena, M., Ellaturu, N., Kumari, T. L., Bambuwala, S., & Rajalakshmi, M. (2024). Ai-Driven Solutions for Supply Chain Management. *J. Inform. Educ. Res*, *4*, 861–868.

Neufville, R., Abdalla, H., & Abbas, A. (2022). Potential of connected fully autonomous vehicles in reducing congestion and associated carbon emissions. *Sustainability, 14*(11), 6910.

Nightview Capital. (2025). How Amazon Robotics is transforming logistics. https://www.nightviewcapital.com

Nisa, U., Shirazi, M., Saip, M. A., & Pozi, M. S. M. (2025). Agentic AI: The Age of Reasoning—. *RE:view*. Advance online publication. DOI: 10.1016/j.jai.2025.08.003

Niu, F. (2021). The role of the digital economy in rebuilding and maintaining social governance mechanisms. *Frontiers in Public Health, 9*, 819727. DOI: 10.3389/fpubh.2021.819727

Oca, A., Cosmas, A., Tunasar, C., & Shah, K. (2024, November). Digital twins: The key to unlocking end-to-end supply chain growth.

OKI. (2025). Advanced AI-powered delivery planning and Remote Operations platform. Retrieved from https://www.oki.com/global/yume_pro/about/logistics/tranceportation.html

Olawuyi, D., & Studies, O. I. for E. (2017). Local content and procurement requirements in oil and gas contracts. https://doi.org/DOI: 10.26889/9781784670955

Ortega Carrasco, P., Iannone, F., Ferrón Vílchez, V., & Testa, F. (2024). Green public procurement as an effective way for sustainable development: A systematic literature review and bibliometric analysis. *Sustainable Development*. Advance online publication. DOI: 10.1002/sd.3234

Pan, Y., Wang, X., & Ye, Q. (2024). Enhancing supply chain management through artificial intelligence: A case study of JD logistics. Advances in Economics. *Management and Political Sciences, 109*(1), 116–121. DOI: 10.54254/2754-1169/109/2024bj0127

Parfenov, A., Shamina, L., Niu, J., & Yadykin, V. (2021). Transformation of distribution logistics management in the digitalization of the economy. *Journal of Open Innovation, 7*(1), 58. DOI: 10.3390/joitmc7010058

Park, J. S., O'Brien, J. C., Cai, C. J., Morris, M. R., Liang, P., & Bernstein, M. S. (2023). Generative Agents: Interactive Simulacra of Human Behavior. DOI: https://arxiv.org/abs/2304.03442

Partner with Monsieur Popp. (2025, January). The new partnership model: Human co-pilots to AI. https://apoppy101.medium.com/the-new-partnership-model-human-co-pilots-to-ai-5a8d5d663de9

Patsavellas, J., Kaur, R., & Salonitis, K. (2021). Supply chain control towers: Technology push or market pull—An assessment tool. *IET Collaborative Intelligent Manufacturing*, *3*(3), 290–302.

Pawlicka, K., & Bal, M. (2022). Sustainable Supply Chain Finances implementation model and Artificial Intelligence for innovative omnichannel logistics. *Management*, *26*(1), 19–35. DOI: 10.2478/manment-2019-0082

Perugini, C., & Signorelli, M. (2022). Robotics in manufacturing and labor market consequences: Displacement and productivity effects. *Technological Forecasting and Social Change*, *175*, 121341.

Piccialli, F., Chiaro, D., Sarwar, S., Cerciello, D., Qi, P., & Mele, V. (2025). AgentAI: A comprehensive survey on autonomous agents in distributed AI for Industry 4.0. DOI: https://doi.org/DOI: 10.1016/j.eswa.2025.128404

Pinheiro, A. B., dos Santos, J. I. A. S., Cherobim, A. P. M. S., & Segatto, A. P. (2024). What drives environmental, social and governance (ESG) performance? The role of institutional quality. *Management of Environmental Quality*, *35*(2), 427–444. DOI: 10.1108/meq-03-2023-0091

Polo, L. (2025). The role of AI and OCR-based label verification systems in enhancing food traceability and supply chain transparency. *International Journal For Multidisciplinary Research*, *7*(2). Advance online publication. DOI: 10.36948/ijfmr.2025.v07i02.41577

PumpEdu. (n.d.). *AI in practice: DHL has accelerated the delivery of parcels*. https://www.pumpedu.cz/en/news/ai-in-practice-dhl-has-accelerated-the-delivery-of-parcels-114n?utm

Qadeer, A., & Awad, A. (2025). AI-powered ChatGPT in branding: Benefits, challenges, and future directions. In *Impacts of AI generated content on brand reputation* (pp. 1–26). IGI Global., DOI: 10.4018/979-8-3373-4327-3.ch001

Qadeer, A., Awad, A., & Ali, A. (2025). Understanding generative AI implementation in digital advertising among retail SMEs in Pakistan. In Hussain, Z., Khan, A., & Uzir, M. U. H. (Eds.), *Impacts of AI-generated content on brand reputation* (pp. 177–201). IGI Global., DOI: 10.4018/979-8-3373-4327-3.ch007

Qiu, R., Li, X., Sun, M., Sun, Y., & Fan, Z.-P. (2025). Online platform demand information sharing with upstream suppliers under the imbalanced market power structure. *European Journal of Operational Research*, *S037722172500726X*, •••. DOI: 10.1016/j.ejor.2025.09.009

Qu, C., & Kim, E. (2024). Reviewing the roles of AI-integrated technologies in sustainable supply chain management: Research propositions and a framework for future directions. *Sustainability*, *16*(14), 6186. DOI: 10.3390/su16146186

Queiroz, M. M., Ivanov, D., Dolgui, A., & Wamba, S. F. (2022). Impacts of epidemic outbreaks on supply chains: Mapping a research agenda amid the COVID-19 pandemic through a structured literature review. *Annals of Operations Research*, *319*, 1159–1196. DOI: 10.1007/s10479-020-03685-7 PMID: 32836615

Qureshi, M. R. N. M. (2022). Evaluating Enterprise Resource Planning (ERP) implementation for sustainable supply chain management. *Sustainability*, *14*(22), 14779. DOI: 10.3390/su142214779

Radanliev, P., De Roure, D., Page, K., Nurse, J. R. C., Mantilla Montalvo, R., Santos, O., Maddox, L., & Burnap, P. (2020). Cyber risk at the edge: Current and future trends on cyber risk analytics and artificial intelligence in the industrial internet of things and industry 4.0 supply chains. *Cybersecurity*, *3*(1).

Rahwan, I., Cebrian, M., Obradovich, N., Bongard, J., Bonnefon, J., Breazeal, C., Crandall, J., Christakis, N., Couzin, I., Jackson, M., Jennings, N., Kamar, E., Kloumann, I., Larochelle, H., Lazer, D., McElreath, R., Mislove, A., Parkes, D., Pentland, A., … Wellman, M. (2019). Machine behavior. DOI: https://doi.org/DOI: 10.1038/s41586-019-1138-y

Rana, R., & Bhambri, P. (2025). Harnessing block chain digital twins for sustainable business operations. In *Practical Frameworks for New-Age Digitalization Business Strategy* (pp. 413–446). IGI Global., DOI: 10.4018/979-8-3373-2018-2.ch013

Rao, P., Balasubramanian, S., Vihari, N., Jabeen, S., Shukla, V., & Chanchaichujit, J. (2021). The e-commerce supply chain and environmental sustainability: An empirical investigation on the online retail sector. *Cogent Business & Management*, *8*(1), 1938377. DOI: 10.1080/23311975.2021.1938377

Ravikumar, A. S., Kalandarov, A., Djumaniyazova, M., & Habib, M. (2025). A roadmap to a sustainable future. In Advances in Computational Intelligence and Robotics (pp. 267–302). IGI Global Scientific Publishing. https://doi.org/DOI: 10.4018/979-8-3373-3017-4.ch010

Ravikumar, R. N., & Aarthi, S. (2025). Digital Twin-driven green energy systems. In *The Future of Green Energy* (pp. 1–28). IGI Global Scientific Publishing., DOI: 10.4018/979-8-3373-3226-0.ch001

Ravikumar, R. N., Aarthi, S., Dilshodbek, A., Satheesh Kumar, A., Eshkaraev, S., & Shanmugam, K. B. (2025). Integrating blockchain, smart contracts, and AI for decentralized healthcare in the metaverse. In *Blockchain-Based Healthcare Management in the Metaverse* (pp. 261–294). IGI Global Scientific Publishing., DOI: 10.4018/979-8-3373-1225-5.ch010

Ravikumar, R. N., Aarthi, S., Masharipova, G., Niyazova, N., Salaeva, N., & Buriyeva, D. (2025). Enhancing clinical decision-making and operational efficiency in healthcare using edge computing. In *Building Data-Driven Edge Systems for Business Success* (pp. 191–224). IGI Global Scientific Publishing., DOI: 10.4018/979-8-3373-1147-0.ch008

Reddy, T. T., Devi, Y. R., & Kavita, G. (2023). Logistics, traceability in food supply chain management. E3S Web Conf., 391, 1075.

Reinhardt, K. (2023). Trust and trustworthiness in AI ethics. *AI and Ethics*, *3*(3), 735–744. DOI: 10.1007/s43681-022-00200-5

Rendon-Benavides, R., Perez-Franco, R., Elphick-Darling, R., Plà-Aragonés, L. M., Gonzalez Aleu, F., Verduzco-Garza, T., & Rodriguez-Parral, A. V. (2023). In-transit interventions using real-time data in Australian berry supply chains. *The TQM Journal*, *35*(3), 759–777.

Rice, A. J. (2024). The rise of intelligent procurement: Embracing AI and data analytics for crossfunctional synergy. Journal of Supply Chain Management. *Logistics and Procurement*, *6*(4), 319. DOI: 10.69554/zgfa3030

Richey, R. G.Jr, Chowdhury, S., Davis-Sramek, B., Giannakis, M., & Dwivedi, Y. K. (2023). Artificial intelligence in logistics and supply chain management: A primer and roadmap for research. *Journal of Business Logistics*, *44*(4), 532–549. DOI: 10.1111/jbl.12364

Russell, S., & Norvig, P. (2022). Artificial Intelligence: A Modern Approach (4th US ed.). https://aima.cs.berkeley.edu/

Saberi, S., Kouhizadeh, M., Sarkis, J., & Shen, L. (2019a). Blockchain technology and its relationships to sustainable supply chain management. *International Journal of Production Research*, *57*(7), 2117–2135.

Satır, B., Erenay, F. S., & Bookbinder, J. H. (2018). Shipment consolidation with two demand classes: Rationing the dispatch capacity. *European Journal of Operational Research*, *270*(1), 171–184. DOI: 10.1016/j.ejor.2018.03.016

Savelsbergh, M., & Van Woensel, T. (2016). 50th Anniversary Invited Article—City Logistics: Challenges and Opportunities. *Transportation Science*, *50*(2), 579–590. DOI: 10.1287/trsc.2016.0675

Savushkin, N. (2024). Warehouse automation in logistics: Case study of Amazon. Theseus Repository. https://www.theseus.fi/bitstream/handle/10024/857682/Savushkin_Nikolai.pdf

Selter, J.-L., Schmitz, J., & Schramm-Klein, H. (2024). Sustainability assessment of last-mile electrification: A qualitative study in Germany. *Transportation Research Part D, Transport and Environment*, *126*, 104019. DOI: 10.1016/j.trd.2023.104019

Sen, A., & Sauter, R. (2021). Integrated Automation in Supply Chains: Implications and Workforce Transitions. *The Journal of Supply Chain Management*, *57*(3), 45–62.

Shams Eldin, A. Y., Elnour, A., Hassan, R. O. A., & Awad, A. (2025). The role of technological and environmental factors in creating business value from social media dynamic capabilities for SMEs in Saudi Arabia. *Humanities & Social Sciences Communications*, *12*, 1431. DOI: 10.1057/s41599-025-05784-x

Shang, X., Guo, E., Song, Y., & Li, Y. (2023). Design and implementation of smart logistics big data management service platform. In *Atlantis Highlights in Engineering* (pp. 97–101). Atlantis Press International BV., DOI: 10.2991/978-94-6463-210-1_12

Sharabati, A. A.. (2022). The use of supply chain control tower in pharmaceutical industry to create a competitive advantage. *International Journal of Pharmaceutical Research & Allied Sciences*, *11*(3), 145–154.

Sharma, A., & Khanna, P. (2020). Relevance of adopting emerging technologies in outbound supply chain: New paradigm for cement industry. Oper. Supply Chain Manag. Int. J., 210–221.

Sharma, S. N., Singh, D., & Dehalwar, K. (2024). Surrogate Safety Analysis- Leveraging Advanced Technologies for Safer Roads. *Suranaree Journal of Science and Technology, 31*(4), 010320(1-14). https://doi.org/DOI: 10.55766/sujst-2024-04-e03837

Sharma, U. K. (2025, April). Digital twins in the supply chain: Transforming operations with real-time simulation and ai.

Sharma, S. N., & Dehalwar, K. (2025a). A Systematic Literature Review of Pedestrian Safety in Urban Transport Systems. *Journal of Road Safety*, *36*(4). Advance online publication. DOI: 10.33492/JRS-D-25-4-2707507

Sharma, S. N., & Dehalwar, K. (2025b). A Systematic Literature Review of Transit-Oriented Development to Assess Its Role in Economic Development of City. *Transportation in Developing Economies*, *11*(2), 23. DOI: 10.1007/s40890-025-00245-1

Sharma, S. N., & Dehawar, K. (2025). Review of Landuse Transportation Interaction Model in Smart Urban Growth Management. *European Transport. Trasporti Europei*, *103*, 1–15. DOI: 10.5281/ZENODO.17315313

Sharma, S. N., Lodhi, A. S., Dehalwar, K., & Jaiswal, A. (2024). Life Cycle Assessment (LCA) of Recycled & Secondary Materials in the Construction of Roads. *IOP Conference Series. Earth and Environmental Science*, *1326*(1), 012102. DOI: 10.1088/1755-1315/1326/1/012102

Shneiderman, B. (2020). Human-Centered Artificial Intelligence: Three Fresh Ideas. *DOI:* https://doi.org/DOI: 10.17705/1thci.00131

Shortliffe, E. H. (1976, October). Computer-based medical consultations: MYCIN. *Journal of Clinical Engineering*, *388*(1). Advance online publication. DOI: 10.1097/00004669-197610000-00011

Siemens, A. G. (2017, February 22). *Siemens technology enables Gestamp to cut energy consumption at its plants by 15 percent [Press release]*. Siemens. https://press.siemens.com/global/en/pressrelease/siemens-technology-enables-gestamp-cut-energy-consumption-its-plants-15-percent?utm

Siemens, A. G. (2025, April 9). *Siemens Xcelerator: Up to 20 percent in energy savings with Drivetrain Analyzer Cloud thanks to AI-based drive optimization [Press release]*. Siemens. https://press.siemens.com/global/en/pressrelease/siemens-xcelerator-20-percent-energy-savings-drivetrain-analyzer-cloud-thanks-ai-based?utm

Silsand, L., Kannelønning, M., Severinsen, G.-H., & Ellingsen, G. (2024). Enabling AI in radiology: Evaluation of an AI deployment process. *Studies in Health Technology and Informatics*, *316*, 580–584. DOI: 10.3233/SHTI240480

Silver, D., Huang, A., Maddison, C. J., Guez, A., Sifre, L., van den Driessche, G., Schrittwieser, J., Antonoglou, I., Panneershelvam, V., Lanctot, M., Dieleman, S., Grewe, D., Nham, J., Kalchbrenner, N., Sutskever, I., Lillicrap, T., Hassabis, D. (2016). Mastering the game of Go with deep neural networks and tree search. DOI: https://doi.org/DOI: 10.1038/nature16961

Sina Mohri, S., Mohammadi, M., & Van Woensel, T. (2024). Designing zero-emissions containerized last-mile delivery systems: A case study for melbourne. *Transportation Research Part C, Emerging Technologies*, *159*, 104492. DOI: 10.1016/j.trc.2024.104492

Singh, P. K. K. (2024). Measuring the broader value proposition of digital transformation in supply chains. *Int. J. Supply Chain Manag.*, *13*(1), 16–24.

Sirilertsuwan, P., Thomassey, S., & Zeng, X. (2020). A strategic location decision-making approach for multi-tier supply chain sustainability. *Sustainability*, *12*(20), 8340.

Smith, B. W. (2020). Psychology of job displacement in autonomous vehicle adoption. *Journal of Occupational Health Psychology*, *25*(3), 125–139.

Smith, B. W., Fridman, L., & Mukhtar, A. (2022). Autonomous vehicle regulatory frameworks in the U.S.: A state-level comparison. *Transport Policy*, *114*, 74–86.

Smyth, C.. (2024). Artificial intelligence and prescriptive analytics for supply chain resilience: A systematic literature review and research agenda. *International Journal of Production Research*.

Sodhi, M. S., & Tang, C. S. (2021). *Supply-chain risk management*. Springer. https://doi.org/DOI: 10.1111/j.1937-5956.2011.01251.x

Solakivi, T., Paimander, A., & Ojala, L. (2022). Cost competitiveness of alternative maritime fuels in the new regulatory framework. *Transportation Research Part D, Transport and Environment*, *113*, 103500. DOI: 10.1016/j.trd.2022.103500

Srivastava, Y. C., et al. (2022, November 3). Digital Control Tower – Instantaneous visibility, granularity and decision support for an LNG mega project. *Conference presentation*.

Subiyanto, E., & Suyoto, Y. T. (2020). Determining value of logistics costs in projects: Empirical findings based-on executing several cement projects in Indonesia. *Heliyon*, *6*(7), e04352. DOI: 10.1016/j.heliyon.2020.e04352 PMID: 32695900

Susan, W., Carsten, M., Daqiang, C., & Rosario, M. (2017). An IoT-enabled supply chain integration framework: Empirical case studies. In *Advances in Transdisciplinary Engineering*. IOS Press.

Sutton, R. S., & Barto, A. G. (2018). *Reinforcement learning: An introduction* (2nd ed.). The MIT Press., http://incompleteideas.net/book/the-book-2nd.html

Talić, T., ... (2021). Control towers in supply chain management: Standardization and documentation preparation. *White paper*.

Tanaka, T., & Saito, Y. (2023). Workforce upskilling for AI-enabled logistics: The Japanese experience. *Journal of Human Resources and Technology*, *24*(4), 321–346.

Tang, H., Jiao, R., Xue, F., Cao, Y., Yang, Y., & Zhang, S. (2024). Task scheduling strategy of logistics cloud robot based on edge computing. *Wireless Personal Communications*, *137*(4), 2339–2358. DOI: 10.1007/s11277-024-11498-1

Tao, F., Qi, Q., Liu, A., & Kusiak, A. (2019). Digital twins and cyber-physical systems toward smart manufacturing and Industry 4.0. *Engineering*, *5*(4), 653–661. DOI: 10.1016/j.eng.2019.01.014

Taufani, M., & Widjaja, A. W. (2023). The manifestation of digital transformation concept in Indonesian logistic firms. *Jurnal Manajemen*, *27*(3), 428–448. DOI: 10.24912/jm.v27i3.1383

Teece, D. J. (2018). Dynamic capabilities as (workable) management systems theory. *Journal of Management & Organization*, *24*(3), 359–368. DOI: 10.1017/jmo.2017.75

Tonsakun-aree, C., Juturat, N., & Kuntonbutr, C. (2020). Integration of information in the ERP system affecting the efficiency of the supply chain performance of the frozen food industry in Thailand. *Journal of Business Administration, Rajamangala University of Technology Thanyaburi, 10*(2), May–August.

Topan, E., Van Houtum, G.-J., & Basten, R. J. I. (2019). A review of operational spare parts service logistics. *European Journal of Operational Research*, *276*(1), 1–24.

Truant, E., Borlatto, E., Crocco, E., & Sahore, N. (2024). Environmental, social and governance issues in supply chains. A systematic review for strategic performance. *Journal of Cleaner Production*, *434*, 140024. DOI: 10.1016/j.jclepro.2023.140024

Tsang, Y. P., Wu, C. H., Wang, Y., & Ip, W. H. (2025). Semantic-driven internet of behaviours for enhancing supply chain ESG capabilities through generative AI. *International Journal on Semantic Web and Information Systems*, *21*(1), 1–33. DOI: 10.4018/ijswis.385572

Tulli, S. K. C. (2024). Enhancing supply chain efficiency in the oil and gas industry: The role of digital transformation in ERP systems for real-time analytics and decision-making. *Research and Analysis Journals*, *7*(3), 1–27.

U.S. Bureau of Labor Statistics. (2023). Employment projections for truck drivers and related occupations.

Udeh, E. O., Amajuoyi, P., Adeusi, K. B., & Scott, A. O. (2024). The role of IoT in boosting supply chain transparency and efficiency. *Magna Sci. Adv. Res. Rev.*, *12*(1), 178–197.

Ul Akram, M., Islam, N., Chauhan, C., & Zafar Yaqub, M. (2024). Resilience and agility in sustainable supply chains: A relational and dynamic capabilities view. *Journal of Business Research, 183*, 114855. DOI: 10.1016/j.jbusres.2024.114855

Unilever, P. L. C. (2023, March 9). *Annual Report and Accounts 2022: Strategic Report – About Unilever*. https://www.unilever.com/files/92ui5egz/production/784a6fcfcf077e7c586832eddd7a923e16c66430.html

van Hoek, R. (2024). Insight from industry-early lessons learned about AI adoption in core procurement processes, directions for managers and researchers. *Supply Chain Management, 29*(4), 794–803. DOI: 10.1108/scm-02-2024-0143

Verbivska, L., Zhygalkevych, Z., Fisun, Y., Chobitok, I., & Shvedkyi, V. (2023). Digital technologies as a tool of efficient logistics. *Revista de La Universidad Del Zulia, 14*(39), 492–508. DOI: 10.46925//rdluz.39.28

Verdecchia, R., Sallou, J., & Cruz, L. (2023). A systematic review of Green AI. *Wiley Interdisciplinary Reviews. Data Mining and Knowledge Discovery, 13*(4). Advance online publication. DOI: 10.1002/widm.1507

Verdouw, C. N., Wolfert, S., & Pérez Mesa, J. C. (2021). Digital twins in agri-food logistics: A framework for real-time monitoring. *Computers and Electronics in Agriculture, 184*, 106130. DOI: 10.1016/j.agsy.2020.103046

Vieira, L. C., Longo, M., & Mura, M. (2024). Impact pathways: The hidden challenges of Scope 3 emissions measurement and management. *International Journal of Operations & Production Management, 44*(13), 326–334. DOI: 10.1108/ijopm-01-2024-0049

Vlachos, I. (2023). Implementation of an intelligent supply chain control tower: A socio-technical systems case study. *Production Planning and Control, 34*(15), 1415–1431. DOI: 10.1080/09537287.2021.2015805

Waller, M. A., & Fawcett, S. E. (2013). Data science, predictive analytics, and big data: A revolution that will transform supply chain design and management. *Journal of Business Logistics, 34*(2), 77–84.

Wang, J., Luo, L., & Wang, J. (2024). Logistics supply chain management and control based on mobile communication technology. *IEEJ Transactions on Electrical and Electronic Engineering, 19*(9), 1475–1482. DOI: 10.1002/tee.24138

Wang, J., Mao, W., & Wenjie, W. (2023). The ethics of artificial intelligence: Sociopolitical and legal dimensions. *Interdisciplinary Studies in Society, Law, and Politics, 2*(2), 27–32. DOI: 10.61838/kman.isslp.2.2.6

Wang, Y., & Disney, S. M. (2016). The Bullwhip Effect: Progress, Trends and Directions. *European Journal of Operational Research, 250*(3), 691–701.

Wang, Z., Hu, H., Gong, J., & Ren, Y. (2020). Blockchain-based framework for improving supply chain traceability and information sharing in precast construction. *Automation in Construction, 111*, 103063.

Wright, L., & Davidson, S. (2020). How to tell the difference between a model and a digital twin. *Advanced Modeling and Simulation in Engineering Sciences, 7*(1), 13. DOI: 10.1186/s40323-020-00147-4

Wu, L., Wang, M., Kumar, A., & Choi, T.-M. (2024). Mitigating the bullwhip effect through supply chain ESG transparency: Roles of digitalization and signal strength. *International Journal of Operations & Production Management, 44*(9), 1707–1731. DOI: 10.1108/ijopm-08-2023-0667

Wulfraat, M. (2021). *Trends and impacts of warehouse automation*. Logistics Management Review.

Xia, X., & Li, P. (2022). A review of the life cycle assessment of electric vehicles: Considering the influence of batteries. *The Science of the Total Environment, 814*, 152870. DOI: 10.1016/j.scitotenv.2021.152870 PMID: 34990672

Xu, J., Lu, J., Chai, L., Zhang, B., Qiao, D., & Li, S. (2024). Untangling the impact of ESG performance on financing and value in the supply chain: A congruence theory perspective. *Business Strategy and the Environment*. Advance online publication. DOI: 10.1002/bse.4098

Xu, X., Zhang, M., & He, P. (2020). Coordination of a supply chain with online platform considering delivery time decision. *Transportation Research Part E, Logistics and Transportation Review, 141*, 101990. DOI: 10.1016/j.tre.2020.101990

Xu, Z., Yang, T., & Li, Q. (2023). Explainable MARL for logistics resilience. *Computers & Operations Research, 157*, 106270. DOI: 10.1016/j.cor.2023.106270

Yadav, K., Dehalwar, K., & Sharma, S. N. (2025). Assessing the factors affecting first and last mile accessibility in transit-oriented development: A literature review. *GeoJournal, 90*(6), 298. DOI: 10.1007/s10708-025-11546-8

Yang, C. (2023). Research on the decision-making mechanism of digital transformation of small and medium-sized logistics enterprises in China based on evolutionary game. *Academic Journal of Management and Social Sciences, 5*(2), 126–132. DOI: 10.54097/ajmss.v5i2.28

Yang, Q., Bolaji Samson, A., Muhammad Gummi, U., & Chen, D. (2023). Study on the use of industry 4.0 technology for the textile industry sustainable supply chain process. *Advances in Engineering Technology Research*, *4*(1), 140.

Yang, W., Li, W., Cao, Y., Luo, Y., & He, L. (2020). An information theory inspired real-time self-adaptive scheduling for production-Logistics Resources: Framework, principle, and implementation. *Sensors (Basel)*, *20*(24), 7007. DOI: 10.3390/s20247007

Yang, Y., Luo, R., & Li, W. (2021). Emergent behaviour and scalability in multi-agent reinforcement learning systems. *Neural Networks*, *142*, 222–234. DOI: 10.1016/j.simpat.2017.03.003

Yazdani, A., & Darbani, S. (2023). The impact of AI on trends, design, and Consumer Behavior. *AI and Tech in Behavioral and Social Sciences*, *1*(4), 4–10. DOI: 10.61838/kman.aitech.1.4.2

Yıldız, B., & Çiğdem, Ş. (2022). Digital transformation in logistics: Lights-out logistics. In *Financial and Economic Issues in Emerging Markets*. Özgür Yayınları., DOI: 10.58830/ozgur.pub1.c41

Yuan, H., Ma, M., Zhou, N., Deng, Y., Liu, J., Zhang, S., & Ma, Z. (2025). Planning future charging infrastructure for private EVs: A city-scale assessment of demand and capacity. *Advances in Applied Energy*, *100258*. Advance online publication. DOI: 10.1016/j.adapen.2025.100258

Yuhanna, N. (2023, September). *Supercharging data fabrics with generative ai*. Forrester. https://www.forrester.com/blogs/supercharging-data-fabrics-with-generative-ai/

Yuhanna, N. (2024, February). The forrester wave™: Enterprise data fabric, q1 2024. Forrester. https://www.forrester.com/report/the-forrester-wave-tm-enterprise-data-fabric-1-2024/RES180529

Yu, L., Xu, J., & Yuan, X. (2024). Sustainable digital shifts in Chinese transport and logistics: Exploring green innovations and their ESG implications. *Sustainability*, *16*(5), 1877. DOI: 10.3390/su16051877

Yu, W., Li, Z., & Hu, C. (2024). Carbon reduction and corporate sustainability: Evidence from low-carbon city pilot policy. *Heliyon*, *10*(7), e28992. DOI: 10.1016/j.heliyon.2024.e28992 PMID: 38601564

Zamani, E. D., Smyth, C., Gupta, S., & Dennehy, D. (2022). Artificial intelligence and big data analytics for supply chain resilience: A systematic literature review. *Annals of Operations Research*, •••, 1–28. Advance online publication. DOI: 10.1007/s10479-022-04983-y PMID: 36212520

Zarembo, I., Kodors, S., Apeināns, I., Lācis, G., Feldmane, D., & Rubauskis, E. (2023). Digital Twin: Orchard management using uav. Environment Technology Resources Proceedings of the International Scientific and Practical Conference, 1, 247–251. https://doi.org/DOI: 10.17770/etr2023vol1.7290

Zeng, H., Li, R. Y. M., & Zeng, L. (2022). Evaluating green supply chain performance based on ESG and financial indicators. *Frontiers in Environmental Science*, *10*. Advance online publication. DOI: 10.3389/fenvs.2022.982828

Zhang, Z., Wen, F., Sun, Z., Guo, X., He, T., & Lee, C. (2022). Artificial intelligence-enabled sensing technologies in the 5G/Internet of Things era: From virtual reality/augmented reality to the digital twin. Advanced Intelligent Systems (Weinheim an Der Bergstrasse, Germany), 4(7), 2100228. https://doi.org/DOI: 10.1002/aisy.202100228

Zhang, J., & Chen, J. (2013). Coordination of information sharing in a supply chain. *International Journal of Production Economics*, *143*(1), 178–187.

Zhang, K., Yang, Z., & Başar, T. (2021). Multi-agent reinforcement learning: A selective overview of theories and algorithms. In *Handbook of reinforcement learning and control* (pp. 321–370). Springer., DOI: 10.1007/978-3-030-60990-0_12

Zhao, R., Mashruwala, R., Pandit, S., & Balakrishnan, J. (2019). Supply chain relational capital and the bullwhip effect. *International Journal of Operations & Production Management*, *39*(5), 658–689. DOI: 10.1108/ijopm-03-2018-0186

Zhao, X., Li, X., Jiao, D., Mao, Y., Sun, J., & Liu, G. (2024). Policy incentives and electric vehicle adoption in China: From a perspective of policy mixes. *Transportation Research Part A, Policy and Practice*, *190*, 104235. DOI: 10.1016/j.tra.2024.104235

Zhou, Y. (2024). Lifecycle battery carbon footprint analysis for battery sustainability with energy digitalization and artificial intelligence. *Applied Energy*, *371*, 123665. DOI: 10.1016/j.apenergy.2024.123665

Zhou, Y., Zhang, N., Wu, C.-H., Wang, Y., Zhang, X., & Zhang, D. (2024). The impact of supply chain ESG management on supply chain resilience with emerging IT technologies. *Journal of Organizational and End User Computing: An Official Publication of the Information Resources Management Association*, *36*(1), 1–31. DOI: 10.4018/joeuc.356497

Zhu, G., Chou, M. C., & Tsai, C.-W. (2020). Lessons learned from the COVID-19 pandemic exposing the shortcomings of current supply chain operations: A long-term prescriptive offering. *Sustainability*, *12*(14), 5858.

Zou, X., & Peng, Y. (2025). Application of NLP and deep learning in enhancing the resilience of cross-border e-commerce supply chain for agricultural products. *In Proceedings of the 2025 4th International Conference on Big Data, Information and Computer Network (BDICN '25)* (pp. 36–40). Association for Computing Machinery. https://doi.org/DOI: 10.1145/3727353.3727360

Zschausch, F., Rosenberger, S., & Halbe, J. (2025). Quantitative evaluation of environmental impacts and mitigation measures for transport logistics companies—Insights through modeling of an exemplary site. *Energy Reports*, *13*, 3291–3311. DOI: 10.1016/j.egyr.2025.02.037

About the Contributors

Abdelrehim Awad is an Associate Professor of Business Administration at the University of Bisha, Saudi Arabia, with extensive academic, research, and administrative experience. His work spans marketing, digital transformation, artificial intelligence applications, supply chain innovation, and customer knowledge management. Dr. Awad has published widely in leading Scopus and Web of Science indexed journals and serves on several editorial boards and review committees. He is also Vice President of the Innovation and Entrepreneurship Center and Coordinator of the Master's Program for Accreditation at the College of Business. His research and teaching portfolio covers marketing strategy, digital marketing, analytics, and organizational development, supported by diverse professional training and contributions to international conferences.

Dhafer Alahmari Assistant professor, Academic–practitioner in public procurement and supply chain management; leads procurement transformation initiatives and supervises theses; also serves as a logistics consultant. Dr. Dhafer collaborates extensively with regional and international scholars and plays an active role in advancing high-impact research across domains related to artificial intelligence, strategic management, and operational excellence. His commitment to academic rigor and thought leadership is reflected in his contributions to peer-reviewed publications, editorial activities, and academic development initiatives, reinforcing his reputation as a leading voice in technology-enabled business research.

***

Suzan Bakr As a Professor of Business Administration and Director of the Quality Assurance Unit at Al-Azhar University's Faculty of Commerce, I have dedicated my career to academia. A proud Al-Azhar alumna, I graduated first in my class with a Bachelor's in Business Administration. My journey with the university began as a Demonstrator, and I have since progressed to Professor. I hold a Master's degree and a PhD in Business Administration. My research focuses on contemporary management issues like strategic intelligence and digital transformation. I am passionate about teaching and mentoring scholars and have taught at all levels, supervising many theses. In my administrative role, I lead curriculum development and quality assurance initiatives to advance our faculty's standards.

Susanta Das is a seasoned educator with a proven record of teaching and mentoring diverse students, working at multiple institutions, and providing service to the various initiatives of organizations. He received his Ph.D. and M.A. degrees from Western Michigan University (WMU), USA, and M.Sc. degree from Banaras Hindu University (BHU), India all in Physics. He continued his research as a Marie-Curie post-doctoral fellow at Stockholm University, Stockholm, Sweden on beam diagnostics for the DESIREE (Double ElectroStatic Ion Ring ExpEriment) in the project DITANET (Diagnostic Techniques for particle Accelerators – a Marie-Curie initial training NETwork), at the Indian Institute of Science Education and Research-Kolkata, India on high-pressure physics as a Project Scientist-B, and at the University of Electro-Communications, Tokyo, Japan on ion-surface interactions as a Post-doctoral fellow. Throughout his career, Dr. Das worked and collaborated with many researchers, Ph.D., master, and visiting students from different countries. He further visited many countries to discuss research and an international conference participant (UK, Italy, Germany, Greece, Belgium, Bulgaria, Romania, Brazil etc.). He worked at several institutions before assuming his current role at Ajeenkya D Y Patil University. He received the Marie-Curie post-doctoral fellowship in Sweden, Science Academies' Summer Research Fellowship in India, Gowen Frostic Doctoral Fellowship, Department Graduate Research and Creative Scholar Award by WMU, and Leo R. Parpart Doctoral Fellowship by Dept. of Physics, WMU, among many others, throughout his academic journey. He co-authored several research articles in WoS/Scopus indexed international journals, conference proceedings, and scholarly book chapters and co-edited several books published by renowned international publishing houses (IGI-Global, Springer Nature, Nova Science Publishers, Wiley, Scrivener-Wiley, Notion Press). At present, Dr. Das continues to delve into cutting-edge fields, with a keen interest in nanotechnology, UN SDGs, and data science. His multifaceted contributions, spanning teaching, research, and administrative leadership, showcase a dedicated professional who is instrumental in advancing the vision and mission of the institutions he serves.

AlMoatassem Mohmmed Experienced Assistant Professor Of Economics with a demonstrated history of working in the higher education industry. Skilled in Food Security, Sustainable Development, Climate Change, Climate Change Adaptation, and Environmental Economics. Strong education professional with a Doctor of Philosophy (Ph.D.) focused in Environmental Economics from Crawford School of Public Policy, the Australian National University.

Ravikumar R. Natarajan is an experienced academician with over 12+ years of teaching and research expertise across institutions in India, the UAE, and the Maldives. He currently serves as an Assistant Professor at Marwadi University, Rajkot, specializing in Machine Learning, Recommender Systems, and AI-driven applications in healthcare and security. He holds a Ph.D. in Machine Learning and Recommender Systems from Amity University, Jaipur, a Master of Engineering in CSE from VMRF University, Salem, and a Bachelor of Engineering in CSE from Anna University. He also has a MiniMBA from the Swiss eLearning Institute. Dr. Ravikumar has authored more than 8+ multiple SCIE/Scopus-indexed journal articles, 25+ IEEE/Springer conference papers, and co-authored a book on Artificial Intelligence. He has also published 9 patents and contributed 10+ book chapters in emerging domains such as Federated Learning, Blockchain, and Digital Twins for IGI Global, Wiley and Springer publisher. He actively mentors students through initiatives like the Research Activities Club (RAC) and Student Research Internship Training (SRIT), promoting innovation and research culture.

Aarthi S is a dedicated Assistant Professor in Computer Science with over six years of teaching experience. She is currently pursuing her Ph.D. at Marwadi University, Gujarat, and holds an M.Phil. and MCA from Bharathiar University, Tamil Nadu. Throughout her academic career, Aarthi has specialized in programming languages such as C++, Java, and C, and contributed to research in recommender systems and AI-related data privacy. She has published journal articles, contributed to book chapters, and actively participated in technical workshops. Known for her student mentorship and engagement in academic events, Aarthi remains committed to fostering innovation and excellence in computer science education.

Atharva Saraf is currently pursuing a B. Tech degree in Computer Science Engineering at Ajeenkya D Y Patil University. Throughout his academic journey, he has developed a strong foundation in various programming languages, including C, C++, and Python. His interests and focus areas lie in algorithm-based programs, artificial intelligence (with a special emphasis on neural networks), and cybersecurity. His has successfully undertaken several projects that reflect my proficiency and passion in these domains. For instance, he developed a PC-Tuner application aimed at optimizing system performance by employing various methods such as defragmentation. Additionally, he created an automated backup utility capable of securely backing up selected files, folders, and stores them in compressed backup folder in system itself it can also store backups on external hard disk and cloud storages. Beyond project work, he has contributed to the academic community through research articles and book chapters. Notable among these is my co-authored chapter on federated learning techniques, exploring their applications and advancements in the field of machine learning. Moreover, he is currently working on writing a book chapter focusing on federated learning, delving deeper into its methodologies and practical implementations. His academic experiences have honed his skills in problem-solving, critical thinking, and collaborative teamwork. He is eager to further expand His knowledge and expertise in computer science, particularly in areas that intersect with his interests in algorithms, artificial intelligence, and their practical applications.

Shashikant Nishant Sharma is a distinguished scholar and practitioner in the field of development studies, widely recognized for his contributions to planning, management, and sustainable development. He is the author of 12 books that critically engage with issues of urban planning, policy, and governance. Currently, he serves as the Research Head at Track2Training, an NGO he co-founded to advance training, capacity building, and skill development initiatives. PhD in Urban Planning from MANIT, Bhopal, and has also contributed to academia as an Assistant Professor at NIT Calicut, Guest Faculty at UPES Dehradun, where he taught and mentored future professionals. His work bridges the gap between academic research and practice, making him a prominent voice in contemporary development discourse.

Index

A

D

E

G

I

K

L

M

N

O

P

R

S

U

W

www.ingramcontent.com/pod-product-compliance
Lightning Source LLC
LaVergne TN
LVHW081533300926
849161LV00006B/1406